The
Testimony
of the Beloved
Disciple

THE
TESTIMONY
OF THE BELOVED
DISCIPLE

Narrative, History, and Theology
in the Gospel of John

RICHARD BAUCKHAM

Baker Academic
Grand Rapids, Michigan

© 2007 by Richard Bauckham

Published by Baker Academic
a division of Baker Publishing Group
P.O. Box 6287, Grand Rapids, MI 49516-6287
www.bakeracademic.com

Second printing, April 2008

Printed in the United States of America

Library of Congress Cataloging-in-Publication Data

Bauckham, Richard.
    The testimony of the beloved disciple : narrative, history, and theology in the Gospel of John / Richard Bauckham.
        p.   cm.
    Includes bibliographical references (p.   ) and indexes.
    ISBN 10: 0-8010-3485-X (pbk.)
    ISBN 978-0-8010-3485-5 (pbk.)
        1. Bible. N. T. John —Criticism, interpretation, etc. I. Title.
BS2615.52.B38 2007
226.5′06—dc22   2007027842

To Martin Hengel
with gratitude
for his immense contribution
to New Testament research

CONTENTS

1

INTRODUCTION

The essays collected in this volume cover a wide variety of aspects of the study of the Gospel of John, but they cohere within an approach to the Gospel that differs very significantly from the approach that has been dominant in Johannine scholarship since the late 1970s, though there are signs that this dominant approach is now being undermined or at least considerably modified by very recent trends in Johannine scholarship. The purpose of this introductory chapter is to relate my essays in this volume to current and recent Johannine scholarship, and also to explain their relationships and coherence within the alternative approach to John that they exemplify.

The Dominant Approach

In the last three decades of the twentieth century,[1] Johannine scholarship was characterized by a dominant approach to questions about the origin and character

1. A major transition in Johannine scholarship is widely acknowledged, following John Ashton, *Understanding the Fourth Gospel* (Oxford: Clarendon, 1991), 107–9, to have been effected by J. Louis Martyn, *History and Theology in the Fourth Gospel* (1st ed., New York: Harper & Row, 1968; 2nd revised ed., Nashville: Abingdon, 1979). The dominant approach could also be said to have come of age when Raymond Brown, who had laid some of its foundations in his major commentary (1966, 1970), came fully on board with the publication of his *The Community of the Beloved Disciple* (New York: Paulist Press, 1979), which John Painter, *The Quest for the Messiah: The History, Literature and Theology of the Johannine*

of the Gospel of John. This is certainly not to say that all Johannine scholarship adopted this approach,[2] but, to say the least, the dominant approach could not be ignored by any Johannine scholar. The main elements of the dominant approach are:

1. Little if any credit is given to the traditions of the early church about the origins and authorship of the Gospel, since they are held to be incompatible with the internal evidence of the Gospel itself. The external evidence is assumed to attribute the Gospel to the apostle John the son of Zebedee, but the dominant approach, though it usually presumes that the figure of the Beloved Disciple in the Gospel is based on a historical figure who played a part in the history of the Gospel's community and traditions, considers the Beloved Disciple neither John the son of Zebedee nor the author of the Gospel. The early Christian tradition's location of the Gospel's origin in Ephesus is usually thought to be merely a corollary of the erroneous attribution of the Gospel to John the son of Zebedee. For most exponents of the dominant approach the community behind the Gospel was far too marginal a Christian group to be located in a city such as Ephesus, with its well-known Christian community, associated with Paul, and its position at the hub of many channels of communications.[3]

2. As an account of the history of Jesus this Gospel is far less reliable than the Synoptics, since its traditions have been so thoroughly shaped by the history of the highly distinctive Christian community in which they evolved. The dominant approach takes up the much older (nineteenth-century) scholarly judgment that this Gospel is theology rather than history, but gives it a much more sociohistorical or sociological character. The dominant approach, since it generally regards this Gospel as independent of the Synoptics, is actually more ready than its nineteenth-century precursors to admit that the Gospel may preserve genuinely historical traditions about Jesus that are not to be found in the Synoptics. They would seem, however, to have been preserved in spite of, rather than because of, the character of this Gospel.

3. The Gospel of John is the product of a complex history of literary composition which has left the marks of its various stages on the text as we have it, making it possible to reconstruct its literary prehistory. This confidence in source criticism as a key to understanding the Gospel has Bultmann's commentary as its most influential forebear, even though Bultmann's specific theories have not survived

---

Community, 2nd ed. (Edinburgh: T. & T. Clark, 1993), 2, calls a "daringly fertile monograph." For a brief survey of scholarship adopting the dominant approach since Martyn, see David Rensberger, Overcoming the World: Politics and Community in the Gospel of John (London: SPCK, 1989), 22–24.

2. Major works of Johannine scholarship published in that period and largely dissenting from the dominant approach include John A. T. Robinson, The Priority of John (London: SCM Press, 1985); Don A. Carson, The Gospel according to John (Grand Rapids: Eerdmans, 1991); Martin Hengel, Die johanneische Frage, WUNT 67 (Tübingen: Mohr Siebeck, 1993); Thomas L. Brodie, The Gospel According to John (New York: Oxford University Press, 1993).

3. Brown, The Community, 179, was one who thought the traditional location in Ephesus remained plausible.

well. In the face of more synchronic, literary-critical approaches to reading the Gospel, the dominant approach continues to appeal to the well-known "aporias," the repetitions and incoherences in the literary sequence of the text, as well as to the inconsistencies in its ideology, that require diachronic explanation.

4. The Gospel is the product of and written for the so-called Johannine community, a small and idiosyncratic branch of early Christianity, sectarian in character, isolated from the rest of the early Christian movement, and formed by its own particular history and conflicts. This aspect of the dominant approach corresponds to the importance given in the same period to the community of each Gospel (understood as both the context of origin and the audience of that Gospel) in study of the Synoptic Gospels. But for several reasons, including the existence of the Johannine letters, reconstruction of the Johannine community has flourished even more than those of the Matthean, Markan, and Lukan communities.

5. Elements 3 and 4 coalesce in that the various stages of the composition of the Gospel are held to reflect developments in the history of the Johannine community. In the dominant approach, the reconstructed history of the text and the reconstructed history of the community are inseparable.[4] This is where the dominant approach of the last three decades of the twentieth century differs from the older (and numerous) theories of multiple sources, authors and redactions. Such theories go back to the nineteenth century, but only from the late 1960s have they been closely connected with the notion of a special Johannine community and the reconstruction of its history.

6. The reconstruction of the history of the community is partly based on the so-called "two-level" reading of the Gospel narrative, which assumes that the Gospel's story of Jesus is also to be understood as the story of the Johannine community. The parade example, with which J. Louis Martyn initiated the enterprise of reconstructing the community's history from the Gospel, is the story of the healing of the blind man in chapter 9. Here Jesus stands for a Christian prophet in the community's present, the blind man is a Christian convert, and "the Jews" are the authorities of the synagogue to which the Johannine community had belonged until it had been expelled, like the blind man in the story. That the traumatic event in the community's history that accounts for much of the character of the Gospel as we have it was expulsion from its local synagogue is concluded from this episode in the Gospel (along with 16:2). Similarly the story of Jesus in Samaria in chapter 4 reflects an earlier stage in the community's history that included successful mission to Samaritans.

7. Reconstructions of the history of the Johannine community are many and diverse, but there is broad agreement that this history focuses on the community's

---

4. Martinus C. de Boer, *Johannine Perspectives on the Death of Jesus*, Contributions to Biblical Exegesis and Theology 17 (Kampen: Kok Pharos, 1996), 44: "communal history and composition history are inseparable. The communal history is reflected in the composition history of the Gospel and Epistles while the composition history documents, both directly and indirectly, the communal history of those for and by whom this literature came to be."

relationship to the Jewish matrix in which it arose and from which it later painfully separated. The character of the Gospel is intimately related to the origin of the community within the synagogue, its attempts to persuade other members of the synagogue of the messiahship of Jesus, its expulsion from the synagogue and its increasingly bitter and polemical attitude to the parent body from which it had separated. On most accounts, the background, context and membership of the Johannine community are Jewish, though Gentiles play a minor part in some reconstructions. In this respect, the dominant approach is indebted to the effect the publication of the Dead Sea Scrolls had in highlighting the Jewishness of the Fourth Gospel in place of the Hellenistic character regularly attributed to it in most earlier scholarship.

Something Completely Different

Over the two decades during which I have pursued serious work on the Gospel, I have found myself abandoning one by one all of these elements of the dominant approach. In my view, the Gospel is an integral whole, including both the prologue and the epilogue, and was designed as such by a single author. I have returned to the traditional view that the distinctiveness of this Gospel, which I certainly do not wish to minimize, is due not to a distinctive community from which it emerged and to which it was addressed, but primarily to a theologically creative and literarily skilled author who produced this distinctive version of the story of Jesus. This author was a personal disciple of Jesus, though not one of the Twelve, who has depicted himself within the narrative as the "disciple Jesus loved." This seems to me the best interpretation of both the internal evidence of the Gospel and the external evidence, the most reliable of which, properly understood, attributes the Gospel to a John who was not the son of Zebedee but a disciple of Jesus who died in Ephesus, having survived longer than most of Jesus' disciples.

This Beloved Disciple, from his own memories of Jesus, together with those of the circle of Jesus' disciples to whom he was closest, and drawing on the resources of the Jewish traditions he knew well, developed a distinctive interpretation of Jesus and his story. This interpretation he embodied in a Gospel on which he must have worked for many years before releasing it to a Christian audience that was certainly not confined to the community in which he lived. My view of both this Gospel and the Synoptics is that they were written for general circulation around all the churches,[5] and that they did quite soon circulate widely. As the author's lifework, the permanent embodiment of his personal calling to testify to Jesus, the Gospel of John was not occasioned by fluctuating local circumstances but by the author's convictions about the universal significance of Jesus and his story.

5. See Richard Bauckham ed., *The Gospels for all Christians: Rethinking the Gospel Audiences* (Grand Rapids: Eerdmans, 1998).

Indeed, I think it likely that, as well as addressing Christians, the author deliberately made his work accessible enough to outsiders for it to be read with profit by nonbelievers, Jewish or Gentile, who might be introduced to it by Christian friends.[6] There is nothing esoteric about this Gospel, though it is a work of richly packed meaning available to further study by readers who studied it in the way the author and other Jewish exegetes studied the Hebrew Bible.

Generically, like the Synoptic Gospels, this Gospel is a biography of Jesus—not, of course, a biography in the modern sense, but a Greco-Roman *bios*. John has adapted the genre to his purpose in somewhat different ways from those adopted by the Synoptic evangelists, but readers would have taken it to be a life of Jesus. They would have read it to find out about Jesus, not in order to find in it an allegorized version of their own community history. Doubtless the author, like all authors, was influenced by the contexts in which he lived and worked, but those contexts are largely unknown to us and, as in the case of most creative works, their influence on the author is not predictable and cannot be reconstructed, except in the most general terms. Reconstructions of the Johannine community from the Gospel are largely fantasy,[7] and even the evidence of the Johannine letters must be used cautiously in interpreting a work that was not, like them, occasioned by specific community concerns,[8] but its author's gift to all the churches for however long there might be before the coming of the Lord.

Recent scholarship, skeptical of any attempt to reconstruct the historical Jesus from this Gospel, has instead poured its energies and its desire for historical specificity into reconstructing the historical Johannine community. Like the quest of the historical Jesus, the quest of the historical Johannine community has produced a wide variety of results, but, unlike the former quest, that of the Johannine community has yet to produce criteria of authenticity and critical methodological reflection. The undisciplined way in which it treats the Gospel as evidence of the history of the community, along with the complexity of possible combinations of different analyses of sources and redactions with different views of the community, make its results unfalsifiable and infinitely variable. Since the Johannine community is understood to be isolated from the rest of the early Christian movement and since it has left no mark either on the non-Johannine literature in the New Testament or on other early Christian sources, there is no external evidence that can act as a control on imaginative reconstruction. Even Martyn's appeal to one

6. See chapter 5 below.

7. For similarly harsh judgments, cf. Ruth Edwards, *Discovering John* (London: SPCK, 2003), 102: "The idea of the Johannine 'community' at loggerheads with other Christians is a scholarly construct arising from a surfeit of sociological speculation" (cf. also 41–44); Thomas L. Brodie, *The Quest for the Origin of John's Gospel* (New York: Oxford University Press, 1993) 21: "When one looks at these various reconstructions [of the history of the Johannine community], these intriguing buildings, the question is not how many bricks in this or that wall are solid but whether there is any solidity to the foundation of the entire house" (cf. 15–21).

8. Even so, 1 John may well be addressed to quite a wide range of churches, a compendium of its author's teaching rather than an occasional letter like 2 and 3 John.

piece of external evidence—the supposed promulgation of the *Birkat ha-Minim* (a liturgical curse against heretics to be recited in synagogues) by the rabbis at Jamnia[9]—as a key to the history of the Johannine community has been very largely abandoned by proponents of the dominant approach.[10]

The widely prevalent assumption that the Gospel is primarily a source for the history of the community and only secondarily a source for the history of Jesus is misconceived. At least we have overwhelming evidence that there was a historical Jesus, and we have other sources with which to compare the Gospel of John. The genre of the work also requires us to read it as a book about Jesus. But what most Johannine scholars have notably failed to take seriously is that *the Gospel's theology itself requires a concern for history*. The theological claim of the prologue that '"the Word became flesh and dwelt among us" (1:14) presupposes that Jesus was a real human person in real history.[11] This is not negated by the degree of reflective interpretation that the author incorporates—certainly a greater degree than in the Synoptic Gospels—because the interpretation is in search of the profoundest meaning of what Jesus said and did. We should not expect the history to have been lost behind the interpretation but rather to have been highlighted by the interpretation.

The present collection of essays is not a systematic presentation or demonstration of this approach to the Gospel of John in all its interconnected aspects. It devotes far more attention to some aspects than others. But the rest of this introductory chapter will place the essays within the context of the overall approach that has just been sketched.

Authorship

Chapters 2 and 3 deal, respectively, with external and internal evidence of the authorship of the Gospel. The external evidence has usually (despite some dissenters with whom I agree) been held to be unanimous in identifying the author as John the son of Zebedee, one of Jesus' twelve apostles. I present the case for a

9. Martyn, *History* (1979 ed.), 50–62, 156–57.

10. Rensberger, *Overcoming*, 26; Ben Witherington, *John's Wisdom: A Commentary on the Fourth Gospel* (Louisville: Westminster John Knox, 1995), 29; de Boer, *Johannine Perspectives*, 69; Andrew T. Lincoln, *Truth on Trial: The Lawsuit Motif in the Fourth Gospel* (Peabody, MA: Hendrickson, 2000), 266–85; Raymond E. Brown, *An Introduction to the Gospel of John*, ed. Francis J. Moloney (New York: Doubleday, 2003), 68–69 n. 65 (editor's note); Andrew T. Lincoln, *The Gospel According to St John*, BNTC (London: Continuum, 2005), 83–84. Andreas J. Köstenberger, "The Destruction of the Second Temple and the Composition of the Fourth Gospel," in John Lierman ed., *Challenging Perspectives on the Gospel of John*, WUNT 2/219 (Tübingen: Mohr Siebeck, 2006), 69–108, here 75, claims that, although "quite a few versions of the Johannine community hypothesis . . . do without the *birkat ha-minim*," the latter did provide "vital plausibility for reconstructions in the Martyn mold, and its loss throws open the door to other possibilities."

11. Lincoln, *Gospel*, 48–49, recognizes but minimizes the point.

different reading of the best of the second-century evidence, that which can be traced to Papias of Hierapolis and to the local tradition of the church of Ephesus. This evidence I think points instead to another disciple of Jesus, not one of the Twelve, but also called John (which was one of the commonest of Palestinian Jewish male names). It was doubtless inevitable that this relatively unknown John should come to be identified with the famous John the son of Zebedee. This interpretation of the external evidence is, in my view, much easier to square with the internal evidence of the Gospel. Despite the classic case made by B. F. Westcott in 1889[12] and often repeated since then,[13] to the effect that the internal evidence of the Gospel points to the identification of the beloved disciple as John the son of Zebedee, I take the view of many other scholars[14] that the Gospel's portrayal of the beloved disciple makes most sense if he was not one of the Twelve, not one of the itinerant disciples who traveled around with Jesus, but a disciple resident in Jerusalem, who hosted Jesus and his disciples for the Last Supper[15] and took the mother of Jesus into his Jerusalem home (19:27). Westcott's case relied too heavily on a view of the exclusive importance of the Twelve drawn overliterally from Mark. Though Mark concentrates his attention on the Twelve and rarely mentions any other disciples of Jesus, Luke's Gospel in particular makes it clear that Jesus had large numbers of disciples, both those who traveled with him and the Twelve (e.g., 6:17; 10:1; 19:37) and others who stayed at home (e.g., 10:38–42). There is no

12. B. F. Westcott, *The Gospel according to St. John* (London: Murray, 1889), v–xxxiv.

13. E.g., Craig S. Keener, *The Gospel of John: A Commentary*, 2 vols. (Peabody, Massachussetts: 2003), 1:84–91.

14. E.g., F. C. Burkitt, *The Gospel History and Its Transmission* (Edinburgh: T. & T. Clark, 1911), 247–50; A. E. Garvie, *The Beloved Disciple* (London: Hodder & Stoughton, 1922), 202–4; J. N. Sanders, *The Fourth Gospel in the Early Church* (Cambridge: Cambridge University Press, 1943), 43–45; P. Parker, "John the son of Zebedee and the Fourth Gospel," *JBL* 81 (1962): 35–43; Oscar Cullmann, *The Johannine Circle*, trans. J. Bowden (London: SCM, 1976), 63–85; Raymond E. Brown, *The Community of the Beloved Disciple* (London: G. Chapman, 1979), 31–34 (a change of view from that in Brown's commentary: *The Gospel According to John I–XII*, AB 29A [New York: Doubleday, 1966] xcii–xcviii); Rudolf Schnackenburg, *The Gospel according to St John*, trans. K. Smyth (New York: Crossroad, 1968–1982), 3:375–88 (also a change from his earlier position: *The Gospel according to St John*, vol. 1, chapter 5); D. E. H. Whiteley, "Was John Written by a Sadducee?" in W. Haase ed., *Aufstieg und Niedergang der Römische Welt* 2.25.3 (Berlin: W. de Gruyter, 1985), 2481–2505; G. R. Beasley-Murray, *John*, WBC 36 (Waco, TX: Word, 1987), lxx–lxxv; Martin Hengel, *The Johannine Question*, trans. J. Bowden (London: SCM Press, 1989), 76–80; idem, *Die johanneische Frage*, WUNT 67 (Tübingen: Mohr Siebeck, 1993), 210–19; John W. Pryor, *John: Evangelist of the Covenant People* (London: Darton, Longman & Todd, 1992), 3; J. A. Grassi, *The Secret Identity of the Beloved Disciple* (New York: Paulist Press, 1992); R. Alan Culpepper, *John the Son of Zebedee: The Life of a Legend* (Columbia, SC: University of South Carolina Press, 1994), 84–85; Ben Witherington, *John's Wisdom* (Louisville: Westminster John Knox, 1995), 14–15. I cannot here discuss the views of those who identify the beloved disciple with a disciple elsewhere named in the Gospel (Thomas, Lazarus, Nathanael and others).

15. Whiteley ("Was John Written by a Sadducee?") shows how the seating arrangements implied by John 13:23–27 make sense if the beloved disciple is the host, Jesus is placed next to him to his left in the position of guest of honour (in that position, Jesus, reclining on left elbow, would be able to talk most easily to him) and Peter to his right in the position of the next most eminent guest.

reason to suppose that no more than the Twelve were present at the Last Supper just because they are the only disciples Mark is interested in. The Twelve were selected for a special role of leadership in the renewed Israel. That the beloved disciple was not called to that role is no reason why he should not have been someone to whom Jesus was close (as he was to the Bethany family, according to John) and in whom Jesus sometimes confided when he was in Jerusalem. The special value of the Gospel of John may be in part that it embodies a different perspective on Jesus, one from outside the circle of the Twelve (see further below: "Issues of Historicity").

Chapter 2 is confined to one crucial aspect of the internal evidence. Against many who see the role of the beloved disciple in the Gospel as that of the ideal disciple, the one believing readers of the Gospel may emulate, I argue that very little of what is said about the beloved disciple can be read as a model of discipleship for others. Rather, it puts the beloved disciple in a unique position, as a disciple uniquely close to Jesus, present at key events in the story, a witness who proved especially perceptive, able to perceive the true meaning of what he saw and heard. In other words, he is portrayed as the ideal witness to Jesus and his history, and therefore as the disciple ideally qualified to write a gospel. The portrayal of the beloved disciple is designed to authenticate him as the author of the Gospel, gaining, in the course of the narrative, his readers'/hearers' confidence that, despite the fact that for many of them he would be an obscure or even unknown disciple of Jesus, he really is qualified to bear his own special witness to Jesus. (I have taken my discussion of the beloved disciple a little further in my book *Jesus and the Eyewitnesses*.)[16]

Genre

As Mark Stibbe remarked in 1994, "Discussion of the literary genre of the fourth gospel has been remarkably rare in twentieth century scholarship."[17] None of the major commentaries on the Gospel published in the second half of the twentieth century included a discussion of genre; it was not part of the expected contents of an introduction to a commentary. The longstanding scholarly supposition that the New Testament Gospels are *sui generis* was doubtless taken for granted by the scholars of the dominant approach to the Gospel of John, though proposals such as the "two-level" reading of the story really ought have raised generic questions. How could the first readers/hearers have been expected to recognize the additional level in a story ostensibly about Jesus? What, in the literature with which they were familiar, could have provided a precedent for such a literary device? These are generic questions. It should also have been an issue for those, including most

16. Richard Bauckham, *Jesus and the Eyewitnesses: The Gospels as Eyewitness Testimony* (Grand Rapids: Eerdmans, 2006), chapters 14–15.

17. Mark W. G. Stibbe, *John's Gospel*, New Testament Readings (London: Routledge, 1994) 54.

of these scholars, who thought John entirely independent of all three Synoptic Gospels. If Mark invented the Gospel genre *ex nihilo*, did John reinvent it? For all the differences, there are striking generic similarities between the two gospels.

At the end of his life, Raymond Brown had almost completed an introduction to a projected revision of his major commentary. Published in 2003, this introduction still lacks any discussion of genre, and the lack was neither supplied nor pointed out by the editor, Frank Moloney.[18] In the new century, however, genre has acquired its rightful place in commentary introductions. In Andrew Lincoln's commentary it is the third topic discussed in the introduction,[19] while in Craig Keener's commentary, a masterly two-volume work that now rivals Brown's, the first, very substantial section of the introduction is devoted to genre.[20] Both rightly recognize that the issue of historicity cannot be adequately discussed in isolation from that of genre.[21]

Genre deserves a prominent place near the beginning of any introduction to a Gospel because it is genre that determines what readers' expectations of a work will be and how they will be disposed to interpret it. In the words of literary critic E. D. Hirsch, "an interpreter's preliminary generic conception of a text is constitutive of everything that he [*sic*] subsequently understands."[22] Mistaking the genre of a work can lead to serious misreadings of it. While genre recognition is normally straightforward, even unconscious, relying on the readers' previous reading experience (or hearers' hearing experience), for cross-cultural reading, like modern reading of the Gospels, it needs to be done deliberately and through well-informed comparison with other literature from the culture in question. It is one of the most useful things a scholarly introduction to a biblical book can do for modern readers.

Both Lincoln and Keener acknowledge the landmark significance of Richard Burridge's work on Gospel genre,[23] which has convinced many, perhaps most,[24]

---

18. Brown, *An Introduction*, 7 (Moloney) and 90 (Brown) seem the only allusions to the matter and seemingly presuppose that the Gospels are *sui generis*.

19. Lincoln, *The Gospel*, 14–17. There are also brief discussions of genre in Charles H. Talbert, *Reading John: A Literary and Theological Commentary on the Fourth Gospel and the Johannine Epistles* (New York: Crossroad; London: SPCK, 1992), 62–63 (Talbert was one of the pioneers of the recent recognition that the Gospels belong to the genre of ancient biography); Mark W. G. Stibbe, *John*, Readings: A New Biblical Commentary (Sheffield: Sheffield Academic Press, 1993), 13; D. Moody Smith, *John*, Abingdon NT Commentaries (Nashville: Abingdon, 1999), 22–23.

20. Keener, *The Gospel of John*, 1:3–52.

21. On this point, see also Craig L. Blomberg, *The Historical Reliability of John's Gospel* (Downers Grove, Illinois: InterVarsity Press, 2001), 57–61.

22. Quoted in Mark W. G. Stibbe, *John as Storyteller: Narrative Criticism and the Fourth Gospel*, SNTSMS 73 (Cambridge: Cambridge University Press, 1992), 31.

23. R. A. Burridge, *What Are the Gospels? A Comparison with Graeco-Roman Biography*, SNTSMS 70 (Cambridge: Cambridge University Press, 1992; 2nd edition: Grand Rapids: Eerdmans; Dearborn: Dove Booksellers, 2004). The 2004 edition contains a review and discussion of reactions to and developments of his argument since its first publication in 1992 (chapter 11).

24. Two scholars who dissent are Willard M. Swartley, *Israel's Scripture Traditions and the Synoptic Gospels: Story Shaping Story* (Peabody, Massachusetts: Hendrickson, 1994), 283–84; John Riches,

Gospels scholars that to their contemporary audiences the Gospels would have been recognized as lives (*bioi*) of Jesus, i.e. belonging to the broad generic category of Greco-Roman biography. For our purposes it is very notable that Burridge found no difference between the Synoptics and John's Gospel in this respect. The latter conforms just as well to the numerous criteria of genre that Burridge applied. An immediate and obvious implication of this understanding of the genre of the Gospels is that they "are about a person rather than about community ideas or problems."[25] The "two-level" reading of the Gospel of John is thus immediately rendered suspect by this recognition of genre, as is any expectation that the Gospel is actually *about* the Johannine community (of course, the genre does not preclude the influence of the writer's context on the way he portrays his subject). When we escape the dominant approach's obsession with the community and its history, we can see that surely the most obvious feature of the Gospel, as has always been recognized, is its intense focus on the figure of Jesus and the christological issue of who he is and what he has achieved. The fact that this focus entails a highly theologically interpretative telling of the story of Jesus is not at all an obstacle to recognizing the biographical genre of the Gospel, for all ancient biographies, to one degree or another, were interpretative projects that present the writer's convictions about the significance of his subject.

However, recognizing the genre of the Gospel of John as ancient biography gets us only so far. The genre, as Burridge fully recognizes, is a broad and flexible one, which, like many genres, may overlap with other genres such as moral philosophy, novel, history, and encomium.[26] Biography, in the view of the ancients, was different from historiography in the strict sense (for them, mainly political history) with its high ideals of accuracy (even if these ideals were often not realized). At one end of the spectrum of types of *bioi* are biographies that aspire to the methods and ideals of good historiography, but at the other are largely legendary or fictional accounts of famous persons about whom very little was genuinely known but who were held to deserve biographies nonetheless. Burridge's generic classification of the Gospels as biography does not in itself enable us to locate the Gospels on the spectrum of types of biography. He himself is content to establish the major point that they do belong on that spectrum. Unfortunately we still lack anything approaching a usable, detailed typology of ancient biographies.[27]

"Introduction," in Karl Ludwig Schmidt, *The Place of the Gospels in the General History of Literature*, trans. Byron R. McCane (Columbia: University of South Carolina Press, 2002), vii–xxviii.

25. Richard A. Burridge, "About People, by People, for People: Gospel Genre and Audiences," in Bauckham, ed., *The Gospels*, 113–45, here 125.

26. Burridge, *What*, 46.

27. The old and influential proposal of Friedrich Leo (writing in 1901) to identify two different traditions of ancient biographies, the Peripatetic and the Alexandrian, depends on a speculative and probably mistaken reconstruction of the development of the genre, and has been widely criticized. Justin M. Smith is currently writing a doctoral dissertation, under my supervision, in which he establishes a typology of ancient biographies in connection with an attempt to situate the Gospels within it.

Andrew Lincoln's judgment is that we should compare the Gospel of John with the ancient lives of philosophers, religious leaders or holy men, with the result that

> [W]hat we know of the genre should lead us to expect, as ancient readers would also have done, a narrative which contained a substratum of core events from the tradition with substantial correspondence to what happened in the past but which was now shaped by an interpretive superstructure with varying amounts of embellishment, including some legendary or what we would call "fictive" elements.[28]

Craig Keener, on the other hand, classifies the canonical Gospels in general, including the Fourth Gospel, as "historical biographies," differentiating all four from the more novelistic noncanonical narrative Gospels. But he finds it difficult, in the absence of "a single, precise parallel to John's interpretation of Jesus," to determine "the *degree* of the historical character of the Fourth Gospel."[29]

My own present contribution to this matter is chapter 4 below ("Historiographical Characteristics of the Gospel of John"), which breaks new ground by comparing the Gospel with the characteristics of good historiographical method, as generally recognized in the Greco-Roman world, and showing that, however surprising this may be in the light of most scholarly evaluations of the Gospel of John, it would have looked to contemporaries more like historiography than the Synoptics would have done. The argument serves to place John's Gospel squarely within that part of the spectrum of types of ancient biographies where the genre of biography overlapped with that of historiography. It does not look at all like the largely fictive lives of philosophers and holy men, usually written long after their lifetimes, with which Lincoln compares it, but in fact more like the biographies of political figures written within living memory. The contemporaneity of the Gospel with the history it recounts—in the sense that the events were still within the memory of at least one still living witness, the author—must be a decisive factor in the audience's perception of its genre. In the view of the ancients, history could really only be written within the period in which the author could, if not himself an eyewitness, at least interview still living eyewitnesses. Similarly, it was biographies that also fulfilled this condition that tended to approximate to historiography and would be expected to have the kind of accuracy that properly

---

28. Lincoln, *Gospel*, 17. His characterization of the lives of philosophers, religious leaders or holy men is too general to be really useful in relation to the Gospels. In particular, he does not consider the case of a contemporary life, one written within living memory by a disciple. In this respect, Lucian's *Life of Demonax* and Porphyry's *Life of Plotinus* might be more appropriate examples to compare with the Gospels. Lawrence M. Wills, *The Quest of the Historical Gospel* (London: Routledge, 1997), very implausibly compares both Mark and John with the *Life of Aesop*.

29. Keener, *The Gospel*, 1:33–34, cf. 79–80. There also is an important study of the genre of the Gospel, which pays attention to the spectrum from fiction to history in ancient narrative genres, in Derek Tovey, *Narrative Art and Act in the Fourth Gospel*, JSNTSup 151 (Sheffield: Sheffield Academic Press, 1997), chapter 6.

researched historiography could have. It was precisely because biographies written long after the time of their subjects could *ipso facto* not be properly historiographical (though they could draw on historiographical sources if such were available) that legend and even outright fiction were acceptable in their case.

The claim to eyewitness authorship made by the Gospel of John is therefore far more important for its audience's perception of its genre than has recently been recognized. It is why, despite Lincoln's claim that an ancient audience would have expected all manner of legendary and fictive embellishment of the core story in a work of this kind, this is not at all what the evidence of second-century readers of the Gospel suggests. Given the evidence set out in my essay that this Gospel, with its topological and chronological precision, its selectivity and narrative asides, would have looked like a biography of strongly historiographical character, it is not likely that the original readers "would not have had any difficulty in recognizing elements in a narrative as a literary device," realizing that "the convention of having eyewitness elements in a narrative frequently served as a way of lending that narrative verisimilitude and of authenticating its writer's later perspective."[30] Once more, we need more generic precision. Doubtless Jewish readers of pseudepigraphal works attributed to figures such as Abraham and Moses could take the attribution with a pinch of salt while valuing the works for their religious or entertainment value. But these were ancient, not contemporary figures. The Greek novels employed some of the rhetorical features of historiography in the same way that a modern historical novel might, but such fictional imitation of history was patently for the sake of entertainment, and the overwhelmingly serious nature of the Gospel of John would certainly preclude its being read as a novel. Finally, there were indeed "lying historians" who made false claims about their eyewitness sources as a rhetorical device of audience persuasion,[31] but this does not mean that readers/hearers would regard this as merely an acceptable literary convention. They might be more or less taken in but would not have deliberately colluded in such rhetorical fabrication.

It is important to stress that my argument in this essay is about genre. It can tell us about readers'/hearers' expectations of the work. It cannot in itself confirm that the Gospel actually has the degree of historical accuracy that its genre would lead readers to expect. It is important also to stress that these reader expectations were not those of modern readers of historiography. This is partly because all historiography in the ancient world was narrative, and skillful storytelling was a necessary and expected means of holding the readers' attention while also instructing them. Even such a scrupulous historian as Polybius exercises, as a matter of course, the ordinary freedom of a narrator to tell a story in his own way. But there is also the special case of discourses. The ancient historical writers' *relative*

30. Lincoln, *Gospel*, 25.

31. S. Byrskog, *Story as History—History as Story: The Gospel Tradition in the Context of Ancient Oral History* (WUNT 123; Tübingen: Mohr Siebeck, 2000; reprinted Leiden: Brill, 2002), 200–23.

freedom to compose discourses appropriate to the speaker and the context is probably the feature of ancient historiography that diverges most from the practice of serious modern history, though we should also note that it is common practice in television docudramas on historical topics or persons. In ancient historiography, discourses were a mandatory part of the genre and had to be supplied even if the historian had very little actual information about what someone said in a context important for the narrative. Keener has already provided a good discussion of the discourses of Jesus in John in relation to ancient practice.[32] My own contribution in this essay is to show how the very different practices of the Synoptic authors and John in composing discourses of Jesus are different ways of solving the issue of how to represent discourses of Jesus within a narrative context. Such discourses could not be reported, only represented. The Synoptic solution, forming a collection of traditional sayings of Jesus, is, as a historiographical technique, no more historically factual than John's alternative method of himself composing extended discourses of Jesus based around traditional sayings. Both practices are to a significant degree fictive, but not in a way that breaches the historiographical character of these Gospels.

Audience and Influences

The question of the target audience of the Gospel (the topic of chapter 5 below) is not unrelated to that of genre. As we have noticed, the most obvious implication of the biographical genre is that the book is about Jesus. In the case of a book that not only focuses relentlessly on Jesus but also constantly depicts him as a figure of universal significance, it would seem odd to write for an audience confined to a small sectarian group isolated from the rest of the Christian movement.[33] This latter concept of the audience seems to me to have been one of the most misleading aspects of the dominant approach to the Gospel. It has led to the notion that the language and ideas of the Gospel are meant to be understood only within the sectarian group and that the socio-ideological purpose of the work is to shore up the group's defensive isolation from outsiders by imparting a sense of the privileged superiority of the in-group. In my view, this view entirely mistakes the literary strategy of the book, which is to introduce readers into its world, with its characteristic language and ideas, by a process of challenging and engaging their interest. The riddles are there to be solved, not by those who already

32. Keener, *The Gospel*, 1:53–80.

33. Cf. Brown, *An Introduction*, 180: "Whatever conflicts in the past history of the community may have shaped the tradition, whatever was the varied and disunited situation among Christian communities reflected in the Gospel, the evangelist was not writing primarily to them or even about them." This seems a major qualification of the hermeneutical significance of Brown's reconstruction of the history of the community.

know the solution,[34] but by those provoked to tease out their meaning, usually with a good deal of help from the author. The constant misunderstandings of Jesus by his opponents in the story are meant to challenge readers to do better. The Gospel's major images seem designed to make contact with the widest possible audience, and the author's storytelling skill is deployed to draw all sorts of readers into the Gospel's "quest for the Messiah."[35] The "special language" of the Gospel (and 1 John) is less like the "anti-language" of a sectarian group systematizing its alienation from the rest of society,[36] more like the work of a poet or artist who stretches everyday meanings in order to shift the audience's perception.[37] These are the issues that are explored, all too briefly, in chapter 5 below, where I take up the thesis of *The Gospels for All Christians*,[38] to the effect that John, like the Synoptics, wrote his Gospel not for a specific community, sectarian or not, but to circulate around all the churches, but also find myself drawn by the special character of this Gospel to suggest that it was written, not for a narrower audience than for the Synoptics, but for an even wider audience, encompassing interested nonbelievers as well as believers in general.

However, I must distinguish my approach from the one that was once common: that John has put the Gospel message into Hellenistic philosophical or religious terms intended to connect with the ideas of educated people in the Greco-Roman world.[39] Charles Dodd could still take this approach in 1953.[40] Dodd argued that the Hermetic literature as well as the strongly Hellenized Jewish thought of Philo are significant backgrounds for understanding the thought world of this Gospel. But the notion that Hellenistic philosophical or mystical ideas or even the kind of Jewish thought, like Philo's, that had adopted major aspects of sophisticated Hellenism, were formative influences on the Gospel has by now given way to a widespread acceptance of the view that the roots of John's particular modes of thought and expression lie in Palestinian Jewish and Jewish-Christian tradition. The thesis that the theological distinctives of the Gospel are to be ascribed to a putative pre-Christian Gnosticism—the view of Bultmann and others—has also been generally abandoned in the face of insuperable difficulties posed by the dates

---

34. *Contra* Tom Thatcher, *The Riddles of Jesus in John: A Study in Tradition and Folklore*, SBLMS 53 (Atlanta: SBL, 2000), despite the importance of this book in other respects.

35. Cf. Painter, *The Quest for the Messiah*. Painter's use of this image is fruitful even if one dissents from his association of it with the thesis of a highly distinctive, sectarian community (e.g., 466).

36. The view of, e.g., Norman R. Petersen, *The Gospel of John and the Sociology of Light: Language and Characterization in the Fourth Gospel* (Valley Forge, PA: Trinity Press International, 1993); Bruce J. Malina and Richard L. Rohrbaugh, *Social-Science Commentary on the Gospel of John* (Minneapolis: Fortress Press, 1998), 7–16.

37. I find much that is conducive to this view in Craig R. Koester, *Symbolism in the Fourth Gospel* (Minneapolis: Fortress, 1995), despite his commitment to the Johannine community hypothesis.

38. See n. 5 above.

39. E.g., E. F. Scott, *The Fourth Gospel: Its Purpose and Theology* (Edinburgh: T. & T. Clark, 1908).

40. Charles H. Dodd, *The Interpretation of the Fourth Gospel* (Cambridge: Cambridge University Press, 1953), 8–9.

of the sources. The turning point in Johannine scholarship's increasing emphasis on the Jewishness of the Gospel came with the publication of major texts from the Dead Sea Scrolls, which apparently revealed a world of Palestinian Jewish thought with parallels precisely to those aspects of Johannine theology—especially its "dualism"—that had been thought to require Hellenistic or Gnostic sources. Johannine scholarship felt the influence of study of the Scrolls in the mid-1950s,[41] and it soon became an accepted conclusion that John "has very special links with the thought of the Dead Sea Scrolls."[42] For some scholars this meant a specific historical or literary relationship with the Qumran community and its writings; for others the parallels pointed only to a common background in certain currents of Palestinian Judaism.

What I have called the dominant approach took this connection with Qumran on board, sometimes in specific features of its varied reconstructions of the history of the Johannine community, more generally in its belief in a more or less exclusively Jewish (including Jewish Christian) background and context for the Gospel. The contrast with the views of scholars in the first half of the twentieth century, for most of whom John was obviously the distinctively Hellenistic Gospel among the four, is remarkable and should perhaps counsel humility in relation to the views of a scholarly consensus at any time. But many scholars in the dominant approach were much less interested in specific ideological influences on the author(s) of the Gospel than in the social and sociological aspects of the community's relationship with the synagogue. The assumption of a special link with Qumran, though very congenial to the dominant approach's construction of the Johannine community as sectarian,[43] has not been reexamined to any great extent since it gained its ascendancy in Johannine studies in the 1960s.

In his revised introduction to the Gospel, shortly before his death in 1998, Raymond Brown, ever the moderate exponent of the dominant approach, opined: "What can be said is that for *some* features of Johannine thought and vocabulary the Qumran literature offers a closer parallel than any other contemporary or

41. See the essays collected in Krister Stendahl ed., *The Scrolls and the New Testament* (New York: Harper, 1957); and James H. Charlesworth ed., *John and Qumran* (London: Chapman, 1972). W. F. Albright and Raymond E. Brown were pioneers in recognizing the importance of the scrolls for Johannine studies.

42. Barnabas Lindars, *The Gospel of John*, NCB (London: Marshall, Morgan & Scott, 1972), 37. One major Johannine scholar who has long been skeptical of any particular relationship between John and the Scrolls is Charles Kingsley Barrett, *The Gospel according to St John*, 2nd ed. (London: SPCK, 1978), 34: "When the passages in John . . . which are really illuminated, and whose exegesis is in any degree determined, by the Scrolls are counted up the result is extremely meagre. Now that the excitement of the first discoveries is past it is possible to see that Qumran has not revolutionized the study of the New Testament—certainly it has not revolutionized the study of John."

43. See Philip F. Esler, *The First Christians in Their Social Worlds: Social-Scientific Approaches to New Testament Interpretation* (London: Routledge, 1994), chapter 5: "Introverted Sectarianism at Qumran and in the Johannine community."

earlier non-Christian literature either in Judaism or in the Hellenistic world."[44] This relatively restrained claim is one that I challenge, along with stronger claims to the connection between John and Qumran, in chapter 6. Perhaps not surprisingly, since he was a pioneer, as early as 1955,[45] in stressing such a connection, Brown reacted strongly against my contention when I gave it a first airing at an annual meeting of the Society of Biblical Literature. But I am convinced that a careful comparison shows that, in the so-called dualistic worldview expressed especially in the terminology of light and darkness, which has been the central common feature in all comparative arguments, the differences between John and the Qumran community's own writings are more impressive than the similarities. I also show that the Johannine material can be more satisfactorily explained from its roots in exegesis of the Hebrew Bible and parallels in other Jewish literature of the late Second Temple period. The influence of Qumran is redundant, and even a common Jewish background other than the most general one is not a helpful hypothesis in view of the differences.

Recently Jörg Frey has published a very thorough and convincing reexamination of the relationship between the Johannine writings and the Qumran writings which similarly concludes that the "dualism" is considerably different in each case, that the terminological parallels are insufficient to demonstrate any special relationship, and that the Dead Sea Scrolls are relevant to the interpretation of the Gospel of John only in the sense that they (including, of course, the literature not written by the community) illuminate our understanding of first-century Judaism in general.[46]

Barnabas Lindars wisely remarked: "The lasting effect of the discovery of the Scrolls is not to range John alongside Qumran, but to give decisive support to the Jewish character of John and the Johannine church."[47] Ironically, the focus on the Scrolls and the assumption that the Jewish background of the Gospel had been "solved" by the Qumran parallels have distracted attention from exploration of more relevant Jewish material. In my view, John's Gospel is Jewish primarily through its pervasive roots in exegesis of the Hebrew Bible in ways that can be illuminated by Jewish exegetical practice of the period. In this sense, John has done what all early Christian writers did: he has understood Jesus better by relating him to the Hebrew Bible. John has done so in ways that are in many (not all) cases rather distinctive. There are parallels in Second Temple Jewish literature that may help us understand some of the more specific influences on him from the variegated Jewish theology of his time. But he was also a highly creative thinker, and his debts

---

44. Brown, *Introduction*, 142.

45. Raymond E. Brown, "The Qumran Scrolls and the Johannine Gospel and Epistles," *CBQ* 17 (1955): 403–19, 559–74.

46. Jörg Frey, "Licht aus den Höhlen? Der 'johanneische Dualismus' und die Texte von Qumran," in Jörg Frey and Udo Schnelle, eds., *Kontexte des Johannesevangelium: Das vierte Evangelium in religions- und traditionsgeschichtlicher Perspektive*, WUNT 175 (Tübingen: Mohr Siebeck, 2004), 117–203.

47. Barnabas Lindars, *John*, New Testament Guides (Sheffield: Sheffield Academic Press, 1990), 49.

to the thought world of his context are therefore selective and idiosyncratic. The threads he has selected have been woven into his own very special tapestry. His Gospel defies ideological pigeonholing.

Issues of Historicity

Chapters 7–10 are arguments in favor of the historical reliability of four aspects or sections of the narrative of the Gospel of John. The methodology deployed is different in each case, since the four topics offer different kinds of opportunity for historical discussion. As such, they may serve to model the various different kinds of historical investigation that are needed if the degree of historical reliability of this Gospel's account of Jesus is to be properly assessed. The fact that all four essays break new ground may show how much there is still to be done along these lines once we put aside the deep-rooted scholarly prejudice against historicity in John, including the dogma that it tells us far more about the Johannine community than it does about Jesus, and get to work on the extensive evidence we have for the Palestinian Jewish world in which the Gospel's narrative is actually set. Johannine scholars cannot expect the historians of late Second Temple Jewish Palestine to hand them on a plate the material relevant to the Gospel. Much of this will only come to light as those who work on the Gospel also immerse themselves in the sources.

Nicodemus is a character unique to John's Gospel and not a few Johannine scholars have therefore supposed that the author probably invented him to serve his own theological or narrative purposes. In chapter 7 ("Nicodemus and the Gurion Family") I study in some detail (readers impatient with this may wish to read first of all the conclusions at the end of the chapter) the few occurrences in Josephus and rabbinic traditions of the name Nicodemus borne by Palestinian Jews in the relevant period. This enables me to reconstruct an aristocratic family of Pharisaic allegiance which was prominent in Jerusalem in the period before 70 CE, and in which the names Nicodemus and Gurion recur over several generations. There have been previous attempts to identify John's Nicodemus with one of these men, but they have lacked the necessary clue to the real significance of the coincidence of names. This is that the Gurion family was one of those Jewish families that used one or two very unusual names, naming sons after grandfathers or after uncles, in order to maintain the identity of the family across the generations. John's Nicodemus is unlikely to be one of the two that we know from the other sources, but he is very likely to have been another member of the same family. What we know of him from the Gospel fits very well the profile of the family as we know it from the other sources. If John invented him, then he would have invented a fictitious member of this well-known family.

Chapter 8 ("The Bethany Family in John 11–12: History or Fiction?") tackles the historicity of another uniquely Johannine character, Lazarus, and of the events in which Lazarus and his two sisters appear in John's narrative. The raising of Lazarus has always been major evidence for the view that John invents characters and events, not simply because the Synoptics say nothing about this miracle but also because it is so important in John's account of the events that led to Jesus' execution, that it is hard to believe that the Synoptic evangelists did not know of it or, knowing of it, omitted it. I draw on Gerd Theissen's identification of "protective anonymity" in Mark's passion narrative in order to suggest why the other evangelists do not (as John does) identify the woman who anointed Jesus as Mary of Bethany and do not narrate the raising of Lazarus at all.

In chapter 9 ("Did Jesus Wash His Disciples' Feet?") I employ not only careful comparisons with the Synoptic Gospels but also the evidence we have for the practice of foot-washing in early Christianity, a strikingly countercultural practice (since outside Christian circles only slaves washed other people's feet). I suggest that this practice is most likely to have originated from Jesus' own example.[48] This is therefore a case where material from patristic literature can illuminate an issue of historicity in John's Gospel.

In chapter 10 ("Jewish Messianism according to the Gospel of John") I show that the expectations of eschatological figures—the prophet like Moses and the Davidic Messiah—which John attributes to the characters in his Gospel correspond very well to what we know of such beliefs from the Jewish sources, and do so with more accurate detail than do the vaguer accounts in the Synoptics. In particular, the expectation of a wonder-working liberator-prophet like Moses was very probably popular among ordinary people but not among the religious experts and leaders, and this is how John's Gospel represents it. We have no reason to think that this kind of expectation was popular in the Jewish diaspora at the end of the century. So this is another major indication (along with such matters as accurate topography and knowledge of temple rituals) that the author really knew very well the Palestinian Jewish context in which Jesus lived. This by no means guarantees the historicity of his story of Jesus, but it does show that he thinks historically in the sense of placing his narrative in a different place and time from that in which he and his readers lived. A writer concerned only to address his own community's conflicts and problems would not have done this. Not even a writer concerned only with the risen and exalted Christ would have set his exposition of Jesus' own messiahship in a context where it is debated, confessed, and denied by characters who accurately reflect the expectations not of the time and place in which he wrote but of the time and place in which Jesus lived.

---

48. Rather predictably the two most recent major commentaries take opposing positions on the historicity of this narrative. Lincoln, *Gospel*, 375, thinks John has created the event out of Synoptic sayings, while Keener, *Gospel*, 2:901, thinks those sayings contribute to the plausibility of the event in John.

I do not think that everything in John's Gospel can be verified historically in these ways. As with any other historical source, what needs to be assessed is its general reliability. (This is the best reason why commentators are either consistently skeptical of historicity in John or consistently inclined to accept it.) If the Gospel is judged trustworthy so far as we can test it, then we should trust it for what we cannot verify. That is ordinary historical method. Probably the many points where the narrative reflects a historical context in first-century Jewish Palestine offer the most promising opportunities for testing, given how much we now know about that context. But judgments about the general reliability of the Gospel as history must also be affected by quite different factors.

The genre of the Gospel, discussed above and in chapter 4, is crucially important, because it shows that readers would have expected a historical narrative, as opposed to some other kind of narrative. They would expect to read of real historical events and real historical persons, of course within the conventions that allowed even the most scrupulous of historians degrees of freedom in certain respects. If we take the genre seriously, then we should not suppose that good historical traditions have survived in this Gospel only by accident, taken over by a writer whose concern was wholly otherwise. In adopting generic features that biographies of the more historiographical kind displayed, John has indicated that he takes seriously his own programmatic statement of the theological significance of real history: "the Word became flesh" (1:14). He intends to be faithful to the history.

The question of authorship is also important to historicity. Of course, the question whether the Gospel really does embody eyewitness testimony, as it claims, and the question of the historical value of its account of Jesus can be played off against each other rather fruitlessly: either (a) such a manifestly unhistorical account cannot have come from an eyewitness, or (b) we can trust the account because it does come from an eyewitness.

In the end, the historical problem of John's Gospel is: how can its differences from the Synoptics be explained? It is worth considering whether the attribution of the Gospel, not just to an eyewitness as such, but to this particular witness, the beloved disciple, can help answer that question. If the beloved disciple is not John the son of Zebedee, but a disciple who was not one of the Twelve, then I believe it can. Mark's Gospel, in my view,[49] is shaped by the Jesus traditions in the form in which they were formulated in the early Jerusalem church by the Twelve, and Matthew and Luke, while adding other traditions from other sources, take over Mark's framework and much of Mark's content. If the Gospel of John were based on the eyewitness testimony of one of the Twelve, moreover one who belonged to the inner circle of the Twelve (Peter and the two sons of Zebedee), then it would be incomprehensible that the story it tells is so different from the Synoptics. But it is comprehensible if the beloved disciple was not one of the Twelve but a nonitinerant disciple of Jesus, resident in Jerusalem, who moved in

---

49. Bauckham, *Jesus and the Eyewitnesses*, chapters 5–7.

circles of disciples rather different from that of Peter and the sons of Zebedee: other disciples outside the number of the Twelve (Nathanael; Mary, Martha and Lazarus; Nicodemus) and members of the Twelve who are prominent in John but not in the Synoptics (Philip, Thomas, Andrew, the other Judas). John provides a different angle on Jesus' story, other memories of Jesus, a different selection of events, because his sources are different, though not inferior. This is the direction in which the dominant approach's emphasis on the independence of John from the Synoptics should have pointed, rather than generating the fantasy of a sectarian history of the community.

The Gospel of John also differs from the Synoptics, unquestionably, in being a much more interpretative account. It is not at all clear, however, why this should be considered an argument against its authorship by an eyewitness. The beloved disciple is represented in the narrative as someone who, though absent from much of the narrative, was nevertheless close to Jesus, observed things that others did not notice, and acquired an especially perceptive insight into the meaning of it all. Precisely such a disciple could well have felt authorized, by his relationship to Jesus and the events, to write not just his memories, but his reflective interpretation of Jesus and his story. That he had been allowed to "remain" (21: 22–23) when other eyewitnesses, such as Peter, had already died (21:18–19), he surely understood as integral to his vocation to bear the most adequate witness to Jesus, the outcome of his lifetime of reflection on the traditions he had been recounting throughout his long life. The inheritance from nineteenth-century German scholarship still inclines us to believe, when all is said and done, that John does not really take us further into the reality of Jesus but further from it, that his interpretation is actually a gross distortion. I do not see why even an interpretation of that kind *could* not come from a personal disciple of Jesus, but neither do I think that we have to choose between the Synoptic Jesus (or rather the three Jesuses of the Synoptics) and the Johannine Jesus.

Theology

I am quite surprised to realize that only two essays in this collection (chapters 11–12) really deal with the theology of the Gospel. I hope to remedy that in the future. In the meantime, chapter 11 tackles the relationship of John's Christology to the Jewish monotheism to which, in my view, he remained fully committed, like other early Christian writers. The dominant approach makes much of the idea that John's high Christology, along with the alleged traces of "lower" Christological material in the Gospel, developed out of the Johannine community's eventually traumatic conflict with the synagogue to which it once belonged and from which it was ejected, though it is debated whether the Johannine Christology was the cause or the result of the community's conflict with its non-Christian fellow Jews. This picture can be interpreted sympathetically, as in a recent treatment by James

McGrath, who argues that the need to defend the community's Christology was the reason for John's authentic development of the tradition,[50] much as the christological heresies of the fourth and fifth centuries were the reason for the church's development of the Nicene and Chalcedonian definitions of orthodox Trinitarian and Christological doctrine. Alternatively, the relationship of Johannine Christology to the community's conflict with the synagogue can be interpreted much less favorably, as by Maurice Casey who sums up his view trenchantly: "Its Christology has gone higher and higher because this is what the Jewish community cannot accept. . . . [The Gospel of John] gives us an un-Jewish presentation of Jesus, one which was formed in conflict with the Jewish community, to which Jesus and all the first apostles belonged."[51]

I do not wish to deny that debate with non-Christian Jews about the consistency of Christology with Jewish faith in the one God played a part in the development of early (not only Johannine) Christology. Moreover, I share the dominant approach's emphasis on the thoroughly Jewish nature of the context in which high Christology was formulated in the New Testament period, by contrast with the old view that only the influence of Gentile Hellenistic cults can explain the development of divine Christology. But in my view the common and fundamental Christology of all of the New Testament writers is "high" in the sense that it portrays Jesus as sharing the divine identity of the one God of Israel, while at the same time it uses precisely the conceptuality of strict Jewish monotheism in order to formulate such a Christology.[52] In principle, Paul's inclusion of Jesus along with God his Father in a reformulation of the Shema (1 Cor. 8:4–6; cf. Deut. 6:4) is as "high" as anything in John's Gospel. All the New Testament authors were engaged in the formulation of a Christological monotheism that, for them, remained in full continuity with Jewish monotheism while including Jesus in the Jewish definition of the uniqueness of the one God. Johannine Christology has its own distinctive ways of expressing this, but nevertheless has much in common with other New Testament expressions of Christological monotheism. The development of such a Christological monotheism had deeper theological roots than any polemical or apologetic requirements of conflict with non-Christian Jews.

Chapter 12 ("The Holiness of Jesus and His Disciples in the Gospel of John") is a more narrowly focused study which examines John's relationship to Jewish cultic practice and vocabulary in order to give precision to the ideas of holiness and consecration as he applies them both to Jesus and to the disciples.

50. James F. McGrath, *John's Apologetic Christology: Legitimation and Development in Johannine Christology*, SNTSMS 111 (Cambridge: Cambridge University Press, 2001).

51. Maurice Casey, *Is John's Gospel True?* (London: Routledge, 1996), 62.

52. Richard Bauckham, *God Crucified: Monotheism and Christology in the New Testament* (Carlisle: Paternoster, 1998; Grand Rapids: Eerdmans, 1999).

Literary Unity

Synchronic studies of the way the final form of the Gospel is constructed are steadily revealing its intricate design and unity in both literary and thematic ways.[53] In my view, these are demonstrating that the older, diachronic approaches of source and redaction criticism are no longer necessary or convincing explanations for the composition of the Gospel as we have it,[54] although many scholars,[55] including some of those engaged in these synchronic studies,[56] continue to think the two approaches complementary and compatible. The more the so-called aporias in the text are seen to fulfil an intelligible function in the structure and meaning of the text as we have it, the less cogent become the old explanations of them as revealing the seams at which preexisting sources have been sewn together by a redactor. The more the theological tensions in the text are understood as serving the theological strategy of the whole Gospel,[57] the less convincing become the attempts to distinguish a variety of authors and redactors engaged in adjusting or correcting each other's theology.[58] It should also be noticed that studies of the style of the Gospel are increasingly undermining source criticism by demonstrating that no parts of the Gospel are stylistically distinguishable from others.[59]

53. See, for example, the survey of German scholarship in the 1990's, highlighting the trend towards synchronic interpretation, in Klaus Scholtissek, "Johannine Studies: A Survey of Recent Research with Special Regard to German Contributions," in two parts: *Currents in Research: Biblical Studies* 6 (1998): 227–59; 9 (2001): 277–305.

54. Cf. Carson, *The Gospel*, 67–68. John Ashton, *Studying John: Approaches to the Fourth Gospel* (Oxford: Clarendon, 1994), chapter 6, attacks narrative criticism of the Gospels, partly because it "systematically ignores the strong likelihood, to say the least, that the text of the Fourth Gospel, like the other three, had a history, and therefore should not be assumed without further ado to be a single, fully integrated, composition" (165). Certainly, unity should not be "assumed, without further ado," but Ashton ignores the possibility that synchronic study may explain better those features of the text that other critics, like himself, take to be marks of textual development.

55. E.g., Martinus C. de Boer, "Narrative Criticism, Historical Criticism and the Gospel of John," in Stanley E. Porter and Craig A. Evans, *The Johannine Writings: A Sheffield Reader* (Sheffield: Sheffield Academic Press, 1995), 95–108 (first published in *JSNT* 47 [1992]: 35–48).

56. E.g., Wayne Brouwer, *The Literary Development of John 13–17*, SBLDS 182 (Atlanta: SBL, 1999).

57. See, as an outstanding example, Jörg Frey's study of Johannine eschatology in three volumes: *Die johanneische Eschatologie*, WUNT 96, 110, 117 (Tübingen: Mohr Siebeck, 1997, 1998, 2000).

58. In his conclusion to Brown, *Introduction*, which he edited, Francis J. Moloney points out that there are tensions and non sequiturs in this work that Brown wrote by revising the 1966 introduction to his commentary, and asks: 'If Brown's own work—obviously the work of a single author working on the same material across a span of 30 years—can reflect . . . tensions and internal contradictions, is it necessary to develop a hypothesis involving a series of different authors (BD, evangelist, redactor) to explain the composition of the Gospel of John that will demonstrate these tensions and internal contradictions?' (318–9).

59. See the survey in Gilbert van Belle, "Style Criticism and the Fourth Gospel," in Patrick Chatelion Counet and Ulrich Berges, eds., *One Text, A Thousand Methods: Studies in Memory of Sjef van Tilborg*, BIS 71 (Leiden: Brill, 2005), 291–316. But see also, for a defence of Robert Fortna's "signs source" theory, using stylometrics, Tom Felton and Tom Thatcher, "Stylometrics and the Signs Gospel," in Robert T.

Chapter 21 of the Gospel is the last refuge of source criticism. This chapter is widely regarded as "unquestionably a later addition, whether by the original author or a later hand."[60] Such a comment is unintentionally dismissive of scholars who have regarded chapter 21 as an integral part of the Gospel's original design.[61] In chapter 13, I argue for this latter view by investigating aspects of the "numerical composition" of the Gospel. Few scholars yet take numerical composition seriously, but the evidence that biblical authors wrote complex numerical patterns into their work is mounting to the point where it cannot be ignored.[62] While it is still difficult to understand the purpose of numerical composition, it belongs with other evidence of meticulous design in such works as the Gospels. The argument I present in chapter 13 is part of a broader theory of numerical composition throughout the Gospel of John, not yet published.

Fortna and Tom Thatcher ed., *Jesus in Johannine Traditions* (Louisville: Westminster John Knox, 2001), 209–18.

60. D. Moody Smith, "What Have I Learned about the Gospel of John?" in Fernando F. Segovia ed., *"What is John?" Readers and Readings of the Fourth Gospel*, SBL Symposium Series 3 (Atlanta: Scholars Press, 1996), 217–35, here 227. For the view that it was the author of the Gospel himself who added chapter 21 at a late stage, see, e.g., Witherington, *John's Wisdom*, 352.

61. See chapter 13 below, n. 32. These scholars include, most recently, Moody Smith's pupil Craig Keener: *The Gospel*, 2:1219–1222.

62. Note the recent endorsement of these arguments by Birger Gerhardsson, "The Secret of the Transmission of the Unwritten Jesus Tradition," *NTS* 51 (2005), 1–18, here 12 and n. 28.

2

PAPIAS AND POLYCRATES
ON THE ORIGIN
OF THE GOSPEL OF JOHN

Hypotheses of Authorship

The external evidence for the origin of the Fourth Gospel has been reviewed so often[1] that it might be thought there could be no new conclusions to be drawn from it. In recent Johannine studies it has tended to be treated as irrelevant. But Martin Hengel's book, *The Johannine Question*,[2] uses a fairly traditional assessment of the external evidence to support a relatively novel solution to "the

Originally published in a slightly different form in *Journal of Theological Studies* 44 (1993): 24–69. Reprinted by permission of the publisher.

1. E.g., J. B. Lightfoot, *Biblical Essays* (London: Macmillan, 1983), 47–122; V. H. Stanton, *The Gospels as Historical Documents*, part 1 (Cambridge: Cambridge University Press, 1903); B. W. Bacon, *The Fourth Gospel in Research and Debate* (London/Leipzig: T. Fisher Unwin, 1910), 73–154; A. E. Garvie, *The Beloved Disciple* (London: Hodder & Stoughton, 1922), 204–21; C. F. Nolloth, *The Fourth Evangelist* (London: J. Murray, 1925), 37–71; J. E. Carpenter, *The Johannine Writings* (London: Constable, 1927), 208–17; H. P. V. Nunn, *The Authorship of the Fourth Gospel* (Eton: Alden and Blackwell, 1952); F.-M. Braun, *Jean le Théologien et son évangile dans l'église ancienne* (Paris: Gabalda, 1959), 299–392; R. E. Brown, *The Gospel according to John (I–XII)*, AB 29 (Garden City, NY: Doubleday, 1966), lxxxviii–xcii; R. Schnackenburg, *The Gospel according to St. John*, trans. K. Smith (London: Burns & Oates/New York: Herder and Herder, 1968), 1:77–91.

2. M. Hengel, *The Johannine Question*, trans. J. Bowden (London: SCM, 1989).

Johannine question." It is the argument of this chapter that a fresh look at the most important external evidence can show that it supports Hengel's case much more strongly than he realizes.

In essence, Hengel's solution to "the Johannine question" is that John the Elder, to whom Papias refers in the famous fragment of his prologue (ap. Eusebius, *Hist. eccl.* 3.39.4), was both the beloved disciple and the author of the Fourth Gospel (as well as of the Johannine letters).[3] This simple statement of Hengel's position requires two qualifications. First, with regard to the authorship of the Gospel, he regards it as substantially the work of John the Elder, but allows that the form of the Gospel that we have (the only form that was ever "published") is the result of a redaction by members of the Johannine school after John the Elder's death. The editors added at least the closing verses; Hengel leaves open the extent to which their editorial activity may have affected the rest of the Gospel.[4] Second, with regard to the identification of the beloved disciple, Hengel thinks that the portrayal of the disciple in the Gospel is to some extent deliberately enigmatic and may be intended to hint at two possible identifications: John the Elder and John the son of Zebedee.[5] I have argued elsewhere[6] that in this respect Hengel has unnecessarily complicated and compromised his proposal by retaining a relic of the traditional identification of the beloved disciple with John the son of Zebedee. The alleged hints of this identification within the Gospel are illusory. In the present chapter we shall proceed on the basis of the view that the Gospel portrays the beloved disciple not as one of the Twelve, but as a Jerusalem disciple of Jesus. This view is accepted by many of those recent scholars who hold that the beloved disciple is portrayed in the Gospel as a historical individual, not as a purely ideal figure.

The threefold identification of the beloved disciple, the author of the Gospel, and John the Elder, has several major advantages: (1) It accepts the only plausible meaning of John 21:24: that it designates the beloved disciple as the author of the Gospel.[7] An author may, of course, employ a secretary, and an author's work may be edited by others, but he is substantially responsible for the content of the work. This verse designates the beloved disciple the author of the Gospel, not merely the source or guarantor of the tradition behind it. I have argued elsewhere that the references to the beloved disciple within the Gospel also portray him precisely as

---

3. The common authorship of the Gospel and the letters is important to Hengel's overall case, but in this chapter we shall focus almost exclusively on the Gospel.

4. Hengel, *Johannine Question*, 84, 94–96, 99–100, and esp. 105–8.

5. Ibid., 127–32.

6. R. Bauckham, "The Beloved Disciple as Ideal Author," *JSNT* 49 (1993): 21–44, reprinted as chapter 3 of the present volume.

7. The meaning of γράψας, though it can easily accommodate an author's use of a secretary, cannot be so extended as to make the beloved disciple less than the author. G. Schrenk, "γράφω," *TDNT* 1:743, offers no evidence at all for such a usage, while F. R. M. Hitchcock, "The Use of γράφειν," *JTS* 31 (1930): 271–75, shows that the kind of evidence that is sometimes alleged does not meet the need.

the author.[8] (2) This proposal accepts that the Gospel itself does not support the identification of the beloved disciple with John the son of Zebedee. (3) It avoids the supposition that the name of one of the greatest teachers of the early church, author of one of its finest literary products, has inexplicably disappeared without any trace in the historical evidence. (4) It takes account of the fact that there is no evidence that the Gospel was ever regarded as anonymous (unlike the case of Hebrews), and that all the evidence for its attribution ascribes it to "John" (though not always unambiguously to John the son of Zebedee).[9] (5) It can explain the attribution to John the son of Zebedee, which eventually prevailed in the early church, as the result of an assimilation of John the Elder, a disciple of Jesus who was not one of the Twelve, to the better known and more prestigious Apostle John the son of Zebedee.

It is surprising to find that, although John the Elder has in the past enjoyed a certain popularity in Johannine scholarship as a candidate for the authorship of the Gospel, the threefold identification of John the Elder with the author of the Gospel *and* with the beloved disciple has only rarely been proposed before Hengel. Hengel himself refers to no precedents for it,[10] and I know of only three: the arguments of H. Delff[11] (though he distinguished the beloved disciple's work from extensive later interpolations), C. F. Burney[12] (whose case was only very briefly argued), and J. Colson.[13] In the period when authorship of the Gospel by John the Elder was quite often canvassed, the possibility that he could also be the beloved disciple was rarely raised even though it was usually rightly recognized that, according to Papias, he had been a personal disciple of Jesus. This seems to have been because of the continuing strength of the view that the evidence of the Gospel itself indicates the identification of the beloved disciple with John the son of Zebedee. In English scholarship at least, this view was very widely accepted well into this century as a result of Westcott's famous case for it.[14] B. H. Streeter, who in England especially espoused the cause of John the Elder's authorship of the Gospel, also regarded the identification of the beloved disciple with John the

---

8. Bauckham, "Beloved Disciple."

9. The only exception is Gaius's polemical attribution of the Gospel to John's traditional enemy Cerinthus, an attribution obviously parasitic on the attribution to John.

10. Hengel, *Johannine Question*, 200 n. 45, refers to Delff's work, but not as a precedent for the threefold identification.

11. H. K. H. Delff, *Die Geschichte des Rabbi Jesus von Nazareth* (Leipzig: W. Friedrich, 1889); idem, *Das vierte Evangelium: Ein authentischer Bericht über Jesus von Nazareth* (Husum: C. F. Delff, 1890). Delff was followed rather tentatively by W. Sanday, *The Criticism of the Fourth Gospel* (Oxford: Clarendon, 1905), 17–18, 98–99; F. C. Burkitt, *The Gospel History and Its Transmission* (Edinburgh: T. & T. Clark, 1911), 247–55.

12. C. F. Burney, *The Aramaic Origin of the Fourth Gospel* (Oxford: Clarendon, 1922), 133–49.

13. J. Colson, *L'énigme du disciple que Jésus aimait*, Théologie Historique 10 (Paris: Beauchesne, 1969). Cf. now also M.-L. Rigato, "L' 'apostolo ed evangelista Giovanni,' 'sacerdoto' levitico," *Rivista Biblica* 38 (1990): 451–83.

14. B. F. Westcott, *The Gospel according to St. John* (London: J. Murray, 1881), v–xxiv; cf. J. B. Lightfoot, *Biblical Essays* (London: Macmillan, 1893), 41–42.

son of Zebedee as virtually self-evident, and so was obliged to postulate some historical connection between the two Johns and to resort to supposing that in 21:20–23 the author of the Gospel, John the Elder, refers both to himself and to the son of Zebedee.[15] But the real strength of the case for attributing the Gospel to John the Elder could not be appreciated when the beloved disciple was still supposed to be John the son of Zebedee.

More recently, a number of scholars have recognized that the Gospel does not portray the beloved disciple as one of the Twelve, who accompanied Jesus throughout the ministry, but as a Jerusalem disciple.[16] In the meantime, however, the idea of associating the Gospel with John the Elder had fallen out of favor. Whoever the beloved disciple might have been and whoever might have written the Gospel, there seemed no good reason for identifying either or both with the shadowy figure of John the Elder,[17] known only from one reference to him by Papias.[18] Moreover, since the external evidence has usually been thought to offer no identification of the beloved disciple or of the author of the Gospel other than John the son of Zebedee, recent scholars who correctly think the internal evidence tells decisively against his being either have tended to treat the external evidence as wholly unreliable and therefore irrelevant.[19] There have been some challenges to the view that the external evidence points unanimously to John the son of Zebedee as the beloved disciple and the author,[20] but these have not succeeded in disturbing the generally accepted account of the external evidence, which almost all recent Johannine scholarship has presupposed. It is time that the external evidence was reexamined, to see whether after all it may not so completely contradict the internal evidence. In this chapter, we shall argue that the

15. B. H. Streeter, *The Four Gospels* (London: Macmillan, 1924), 430–81; cf. idem, *The Primitive Church* (London: Macmillan, 1929), 89–97. A similar position was taken by A. Harnack, *Die Chronologie der altchristlichen Litteratur bis Eusebius* (Leipzig: J. C. Hinrichs, 1897), 1:659–80.

16. J. N. Sanders, *The Fourth Gospel in the Early Church* (Cambridge: Cambridge University Press, 1943), 43–45; O. Cullmann, *The Johannine Circle*, trans. J. Bowden (London: SCM, 1976), 63–85; R. E. Brown, *The Community of the Beloved Disciple* (London: G. Chapman, 1979), 31–34 (a change of view from that in idem, *Gospel according to John*, xcii–xcvii); G. R. Beasley-Murray, *John*, Word Biblical Commentary 36 (Waco: Word Books, 1987), lxx–lxxv. These hold that the beloved disciple must remain anonymous. For older arguments to this effect, see Burkitt, *Gospel History*, 247–50; Garvie, *The Beloved Disciple*, 202–4. Others who see the beloved disciple as a Jerusalem disciple have identified him with Lazarus or John Mark: see the references and discussion in Cullmann, *Johannine Circle*, 76–77; S. S. Smalley, *John: Evangelist and Interpreter* (Exeter: Paternoster, 1978), 77–78.

17. Of course, the view that in Papias's prologue John the Elder is a distinct person from John the son of Zebedee has been challenged, notably by J. Chapman, *John the Presbyter and the Fourth Gospel* (Oxford: Clarendon, 1911); G. M. Lee, "The Presbyter John: A Reconsideration," in *Studia Evangelica*, ed. E. A. Livingstone, TU 112 (Berlin: Akademie-Verlag, 1973), 311–20. But it remains the most plausible interpretation of Papias and is accepted by the vast majority of scholars.

18. Cf. Cullmann, *Johannine Circle*, 70.

19. E.g., Brown, *Community*, 33–34, abandoning the view that the beloved disciple is John the son of Zebedee, says, "I now recognize that the external and internal evidence are probably not to be harmonized."

20. E.g., Burney, *Aramaic Origin*, 134–40.

best external evidence in fact supports the internal evidence in seeing the beloved disciple, the author of the Gospel, as a disciple of Jesus who was not one of the Twelve. This coincidence with the best reading of the internal evidence strongly suggests that the external evidence is also reliable when it calls this disciple John, indicating a John of Ephesus who must be not the son of Zebedee, but Papias's John the Elder.

The only church, so far as we know, that ever claimed to be the place of origin of the Fourth Gospel was Ephesus. This means that if the external evidence is of any value, the most reliable is likely to be that of writers who can witness to the local tradition of Ephesus and its neighborhood in the second century. Such writers are Papias of Hierapolis and Polycrates of Ephesus. We shall begin with Polycrates, since what he said on this subject is extant, whereas whether Papias said anything on the subject is disputed and what he said will have to be reconstructed from other authors who used his work. In the light of a fresh interpretation of Polycrates and Papias, the rest of the external evidence will fall into a different pattern from the way it has usually been represented.

The Letter of Polycrates

The tradition of the church of Ephesus as to the authorship of the Gospel is preserved for us by Polycrates, bishop of Ephesus, in a letter written in the last decade of the second century to Victor of Rome during the paschal controversy. The purpose of the letter is to defend the quartodeciman observance of Asia as supported by the highest authority in local tradition:

> As for us, then, we keep the day without tampering with it, neither adding, nor subtracting. For indeed in Asia great luminaries have fallen asleep, such as shall rise again on the day of the Lord's appearing, when he comes with glory from heaven to seek out all his saints: to wit, Philip, one of the twelve apostles, who has fallen asleep in Hierapolis, [as have] also his two daughters who grew old in virginity, and his other daughter who lived in the Holy Spirit and rests at Ephesus; and, moreover, [there is] John too, he who leant back on the Lord's breast, who was a priest, wearing the sacerdotal plate (τὸ πέταλον πεφορεκώς), both martyr (μάρτυς) and teacher. He has fallen asleep at Ephesus. Moreover, Polycarp too, at Smyrna, both bishop and martyr; and Thraseas, both bishop and martyr, of Eumenia, who has fallen asleep at Smyrna. And why need I mention Sagaris, both bishop and martyr, who has fallen asleep at Laodicea? or the blessed Papirius, or Melito the eunuch who in all things lived in the Holy Spirit, who lies at Sardis, awaiting the visitation from heaven when he shall rise from the dead? These all observed the fourteenth day for the Pascha according to the Gospel, in no way deviating therefrom, but following the rule of faith. And moreover I also, Polycrates, the least of you all, [do] according to the tradition of my kinsmen, some of whom also I have followed closely (παρηκολούθησα). Seven of my kinsmen were bishops, and I am the eighth. And my kinsmen always kept the day when the people put away the leaven. Therefore I

for my part, brethren, who number sixty-five years in the Lord and have conversed with the brethren from all parts of the world and traversed the entire range of holy Scripture, am not affrighted by threats. (ap. Eusebius, *Hist. eccl.* 5.24.2–7)[21]

Discussions of this passage have usually failed to appreciate its careful artistry. Polycrates adduces *seven* great luminaries of Asia who practiced the quartodeciman observance. As the number of completeness, seven indicates the sufficiency of their evidence.[22] When Polycrates subsequently refers to his seven relatives, who were bishops and to some of whom he had been a disciple (παρηκολούθησα), he is not adducing a second, unnecessary set of witnesses, but claiming the seven great luminaries themselves as his relatives. In the interests of modesty, he does not claim them as his relatives until he has first named them all and then introduced himself, "the least of you all,"[23] as a supernumerary eighth, whose witness is therefore strictly superfluous. In this way he is able to add his own testimony to that of his illustrious relatives in a suitably modest way. Clearly he regards all seven luminaries as bishops, but uses the word in the list only of those to whom he can attach the phrase ἐπίσκοπος καὶ μάρτυς (Polycarp, Thraseas, Sagaris).

Polycrates' claim to some kind of family relationship with all seven luminaries is not in the least improbable. It is surely significant that, whereas the two daughters of Philip who died at Hierapolis are said to have grown old as virgins, this is not said of the third daughter who died at Ephesus and whom we should presume was therefore an ancestor of Polycrates. It may well be that Polycrates' catalog of his illustrious episcopal relatives was not compiled especially for this occasion, but was one he had proudly rehearsed before. The deliberate limitation of the list to his own relatives, as well as to the number seven, explains the omission of other Asian notables who could presumably have been cited in support of the quartodeciman observance, such as Aristion the disciple of the Lord or Onesimus of Ephesus or Papias of Hierapolis.

Polycrates' reference to Philip is of interest before we turn to John. The Philip in question is certainly Philip the evangelist, whose four virgin daughters prophesied, according to Acts 21:8–9.[24] At least two of the daughters had been known to Papias of Hierapolis (Eusebius, *Hist. eccl.* 3.39.9). Polycrates is clearly dependent

---

21. Translation from H. J. Lawlor and J. E. L. Oulton, *Eusebius Bishop of Caesarea: The Ecclesiastical History and the Martyrs of Palestine* (London: SPCK, 1927), 1:169.

22. Cf. the way the *Muratorian Canon* understands the seven churches to which Paul wrote and the seven churches to which John wrote in Revelation as representative of the whole church.

23. All Greek manuscripts have ὑμῶν, but it is tempting to follow the Syriac version of Eusebius in omitting it.

24. The attempt by Chapman, *John the Presbyter*, 64–71, to argue that Polycrates was correct in identifying the Philip who died at Hierapolis with Philip the apostle, rather than Philip the evangelist, fails because he misunderstands the statement of Polycrates that one of Philip's daughters "lived in the Holy Spirit" (ἐν ἁγίῳ πνεύματι πολιτευσαμένη). This phrase, which Polycrates also uses of Melito, means not just that she was "a holy and venerable person" but that she was a prophetess. Consequently the parallel between the Philip of Polycrates and Philip the evangelist (Acts 21:8–9) is not just that they had daughters

on local tradition about the daughters rather than on Acts 21:8–9, in contrast with the Montanist writer Proclus who knew the tradition associating Philip and his daughters with Hierapolis (and therefore no doubt cited them as part of a Phrygian succession of prophets preceding the Montanist prophets) but refers to four daughters, all prophets, as in Acts 21:8–9 (ap. Eusebius, *Hist. eccl.* 3.31.4). But by calling Philip one of the twelve apostles, Polycrates appears to have confused the two Philips, the apostle and the evangelist. Probably it would be more accurate to say that he identified Philip the apostle and Philip the evangelist as the same person.[25] Early Christian exegetes of New Testament writings, following the similar practice in Jewish exegesis of the Old Testament, frequently assumed that scriptural characters bearing the same names were the same person. The identification of the two Philips by Polycrates, no doubt following an exegetical tradition of the church of Ephesus, is very similar to the way Mary Magdalene and Mary of Bethany were treated as the same person by most Christian writers later than the canonical Gospels. Thus, in his reference to Philip, Polycrates follows a tradition that draws both on local memory of the evangelist and his daughters at Hierapolis and Ephesus and also on an exegetical identification of this Philip with the Philip who was one of the Twelve. We shall see that his reference to John displays the same combination of local historical tradition and local exegetical tradition.

The reference to John is as follows: ἔτι δὲ καὶ Ἰωάννης, ὁ ἐπὶ τὸ στῆθος τοῦ κυρίου ἀναπεσών, ὃς ἐγενήθη ἱερεὺς τὸ πέταλον πεφορεκὼς καὶ μάρτυς καὶ διδάσκαλος, οὗτος ἐν Ἐφέσῳ κεκοίμηται. Of the elements of this description, the most puzzling and debated is the reference to John as a priest who wore the πέταλον. This will therefore be left until last in our discussion. The clause ὁ ἐπὶ τὸ στῆθος τοῦ κυρίου ἀναπεσών is drawn virtually verbatim from the Fourth Gospel (13:25: ἀναπεσὼν . . . ἐπὶ τὸ στῆθος τοῦ Ἰησοῦ; 21:20: ὃς καὶ ἀνέπεσεν . . . ἐπὶ τὸ στῆθος αὐτοῦ). The allusion is most likely to 21:20, because here the beloved disciple is introduced for the last time in the Gospel before being identified as the Gospel's author in 21:24. The phrase indicates the special intimacy with Jesus that qualified the beloved disciple to be the author of the Gospel. By means of it Polycrates not only identifies John as the author of the Fourth Gospel, but also suggests the special value of the fourth Gospel as deriving from a disciple who was especially close to the Lord. That Irenaeus uses precisely the same words (*Haer.* 3.1.1 = Eusebius, *Hist. eccl.* 5.8.4: ὁ καὶ ἐπὶ τὸ στῆθος αὐτοῦ ἀναπεσών) to indicate John as the author of

---

(three or, as Chapman thinks, two according to Polycrates, four according to Acts), but also that at least one daughter of the former was a prophetess, as all four daughters of the latter were.

25. When J. J. Gunther, "Early Identifications of Authorship of the Johannine Writings," *JEH* 31 (1980): 417, says, "A learned ecclesiastic would be able to recognize that Philip the Evangelist was not one of the Twelve," he mistakes the character of learned exegesis in this period. Eusebius fully accepts the identification of the two Philips (*Hist. eccl.* 3.31.2–5).

the Gospel probably reflects a traditional Asian way of referring to the author of the Gospel, rather than Polycrates' dependence on Irenaeus.[26]

Reference to John as the author of the Gospel probably continues with the word μάρτυς. It is not κεκοίμηται that prevents μάρτυς from referring to death as a martyr,[27] for κεκοίμηται is also used of Thraseas and Sagaris who, like Polycarp, are designated martyrs. But whereas Thraseas, Sagaris, and Polycarp are all called ἐπίσκοπος καὶ μάρτυς, with μάρτυς appropriately placed second in the pair, John is called ἱερεὺς . . . καὶ μάρτυς καὶ διδάσκαλος, where μάρτυς, if it referred to his death, would be oddly sandwiched between ἱερεύς and διδάσκαλος. It has often been taken to allude to Revelation 1:2, 9, identifying the author of the Fourth Gospel with the author of Revelation, and referring to his sufferings as a witness to the Gospel in exile on Patmos.[28] But it is more likely to allude to his authorship of the Gospel, which in John 21:24 (cf. 19:35) is treated as equivalent to the beloved disciple's witness.[29] The pair of terms μάρτυς καὶ διδάσκαλος may well designate John as respectively the author of the Gospel and the author of the Johannine letters.[30] We do not need to suppose that Ephesian church tradition had yet identified John the seer of Patmos with John the beloved disciple, the author of the Gospel.

Polycrates' stress on John's authorship of the Gospel may well be connected with the importance of the authority of the Fourth Gospel for defense of the quartodeciman observance. Claudius Apollinaris, bishop of Hierapolis, writing a little earlier or contemporaneously, strongly associates the quartodeciman observance with the Johannine chronology of the passion and refers to opponents of it who appealed to the Matthaean chronology (ap. *Chron. pasch.* praef.). He evidently thought that the Gospels do not disagree, but that the proper way to harmonize them was to take the Johannine chronology as authoritative for correctly interpreting the Matthaean.[31] That Polycrates shared this view is suggested by the way he refers to the 14 Nisan, as "the day when the people put away the leaven." This means that for him the date was identified not as the day on which the Jews ate the Passover meal (since, according to the Jewish reckoning of the day from sunset to sunset,

---

26. J. N. Sanders's treatment of the Johannine question is seriously marred by the way he dismisses Polycrates' evidence, without discussion, as merely dependent on Irenaeus and lacking any independent authority (*Fourth Gospel*, 7). He requires us to believe that no one in Asia thought of considering John of Ephesus the author of the Fourth Gospel until Polycrates read Irenaeus, and that this aged bishop of *Ephesus* then accepted this entirely novel idea purely on Irenaeus's authority. Local church tradition counted for more than this in the late second century. In fact, the association of the author of the Fourth Gospel with Ephesus is attested quite independently of Irenaeus by the *Acts of John*. For the superiority of Polycrates' evidence to that of Irenaeus, cf. Colson, *L'énigme*, 35.

27. As Gunther, "Early Identifications," 420, and others think.

28. E.g., Braun, *Jean le Théologien*, 339.

29. J. H. Bernard, *A Critical and Exegetical Commentary on the Gospel according to St. John*, ed. A. H. McNeile, ICC (Edinburgh: T. & T. Clark, 1928), 1:li.

30. The fact that John is called ὁ διδάσκαλος in *Acts of John* 37 is probably coincidental.

31. R. M. Grant, *The Earliest Lives of Jesus* (New York: Harper, 1961), 30.

this took place at the beginning of the 15 Nisan), but as the day of preparation for the Passover (cf. John 19:14), when leaven had to be removed from houses before sunset. In that case, the significance for Polycrates of observing 14 Nisan can only be that, according to the Johannine chronology, it was the day Christ was crucified. Thus his reference to observing the fourteenth day "according to the Gospel" must be to John's Gospel as authoritative on this point.

Polycrates' final statement about John—that he died at Ephesus—is an obvious claim to local tradition. It means that the tomb of this author of the Gospel was known at Ephesus. It corresponds to Irenaeus's statement, doubtless also based on local Asian tradition, that John wrote the Gospel while living at Ephesus (*Haer.* 3.1.1 = Eusebius, *Hist. eccl.* 5.8.4).

On the basis of the information so far discussed, it has occasionally been argued that Polycrates was clearly not thinking of John the son of Zebedee.[32] The arguments used are suggestive, but not fully conclusive. It is pointed out that whereas Philip is explicitly called one of the twelve apostles, this is not said of John. But it could be replied that, if it were generally believed that the John who wrote the Gospel was one of the twelve apostles, Polycrates could take this for granted, while using instead a description (ὁ ἐπὶ τὸ στῆθος τοῦ κυρίου ἀναπεσών) that gave him even greater authority: not just one of the Twelve, but that member of the Twelve who was most intimate with the Lord. However, this reply begs the question whether it was generally accepted that the author of the Gospel was one of the Twelve. It is also pointed out that Philip, first in the list, is given precedence over John, but the order could merely reflect the belief that Philip had died before John, who according to Irenaeus survived until the reign of Trajan.[33] It is possible, though we cannot be sure, that the rest of the list continues in chronological order of death. A decisive argument for the view that Polycrates refers to a John other than the son of Zebedee will emerge only when we establish the correct interpretation of the remaining item in Polycrates' description of him: his priesthood.

Wearing the *Petalon*

To the puzzle of Polycrates' words ὅς ἐγενήθη ἱερεὺς τὸ πέταλον πεφορεκώς a satisfactory solution has not yet been proposed, but one is available. Before proposing this solution, we need to examine the use of the word πέταλον with reference to the vestments of the Jewish priesthood. The word undoubtedly refers to part of the headdress of the high priest, but it is a matter of some confusion precisely which part is indicated.

32. E.g., Delff, *Geschichte*, 69–72; idem, *Das vierte Evangelium*, 2–11; Burney, *Aramaic Origin*, 134; Colson, *L'énigme*, 35–42; Gunther, "Early Identifications," 420–21; cf. Hengel, *Johannine Question*, 7.
33. Cf. Stanton, *Gospels*, 229.

There need be no doubt at all about what the high priests of the late Second Temple period actually wore on their heads. The problem is rather one of terminology. Josephus, who does not use the word πέταλον at all in this connection, provides a detailed description of the high priest's headdress, with which all other briefer descriptions and allusions are entirely consistent. According to Josephus, the high priest wore the ordinary linen turban (πῖλος) of the priests (*Ant.* 3.172; cf. 157–58) and over it another turban embroidered in blue. This was encircled by a golden crown (στέφανος), which had three tiers and was surmounted by a golden "calyx" (κάλυξ) resembling the calyx of a flower (*Ant.* 3.172–78). The part of the crown that covered the forehead was a band (τελαμών) of gold, on which was inscribed the tetragrammaton. This detailed account is not inconsistent with the briefer description in *Jewish War* 5.235, where the high priest's linen turban (τιάρα), wreathed (κατέστεπτο) with blue, is said to be encircled by a golden crown (στέφανος),[34] on which the tetragrammaton is engraved. The major difference is that here Josephus does not specify on which part of the crown the letters of the divine name appear.[35]

The confusion arises as to how the terms in the Pentateuch's account of the vestments of Aaron should be understood to correspond with this high priestly headdress, in particular the crown. In addition to Aaron's linen turban (מצנפת), Exodus and Leviticus refer both to a holy crown (נזר: Exod. 29:6; 39:30; Lev. 8:9) and to a golden object fastened on the front of the turban (Exod. 28:37), which bears the inscription "Holy to YHWH." The latter is the ציץ (Exod. 28:36; 39:30; Lev. 8:9), a word that normally means "flower." It might be understood to be a flower-shaped ornament (cf. NRSV: "rosette") strapped to the forehead and distinct from the crown, but Exodus 39:30 and Leviticus 8:9 appear to identify the two, using the two words ציץ and נזר in apposition. In the Second Temple period, there seem to have been two traditions of interpretation. In the Hebrew text of Sirach 45:12, the ציץ, with the sacred inscription, is mentioned after and in addition to the golden crown (עטרת) (cf. also 40:4,[36] where the ציץ is mentioned along with the turban: צניף). But Josephus, with his elaborate explanation of how the crown has the shape of a flower, seems dependent on a tradition that understood the ציץ ("flower") to be the whole crown.

In both traditions of interpretation, πέταλον could be used to translate ציץ. Thus *Aristeas* 98, distinguishing the ציץ from the נזר as Ben Sira does, refers to "the hallowed diadem (βασίλειον) having in relief on the front in the middle in holy

---

34. Cf. also the reference to the crown in *Ant.* 20.12.

35. Josephus's statement that what was engraved on the front of the crown was the four letters of the divine name (*Ant.* 3.178; *BJ* 5.235) is supported by Philo, *Mos.* 2.114–15, 132; *Aristeas* 98; Clement of Alexandria, *Strom.* 5.6.38.6. However, Exod. 28:36; 39:30 appear to give the inscription as "Holiness to YHWH" (קדש ליהוה). J. E. Hogg, "A Note on Two Points in Aaron's Headdress," *JTS* 26 (1925): 74–75, argues that the texts in Exodus should be interpreted in line with the later evidence.

36. The reference in 40:4a is certainly to the high priest, corresponding to the reference to the king in 40:3a.

letters on a golden leaf (πετάλῳ) the name of God, ineffable in glory." Similarly, the list of the high priestly garments in *Testament of Levi* distinguishes the crown (στέφανος) from the πέταλον (8:2, cf. vv. 9–10, where the διάδημα seems to be the same as the πέταλον of v. 2). But the Septuagint translators of Exodus and Leviticus seem to agree with the tradition of interpretation reflected in Josephus. They clearly took the ץיצ to be the whole crown. They translate ץיצ as πέταλον (Exod. 28:30 [= Heb. 36]; 36:38 [= Heb. 39:30]; Lev. 8:9), and where the Hebrew refers to the רזנ along with the ץיצ, they take שדקה רזנ to describe the ץיצ as a sanctified object (Exod. 36:38: ἀφόρισμα τοῦ ἁγιοῦ, Lev. 8:9: τὸ καθηγιασμένον ἅγιον). But where שדקה רזנ occurs alone (Exod. 29:6), it is translated as τὸ πέταλον τὸ ἁγίασμα. The same tradition of interpretation is found in Philo, who speaks of a gold πέταλον in the form of a crown (χρυσοῦν δὲ πέταλον ὡσανεὶ στέφανος), on which the tetragrammaton was engraved (*Mos.* 2.114, cf. 116, 132), and probably in Clement of Alexandria who, evidently dependent on Jewish information (cf. *b. Yoma* 31b–32a), says that the high priest on the Day of Atonement removes the πέταλον before entering the holy of holies (*Exc. ex Theod.* 27.1;[37] cf. *Strom.* 5.6.38.6). This most likely means that he removes the whole crown, since according to Josephus's description, it is unlikely that the gold band on the forehead could have been worn separated from the crown of which it was part. We should also note that, although the word πέταλον is not used, in the Greek translation of Sirach both occurrences of ץיצ are suppressed (Sir. 40:4; 45:12), presumably because the Hebrew word was understood to mean nothing other than the golden crown (στέφανος) itself, which had already been mentioned.

We cannot tell, therefore, whether the πέταλον is understood by Polycrates to be the whole of the high priest's golden crown or only the part of it that formed a band across the forehead and on which the tetragrammaton was engraved. What is important is that, in either case, the reference is to a distinctively high-priestly, indeed *the* distinctively high-priestly item of headdress. Of the various golden garments distinctive to the high priest, the golden crown bearing on its front the sacred letters is always treated as the most significant. It appears as the climax of the description of the awe-inspiring garments of Eleazar the high priest in *Aristeas* 96–99, and similarly climaxes Sirach's description of the vestments of Aaron (Sir. 45:8–12). He claims that the crown with its engraved frontlet was a spectacular sight (45:12). Josephus similarly ends his descriptions of the high-priestly vestments with the crown and its sacred inscription (*BJ* 5.231–35; *Ant.* 3.159–78). It was the unique privilege of the high priest to bear the divine name, graven in gold, on his forehead. Josephus also indicates that, whereas there could be any number of sets of the other high-priestly vestments (Solomon, he says, made thousands), "the crown on which Moses had inscribed God's name was unique

---

37. On the Jewish background to this passage, see the note by H. A. Wolfson in R. P. Casey, *The Excerpta ex Theodoto of Clement of Alexandria*, Studies and Documents 1 (London: Christophers, 1934), 122–24.

and has remained to this day" (*Ant.* 8.93).[38] There was only one πέταλον, believed to be the original one made for Aaron. To wear the πέταλον, then, was to officiate as high priest. According to a rabbinic tradition in *b. Qidd.* 66a, when King Jannai (John Hyrcanus?) wished to provoke the Pharisees, who objected to his claiming the high priesthood, he made that claim clear to them by wearing the ץיצ. Thus, when Polycrates claims that John ἐγενήθη ἱερεὺς τὸ πέταλον πεφορεκώς, the words state, as precisely and unambiguously as it was possible to do, that he officiated as high priest in the temple. They cannot even make him one of the ἀρχιερεῖς in the broader sense of that term, as used in the New Testament and Josephus, whether it means members of the high priestly families or the holders of a number of higher offices in the temple. Polycrates' words must mean that John held the office of high priest in succession to Aaron.

They are an accurately Jewish way of expressing this. We may compare Polycrates' description of 14 Nisan as the day "when the people remove the leaven" (ὅταν ὁ λαὸς ἤρνυε τὴν ζύμην). This cannot be simply derived from Exodus 15:12, but reflects both the contemporary Jewish practice (of removing leaven from houses before the beginning of the first day of unleavened bread) and the technical language for it (cf. *m. Pesah.* 1–2). The use of the simple ὁ λαός to mean the Jews is diaspora Jewish practice, known from inscriptions in Asia Minor.[39] Living close to the large Jewish community of Ephesus and in a church with a strongly Jewish-Christian background, it is not surprising that Polycrates can speak of things Jewish in an accurately Jewish way. His doing so may even reflect pride in his own at least partly Jewish descent if, as we have suggested, he claimed descent from one of the daughters of Philip.

In any case, there is no evidence that Christian writers of this period ever imagined that the πέταλον was worn by anyone except the Jewish high priest himself when officiating in the temple. A passage that might be thought to mean that ordinary priests wore the πέταλον is *Protevangelium of James* 5:1, in which Joachim goes to offer sacrifice in the temple and is somehow able to tell from the πέταλον of the priest that God has forgiven his sins. Certainly this writer is not too well informed about what went on in the temple (cf. 8:2–3), but it is not necessary to suppose, as has been argued,[40] that he here confuses the πέταλον with the high priest's breastpiece that contained the Urim and Thummim (Exod. 28:30). Rather, he is interpreting Exodus 28:38 (LXX 34), which connects the πέταλον of the high priest with the removal of the guilt of those who offer sacrifice. Nor does the phrase τὸ πέταλον τοῦ ἱερέως indicate that he thinks the πέταλον was worn by a priest other than the high priest. The simple term "the priest" was not infrequently used when the context made clear reference to the high priest

---

38. Presumably Josephus thinks it was taken with other temple treasures (cf. *BJ* 6.387–91) to Rome after the fall of Jerusalem.

39. H. Strathmann, "λαός," *TDNT* 4:39.

40. Bernard, *John*, 2:595 n. 1; A. de Santos Otero, *Los Evangelios Apócrifos*, 6th ed. (Madrid: Biblioteca de Autores Cristianos, 1988), 138.

(e.g., 1 Kings 1:8; Bar. 1:7; 1 Macc. 15:1; *Gos. Heb.* 7). Since the πέταλον was the most distinctively high-priestly accoutrement, the phrase τὸ πέταλον τοῦ ἱερέως is wholly unambiguous and would probably be preferred to the virtually tautologous τὸ πέταλον τοῦ ἀρχιερέως. This is also why Polycrates does not say that John ἐγενήθη ἀρχιερεὺς τὸ πέταλον πεφορεκώς. The sense of the prefix ἀρχ- is actually conveyed more accurately by the phrase τὸ πέταλον πεφορεκώς, since the latter means precisely that he officiated as high priest in the temple.

Among other Christian references to the πέταλον, the most important as a parallel to Polycrates is Epiphanius's claim that James the Lord's brother wore the πέταλον. He makes this statement in two passages:

> For he [James] was Joseph's eldest born and consecrated. Moreover, we have found that he exercised a priestly office (ἱερατεύσαντα) according to the old priesthood. Wherefore it was permitted to him to enter once a year into the holy of holies, as the law enjoined the high priests in accordance with the Scriptures. For so it is recorded concerning him by many before us, Eusebius and Clement and others. Nay, he was allowed to wear the πέταλον on his head (τὸ πέταλον ἐπὶ τῆς κεφαλῆς ἐξῆν αὐτῷ φορεῖν), as the aforementioned trustworthy persons testified in the same memoirs (ὑπομνηματισμοῖς). (*Pan.* 29.4)[41]
>
> Only to this James was it permitted (μόνον τούτῳ τῷ Ἰακώβῳ ἐξῆν) to enter (εἰσιέναι) once a year into the holy of holies (εἰς τὰ ἅγια τῶν ἁγίων), because he was a Nazirite (Ναζωραῖον), and took part in the office of priesthood (μεμίχθαι τῇ ἱερωσύνῃ). . . . This James also wore the πέταλον on his head (πέταλον ἐπὶ τῆς κεφαλῆς ἐφόρεσε) (*Pan.* 78.13–14).[42]

Since the first passage is clearly connected with Hegesippus's statements that James was holy from his mother's womb and that James alone was allowed to enter the sanctuary (ap. Eusebius, *Hist. eccl.* 2.23.6), and since the second passage occurs in a context in which Epiphanius plainly reproduces what Hegesippus said about James's asceticism and his prayer for the people, as well as his death (*Pan.* 78.13–14; cf. Eusebius, *Hist. eccl.* 2.23.5–7, 11–12, 17), Lawlor argued that the information about James in these two passages must also have come from Hegesippus.[43] It is much more likely that they represent an elaboration of what Hegesippus had said, though one that Epiphanius already found in a source. The relevant words of Hegesippus, reported by Eusebius, are:

> To him alone it was permitted to enter the holy place (τούτῳ μόνῳ ἐξῆν εἰς τὰ ἅγια τῶν ἁγίων εἰσιέναι); for he wore nothing woollen, but linen garments. And

41. Translation from H. J. Lawlor, *Eusebiana: Essays on the Ecclesiastical History of Eusebius Pamphili* (1917; repr., Amsterdam: Philo, 1973), 10.

42. Translation partly from Lawlor, *Eusebiana*, 13.

43. Ibid., 9–15. The word ὑπομνηματισμοῖς in *Pan.* 29.4 probably does allude to the ὑπομνήματα of Hegesippus, but this need not mean that Epiphanius knew Hegesippus's work other than as quoted by Eusebius.

alone he entered into the sanctuary, and was found on his knees asking forgiveness on behalf of the people, so that his knees became hard like a camel's, for he was continually bending the knee in worship to God, and asking forgiveness for the people. (Eusebius, *Hist. eccl.* 2.23.6)[44]

Hegesippus probably meant that James, because of his ascetic sanctity and because he dressed like the priests in linen, was the only man other than the priests who was allowed to enter the holy place. But a reader of Hegesippus has thought the reference must be to the privilege of the high priest to be the only man to enter the holy of holies, once a year on the day of atonement. This interpretation was encouraged by Hegesippus's statements that what James did in the holy place was to pray for the people's forgiveness. So the opening statement of the passage quoted above from Epiphanius, *Pan.* 78.13 is clearly an interpretative rewriting of the first nine words of the passage just quoted from Hegesippus. The passage in Epiphanius then proceeds to interpret the reasons Hegesippus gave for James's privilege of being allowed to enter the holy place. It understands James's ascetic practices and holiness from his mother's womb (Eusebius, *Hist. eccl.* 2.23.4–5) to mean that he was a Nazirite, and it takes his wearing only linen to mean that he actually was a priest.

This secondary interpretation of Hegesippus therefore supposes that James was permitted to officiate on the day of atonement as only the high priest may, entering the holy of holies as if he were high priest. This claim that James officiated as high priest is then expressed by the statement that he wore the πέταλον.

It is clear that this statement about James, despite its extremely improbable nature, is meant literally. It offers no support to the view that what Polycrates said of John was meant metaphorically, with reference to his exercise of authority within the Christian church. Nor does it offer any possibility that wearing the πέταλον could mean anything other than officiating as high priest in the temple. It is not clear whether Epiphanius means that James actually held office as high priest. He seems to mean rather that, although not officially appointed high priest, James was allowed to perform the function reserved exclusively for the high priest. The whole point of his reference to the πέταλον is that it was worn only by the high priest. Moreover, comparison between the way Epiphanius speaks of James (τὸ πέταλον ἐπὶ τῆς κεφαλῆς ἐξῆν αὐτῷ φορεῖν) and the way Polycrates speaks of John (ἐγενήθη ἱερεὺς τὸ πέταλον πεφορεκώς) indicates that, whereas Epiphanius's language suggests that James, though not appointed high priest, was permitted to officiate as high priest, Polycrates' language suggests that John was actually appointed high priest.

These claims about James and John probably originated quite independently, and we should resist attempts, such as Bernard's,[45] to find a common explanation

44. Translation from Lawlor and Oulton, *Eusebius*, 57.
45. Bernard, *John*, 2:594–97. Bernard connects these two traditions about James and John with a similar statement about Mark, but the late Latin source of the latter seems to be no longer known. It is

for both. We have seen how the tradition about James derived from a misunderstanding of Hegesippus. It is unnecessary to suppose that Epiphanius or his source was influenced by what Polycrates said about John.[46] This is also unlikely, because Epiphanius states so emphatically the unique privilege of James in this respect.[47] It is also unlikely that the tradition about James influenced the claim that John was high priest, even supposing it antedated Polycrates, which is entirely uncertain. There would be no reason for transferring, without further explanation, this very remarkable claim about James to John. The two traditions are independent, but share the same—evidently stereotyped—way of referring to the exercise of the high priest's office in the temple: wearing the πέταλον.

Attempts to explain Polycrates' words have hitherto fallen into two categories: metaphorical[48] and historical. The idea that Jewish high priesthood is used as a metaphorical way of referring to John's position of authority in the church can claim support from just two allegedly parallel usages. In *Didache* 13:3, Christians are instructed to give the first fruits of their produce to the prophets, "for they are your high priests" (ἀρχιερεῖς ὑμῶν). Hippolytus (*Ref.* 1.prooem.6) claims that the successors of the apostles participate with them in the same grace of high priesthood (τῆς τε αὐτῆς χάριτος μετέχοντες ἀρχιερατείας). This latter passage may actually be based on a misunderstanding of Polycrates' words about John,[49] but in any case neither of these passages really parallels the latter. The general idea of high priesthood might occasionally be used metaphorically of Christian prophets or bishops, whose position in some respects resembled that of Jewish high priests. But in such a usage it would be odd to use the precise expression τὸ πέταλον πεφορεκώς. Polycrates' words are a straightforward statement that John officiated as high priest in the temple. Their context offers no indication that they are meant other than literally, while their place in the sequence of statements about John naturally associates them with his early life in Jerusalem, where he had been a disciple of Jesus and could have been a high priest.

The other form of interpretation takes seriously the apparently intended literal meaning and explains the words as a historical reminiscence of the beloved disciple or the author of the Fourth Gospel who, it is suggested, belonged to a priestly family in Jerusalem and perhaps officiated in the temple in some capacity. The difficulty in interpretations along these lines is that the historical basis they postulate for Polycrates' words is only historically plausible when it is something

---

probably ultimately dependent on Polycrates' statement about John, used to elaborate the existing tradition that Mark was a Levite.

46. Contra Rigato, "Giovanni," 469.

47. This in spite of the fact that he also says that the sons of Zebedee practiced the same kind of ascetic lifestyle as James: *Pan.* 78.13.

48. E.g., Braun, *Jean le Théologien*, 339–40; F. F. Bruce, "St. John at Ephesus," *BJRL* 60 (1978): 343.

49. R. Eisler, *The Enigma of the Fourth Gospel* (London: Methuen, 1938), 55, quotes an apparently unpublished fragment of a lost work of Hippolytus that refers to John as ἀρχιερεὺς Ἐφέσιος. Whether genuine or not, this is certainly dependent on Polycrates. If genuine, it would explain *Ref.* 1.prooem.6.

much less than Polycrates states: that John was high priest. Bernard's speculation that the πέταλον might sometimes have been worn by ordinary Jewish priests in New Testament times[50] is contradicted by all the evidence. Internal evidence from the Fourth Gospel (including 18:15) alleged to show that the author—or the source of the author's tradition—belonged to Jerusalem priestly circles has some force,[51] but does not really explain why Polycrates should have thought John actually held the office of high priest.

The boldest historical speculation is that of Eisler.[52] Following Delff,[53] he identifies John, the author of the Fourth Gospel, with the John who appears as a member of the high-priestly family (ἐκ γένους ἀρχιερατικοῦ) in Acts 4:6. Going further than Delff,[54] he claims that this John actually was high priest by identifying him with Theophilus the son of Annas (Josephus, *Ant.* 18.123), who was high priest from 37 to 41 CE. He suggests that Theophilus was used as the Greek name roughly equivalent in meaning to Yoḥanan. This is possible, but identification of the John of whom Polycrates speaks with the high priest Theophilus is achieved only by a series of unverifiable guesses and requires us to believe that only Polycrates has preserved any reference to the fact that the high priest Theophilus was a disciple of Jesus. In a recent article, Rigato, apparently without knowledge of Eisler's work, has taken Polycrates' statement fully seriously, identified John the author of the Fourth Gospel with the John of Acts 4:6,[55] and supposed that this John must at some time have officiated as high priest.[56] He allows three possibilities:[57] that Josephus's record of the high priests is not complete and does not happen to refer to John (perhaps the name of John, as a Christian, was subject to a kind of *damnatio memoriae*), that John was another name of one of those mentioned by Josephus, or that on one day of atonement John substituted for the reigning high priest (according to the practice of substituting another member of the family if the high priest were ill or ritually impure).[58] Certainly these are possibilities, but it remains surprising that only Polycrates should have preserved any reference to the remarkable fact that a disciple of Jesus, the author of the Fourth Gospel, was or substituted for the high priest.

50. Bernard, *John*, 2:596; cf. Colson, *L'énigme*, 37, who defies all the evidence in stating: "il n'est pas prouvé que l'usage, au temps de Jésus, n'était pas plus étendu."

51. E.g., Burney, *Aramaic Origin*, 133–34; Colson, *L'énigme*, 18–27, 94–97; Hengel, *Johannine Question*, 109–11, 125–26; Rigato, "Giovanni," 469–81.

52. Eisler, *Enigma*, 36–45.

53. Delff, *Geschichte*, 95.

54. Delff, *Das vierte Evangelium*, 9–10, supposed that John stood in for the high priest on one occasion. This possibility is also suggested by Rigato, "Giovanni," 464 n. 33 (see below).

55. Rigato, "Giovanni," 465–66.

56. Ibid., 463–65.

57. Ibid., 464–65 n. 33.

58. J. Jeremias, *Jerusalem in the Time of Jesus*, trans. F. H. and C. H. Cave (London: SCM, 1969), 157.

The improbable and speculative nature of Eisler's proposal has distracted attention from the way in which Acts 4:6 really can explain Polycrates' words about John. The simplest explanation of them is that Polycrates (or the Ephesian church tradition that he followed) identified John the beloved disciple, who had died in Ephesus, with the John of Acts 4:6, not because he had any historical information to this effect, but as a piece of scriptural exegesis.[59] The tradition that John the beloved disciple was a high priest is neither metaphorical nor historical, but exegetical. As we already noted in connection with Polycrates' identification of the two Philips, it was common practice for early Christian exegetes of the New Testament writings to identify characters who bore the same name. Other examples are the identification, in the second-century *Acts of Paul* (written in Asia in Polycrates' time), of the Judas who was Paul's host in Damascus (Acts 9:17) with Judas the Lord's brother (Mark 6:3),[60] or the identification that the *Protevangelium of James* (23–24) makes between Zechariah the father of John the Baptist and the Zechariah who was murdered in the temple (Matt. 23:35). We may also recall how prominent figures of the early postapostolic church—comparable with John of Ephesus—were assumed to be the same as persons of the same name who appear in New Testament writings: Clement of Rome was identified as the Clement of Philippians 4:3 (Eusebius, *Hist. eccl.* 3.4.9), Linus of Rome was identified as the Linus of 2 Timothy 4:21 (Irenaeus, *Haer.* 3.3.3; Eusebius, *Hist. eccl.* 3.4.8), Hermas the prophet, author of the *Shepherd*, was identified as the Hermas of Romans 16:14 (Origen, ad. loc.). These last two instances may have some historical plausibility, but these identifications were made in the same way as the others, as an exegetical procedure.

It is quite likely that the identification of the beloved disciple with the John of Acts 4:6 was facilitated by John 18:15, which, if it is understood to refer to the beloved disciple, depicts him as intimately acquainted (γνωστός) with the high priest. In Acts 4:6, John is listed third after Annas the high priest and Caiaphas. Someone who knew that in the New Testament period the Jewish high priests mostly held office for short periods only, or who was misled by John 18:13 into thinking the office was filled annually, would easily suppose that such a senior member of the high-priestly family as the John of Acts 4:6 appears to be must have himself held the office of high priest at some time. The motive for identifying John the beloved disciple with this John will have been—in addition to the general exegetical tendency already mentioned—the natural desire of the Ephesian church to find their own John, the author of the Gospel they prized, mentioned somewhere else in the writings of the emergent New Testament canon. But the identification also served well Polycrates' particular purpose in his letter to Pope Victor: the justification of the quartodeciman observance in line with the

59. That Polycrates was well acquainted with the early chapters of Acts is shown by his quotation of Acts 5:9 later in his letter.

60. Coptic text of a section of the *Acts of Paul*, in *New Testament Apocrypha*, ed. E. Hennecke, W. Schneemelcher, and R. McL. Wilson (London: Lutterworth, 1965), 2:388.

Johannine chronology of the passion. An eyewitness of the passion who actually himself served as high priest could be expected to remember correctly its precise chronological relation to the Jewish festival.

It is quite likely that Polycrates, who in his letter prides himself on his considerable knowledge of the scriptures, himself made this identification of his own illustrious relative with the John of Acts 4:6. But whether Polycrates made or inherited it, it is of considerable importance. For it is now clear that when the Ephesian church looked for its own John, the beloved disciple, in New Testament writings other than the Fourth Gospel, they did not identify him with John the son of Zebedee. The identification of him with the John of Acts 4:6 makes it impossible to identify him also with John the son of Zebedee, who appears in the same narrative, along with Peter, as one of the two disciples who are there interrogated before Annas, Caiaphas, John, and Alexander. The Ephesian church's own tradition about their own John evidently made them quite sure that he could not be John the son of Zebedee and obliged them, even at the end of the second century, to resist this identification, which was already proving irresistible elsewhere and seems to have become universal in the next century.

The John to whom Polycrates ascribed the Fourth Gospel was a very definite person. His tomb was at Ephesus. Polycrates could have explained how he was related to him. He was not the son of Zebedee, one of the Twelve, but he was a personal disciple of Jesus. He must be John the Elder, a disciple of the Lord, to whom Papias referred in the famous passage of his prologue (ap. Eusebius, *Hist. eccl.* 3.39.4). This John the Elder, who was still teaching when the young Papias was gathering his traditions, lived near enough to Hierapolis for Papias to have heard him in person on occasion (Eusebius, *Hist. eccl.* 3.39.7;[61] cf. Irenaeus, *Haer.* 5.33.4). His association with Ephesus is confirmed by the *Apostolic Constitutions* (7.46), which lists "John," appointed by the apostle John the son of Zebedee, as second bishop of Ephesus after Timothy. At this point in his lists of early bishops, the author of the *Apostolic Constitutions* was probably not dependent on Eusebius, since he would certainly have thought the John of Polycrates' letter was the son of Zebedee and since Eusebius's own association of Papias's John the Elder with Ephesus is tied up with his attribution of the Apocalypse to him (*Hist. eccl.* 3.39.6). He follows, no doubt, the same source of local Asian tradition that led him to associate Ariston (Papias's Aristion) with Smyrna, an association which Streeter showed is probably correct.[62]

The discovery that local Ephesian church tradition attributed the Fourth Gospel to Papias's John the Elder requires us to raise again the question of what Papias himself may have said about the Fourth Gospel. In this case too new light can be shed by a fresh reading of the evidence.

---

61. On this passage, see Chapman, *John the Presbyter* 28–32; Hengel, *Johannine Question*, 22.
62. Streeter, *Primitive Church*, 92–97.

Papias on the Gospels

There should be no doubt that Papias knew the Fourth Gospel.[63] There is his list of seven disciples (ap. Eusebius, *Hist. eccl.* 3.39.4), the first six of whom (Andrew, Peter, Philip, Thomas, James, John) are in a distinctively Johannine order,[64] the order they appear in the Fourth Gospel, with James and John in fifth and sixth place (cf. John 21:2), and Matthew, a non-Johannine disciple important for Papias as a disciple who wrote a Gospel, added in seventh place.[65] There is the quotation from John 14:2 in a passage Irenaeus ascribes to the elders and very probably borrowed from Papias (*Haer.* 5.36.1–2).[66] The Armenian reference to Papias seems to depend on a comment he made on John 19:39.[67] But it does not follow necessarily that Papias said anything about the authorship and origin of the Fourth Gospel.[68] If he merely quoted from and alluded to it occasionally, Eusebius's silence on the matter would be not at all surprising. Eusebius does not say that Papias quoted the Apocalypse, which he certainly did.[69] Eusebius does not say that he quoted Luke's Gospel, as he does in the fragment of Papias in the Armenian version of Andrew of Caesarea[70] (unless we suppose that he knew the saying in Luke 10:18 from oral tradition). But Eusebius's silence will need some explanation if Papias dealt with the origin of the Fourth Gospel in the context of his well-known comments on the origins of the Gospels of Mark and Matthew. A preliminary indication that he did so can be found from a consideration of these comments on Mark and Matthew:

63. Contra, e.g., U. H. J. Körtner, *Papias von Hierapolis* (Göttingen: Vandenhoeck & Ruprecht, 1983), 197.

64. On this list, see Hengel, *Johannine Question*, 17–21.

65. Cf. Grant, *Earliest Lives*, 16.

66. Lightfoot, *Biblical Essays*, 67–68; idem, *Essays on the Work Entitled Supernatural Religion* (London: Macmillan, 1889), 194–202.

67. Fragment 24 in J. Kürzinger, *Papias von Hierapolis und die Evangelien des Neuen Testaments*, Eichstätter Materialien 4 (Regensburg: F. Pustet, 1983), 132–35, = fragment 25 in *The Apostolic Fathers in English*, 3rd ed., trans. and ed. M. W. Holmes after the earlier version of J. B. Lightfoot and J. R. Harmer (Grand Rapids: Baker Academic, 2006), 319.

68. No weight can be given to the so-called Anti-Marcionite Prologue to John (fragment 21 in Körtner, *Papias*, 124–25, = fragment 19 in Holmes, *Apostolic Fathers*, 316–17; cf. also fragment 20 in Kürzinger, *Papias*, 122–23, = fragment 20 in Holmes, *Apostolic Fathers*, 317), which claims to report from Papias that John wrote the Gospel and says that he dictated it to Papias. The latter statement may be based on Irenaeus's that Papias was a hearer (ἀχουστής) of John (*Haer.* 5.33.4). On this Prologue, see Lightfoot, *Supernatural Religion*, 210–14 (who makes the best of the evidence, but admits that it can be allowed no weight); Braun, *Jean le Théologien*, 345–49.

69. Fragments 12, 13, 23 in Kürzinger, *Papias*, 110–23, 128–33, = fragments 10, 11, 24, in Holmes, *Apostolic Fathers*, 313–14, 318–19.

70. Fragment 23 in Kürzinger, *Papias*, 128–33, = fragment 24 in Holmes, *Apostolic Fathers*, 318–19. It is striking that Lightfoot, *Supernatural Religion*, 186, 200–201, already concluded that Papias must have referred to Luke 10:18.

And the Elder[71] used to say this: Mark, having become Peter's interpreter (ἑρμη-νευτής), wrote down accurately everything he remembered, though not in order (οὐ μέντοι τάξει), of the things either said or done by the Lord. For he neither heard the Lord nor followed him, but afterwards, as I said, followed Peter, who adapted his teachings as needed (πρός τὰς χρείας) but not giving, as it were, an ordered account (σύνταξιν) of the oracles[72] of the Lord. Consequently Mark did nothing wrong in writing down single points (ἔνια) as he remembered them, for he made it his own concern not to omit anything which he had heard or to make any false statement in them. (ap. Eusebius, *Hist. eccl.* 3.39.15)

So (οὖν) Matthew composed (συνετάξατο) the oracles in the Hebrew language, but each person interpreted (ἡρμήνευσεν) them as best he could. (ap. Eusebius, *Hist. eccl.* 3.39.16)

It is worth noticing immediately that Eusebius has clearly not given us every-thing Papias said about Matthew and Mark. In the case of Matthew, the οὖν shows that the quoted sentence was preceded by something else, probably to the effect that Matthew (unlike Mark) had been a personal disciple of the Lord. In the case of Mark, we can infer from Eusebius that Papias also quoted 1 Peter 5:13 to substantiate his claim that Mark was a disciple of Peter. This is clear from the comment Eusebius makes after the quotation of Papias on Matthew (3.39.17: "The same writer utilized testimonies from the first letter of John and, likewise, from that of Peter"), taken together with the conclusion to Eusebius's own account of the origin of the Gospel of Mark (2:15). This account is elaborated from those of Papias and Clement of Alexandria. Eusebius concludes:

Clement has given the story in the sixth book of the Hypotyposeis; and the bishop of Hierapolis also, Papias by name, corroborates his testimony (συνεπιμαρτυρεῖ), [saying] that Peter mentions Mark in his first letter; which also it is said (φασίν) he composed at Rome itself, and indicates the fact when he calls the city, some-what metaphorically, "Babylon," in these words: "She who is at Babylon, who is likewise chosen, sends you greetings; and so does my son Mark." (*Hist. eccl.* 2.15.2; cf. 1 Pet. 5:13)

Although the report "that Peter mentions Mark in his first letter" (τοῦ δὲ Μάρκου μνημονεύειν τὸν Πέτρον ...) is not quite unequivocally said to be that of Papias, it is most naturally connected with συνεπιμαρτυρεῖ, while the further implications

71. "The Elder" is presumably John the Elder, but we cannot be quite certain of this, since the fact that the quotation in Eusebius follows a mention of John the Elder by Irenaeus (*Haer.* 3.39.14) may be misleading in this respect and the context from which Eusebius has taken the quotation might have made it clear that another elder is the one referred to. It is not certain how much of the comment on Mark's Gospel Papias attributed to the Elder. Whether the comment on Matthew came from John the Elder there is no way of knowing.

72. Papias's use of λόγια here evidently covers "the things either said or done by the Lord," already mentioned (so Lightfoot, *Supernatural Religion*, 175–76). This is the best guide to the meaning of λόγια both in Papias's comment on Matthew and in the title of his own work.

of 1 Peter 5:13 are unattributed (φασίν). This interpretation is the more probable because it explains Eusebius's reference to Papias's use of 1 Peter in 3.39.17. It was as a "testimony" (μαρτυρία) to the value of Mark's Gospel, as dependent on Peter's preaching, that Papias used a quotation from 1 Peter. This raises the possibility, to which we shall return, that Papias similarly quoted 1 John in order to validate the Fourth Gospel as based on eyewitness testimony. For the moment we conclude that Eusebius, guided by his own interests, has evidently lifted Papias's remarks about Mark and Matthew out of a context in which he said more about both.

Much discussion of Papias's comments about Mark and Matthew, preoccupied either with showing their reliability as evidence for the origins of these Gospels or with emphasizing their apologetic character in order to discredit their reliability, has failed to understand why Papias made these comments. The quoted comments on the two Gospels have two interests in common. First, they are both concerned with the way these Gospels are based on eyewitness authority (Peter's and Matthew's). A concern with reliable access to eyewitness reports of the Lord's deeds and sayings is prominent in the passage Eusebius quotes from Papias's prologue (*Hist. eccl.* 3.39.3–4), and so it is likely to have been a major concern in his discussion of the Gospels. Second, both comments are concerned with "order." Although the use of συνετάξατο of Matthew need not, by itself, be very significant, in the context of the two comments on Mark and Matthew it demands to be connected with the statements that Mark wrote the deeds and sayings of the Lord accurately but not in order (οὐ μέντοι τάξει), and that Peter did not give an ordered account (σύνταξιν) of the oracles of the Lord.

A common mistake has been to suppose that Papias is contrasting the lack of order in Mark's Gospel with the presence of order in Matthew, whether "order" is understood as a matter of chronological sequence or of literary arrangement. But this ignores the fact that Papias's comment on Matthew is by no means wholly positive. He appears to be acknowledging the fact that the Greek Gospel of Matthew known to him and his readers had suffered something in the translation from Matthew's original Hebrew.[73] If we allow the μὲν ... δὲ structure of the statement about Matthew its contrastive sense, then Papias is saying that, although Matthew himself arranged the oracles of the Lord in order when he wrote his Gospel in Hebrew, those who translated his work as best they could (ὡς ἦν δυνατός) cannot be relied on to have preserved this σύνταξις. Quite probably Papias went on to make this more explicit in a further comment, which Eusebius omitted because he did not like the notion that the Greek Gospel of Matthew used by the church diverged rather considerably from Matthew's original Hebrew Gospel. From what we know Papias to have said about Matthew, it is clear that he thought there had been more than one translation of the original Hebrew Gospel into Greek. Probably he knew something about Greek Gospels, under the name of Matthew and related to our Matthew, which were used by Jewish-Christians in Palestine and

---

73. Cf. Lightfoot, *Supernatural Religion*, 208.

Syria.[74] He knew they exhibited major divergences from the Gospel of Matthew used in Hierapolis and neighboring churches. He referred to these various Greek Matthews to show that none of them could be presumed to preserve accurately the σύνταξις of the original Hebrew Matthew.

This probably explains Eusebius's final remark about Papias's work. Following the statement already quoted that Papias used testimonies from 1 John and 1 Peter, he says, "he also related another story about a woman accused of many sins before the Lord, which the Gospel according to the Hebrews contains" (*Hist. eccl.* 3.39.17). The "Gospel according to the Hebrews" is no doubt what Eusebius has called Papias's source. It is the Jewish-Christian gospel in Greek to which he elsewhere refers (*Hist. eccl.* 3.25.5; 3.27.4; 4.22.8), distinguishing it from a Jewish-Christian Gospel in Aramaic of which he also knew (*Hist. eccl.* 4.22.8; cf. *Theoph.* 4.12). There is no evidence in his writings that Eusebius knew the Greek Gospel he calls the Gospel according to the Hebrews other than by report. So he did not have knowledge independent of Papias that it contained Papias's story of the accused woman. Probably Papias said it occurred in a Greek Gospel used by Jewish-Christians[75] and so Eusebius assumed that this Gospel must be the only such Greek Gospel of which he knew: the Gospel according to the Hebrews. But for Papias himself, we may assume that the significance of this Gospel was that he regarded it (probably not without reason) as a version of Matthew. He cited the story of the accused woman, which occurred in this Gospel but not in the Gospel of Matthew generally used in the churches of his area, to show how far the various Greek versions of the Hebrew Matthew differed. It is not surprising that Eusebius does not make this clear, but this explanation of the reason Papias quoted the story of the accused woman has the advantage of allowing us to suppose that all three of the quotations made by Papias to which Eusebius refers immediately after giving Papias's comments on Mark and Matthew (*Hist. eccl.* 3.39.17) he found in Papias in the same context as those comments.

If this explanation of Papias's use of the story of the woman is correct, it would mean that Papias attributed to the translators of the various versions of Matthew not minor differences of translation, but major variations in content. This may be confirmed by the implied contrast between Mark, as Peter's interpreter (ἑρμηνευτής), and those who interpreted (ἡρμήνευσεν) Matthew's Hebrew Gospel. Whereas Mark's accuracy and scrupulosity in recording everything he had heard from Peter, leaving nothing out and falsifying nothing, is stressed, those who interpreted Matthew as best they could were evidently much less careful and competent.

---

74. For the "Gospel of the Ebionites," see now G. Howard, "The Gospel of the Ebionites," *ANRW* 2.25.5:4034–53. For the title "Gospel according to Matthew," see Epiphanius, *Pan.* 30.13.2.

75. It may be significant that Papias's version of the story seems closest to that in the Syriac *Didascalia* (7.2.24); see B. D. Ehrman, "Jesus and the Adulteress," *NTS* 34 (1988): 24–44; Holmes, *Apostolic Fathers*, 303–5, 311. The *Didascalia* certainly used the *Gospel of Peter*, and could have had access to a Jewish-Christian Gospel used in Syria.

We can now see that the purpose of Papias in his comments on both Mark and Matthew is to explain why it is that, although both Gospels are based on eyewitness testimony, neither arranges the λόγια of the Lord "in order." This view of his purpose has the great advantage of doing justice to both of the concerns that we noted are common to the comments on both Gospels—the concerns with eyewitness authority and with "order"—and also of accounting for everything Papias says in both comments, which is not often done by other explanations of his purpose. In the case of Mark, the Gospel is a most valuable record of eyewitness testimony, because Mark carefully and accurately recorded everything he remembered of Peter's preaching, but since Peter in his preaching naturally did not put the λόγια in order, neither does the Gospel of Mark. In the case of Matthew, however, Papias believes that Matthew himself, a disciple and eyewitness, wrote the λόγια and so it must be presumed that he would have arranged them in the correct order. The fact that (as Papias supposes) they are not in order in the Gospel of Matthew known to Papias and his readers is not therefore due to Matthew himself. It results from the fact that Matthew wrote in Hebrew and various different versions of his work were made in Greek. So in the case of Mark, the lack of order is the fault neither of the eyewitness (Peter) nor of the interpreter (Mark), but is due to the oral nature of the eyewitness's testimony, whereas in the case of Matthew, the lack of order is not the fault of the eyewitness (Matthew), although he himself wrote the λόγια, but is due to his translators.

It follows that the "order" with which Papias is concerned must be chronological sequence, not literary arrangement.[76] The latter need not be expected of eyewitnesses, but the former could reasonably be expected of eyewitnesses, and so Papias is at pains to explain why two Gospels that certainly derive from eyewitness testimony do not exhibit it. The only reason Papias could have had for arguing this point is that he knew another Gospel, also recording eyewitness testimony, which in his view did arrange the λόγια of the Lord in the correct order. This must be John.[77] Leaving aside gospels such as Thomas, which do not offer a sequential account of Jesus' ministry, John's is the extant Gospel that differs most markedly in this respect from Matthew and Mark. From later patristic discussions of the differences between the Gospels, we know that the differences of order between the Synoptics did not greatly matter to ancient readers by comparison with the differences between John and the Synoptics.

Thus the context of Papias's comments on Mark and Matthew was not an account of the origins of the Gospels per se, nor an apologetic defense of these two Gospels against attacks, but a discussion of the most obvious difference between those Gospels that were generally accepted—in the churches around

76. The case for the latter is most fully argued by Kürzinger, *Papias*, chaps. 1–3. The critique of Kürzinger by M. Black, "The Use of Rhetorical Terminology in Papias on Mark and Matthew," *JSNT* 37 (1989): 31–41, only deals in passing with τάξις.

77. So also Lightfoot, *Supernatural Religion*, 165; A. Wright, "Τάξει in Papias," *JTS* 14 (1913): 300; Hengel, *Johannine Question*, 157 n. 118.

Hierapolis—as embodying eyewitness testimony. Probably Papias cited the authority of the elders for his view that Matthew, Mark, and John were all, in some sense, eyewitness records, but this was not the point of discussion. If this was accepted, the question of the differences between John on the one hand and Matthew and Mark on the other could not be avoided, and there is no reason why it should not already have become a topic of discussion in the circles Papias knew, where all three of these Gospels were in use. Our best evidence for such discussion comes from perhaps a century later, in the attacks made by Gaius and the Alogi (if the latter are not simply Gaius himself) on the Fourth Gospel,[78] which they attributed to John's heretical adversary Cerinthus.[79] In pointing out the disagreements between John and the Synoptics, they evidently focused especially on John 1:29–2:1, where John's carefully stated sequence of days from the baptism (if 1:32–33 is read as a narrative of it) through the call of the disciples to the miracle at Cana (1:29, 35, 39, 43; 2:1) allows no room for the forty days in the wilderness, which Matthew and Mark place between the baptism and the return to Galilee, where Jesus then calls the disciples.[80] For Gaius and the Alogi, this was evidence against the authenticity of John's Gospel, which they wished to discredit because of its use by the Montanists. But in pointing out this obvious incompatibility in chronological sequence in the early sections of the Gospels, they would no doubt be taking up a question that already had been raised before the Montanist controversy. We may find some evidence of this in the *Epistle of the Apostles*, which should probably not be dated later than circa 150.[81] Though dependent on all four Gospels, it gives precedence to John's by placing John, detached from his brother James, first in the list of the twelve apostles who purport to be the authors (2: John, Thomas, Peter, Andrew, James, Philip . . .). Its extensive catalog of the miracles of Jesus, which fills chapter 5, consists mostly of Synoptic Gospel miracles and follows the order of no particular Gospel, but it emphatically begins with the Johannine miracle at Cana, evidently taking seriously the Fourth Gospel's claim to provide chronological order (John 2:11: "the first of his signs"). Tatian's *Diatessaron* was also no doubt motivated more by the discrepancies in order between the Gospels than by differences between them in parallel pericopes. Tatian did not consistently prefer the Johannine order, but he tended to accept John's authority where his Gospel made explicit chronological statements.[82]

If the question of order focused especially on the events around the beginning of the ministry, it may be that Papias's prologue already indicates which order he

---

78. On the Alogi, see Gunther, "Early Identifications," 413–17 (but most of his paragraph on pp. 416–17 is unfounded speculation); Grant, *Earliest Lives*, 28–29.

79. See fragments 10, 12, and 16 in the collection of fragments in R. M. Grant, *Second-Century Christianity: A Collection of Fragments* (London: SPCK, 1946), 106–8.

80. See fragments 11, 13, 15, and 16 in Grant, *Second-Century Christianity*, 105–8.

81. On the indication of date in chap. 17, see the list of interpretations in J. Hills, *Tradition and Composition in the Epistula Apostolorum*, HDR 24 (Minneapolis: Fortress, 1990), 166 n. 73.

82. Grant, *Earliest Lives*, 23–26.

preferred. We have noticed that his list of seven disciples (Andrew, Peter, Philip, Thomas, James, John, Matthew) is (up to Matthew) a Johannine list and contrasts with the synoptic lists of the Twelve, but it also begins by following the Johannine order in which the disciples were called (Andrew, Peter, Philip...), in contrast to the Matthaean and Marcan order (Peter, Andrew, James, John, Matthew/Levi).

If Papias mentioned Luke in his discussion of the differences of order between the Gospels, he need only have pointed out that Luke's Gospel does not rest as immediately on eyewitness testimony as the others were thought to do. If he mentioned Luke, Eusebius did not report the fact, either because what Papias said about Luke was not significant enough to be worth quoting or because it distanced Luke further from eyewitness testimony than Eusebius would have liked (cf. his own view of the matter in *Hist. eccl.* 3.24.15). But our argument requires that Papias must have said something quite significant about the Fourth Gospel to justify his own preference for its order. There may be two reasons why Eusebius did not report this.[83] In the first place, if (as we shall argue later) Papias ascribed the Fourth Gospel to John the Elder, Eusebius, who emphatically draws attention to Papias's distinction between John the son of Zebedee and John the Elder, in order to suggest that the latter may be the author of the Apocalypse, could not have missed or disguised the fact that, according to Papias, the author of the Fourth Gospel was not the son of Zebedee.

But second, Eusebius would not have liked Papias's solution to the problem of the differences of order between the Gospels: that John's is correct and the others unreliable in this respect. His own understanding of the way the sequences of events in the four Gospels relate (expounded in 3.24.5–16) is that the three synoptic evangelists only record the ministry of Jesus after the imprisonment of John the Baptist. John wrote his Gospel precisely to fill in the gap they had left: he records the ministry before the imprisonment of John the Baptist. This seems to settle the matter. Eusebius apparently sees no need to admit that the order in any Gospel ever needs to be preferred to the order in another. It is significant that, despite his interest in recording what early authors said about the Gospels[84] and despite the fact that the chronological differences between the Gospels were certainly discussed in some of his sources, he never quotes or refers to such discussions. He does not quote Claudius Apollinaris on the chronology of the passion in relation to the quartodeciman question, and his account of the paschal controversy gives no hint that it bore any relation to differences between the Gospels. But his sensitivity on this issue appears especially in his treatment of Gaius. Of the fact that Gaius rejected the Fourth Gospel on the grounds of its discrepancies with the Synoptics and ascribed it to Cerinthus,[85] he gives no hint. In

---

83. See also Lightfoot's discussion of Eusebius's "silence": *Supernatural Religion*, 36–52.

84. Cf. *Hist. eccl.* 3.3.3; 3.24.16.

85. See fragments 10 and 11 (from Dionysius Bar Salibi) in Grant, *Second-Century Christianity*, 106. In both of these, Gaius is named. On the reliability of this ascription to Gaius, see J. R. Harris, *Hermas in Arcadia and Other Essays* (Cambridge: Cambridge University Press, 1896), 43–57.

his account of Cerinthus, he quotes Gaius's attribution of the Apocalypse to him, but not the similar attribution of the Fourth Gospel (3.28.2). More significantly, when giving his account of Gaius's work (6.20.3), he refers to the questions of the authenticity of the thirteen Pauline epistles and the authorship of Hebrews, but makes no reference to the Gospels. Clearly Eusebius did not record everything his sources said about the origins of the Gospels, but only those comments with which he agreed.

Papias's comment on Mark is the only admission of a lack of correct order in any of the Gospels that Eusebius has allowed into his work. It has slipped through his net because what Papias said about Mark's accuracy in recording Peter's preaching was too valuable to omit. But he has obscured the importance of the question of order in Papias's quoted comments on Mark and Matthew by drastically censoring the context from which he selects these quotations. We can well imagine that he would not quote a statement about John's Gospel that was inextricable from Papias's assertion of its superiority to Matthew and Mark in the question of order.

Papias and the *Muratorian Canon*

If Papias wrote something about the origin of the Fourth Gospel that Eusebius did not record, we might expect it to have left some trace in other writers who knew Papias's work. In search of such a trace we may turn first to the *Muratorian Canon*,[86] whose relation to Papias has been occasionally noticed[87] but insufficiently examined. The section dealing with the Gospels unfortunately preserves only the last six words of the comment on Mark, followed by the comments on Luke and John:

> . . . at which he was present, and thus he wrote them down.
> The third book of the gospel is according to Luke. Luke the physician, when Paul had taken him with him after the ascension of Christ, as one skilled in writing, wrote from report in his own name, though he did not himself see the Lord in the flesh; and on that account, as he was able to ascertain [events], so [he set them down]. So he began his story from the birth of John.

86. The usual dating of the *Muratorian Canon* in the late second century was challenged by A. C. Sundberg, "Canon Muratori: A Fourth-Century List," *HTR* 66 (1973): 1–41, but his challenge has not been regarded as successful: see E. Ferguson, "Canon Muratori: Date and Provenance," *Studia Patristica* 18 (1982): 677–83; F. F. Bruce, "Some Thoughts on the Beginning of the New Testament Canon," *BJRL* 65 (1983): 56–57; B. M. Metzger, *The Canon of the New Testament: Its Origin, Development, and Significance* (Oxford: Clarendon, 1987), 193–94.

87. Lightfoot, *Biblical Essays*, 100; idem, *Supernatural Religion*, 205–7; Braun, *Jean le Théologien*, 355; A. Ehrhardt, "The Gospels in the Muratorian Fragment," in *The Framework of the New Testament Stories*, ed. A. Ehrhardt (Manchester: Manchester University Press, 1964), 12–13.

The fourth of the gospels is of John, one of the disciples. To his fellow-disciples and bishops, who were encouraging him, he said, "Fast with me today for three days, and whatever will be revealed to each of us, let us tell to one another." The same night it was revealed to Andrew, one of the apostles, that all should certify what John wrote in his own name.

Therefore, while various elements may be taught in the several books of gospels, it makes no difference to the faith of believers, for by the one chief Spirit all things have been declared in all: concerning the nativity, the passion, the resurrection, the life with his disciples, and his double advent, first in lowliness and contempt (which has taken place), second in glorious royal power (which is to be).

Why, then, is it remarkable that John so constantly brings forth single points even in his epistles, saying of himself, "What we have seen with our eyes and heard with our ears and our hands have handled, these we write to you"?[88] Thus he professes himself not only an eyewitness and hearer but also a writer of all the miracles of the Lord in order.[89]

The words with which the fragment begins (*quibus tamen interfuit et ita posuit*) are most easily intelligible as dependent on what Papias said about Mark. They cannot mean that Mark was present at the events he recorded, not only because no early tradition suggests this, but also because the subsequent statement about Luke, that "he did not himself see the Lord in the flesh" (*dominum tamen nec ipse vidit in carne*), should probably be translated: "he also did not see. . . ." In other words, Luke, like Mark, was not an eyewitness of the ministry of Jesus.[90] Therefore the comment on Mark was probably to the effect that (as Papias said) he had not been a disciple of Jesus, but he had been present at Peter's preaching and set down in writing what he heard from Peter. If the surviving words mean that Mark set down what Peter said just as he heard it, this reflects Papias's own account, not the accounts of Irenaeus and Clement of Alexandria dependent on Papias. The whole *Muratorian Canon* is, in fact, notable for the lack of any sign of Irenaeus's influence.[91]

The last sentence of the quoted section should also be compared with Papias on Mark. That John was not only an eye and ear witness but also wrote all the miracles of the Lord in order (*non solum uisurem sed et auditorem sed et scriptorem omnium mirabilium domini per ordinem*) corresponds to Papias's assertion that Mark "neither heard the Lord nor followed him" and did not write "in order" what was said and done by the Lord. Because John, unlike Mark, was an eyewitness he was able to write "in order" (*per ordinem*, surely corresponding to τάξει in Papias). Moreover, the order thus validated is that of the Lord's miracles, referring to the

88. Cf. 1 John 1:1, 4.
89. Translation from Grant, *Second-Century Christianity*, 118 (slightly adapted).
90. Lightfoot, *Supernatural Religion*, 206; Ehrhardt, "Gospels," 13.
91. Ehrhardt rather oddly comments: "Irenaeus' influence upon the *Muratorian Canon* scarcely extended beyond a commendation of Papias" ("Gospels," 14). There is no reason why the author should not have known Papias's work without Irenaeus's commendation.

most obvious way in which the Fourth Gospel appears to insist on chronological order: in specifying the first two signs as the first and the second of a sequence (2:11; 4:54). Though we do not know what the *Muratorian Canon* said about Matthew, this concluding statement clearly makes John superior to Mark and Luke when it comes to order.

Such a statement is the kind of claim we have already concluded that Papias probably made about the Fourth Gospel. The suspicion that the *Muratorian Canon* is here borrowing from Papias is confirmed by the quotation from 1 John, which is used to substantiate the claim that John wrote as an eyewitness and therefore "in order."[92] This can be related to Eusebius's statement that Papias cited testimonies from 1 John and 1 Peter (*Hist. eccl.* 3.39.17).[93] If, as we have argued, the testimony from 1 Peter was a quotation of 1 Peter 5:13, adduced in support of what Papias said about Mark's Gospel, a quotation of 1 John 1:1–4, in support of what he said about John's Gospel, would be an appropriate parallel.

Thus it is likely that the last paragraph in our quoted section of the *Muratorian Canon* is closely dependent on Papias. The preceding paragraph reflects the author's own apologetic concern about the differences between the Gospels.[94] It is not out of place in the middle of the comments on John, because no doubt the author was particularly conscious of the differences between John and the Synoptics. He makes the observation immediately after the story he has told about the origin of John's Gospel, because the story tells how John's fellow disciples certified John's own account. He takes this to mean that John's Gospel cannot really be in disagreement with others, as the Alogi, for example, alleged. But it is notable that his own concern (which he shares with Tertullian, *Marc.* 4.2) seems to be to stress that on the essential points in the story of Jesus (including presumably their sequence) the four Gospels agree. This is rather different from the point his subsequent statement about John's Gospel seems to make: that, as far as order is concerned, John is superior. This confirms that the latter point comes from his source.

Echoes of Papias in Irenaeus and Clement

If the *Muratorian Canon*'s quotation from 1 John and the conclusions drawn from it about the Fourth Gospel very probably follow Papias quite closely, the

---

92. In his discussion of this section of the *Muratorian Canon*, Ehrhardt, "Gospels," 26–36, is led astray by connecting the quotation from 1 John with 1 Cor. 2:9 and regarding the latter as a Pauline slogan. The quotation in 1 Cor. 2:9 was much too widely used to have been considered a Pauline slogan: see M. E. Stone and J. Strugnell, *The Books of Elijah: Parts 1–2* (Missoula, MT: Scholars Press, 1979), 42–73.

93. Already suggested by Lightfoot, *Supernatural Religion*, 206.

94. Ehrhardt, "Gospels," 26, is mistaken in seeing the influence of Papias on this passage.

Muratorian Canon's story about the origin of the Gospel is more problematic.[95] Papias is likely to have had some account of the origin of the Gospel. Just as his quotation of 1 Peter 5:13 was most likely used to substantiate the account he had given of the origin of Mark's Gospel, so we should expect that the quotation from 1 John would have been used to substantiate something he had already said about the origin of the Fourth Gospel. But we should also be alert to the possibility that the *Muratorian Canon*'s story may be a considerably embroidered version of what Papias said, if the fortunes of his account of the origin of Mark are anything to go by. This was elaborated by Clement of Alexandria and then further by Eusebius (*Hist. eccl.* 2.15.1–2), even while the latter claimed only to be repeating Papias's and Clement's account. The elaborations served the apologetic purpose of enhancing the apostolic authority of the Gospel. The same could be true of the *Muratorian Canon*'s story of the origin of the Fourth Gospel.

We should notice, in the first place, that there is good reason for supposing that this story bears some relation to Papias, and that it treats not John the son of Zebedee, but Papias's John the Elder, as the author of the Gospel.[96] This is shown by the terminology. John himself is "one of the disciples" (*ex decipolis*). He is encouraged to write by his "fellow-disciples and bishops" (*condescipulis et episcopis*), one of whom is Andrew, "one of the apostles" (*ex apostolis*). The contract between John, one of the disciples, and Andrew, one of the apostles, is striking. We recall that in the passage from his prologue that Eusebius quotes (*Hist. eccl.* 3.39.4), Papias uses the term "disciples of the Lord" for all who had been personal disciples of the Lord, whether members of the Twelve (such as the seven he lists) or others (such as Aristion and John the Elder). He uses the term for those who were members of the Twelve, in preference to the term "apostle," no doubt because it is the fact that they had been personal disciples of Jesus that matters to him. The term "apostle" as such did not necessarily convey this meaning, especially as in Asia, even for Papias, Paul was "the Apostle."[97] But in the passage from the prologue Papias uses no term that distinguishes members of the Twelve from other disciples of the Lord. The author of the *Muratorian Canon* makes this distinction by calling John "one of the disciples" and Andrew "one of the apostles." He did not need to call Andrew this to distinguish him from some other Andrew, but evidently did so to distinguish a member of the Twelve from John, who was not a member of the Twelve. This is the distinction Papias

95. There is no evidence to support the suggestion (cf. B. W. Bacon, *The Gospel of the Hellenists* [New York: H. Holt, 1933], 37) that the story comes from the *Acts of John*. In that case we should expect it to be more widely known, whereas in fact it is extant only in the *Muratorian Canon*.

96. That Streeter, *Four Gospels*, 439–40, was able to quote the *Muratorian Canon* without noticing its support for his own view that the author of the Fourth Gospel was John the Elder is remarkable, and illustrates how far study of the external evidence has been dominated by an uncritical assumption that second-century references to "John" as the author of the Fourth Gospel must be to the son of Zebedee.

97. Papias refers to Paul as "the Apostle" in fragment 23 in Kürzinger, *Papias*, 128–29, = fragment 24 in Holmes, *Apostolic Fathers*, 318–19 (fragment 24.7).

in fact makes, in the prologue, between Andrew and John the Elder—although he does not there need to use the word "apostle" to do so. That the author of the *Muratorian Canon* is deliberately working with the categories of disciples Papias distinguishes in the prologue is further suggested by the fact that the apostle he singles out is Andrew, who heads Papias's list of seven disciples.

Thus the author of the *Muratorian Canon* evidently means that John, who was a disciple but not a member of the Twelve, met with his fellow disciples, who would include both members of the Twelve and other personal disciples of Jesus, and it was to Andrew, the foremost member of the Twelve who was present, that the revelation came. The greatest obstacle to supposing that this account as such derives from Papias is that it presupposes that when the Fourth Gospel was written not only Andrew but also a number of other disciples of Jesus were still alive. Papias in his prologue clearly implies that at the time when he was collecting oral traditions not only Andrew but also all other disciples of the Lord whose teaching could have been accessible to him, with the exception of Aristion and John the Elder, were already dead. It is possible that he dated the writing of the Fourth Gospel considerably earlier than this, but unlikely, in view of the fact that Irenaeus and Clement of Alexandria, who both knew Papias's work, both thought John's the last Gospel to be written.

In order to discern just what the *Muratorian Canon* owes to Papias, it will be useful to notice that, whereas its story of the origin of the Fourth Gospel does not as a whole occur in any other extant source, two elements of the story are found elsewhere. These are the two aspects of the part that the other disciples play in the origin of the Gospel: they encourage (*cohortantibus*) John to write and they certify (*recogniscentibus*) what John writes as true. The second aspect is most likely, as has long been recognized, an interpretation of John 21:24.[98]

This second aspect can also be found in Irenaeus, whose evidence is important because he undoubtedly knew Papias's work very well. In *Haer.* 2.22, Irenaeus is arguing against the Valentinians who laid great stress on the symbolism of the number "30." On the basis of Luke 3:23 and the supposition, which could be made on the basis of the Synoptics, that Jesus' ministry lasted only one year, they thought that Jesus was no more than thirty years old when he died. Irenaeus appeals to the Johannine chronology to support a ministry of several years, and argues that in fact Jesus was between forty and fifty when he died. The point has theological importance for him, because it enables him to claim that Jesus entered the last of the periods of human life, and so passed through all the stages of human life (2.22.4). But he also has evidence that Jesus lived beyond forty:

> For everyone will admit that the age of thirty is that of someone still young and this period of youth extends to the fortieth year.[99] It is only from the fortieth and

98. Bacon, *Gospel of the Hellenists*, 36–37.

99. The Latin text of this sentence is corrupt: see the note in A. Rousseau and L. Doutreleau, *Irénée de Lyon: Contre les hérésies, Livre II*, vol. 1, Sources chrétiennes 293 (Paris: Cerf, 1982), 288.

fiftieth year that a person begins to decline towards old age. This is the age which our Lord possessed while he was still teaching, as the Gospel testifies and all the elders who associated (συμβεβληκότες) with John the disciple of the Lord in Asia testify (μαρτυροῦσιν), [saying that] John transmitted [to them the same tradition]. For he remained with them until the time of Trajan. Some of them saw not only John but also other apostles, and heard the same things from them, and testify to the truth of this report (*testantur de huiusmodi relatione*). Whom then should we rather believe? Such men as these, or Ptolemaeus, who never saw the apostles and even in his dreams never followed even the footprint of an apostle? (*Haer.* 2.22.5; Greek text partly in Eusebius, *Hist. eccl.* 3.23.3)

Irenaeus goes on (in 2.22.6) to expound John 8:57 ("You are not yet fifty years old") as implying that Jesus had passed forty (otherwise the Jews would have said, "You are not yet forty years old"). Clearly it is to this text that he refers in the passage just quoted ("as the Gospel testifies"). His further reference to the elders has commonly been taken to mean that he knew a tradition from the elders that *also* affirmed that Jesus lived beyond forty years.[100] Irenaeus, of course, several times quotes traditions of the elders, and sometimes, if not always,[101] derives them from Papias. But in this case the more probable explanation, though it seems to have gone unnoticed, is that Irenaeus is referring to John 21:24 ("we know that his testimony is true"). He takes the "we" of that verse to be the elders who knew John in Asia, and by that statement testified to the truth of all he had written in the Gospel. Thus they testified to the truth of John 8:57 along with every other part of the Gospel record of Jesus. They were able to certify the truth of all that John had written, both by testifying that it was John the disciple of the Lord who transmitted these traditions and because some of them had in the past also known other apostles and were able to testify that John's record agreed with what they had heard from other apostles. Irenaeus gives this explanation of John 21:24 here because it is at this point very important to him to maintain the eyewitness authority of a statement peculiar to the Fourth Gospel.

So far as it goes, this report that the elders certified the truth of John's Gospel coincides with the story in the *Muratorian Canon*. What they have in common may well go back to Papias. But there are two important differences. First, Irenaeus, by placing John the disciple of the Lord alongside "the other apostles" (*alios apostolos*) seems to include John among the apostles in a way that he does very occasionally elsewhere. We shall return later to Irenaeus's identification of John. But his language thus differs from that of the *Muratorian Canon*, in which John and Andrew are contrasted as "one of the disciples" and "one of the apostles." The latter must preserve Papias's attribution of the gospel to John the Elder. Second,

---

100. Lightfoot, *Biblical Essays*, 56–58; idem, *Supernatural Religion*, 245–47; J. Chapman, "Papias on the Age of Our Lord," *JTS* 9 (1908): 53–61 (who thinks Irenaeus misunderstood a statement of Papias); Gunther, "Early Identifications," 408.

101. Cf. Chapman, *John the Presbyter*, 16, for the view that he always derives them from Papias.

those who certify the Gospel are, in Irenaeus, the elders who knew John, but in the *Muratorian Canon* they are John's "fellow-disciples and bishops." An explanation of this difference will confirm that both writers are indebted to Papias.

In Irenaeus "the elders" are usually the generation of Christian teachers in Asia who had known the apostles but outlived them.[102] There is good reason to think that this is also how Papias used the term. The elders were those who were teaching in the churches of Asia in the late first century and whose traditions, which they had received from those who had been personal disciples of the Lord, Papias recorded in his work. At the time when he was collecting his oral traditions, the only personal disciples of Jesus still alive were Aristion and John the Elder.[103] These were elders in the sense that at that time they belonged to the same circle of senior teachers as the rest of the elders, but unlike the rest they had themselves been disciples of Jesus. Thus John the Elder was so called to distinguish him from the other disciple of Jesus called John, who was one of the Twelve. Papias collected both the traditions of the elders who had known disciples of the Lord no longer alive and the traditions of Aristion and John the Elder who were at that time still alive. But Papias's use of the term "elders" in the famous sentence of his prologue about the disciples of the Lord is notoriously ambiguous: εἰ δέ που καὶ παρηκολουθηκώς τις τοῖς πρεσβυτέροις ἔλθοι, τοὺς τῶν πρεσβυτέρων ἀνέκρινον λόγους, τί Ἀνδρέας ἢ Πέτρος εἶπεν ... (Eusebius, *Hist. eccl.* 3.39.4). The most probably meaning, which makes Papias's use of the term "elders" here consistent with that of Irenaeus who knew his work well, is that the elders are not the same people as Peter and Andrew and the other disciples listed.[104] The elders are the senior Christian teachers in various cities of Asia at the time when Papias was collecting traditions. Papias, living at Hierapolis, did not normally have the opportunity to hear them himself, but when any of their followers visited Hierapolis "he inquired about the words of the elders, [that is] what [according to the elders] Andrew and Peter had said." This interpretation is much more obviously consistent with the statement Papias had made just before, that he himself had learned from the elders (παρὰ τῶν πρεσβυτέρων ... ἔμαθον), than is the interpretation that equates the elders with Andrew and Peter and the rest of the disciples of the Lord. Papias's words are ambiguous only because he takes it for granted that the words of the elders in which he would be interested are those that transmit traditions from Andrew and Peter and the other disciples of the Lord.

---

102. See the references and discussion in ibid., 13–16.

103. Carpenter, *Johannine Writings*, 214; and Schnackenburg, *John*, 1:89–90, deny that Aristion and John the Elder had been personal disciples of Jesus, apparently because they think Papias means that they were still alive when he wrote his book. The date of Papias's work is very uncertain, but his statement in the prologue need mean only that they were still alive when he was collecting oral traditions. This could have been as early as the 80s.

104. The interpretation of Papias's statement by Chapman, *John the Presbyter*, 9–27, is in this respect convincing. Cf. also Körtner, *Papias*, 114–22, who agrees, but also, more questionably, sees the elders as itinerant teachers.

However, it is possible to read Papias's words as equating the elders with Andrew and Peter and the rest. This seems to have been how Eusebius read them (*Hist. eccl.* 3.39.7).[105] If we suppose that this is also how the author of the *Muratorian Canon* read them, we can see why his identification of those who certified John's Gospel differs from Irenaeus's. Papias, we may suppose, said that John's Gospel was certified by the elders. Perhaps he even called them John's fellow elders (συνπρεσβύτεροι). The author of the *Muratorian Canon*, guided by a misunderstanding of Papias's words in the prologue, assumed that these elders were the other disciples of the Lord whom Papias there names. He therefore calls them John's "fellow-disciples." Asking himself why they were called elders and perhaps remembering 1 Peter 5:1–2, he assumes this must be because they were also bishops.[106] So he calls them John's "fellow-disciples and bishops," and when he wishes to name one of them, he naturally selects the first name in Papias's list of these supposed elders: Andrew.

Irenaeus, on the other hand, correctly understood Papias. The elders could vouch for the truth of John's Gospel, not because they themselves had been disciples of the Lord, but because some of them had known other disciples of the Lord besides John. When Irenaeus adds that John survived to the reign of Trajan (also in *Haer.* 3.3.4),[107] it is possible he drew this from Papias's account of the origin of the Fourth Gospel, but chronological indications of this kind do not seem to be characteristic of Papias. So it is also quite possible that Irenaeus calculated this one himself, knowing that John's was the last of the four Gospels to be written (*Haer.* 3.1.1) and believing that the same John wrote the Apocalypse in the reign of Domitian (*Haer.* 5.30.3). Such a deduction would be comparable with the way he adds greater chronological precision to Papias's accounts of the origins of the Gospels of Matthew and Mark, doubtless by intelligent deduction rather than because he had additional information (*Haer.* 3.1.1).[108] Thus John the Elder need not have been quite so young at the time of Jesus' ministry or quite as old at the end of his life when he wrote the Gospel as Irenaeus's calculation would require.

The other aspect of the role of John's fellow disciples in the story in the *Muratorian Canon* is that they urged (*cohortantibus*) him to write. This has a kind of parallel in Clement of Alexandria, another writer who seems to have known Papias's work, since his account of the origin of Mark's Gospel (ap. Eusebius, *Hist. eccl.* 6.14.6) is dependent on Papias. Of the Fourth Gospel he said:

105. But cf. Chapman, *John the Presbyter*, 17–19.

106. That the elders are bishops is also the interpretation of Irenaeus, *Haer.* 2.22.5, in the passages of Victorinus, Jerome, and the *Monarchian Prologue* quoted in "Some False Leads," below.

107. The recurrence of the same phraseology in 2.22.5 and 3.3.4 could indicate a common literary source (Papias: so Chapman, "Papias," 57 n. 1) or a traditional Asian way of speaking of John of Ephesus, but could merely mean that Irenaeus repeats himself.

108. Cf. R. Bauckham, "The Martyrdom of Peter in the New Testament and Early Christian Literature," *ANRW* 2.26.1:539–95. J. Chapman, "St. Irenaeus and the Dates of the Gospels," *JTS* 6 (1905): 563–69, agrees that Irenaeus had only Papias's information, but denies that he intends to give greater chronological precision than Papias.

that John, conscious that the outward facts (τὰ σωματικά) had been set forth in the [other] Gospels, was urged on by his disciples[109] (προτραπέντα ὑπὸ τῶν γνωρίμων), and, divinely moved by the Spirit, composed a spiritual (πνευματικόν) Gospel. (*Hypotyposeis*, ap. Eusebius, *Hist. eccl.* 6.14.7)

The contrast here between the Synoptics, as recording τὰ σωματικά, and the Fourth Gospel, as a spiritual Gospel, is certainly Clement's own. This leaves, as the only detail that could be derived from Papias, the comment that John was urged to write by his disciples. However, we should note that in his account of the origin of Mark's Gospel, Clement (ap. Eusebius, *Hist. eccl.* 6.14.6) added to what he knew from Papias the information that those who had heard Peter's preaching exhorted (παρακαλέσαι) Mark to write a record of what he had said (cf. the further elaboration of this point by Eusebius, *Hist. eccl.* 2.15.1). So although the coincidence between Clement and the *Muratorian Canon* is notable and may well indicate that Papias said the elders urged John to write his Gospel, as well as certifying it when it was written, it is possible that this is a conventional topos to explain why an author put pen to paper and that the agreement between Clement and the *Muratorian Canon* is just a coincidence. If Clement read in Papias that the elders certified John's Gospel, it is not surprising that he did not reproduce this. He would not have seen why John should need to have the truth of his Gospel authenticated by mere elders.[110] But Clement's account of the origin of the Gospel confirms that Papias provided no more interesting detail about this matter than we have so far reconstructed.

We conclude that what Papias said about the origin of the Fourth Gospel was that John the Elder, the disciple of the Lord, wrote it.[111] He may have said he was urged to do so by the elders of Asia. He certainly said that the elders vouched for the truth of the Gospel (referring to John 21:24). (Papias's readers knew from his prologue, if not from elsewhere in his work, that these elders were able to do so because they had known other very prominent disciples of the Lord and themselves passed on traditions from them.) He then quoted part of 1 John 1:1–4 to show that John the Elder was both an eyewitness of the events of the Gospel history and wrote them in his Gospel. Therefore he (alone of the evangelists) wrote the λόγια of the Lord in order.

109. The translation given by Ehrhardt ("Gospels," 20) has "urged on by the 'Elders.'" This must be a mistake, but it is a serious one because it makes Clement's statement look closer to the elders of Papias and Irenaeus than it is. John's disciples no doubt are the elders, but Clement does not here call them so.

110. This is also why in the passages from Victorinus, Jerome, and the *Monarchian Prologue*, quoted in "Some False Leads" below, there is no reference to certification by the bishops, even though these passages are dependent on Irenaeus, *Haer.* 2.22.5. They have followed Clement in substituting encouragement to John to write for certification of what John had written.

111. There is no need in this context to adjudicate the vexed question of whether Papias referred to the martyrdom of John the son of Zebedee (and so is not likely to have ascribed the Fourth Gospel to him). For recent arguments in favor of the authenticity of such a reference, see Colson, *L'énigme*, 65–84; Hengel, *Johannine Question*, 158–59.

It might be objected that surely Papias, who was in a good position to know about the origin of the Fourth Gospel, could have given more information than this. In reply, we recall that it was not Papias's purpose to state all he may have known about the origins of the Gospels. What we have reconstructed serves precisely his purpose in proving the superiority of the Fourth Gospel, as far as order is concerned, over the other two Gospels believed to derive from eyewitness testimony.

Some False Leads

It remains to consider three related passages in later writers, which at first sight look as though they may be dependent on Papias but will turn out not to be:

> For when Valentinus, Cerinthus and Ebion and the others of the school of Satan were spread over the world, all the bishops came together to him (*conuenerunt ad illum*) from the most distant provinces and compelled (*compulerunt*) him to write a testimony. (Victorinus of Pettau, *In apoc.* 11.1)[112]

> John, the apostle whom Jesus most loved, the son of Zebedee and brother of James the apostle, whom Herod, after the Lord's passion, beheaded, was the last one to write a Gospel, at the request (*rogatus*) of the bishops of Asia, against Cerinthus and other heretics and especially against the then growing doctrine of the Ebionites, who asserted that Christ did not exist before Mary. For this reason he was compelled (*compulsus est*) also to announce his divine nativity. (Jerome, *Vir. ill.* 9)[113]

> When, however, after the death of Domitian, [John] was set free and returned from exile to Ephesus, and the seeds of the heretics—of Cerinthus, Ebion, and others who deny that Christ existed before Mary—already budded forth at that time, he was compelled (*compulsus est*) by almost all the bishops at that time in Asia and embassies from many churches to write about the divinity of Christ in a more profound way. (*Monarchian Prologue to John*)[114]

These passages, like many later patristic statements about the origins of the Gospels, result from bringing together the bits of information that could be gathered from early sources. In this case, information is drawn from three sources: (1) a statement by Irenaeus that John wrote his Gospel against Cerinthus (*Haer.* 3.11.1); (2) the passage in Irenaeus, *Haer.* 2.22.5, which we have already discussed (and which it is interesting to find was understood correctly as a reference to the origin of the Fourth Gospel): this supplied the information about the bishops;

---

112. Translation adapted from A. F. J. Klijn and G. J. Reinink, *Patristic Evidence for Jewish-Christian Sects*, Supplements to *Novum Testamentum* 36 (Leiden: Brill, 1973), 137.
113. Translation adapted from ibid., 211.
114. Ibid., 235.

and (3) Clement of Alexandria's statement that John was urged to write by his disciples (ap. Eusebius, *Hist. eccl.* 6.14.7). In the case of Victorinus,[115] it can be demonstrated that any debt to Papias is only indirect, via Irenaeus (*Haer.* 2.22.5). In that passage, the Greek text that Eusebius preserves says that the elders οἱ κατὰ τὴν Ἀσίαν Ἰωάννῃ τῷ τοῦ Κυρίου μαθητῇ συμβεβληκότες (*Hist. eccl.* 3.23.3), but the Latin translator of Irenaeus evidently read συμβεβηκότες for συμβεβληκότες, and so translated: *qui in Asia apud Johannem discipulum domini conuenerunt.* That Eusebius has the correct text can be seen from the parallel statement about Clement of Rome that Irenaeus makes in *Adversus haereses* 3.3.3 (συμβεβληκὼς αὐτοῖς, i.e., the apostles).[116] Victorinus evidently understood the Latin version of Irenaeus to mean that bishops from outside Asia came together to John in Asia. Jerome's statement, because it does not make the same mistake about the identity of the bishops but speaks of "the bishops of Asia," must be based not on Victorinus but on a common source used by both Victorinus and Jerome. They cannot be independently based on Irenaeus, because both take the elders in Irenaeus to be bishops, and both combine information from this passage of Irenaeus with information from *Adversus haereses* 3.11.1, adding Ebion or the Ebionites to Irenaeus's mention of Cerinthus,[117] and with information from Clement of Alexandria. The *Monarchian Prologue* is probably directly dependent on Jerome.

John the Elder Conflated with John the Son of Zebedee

The Fourth Gospel was never anonymous. As Hengel has shown,[118] as soon as Gospels circulated in the churches, they must have been known with authors' names attached to them. The Fourth Gospel was known as John's. In Asia, the tradition from Papias early in the second century to Polycrates at its end was that this John, the beloved disciple and the author of the Gospel, was John the Elder, a disciple of the Lord but not one of the Twelve, who had died in Ephesus.

115. Chapman ("Papias," 47–53) argues that Victorinus was dependent on Papias. Not all of his evidence is convincing, but some of it is, especially Victorinus's account of Mark's authorship of his Gospel. However, it is not certain that Victorinus knew Papias's work directly. If he did, he need not be dependent on Papias in the quoted passage.

116. See the discussion in Rousseau and Doutreleau, *Irénée de Lyon*, 1:288.

117. That John wrote his Gospel against the Cerinthians and the Ebionites is also found in Epiphanius, *Pan.* 51.2; 69.23; cf. 51.12. In 51.12 it is not clear whether Epiphanius means that John was compelled (ἀναγκάζεται) to write the Gospel by the Holy Spirit (already mentioned) or the bishops (not mentioned).

118. Hengel, *Johannine Question*, 74–76; cf. also, in more detail, Hengel, *Studies in the Gospel of Mark* (London: SCM, 1985), 64–84, and the criticism of his view by H. Koester, *Ancient Christian Gospels: Their History and Development* (London: SCM, 1990), 26–27. But it is noteworthy that Koester's objection is to the view that the Gospels originally bore titles of the form, "The Gospel according to . . ." (τὸ εὐαγγέλιον κατά . . .). He allows that Hengel may be correct in arguing that the Gospels must have circulated under the names of specific authors from the beginning.

We know of no dissent from this tradition in Asia before the third century. It is not certain when the identification of this John of Ephesus with John the son of Zebedee was first accepted in Asia,[119] but it does not appear to have happened for more than a century after the writing of the Gospel.

The identification of John of Ephesus, the beloved disciple and the author of the Fourth Gospel, with John the son of Zebedee seems to have been first made in Egypt. The only unambiguous identifications of the author of the Fourth Gospel with John the son of Zebedee in second-century literature are in the *Epistle of the Apostles* and the *Acts of John*, which both appear to be Egyptian works[120] from around the middle of the century.[121] In addition, Valentinian teachers of the second half of the second century—Ptolemy[122] and Theodotus[123]—call the author of the Fourth Gospel an apostle. Probably the Valentinian school derived from Egyptian Christian tradition the view that the author of the Fourth Gospel was the apostle John the son of Zebedee. Admittedly, the term "apostle" was sufficiently flexible to leave this in some doubt, as is also the case when Clement of Alexandria refers to John of Ephesus, author of the Apocalypse and presumably also of the Fourth Gospel (cf. Eusebius, *Hist. eccl.* 6.14.7) as "John the apostle" (*Quis div.* 42 = Eusebius, *Hist. eccl.* 3.23.6). After all, Clement of Alexandria can refer to Clement of Rome as "the apostle Clement" (*Strom.* 4.17.105.1). But probably these references to John as the apostle belong to an originally Egyptian tradition of identifying the author of the Fourth Gospel with John the son of Zebedee. This tradition will have originated quite naturally from an attempt to relate the Fourth Gospel to other traditions about the disciples of Jesus, among whom only one, the son of Zebedee, was known by the name of John. It was not that in Egypt nothing was known of the author of the Fourth Gospel except his name John. The *Acts of John* show that he was known to have lived and died at Ephesus, and Clement of Alexandria knew traditions about the John of Ephesus

119. Eusebius, *Hist. eccl.* 5.18.14, reports that Apollonius, the anti-Montanist writer, who was probably writing at Ephesus at the beginning of the third century, quoted the Apocalypse and told a story about a resurrection performed by John of Ephesus, but Eusebius is suspiciously silent about his views on the Fourth Gospel. It is possible that the Montanist writer Proclus thought that John the son of Zebedee wrote the Fourth Gospel and the Apocalypse, since his opponent Gaius seems to be rejecting the authorship of both by an apostle (fragments 2, 10, in Grant, *Second-Century Christianity*, 105–6), but is not certain that Proclus came from Asia.

120. For the Egyptian origin of the *Epistle of the Apostles*, see M. Hornschuh, *Studien zur Epistula Apostolorum* (Berlin: de Gruyter, 1965). For the Egyptian origin of the *Acts of John*, see E. Junod and J.-D. Kaestli, *Acta Johannis*, Corpus Christianorum Series Apocryphorum 2 (Turnhout: Brepols, 1983), 692–94; they consider Syria also possible (691–92), but Asia Minor impossible (691).

121. For the date of the *Acts of John*, see Junod and Kaestli, *Acta Johannis* 694–700. Colson, who attributes the confusion of the author of the Fourth Gospel with John the son of Zebedee to Irenaeus's confusion of them in his memory of what in his youth he had heard Polycarp say (*L'énigme*, 32–34, 55–56, 113), ignores the *Epistle of the Apostles* and the *Acts of John*.

122. *Letter to Flora*, ap. Epiphanius, *Pan.* 33.3.6. He also called the author of the Fourth Gospel, as Irenaeus did, "John the Lord's disciple" (ap. Irenaeus, *Haer.* 1.8.5).

123. Clement of Alexandria, *Exc.* 7.3; 35.1.1; 41.3.

whom he took to be the author of the Gospel (*Quis div.* 42 = Eusebius, *Hist. eccl.* 3.23.5–19).[124] The Gospel must have come to Egypt, as we should expect, along with some oral information about its author, though not enough to prevent his identification with the son of Zebedee. The ascription of the Gospel to John the son of Zebedee probably spread through the churches from the late second century through the influence of the *Acts of John*, Clement of Alexandria, and other representatives of the Egyptian tradition.[125]

The writings of Irenaeus help to show us why this ascription would prove acceptable. It has been commonly assumed and sometimes argued[126] that Irenaeus identified the author of the Fourth Gospel with John the son of Zebedee, but this has also been vigorously contested.[127] Decisive evidence is surprisingly and significantly elusive, despite Irenaeus's frequent references to the Fourth Gospel and its author. Irenaeus knew of John of Ephesus both from Papias and independently from the Asian traditions he learned in Smyrna as a young man (ap. Eusebius, *Hist. eccl.* 5.20.6; 5.24.16; *Haer.* 3.3.4).[128] He refers to John (regarding him as the author of all the Johannine writings, including the Apocalypse)[129] twenty-two times as "the disciple of the Lord" (and thirty-four times as just "John"), never as "John the apostle," by contrast with his references to Paul, who is quite frequently "Paul the apostle" (and much more frequently just "the Apostle"), Matthew (once "Matthew the apostle," usually just "Matthew"), and Peter (three times "Peter the apostle," usually just "Peter").[130] No doubt "John the disciple of the Lord" is

124. Identification of the author of the Fourth Gospel with the author of the Apocalypse would not necessarily lead to any special relationship with Ephesus, which is only one of the seven churches of Asia addressed in Revelation.

125. In North Africa, Tertullian, ca. 200, considered the author of the Fourth Gospel and the Apocalypse to be John the son of Zebedee: *Praescr.* 22, 36. But from Theophilus, *Autol.* 2.22, it is impossible to tell whether the identification of the author of the Fourth Gospel with the son of Zebedee was yet current in Syria.

126. E.g., Chapman, *John the Presbyter*, 42–43.

127. E.g., Burney, *Aramaic Origin*, 138–42; Gunther, "Early Identifications," 418–19; cf. Colson, *L'énigme*, 29–34.

128. For Irenaeus's age when he knew Polycarp, see Chapman, *John the Presbyter*, 44; Colson, *L'énigme*, 32–33.

129. The development of views on the authorship of the Apocalypse is even more difficult to trace than that of views on the authorship of the Fourth Gospel. From Irenaeus onward, common authorship of all the Johannine writings seems to have been widely accepted, but there is no evidence for this before Irenaeus. Justin, *Dial.* 81.4, ascribes the Apocalypse to the apostle John, but his view of the authorship of the Fourth Gospel is unknown. I am inclined to think that the two tombs of two Johns at Ephesus, of which Dionysius of Alexandria had heard and which he thought were those of John the son of Zebedee (author of the Gospel) and John the Elder (author of the Apocalypse), were actually those of John the Elder (author of the Gospel) and John the prophet (author of the Apocalypse). But it is possible that the association of the author of the Apocalypse with Ephesus in particular is a mistake resulting from the late second-century identification of him with the author of the Gospel.

130. The calculations are my own.

traditional Asian usage,[131] firmly fixed in Irenaeus's terminology from his early days in Smyrna. The term itself merely indicates a personal disciple of Jesus and could apply, as in Papias, to members of the Twelve as well as to others. In the Asian tradition of emphasizing tradition from the eyewitnesses of the ministry of Jesus, which Irenaeus's references to John continue (cf. especially Eusebius, *Hist. eccl.* 5.20.6), the term "disciple of the Lord" was preferable to "apostle," which, as in the case of "*the* Apostle" (Paul), need not imply this. But it is significant that Irenaeus applies this term to no individual except John (while in *Haer.* 3.12.5 the plural seems to refer to disciples who were explicitly not apostles).

However, Irenaeus twice calls the author of the Fourth Gospel "the apostle" (*Haer.* 1.9.2–3), twice puts John alongside "the other apostles" (*Haer.* 2.22.5; *Letter to Victor*, ap. Eusebius, *Hist. eccl.* 5.24.16), and in one other passage clearly includes John in the category of the apostles (*Haer.* 3.3.4). We can see why he does so.[132] In *Haer.* 1.9.2–3 he is arguing with the Valentinian Ptolemy (who himself calls the author of the Fourth Gospel "the apostle"[133] and from whom Irenaeus may in this context have borrowed the usage). In *Haer.* 2.22.5, he is concerned with the elders' certification of the eyewitness authority of John's Gospel. In the other two passages he is concerned with Polycarp's role as the next link after the apostles in a chain of apostolic tradition. All these passages reflect Irenaeus's concern with apostolicity as the criterion of truth against the Gnostics, including both the apostolicity of the reliable scriptures of the New Testament and the succession of public teaching from the apostles through the bishops of the apostolic sees. In these contexts, the term "apostle" indicates reliable authority, authorized by Christ, publicly recognized, by contrast with the chains of secret tradition from disciples of Jesus that the Gnostics claimed.[134] It is understandable that Irenaeus should assimilate to this concept of apostolicity his own favorite evangelist and the most important source of eyewitness tradition from the ministry of Jesus in his native Asia. But since Irenaeus can treat the seventy as "other apostles" in addition to the Twelve (*Haer.* 2.21.1), there is no need to suppose he included the fourth evangelist among the Twelve. He himself valued the Asian tradition too highly to identify John of Ephesus with John the son of Zebedee, but it is understandable that others, influenced by the same concept of apostolicity, should have welcomed the opportunity to do so. Increasing (and related) use of the terms, found in the *Muratorian Canon,* "the prophets" and "the apostles" to refer respectively to the Old and New Testament scriptures would have the same effect. Mark and Luke qualified as New Testament authors by being considered disciples of the apostles, but the notion of a writer of scripture who was a disciple of Jesus but not an apostle

131. It is also found, outside Asia, in Ptolemy (ap. Irenaeus, *Haer.* 1.8.5), and Heracleon (ap. Origen, *Comm. Jo.* 6.3); cf. the apocryphal letter of John quoted by Pseudo-Cyprian, *De Montibus Sina et Sion* 13; also *Apocryphon of John* 1.4.

132. Cf. Carpenter, *Johannine Writings*, 208.

133. *Letter to Flora,* ap. Epiphanius, *Pan.* 33.3.6.

134. Cf. also Tertullian, *Marc.* 4.5.

must have been too anomalous to persist. Once he was considered an apostle, John of Ephesus easily became indistinguishable from the son of Zebedee.

Martin Hengel writes, "In Asia Minor there was a special interest in the 'promotion' of the 'elder John' and 'disciple of the Lord' to an 'apostle and member of the Twelve.' Like Rome and Antioch, their great competitors, they now possessed two apostles as founders."[135] The more plausible this seems, the more remarkable it is that this "promotion" did not in fact take place in Asia before the third century. This gives the Asian tradition that the beloved disciple who wrote the Fourth Gospel was John the Elder a right to be taken very seriously.[136]

---

135. Hengel, *Johannine Question*, 31–32; cf. Sanders, *Fourth Gospel*, 38–39.

136. In *Jesus and the Eyewitnesses: The Gospels as Eyewitness Testimony* (Grand Rapids: Eerdmans, 2006), chapter 16 ("Papias on John") and chapter 17 ("Polycrates and Irenaeus on John"), I have summarized the main arguments of the present chapter and added some additional discussion of John the Elder as author of the Gospel of John. In the appendix to chapter 16, I have discussed Charles Hill's argument (Charles E. Hill, "What Papias Said about John [and Luke]: A 'New' Papias Fragment," *JTS* 49 [1998], 582–629) that Papias's views on John's Gospel are preserved in Eusebius, *Hist. eccl.* 3.14.5–13. In *Jesus and the Eyewitnesses*, chapter 17, I have provided a more extensive and detailed discussion of Irenaeus, strengthening the case for thinking he did not identify John, the author of the Gospel, with John the son of Zebedee. Hill may be correct in locating the *Epistle of the Apostles* in Asia Minor (Charles E. Hill, "The *Epistula Apostolorum*: An Asian Tract from the Time of Polycarp," *JECS* 7 [1999], 1–53), in which case my view that the identification of John the author of the Gospel with John the son of Zebedee originated in Egypt would need some qualification. The identification could well have originated independently in more than one context. On the very debatable issue of Gaius and the Alogi, reference should now be made to Charles E. Hill, *The Johannine Corpus in the Early Church* (Oxford: Oxford University Press, 2004), chapter 4.

3

THE BELOVED DISCIPLE
AS IDEAL AUTHOR

Hengel on Authorship of the Fourth Gospel

This chapter presupposes Martin Hengel's solution to the Johannine question.[1] For this solution Hengel has made a very impressive case, argued with a characteristic wealth of relevant learning and a characteristically sound historical judgment. In essence the solution is that John the Elder, to whom Papias refers in the famous fragment of his prologue (ap. Eusebius, *Hist. eccl.* 3.39.4), was both the beloved disciple and the author of the Fourth Gospel, as well as the author of the three Johannine letters. This simple statement of Hengel's position would, to be fully accurate, require some minor qualifications, in respect both of the identity of John the Elder with the beloved disciple and of the extent of his authorship of the Fourth Gospel. We shall return to these qualifications later. But much of the cogency of Hengel's proposal lies in its essential simplicity, which, of course, runs quite counter to recent trends in Johannine studies, with their speculative reconstructions of the complex history of the Johannine community in relation

Originally published in a slightly different form in *Journal for the Study of the New Testament* 49 (1993): 21–44. Reprinted by permission of the publisher. A reprint appears in S. E. Porter and C. A. Evans, eds., *The Johannine Writings*, Biblical Seminar 32 (Sheffield: Sheffield Academic Press, 1995), 46–68.

1. M. Hengel, *The Johannine Question* (London: SCM/Philadelphia: Trinity, 1989). Since Hengel's book provides abundant references to the relevant scholarly literature, such references will be kept to a minimum in the footnotes to this chapter.

to a variety of postulated Johannine authors and a variety of postulated stages of composition and redaction of the Gospel. Of course, simplicity is by no means self-evidently a virtue in historical reconstruction, since historical reality is often complex. In this case, the simplicity of Hengel's solution is attractive because it adequately explains both the internal evidence of the Gospel and the external evidence about the Gospel, whereas by contrast other solutions tend to set internal and external evidence against each other. The traditional attribution to John the son of Zebedee attempts to do justice to the external evidence, but at the price of imposing on the internal evidence an interpretation it can scarcely bear. More recent theories that tend to rely in principle on the internal evidence alone make the external evidence very difficult to explain.

The present chapter is one of a pair that take Hengel's position as their starting point. In the other[2] I have offered a detailed reassessment of the external evidence for the origin of the Gospel, demonstrating that the best external evidence supports Hengel's basic proposal much more strongly than he himself realized. Here we are concerned with his treatment of the Fourth Gospel's own portrayal of the beloved disciple. It is in this area that criticism will be offered and a somewhat different interpretation, which will strengthen rather than detract from his overall proposal, will be advanced.

Deliberate Ambiguity?

We noted above that our simple statement of Hengel's solution to the Johannine question requires some qualifications. First, with regard to the authorship of the Gospel, Hengel clearly regards it as substantially the work of John the Elder, but he allows that the form of the Gospel that we have (the only form that was ever "published") is the result of a redaction by members of the Johannine school after John the Elder's death. The editors at least added the closing verses; Hengel leaves open the extent to which their editorial activity may have affected the rest of the Gospel.[3] This is relevant to the Gospel's portrayal of the beloved disciple, since Hengel tends to speak of major aspects of this portrayal as the work of the redactors and seems by no means decided how far John the Elder himself was responsible for the way the beloved disciple is portrayed.[4] Second, with regard to the identification of the beloved disciple, the sense in which the beloved disciple is intended to represent John the Elder himself is qualified in Hengel's argument by three converging considerations: (1) He accepts the common view that the beloved disciple in the Gospel represents the ideal disciple.[5] This does not mean

2. Chapter 2 above.
3. Hengel, *Johannine Question*, 84, 94–96, 99–100, and especially 105–8.
4. Ibid., 3, 78, 127–32.
5. Ibid., 78, 125.

that the beloved disciple is not also a historical figure,[6] but it means that the portrayal of the figure has been idealized in the interests of portraying him as the ideal disciple. (2) Hengel emphasizes the enigmatic nature of the references to the beloved disciple, which leave his identity ambiguous: "The editors—like the author—want the riddle to remain unsolved, the issue to be left open."[7] But since he argues that the Gospel was "published" (i.e., circulated to other churches by its editors) with the title "the Gospel according to John,"[8] as well as with a clear identification of the beloved disciple as the author of the Gospel in 21:24, this ambiguity, at least on the part of the editors, cannot leave the identity of the beloved disciple entirely open. (3) Hengel thinks that in some respects the Gospel seems to hint at an identification of the beloved disciple with John the son of Zebedee, and thinks that certainly the redactors, perhaps even John the Elder himself, deliberately allowed the figure of the beloved disciple to suggest both John the Elder and John the son of Zebedee.[9] Hengel's discussion at this point is full of questions and conjectures, especially as to the respective intentions of John the Elder and the redactors, but it is clear at least that he thinks the ambiguity of the beloved disciple, for the first readers or hearers, consisted in the possible reference to either of the two Johns, combined with the idealization of the figure.[10]

In my view, Hengel has quite unnecessarily complicated and compromised his proposal by allowing a relic of the old attribution to John the son of Zebedee back into his argument. In this context, John the son of Zebedee is a phantom that needs to be finally and completely exorcised. Hengel is, in a way, obliged to reintroduce the son of Zebedee into the Gospel by his conviction that the figure of the beloved disciple is deliberately enigmatic and ambiguous. I shall argue that the beloved disciple is not an ambiguous figure. Insofar as there is anything enigmatic about him, the enigma is dispelled at the end of the Gospel, which functions clearly to identify him as John the Elder who wrote the Gospel. This is not to deny an element of idealization, but the idealization by no means produces ambiguity because it is not as the ideal disciple that the beloved disciple is idealized, but as the ideal author. By this term I mean that the beloved disciple is portrayed in the Gospel narrative in such a way as to show that he is ideally qualified to be the author of the Gospel.

6. Ibid., 78–80.

7. Ibid., 128, cf. 3, 77–78.

8. Ibid., 74–76; cf. also, in more detail, Hengel, *Studies in the Gospel of Mark* (London: SCM, 1985), 64–84, and the criticism of his view by H. Koester, *Ancient Christian Gospels: Their History and Development* (London: SCM; Philadelphia: Trinity, 1990), 26–27. But it is noteworthy that Koester's objection is to the view that the Gospels originally bore titles of the form, "The Gospel according to . . ." (τὸ εὐαγγέλιον κατά . . .). He allows that Hengel may be correct in arguing that the Gospels must have circulated under the names of specific authors from the beginning.

9. Hengel, *Johannine Question*, 127–32.

10. Ibid., 130–32.

The Sons of Zebedee in the Fourth Gospel

It will be convenient first to dispose of the supposed deliberate hints that the beloved disciple might be John the son of Zebedee. We need not repeat Hengel's argument that the beloved disciple is portrayed as a Jerusalem disciple, not one of the Twelve.[11] But in his argument that, nevertheless, the reader is meant to have the option of thinking of John the son of Zebedee, Hengel is too impressed both by the absence of the sons of Zebedee from the Gospel apart from 21:2 and by their presence in 21:2.

The argument about the absence of the sons of Zebedee assumes that the author of the Fourth Gospel presupposes knowledge of the Synoptic Gospels on the part of his readers, who would therefore mark the absence of these disciples who were prominent in the Synoptics.[12] This is a large assumption. It is likely enough that the author knew Mark, but at this date Matthew's and Luke's Gospels need not have reached Ephesus. But whichever Gospels were known to the author, it would be a mistake to suppose that they were necessarily widely used and well known in his community. Written Gospels from elsewhere would not easily have supplanted or even competed with such a church's own oral tradition, of which the author of the Fourth Gospel was the most important exponent. It is possible that the portrayal of the beloved disciple in relation to Peter indicates the superiority of the Gospel over the Petrine gospel, Mark.[13] But even this does not mean that the author is so constantly looking over his shoulder at Mark that his failure to mention James and John needs to be related to their prominence in Mark. It is probable that the Johannine tradition just happened to focus on other disciples. We should remember that the prominence of the sons of Zebedee in the Synoptics is largely due to Mark and to a lesser extent to special Lukan tradition; they never appear in special Matthean tradition. We should also notice that none of the traditions in which the sons of Zebedee appear in the Synoptics occur in the Fourth Gospel. The latter's narrative of the call of the disciples, beginning as it does with those who were disciples of the Baptist, is a quite different tradition from Mark's. If it does not include the sons of Zebedee, nor does it include Thomas, a prominent disciple in the Fourth Gospel. Anyone tempted to identify the anonymous disciple of 1:34–39 as John the son of Zebedee ought to see at once that the presence of John the son of Zebedee without his brother James would be even more surprising here than the absence of John the son of Zebedee. Finally, we may notice that the one place in the Fourth Gospel where we could be justifiably surprised if the sons of Zebedee, as fishermen, did not appear, they do in fact appear (21:2).

11. Ibid., 124–26, cf. 109–11; O. Cullmann, *The Johannine Circle*, trans. J. Bowden (London: SCM, 1976), 63–85; G. R. Beasley-Murray, *John*, Word Biblical Commentary 36 (Waco: Word Books, 1987), lxx–lxxv.

12. Hengel, *Johannine Question*, 129, cf. 75, 91.

13. Ibid., 125.

This simple explanation for the single appearance of the sons of Zebedee in the Fourth Gospel should warn us also against finding their appearance in 21:2 significant for the identity of the beloved disciple. But in fact 21:2, far from allowing the possibility that the beloved disciple is John the son of Zebedee, actually excludes this possibility. The convention that the beloved disciple appears only anonymously in the Gospel is well enough established by this point for the reader not to expect it to be breached here, especially without any indication that it is and when there are no less than two genuinely anonymous disciples to cover the presence of the beloved disciple. To argue that 21:2 refers to four unnamed disciples, any of whom could be the beloved disciple, is specious. Everyone knew the names of the sons of Zebedee, who are quite sufficiently specified by the phrase οἱ τοῦ Ζεβεδαίου. If the beloved disciple could be one of them, he could also just as well be Thomas or Nathanael.

Thus 21:2 excludes the possibility that the beloved disciple is John the son of Zebedee, even as one possibility in a deliberately ambiguous portrayal. But this does not exhaust the interest of the curious way in which the beloved disciple is included in this list of disciples. There are seven disciples. The number seven is the number of completeness, and a list of seven can therefore be representative of all: the seven listed do not exhaust but stand for all. This is probably the significance of the seven churches in the book of Revelation: seven specific churches are selected to represent all churches. It is the significance of the seven signs in the Fourth Gospel itself: they are related as representative of all the many others that are not related (20:30). Thus the seven disciples who make the great catch of fish are representative of all the disciples of Jesus who are to be engaged in the mission of the church (and could not, of course, all appear in person in a story about fishing). From this point of view, it is significant that there are seven, not twelve or eleven (as in some other, though not all, postresurrection commissionings of the disciples). These seven include some of the Twelve, but also Nathanael, and therefore the beloved disciple can be included without the implication that he is one of the Twelve.

It remains puzzling why there should be two anonymous disciples, rather than just one. There seem to be two possible explanations. One is that, in drawing up his list, the evangelist did not wish it to look as though he had deliberately excluded any of the disciples named in his Gospel (Andrew, Philip, Judas not Iscariot). The inclusive representativeness of the list is protected by leaving, as it were, an empty place. The other possibility, suggested by Cullmann,[14] is that the two anonymous disciples are two members of the Johannine school: the beloved disciple and a colleague who had also been a personal disciple of Jesus and to whom, as a colleague of the beloved disciple, the latter's conventional anonymity is here extended. If we wonder what the point of such a reference would be, we might suppose that this other "Johannine" disciple's eyewitness testimony

14. Cullmann, *Johannine Circle*, 76

made a contribution to the Gospel along with the beloved disciple's. We might suppose that the first person plural of eyewitness testimony in John 1:14 (and 1 John 1:1–3?) includes him (along with some others who had not been close enough to the inner circle of the disciples to appear in the Gospel's narrative). We might even wonder whether this second anonymous disciple is the problematic "other disciple" of 18:15–16, who (despite his association with Peter) is hardly introduced in such a way as to encourage the reader's identification of him with the beloved disciple.[15] The reader who thought that he must be the beloved disciple simply because, like the beloved disciple, he is anonymous, would find in 21:2 that the Gospel knows two anonymous disciples. For readers who knew this other "Johannine" disciple, his close association with the high priest (18:15) would probably be sufficient to identify him.[16]

The Fourth Gospel's Statement of Authorship

The next stage of our argument must be to examine the Gospel's own statement of its authorship in 21:24, but before we do so it is necessary briefly to consider the relation of chapter 21, which in more than one respect is crucial for the understanding of the beloved disciple, to the rest of the Gospel. Against the general view that chapter 21, whether or not from the same hand as the rest of the Gospel, is in some sense an appendix to a Gospel originally intended to end at 20:31, Paul Minear, in a significant but neglected article, has made a convincing case for the view that chapter 21 was always an integral part of the design of the Gospel.[17]

Scholarship has been strangely mesmerized by the impression that 20:30–31 read like the original conclusion to the Gospel. These verses are a conclusion of sorts, but there is no reason to regard them as the conclusion to the Gospel. They are the conclusion to the Gospel's account of the signs that manifested Jesus' glory and enable people to believe in him as Messiah and Son of God (20:31). As such, they certainly signal the completion of the Gospel's main purpose, and so chapter 21 could be regarded as an epilogue. But an epilogue need not be an afterthought: it may be integral to the design of a work. This epilogue completes the double story of Peter and the beloved disciple, which began in chapter 13, and thereby indicates the continuing history of the church between the resurrection appearances and the Parousia (cf. 21:22). The story of the great catch of fish does not contradict the indication in 20:30–31 that the account of Jesus' signs is now

15. For a valuable survey of this issue, see F. Neirynck, "The 'Other Disciple' in Jn 18,15–16," in idem, *Evangelica*, BETL 60 (Leuven: Peeters/Leuven University Press, 1982), 335–64.

16. If the beloved disciple is John the Elder, it is not difficult to suggest who the other "Johannine" disciple must be. Aristion, whom Papias places alongside John the Elder as a disciple of the Lord, whom Papias himself had heard (*Apos. Con.* 7.46.8 associates Aristion with Smyrna) and, according to Eusebius, frequently mentioned in his writings (*Hist. eccl.* 3.39.7, 14), is the obvious candidate.

17. P. S. Minear, "The Original Functions of John 21," *JBL* 102 (1983): 85–98.

completed. It is not a sign of the kind that the signs of chapters 2–20 are said to be, that is, signs that manifest Jesus' glory in order to enable belief in him. It has a quite different purpose: to symbolize programmatically the mission in which the disciples are now to engage. After chapter 20, no more needs to be said about Jesus himself: the central, christological purpose of the Gospel has been fulfilled. But more does need to be said about the disciples: the loose ends that the story of Peter and the beloved disciple up till this point has left must be taken up before the Gospel is complete. Minear has convincingly shown how 21:15–19 corresponds closely to earlier material in the Gospel, not in such a way as to indicate a secondary addition to the Gospel, but in such a way as to show that this conclusion to the Gospel's story of Peter must have been presupposed all along.[18] We may add, as of particular interest to our purpose, that the otherwise unnecessarily full way in which the beloved disciple is described in 21:10 (after he has already appeared in 21:7) must form a deliberate inclusio with 13:23–25, indicating that the double story of Peter and the beloved disciple that began there ends here. Of course, the view that chapter 21 is integral to the Gospel cannot tell us whether the last three or two verses of the chapter are an editorial addition. The story of Peter and the beloved disciple could certainly have ended satisfactorily at 21:22. But it could not have ended satisfactorily at 21:19.

The basic significance of 21:24–25 ought to be clear, even though it has been continually debated. A single editor speaks for himself in the first person singular of verse 25 and on behalf of the Johannine school in the first person plural of verse 24. He writes evidently with the concurrence and approval of other members of the school, but there is actually no justification in these verses for even Hengel's constant references to redactors of the Gospel. We know of only one editor, who acted on behalf of the school. More significantly, however, this editor distinguishes both himself and the school from the author of the Gospel (v. 24), who is identified as the beloved disciple to whom the preceding three verses refer. The meaning of γράψας cannot plausibly be so extended as to make the beloved disciple less than the author.[19] Of course, it could mean "had it written by a secretary" (the most that 19:19–22 as a parallel could legitimate), and a secretary could be given more or less freedom by an author. But an author employing a secretary is still an author. It is a long way from authorship in this sense to the idea of the beloved disciple as merely the source or guarantor of the tradition that the Gospel incorporates. John 21:24 designates the beloved disciple the author of the Gospel.

Moreover, we learn from 21:23 that the Johannine school certainly thought they knew very well who the beloved disciple was. The common interpretation of this verse in the light of the expectation that the Parousia would come before

18. See also, on the relation of 13:36–38 and 21:15–19, R. Bauckham, "The Martyrdom of Peter in the New Testament and Early Christian Literature," in *ANRW* 2.26.1: 539–95.

19. G. Schrenk ("γράφω," *TDNT* 1:743) offers no evidence at all for such a usage, while F. R. M. Hitchcock ("The Use of γράφειν," *JTS* 31 [1930]: 271–75) shows that the kind of evidence that is sometimes alleged does not meet the need.

the generation of those who had known Jesus died out (cf. Mark 9:1; 13:30) is compelling. We know that for this reason the passing of the first generation of Christian leaders caused a problem (2 Pet. 3:4), though all the evidence suggests that it was a quite temporary problem of the late first century, the period when the first generation seemed to have almost passed away. As many of those who were well known as personal disciples of Jesus, such as Peter (John 21:18–19), died, attention would have focused on any still known to be alive. That the beloved disciple—as a rare, perhaps finally unique, survivor—should at the end of his life have been rumored to be the subject of a personalized version of Mark 9:1 is easily credible. The rumor would certainly be of no interest if the beloved disciple were regarded as an unknown disciple. It is explicable only if the beloved disciple were a well-known figure. The rumor, of course, must have circulated before the death of the person to whom it referred.

The rumor could have been based on 21:22 in an earlier version of the Gospel that ended at 21:22, or it could have been based on an alleged saying of Jesus that already circulated before the completion of the Gospel and of which 21:22 gives a version. In either case, the conclusion is inescapable that, in light of 21:23, 21:24 designates as the author of the Gospel that specific individual who was generally regarded in the Johannine churches as the disciple to whom the saying in 21:22 refers. Thus these verses allow no ambiguity, for the first readers/hearers of this final form of the Gospel, as to the identity of the author or of the beloved disciple. They presuppose that the identity of the disciple to whom the saying in 21:22 refers is well known and they claim that he wrote the Gospel. Hengel's argument for deliberate ambiguity about the identity of the beloved disciple in the final redaction of the Gospel is at all plausible only because he is thinking of the Gospel's circulating far beyond the circle in which the beloved disciple was well known. But we should probably suppose that, as the Gospel circulated further afield, the common knowledge of the Johannine churches as to the identity of the beloved disciple would spread with it.

Thus the identity of the beloved disciple becomes unambiguous, at least at the end of the Gospel in its finally redacted form. But the closing verses of the Gospel also raise for us the question of the extent of the final redaction. That the editor distinguishes both himself and the Johannine school from the author would be consistent with a degree of editing of the author's work. For our purposes, it is relevant to ask whether the portrayal of the beloved disciple may not be due to the redaction, rather than to the author. This is possible, though it would mean that there was rather extensive redaction. However, we should note that, in light of 21:24, such a portrayal of the beloved disciple by the redactor would be precisely his portrayal of the author of the Gospel. He would be inserting references to the author into the author's own work. Our argument, to be presented below, that the beloved disciple is portrayed as the ideal author would thus be quite consistent with this attribution of the references to the beloved disciple to the redactor.

However, there is one consideration that suggests that not all the references to the beloved disciple within the Gospel are due to the redactor. This is the relation between 21:24 and 19:35 (though the latter is not, of course, a reference to the beloved disciple as the beloved disciple). From the close verbal relationship between these verses, it is clear that the writer of 21:24 modeled his words on 19:35. It is also clear how he understood 19:35. Although modern exegetes debate the identity of both ὁ ἑωρακώς and ἐκεῖνος, the writer of 21:24 clearly took both to be the author of the Gospel. But whereas in 19:35 the author himself vouches for the truth of what he says (ἐκεῖνος οἶδεν), in 21:24 the Johannine school vouches for the truth of his witness (οἴδαμεν). The difference is most easily understood if 19:35 really comes from the hand of the author. The witness's own knowledge that he tells the truth is a remarkably weak way of substantiating his witness (cf. 8:13–18), but it is the only claim a single author can make. The Johannine school's claim that the author speaks the truth carries more weight. The redactor would surely have written οἴδαμεν in 19:35 as he did in 21:24.

This is not quite a compelling argument. It could be said that the nature of the witness in 19:35 is such that no one else could verify it, though this raises the question of the sense in which members of the Johannine school could claim in 21:24 to verify the truth of the Gospel as a whole. They could not themselves have been eyewitnesses of the events, for the rumor of 21:23 must presuppose that the beloved disciple was then one of the very last disciples of Jesus still alive. They could have known other eyewitnesses in the past.

Of course, even if we could be sure that 19:35 is from the hand of the author, not that of the redactor, it would not necessarily follow that the same is true of the passages in which the beloved disciple is so called. However, we shall argue below that, despite its quite different character, 19:35 in fact presupposes and coheres with the other passages in which the beloved disciple appears.

We cannot be certain whether the figure of the beloved disciple is due to the author or the redactor. However, we can be fairly confident that in either case the figure of the beloved disciple represents the author and that in either case it correctly represents the author as a personal disciple of Jesus and eyewitness of some of the events of the Gospel story. The redactor who added 21:24–25, along with the Johannine school on whose behalf he wrote, was in a position to know this. These verses must have been added along with verse 23 and therefore soon after the death of the beloved disciple if verse 23 presupposes this, or even before if it does not. The Gospel could never have ended with verse 23. So banal and anticlimactic an ending to a work of such artistry is inconceivable. It could have ended at verse 22, which would be a highly effective ending, or, if the figure of the beloved disciple is entirely due to the redactor, we cannot tell how the author ended his work. But in either case, verse 23 must have been written along with verse 24. So verse 24, like verse 23, must date from the time when the claim that the beloved disciple would not die either was still believed and needed correcting or had only recently been disappointed by the beloved disciple's death and needed explaining.

To sum up, in 21:24 the redactor of the Gospel, speaking for the Johannine school, identifies as the author of the Gospel a figure well known to his first readers/hearers as the disciple of Jesus to whom the saying in 21:22 referred. He does so, at the latest, soon after the death of this person whom he considers both the beloved disciple and the author of the Gospel. In such a context, he cannot have been mistaken either about the author of the Gospel or about the author's identity with the beloved disciple. If the beloved disciple already appeared in the author's work, the redactor could not have been mistaken in supposing that the author portrayed himself as the beloved disciple. If the figure of the beloved disciple is due to the redactor, he cannot have been mistaken in supposing that the author had been a personal disciple of Jesus who witnessed significant events in the Gospel story. He cannot have been mistaken, and so the only alternative to accepting his claim that the beloved disciple authentically represents the author of the Gospel would be to regard the Gospel as pseudepigraphal.[20] In other words, soon after the beloved disciple's death someone else (whom we must then call the author, not the redactor) wrote the Gospel and represented the beloved disciple as its author. Our reasons for preferring to accept the Gospel's claim to author-ship are largely Hengel's and need not be repeated here. But it should be noted that, even if the Gospel were pseudepigraphal, our argument that it identifies its author unambiguously is unaffected. Whether the beloved disciple was genuinely or only fictionally the author, he was a specific individual well known to the first readers/hearers and for these first readers/hearers the Gospel in its final form pointed unambiguously to that individual as its author.

Having established that the Gospel identifies its author unambiguously, we turn to the way in which the Gospel portrays the beloved disciple as its author.

Ideal Disciple or Ideal Witness?

It is a rather popular notion, taken up by Hengel, that the beloved disciple is portrayed as the ideal disciple.[21] If this means that he represents, as a model for others, the ideal of discipleship, it is certainly misleading. The beloved disciple may sometimes function in this way, just as other disciples (such as Nathanael and Mary Magdalene) in the Fourth Gospel do, but such a function cannot satisfactorily account for most of what is said about him. Even if we confine ourselves to the passages in which the beloved disciple is so called, the only undisputed references

20. One scholar who accepts that the Gospel is pseudepigraphal (though on the basis of 1:14) is J. Ashton, *Understanding the Fourth Gospel* (Oxford: Clarendon, 1991), 437–39.

21. See, for example, K. Quast, *Peter and the Beloved Disciple: Figures for a Community in Crisis*, JSNTS 32 (Sheffield: JSOT Press, 1989), who combines this idea with the view that the beloved disciple represents the Johannine community.

to him, we find an emphasis on an exclusive privilege that is precisely not representative. In 13:23–26, the beloved disciple has the place of special intimacy next to Jesus at the supper, which it is not possible for more than one disciple to occupy, and he is therefore uniquely placed to enquire and be enlightened as to Jesus' meaning and purpose. In 20:1–10, his understanding faith in the resurrection is enabled by his observing the empty tomb and the grave clothes: it relates to the role of eyewitness, which he shares with Peter but not with later disciples. The passage most easily susceptible to an interpretation of the beloved disciple as ideal disciple is 19:26–27, where he is certainly portrayed as the only one of Jesus' male disciples who is faithful enough to be with him at the cross. The scene may well represent the new relationships established by Jesus' death and resurrection (cf. 20:17), but even here the representativeness of the beloved disciple cannot replace his unique and particular privilege. The point is not simply that any faithful disciple becomes the son of Jesus' mother, though to an extent this is true. The beloved disciple uniquely takes the mother of Jesus into his own home.

Most difficult of all for the thesis that the beloved disciple is the ideal disciple is his last appearance (21:20–23). The story of the Gospel undoubtedly ends on a note of discipleship, with Jesus' words, "Follow me!" in verse 19 repeated, as the last words of Jesus in the Gospel, in verse 22. But the words are spoken to Peter and there is no indication here that the beloved disciple is the model of discipleship, either for Peter or for the readers/hearers. The beloved disciple's discipleship is indicated in verse 20 (ἀκολουθοῦντα), but the course it will now take should be of no concern to Peter or, it is implied, to the readers/hearers. Whereas the attention of the readers/hearers is drawn to Peter's future discipleship, as shepherd of Jesus' sheep who will in the end give his life for them, it is pointedly deflected from that of the beloved disciple. Where, if the beloved disciple represents the ideal disciple, we should expect the Gospel to leave the reader with an emphatic indication of this role, we find exactly the opposite. Since the portrayal of the beloved disciple throughout the Gospel is so closely connected with that of Peter and since the inclusio between 13:23–25 and 21:20 deliberately draws attention to the fact that 21:20–22 concludes the story of the two disciples that began in 13:23–25, any interpretation of the role of the beloved disciple in the Gospel must justify itself by a convincing and consistent explanation of this final scene.

In interpretations of the beloved disciple as the ideal disciple, he is usually contrasted with the figure of Peter, understood as a less than ideal disciple. The beloved disciple's relationship to Peter, whose portrayal in the Gospel is much more complex and detailed than that of the beloved disciple, is certainly important for understanding the role of the latter. It must be highly significant that, in almost all cases where the beloved disciple is portrayed in relation to Peter, the beloved disciple in some sense takes precedence (13:23–26; 20:1–10; 21:7; also 1:35–42; 18:15–16, if the anonymous disciple in these cases is the beloved disciple, as I think he must be in 1:35–39 but need not be in 18:15–16),[22] while in 19:26–27 (also 19:35, which in my view must refer to the beloved disciple) Peter's absence similarly gives the beloved disciple a kind of superiority to Peter. However, precisely the consistency of this feature up to and including 21:7 must make it also very significant that in the beloved disciple's final appearance it is not found. John 21:20 offers a subtly ambivalent picture. On the one hand, there seems to be the implication that the beloved disciple is already doing (ἀκολουθοῦντα), as he has done throughout the Gospel, what Peter is now commanded to do (μοι ἀκολούθει), but on the other hand there is the impression that the beloved disciple now lags behind. An adequate interpretation of the relationship between the beloved disciple and Peter must also take account of this.

There is an important sense in which, up to and including 21:7, the beloved disciple is represented as superior to Peter. But the sense in which this is true only becomes apparent when we see that Peter and the beloved disciple represent two different kinds of discipleship: active service and perceptive witness. Peter is portrayed as the disciple who is eager to follow and to serve Jesus (13:6–9, 36–37; 18:10–11, 15). He will not let Jesus serve him until he realizes that he cannot be a disciple otherwise and then his eagerness exceeds Jesus' intention (13:6–9). He is ready to follow Jesus into mortal danger and to lay down his own life to save Jesus from death (13:37). But just as he does not understand that Jesus must wash his feet, so he does not understand that Jesus the good shepherd must lay down his life for him (cf. 13:37 with 10:11, 15; this lack of understanding appears similarly in 18:10–11). Only after Jesus' death (13:36, "afterward"; cf. 13:7) will he be able to follow Jesus to death (13:36). So Peter's love for Jesus, though eager and extravagant, is expressed in ignorant self-confidence that ends in failure when he denies Jesus (13:38; 18:15–27). It is after the resurrection (when Peter's characteristic of active eagerness reappears: 20:3–6; 21:7–8) that Jesus not merely restores Peter to discipleship but enables Peter to become for the first time a disciple who understands what discipleship means for him and can at last truly follow Jesus to death. To Peter's threefold denial of Jesus corresponds the threefold pledge of love that Jesus now draws from him (21:15–17; note the charcoal fire, which links 21:9 with 18:18). To this new Peter, who now loves Jesus as the good shepherd who has given his life for his sheep, can now be given the commission to follow Jesus (21:19, 22; cf. 13:36) as the chief undershepherd of Jesus' sheep, who is to care for the sheep and, following Jesus, give his own life for them (21:18–19; cf. 12:33; 18:32). In this role, Peter's eagerness for service is redeemed, but his self-will is replaced (21:18) by true discipleship. Thus the point of the Gospel's portrayal of Peter—which can really only be appreciated when chapter 21 is understood as integral to the Gospel—is not to denigrate Peter but to show him as the disciple who through failure and grace is enabled by Jesus to become the chief pastor of the church. Although the Gospel does

22. Here I judge the probabilities differently from Hengel, *Johannine Question*, 78–79.

acknowledge a minor role for Peter as witness to the events of the Gospel story (20:6–7), it gives him primarily the role of shepherd. This is not at all the role of the beloved disciple, who therefore becomes at the end irrelevant to Peter's own call to discipleship (21:20–22).

The beloved disciple is given a superiority to Peter only in respects that qualify him for his own role of perceptive witness to Jesus. This understanding of his role also explains the way in which the beloved disciple is portrayed much more adequately than does the idea that he is the ideal disciple. This portrayal can be analyzed as having three elements. In the first place, there is the beloved disciple's special intimacy with Jesus, which is stressed already in 1:35–40. The anonymous disciple here is almost certainly the beloved disciple, who cannot, of course, on first acquaintance be called, as he is later, "the disciple Jesus loved." Of course, to the first-time reader/hearer of the Gospel the anonymous disciple of these verses is enigmatic, but the curiously precise specification of the hour of the day may already be intended to give a hint of eyewitness testimony. Certainly, the reader/hearer is bound to notice the anonymity of this disciple, since all other disciples in 1:35–51 are named and the reader/hearer would naturally expect one of the first two of Jesus' disciples to be a disciple already well known to those acquainted with the Gospel tradition. Thus the reader/hearer who subsequently encounters the anonymous disciple Jesus loved in 13:23 would have no difficulty in retrospectively identifying him with the anonymous disciple of 1:35–40. But what is important about the little that is already said of this disciple in 1:35–40 is that it stresses the opportunity he and Andrew had to get to know Jesus, a point that is not made about the disciples who are recruited subsequently. Although the beloved disciple then disappears from the narrative until chapter 13, the point has been made that he was able to get to know Jesus before any other disciple except Andrew. When he reappears in 13:23–26, it is his intimacy with Jesus that is stressed, so that he alone is in a position to ask Jesus a delicate question and to hear and observe the way Jesus answers it. His specially close relationship with Jesus again emerges in 19:26–27.

Second, the beloved disciple is present at key points in the story of Jesus. Again, his initial appearance at 1:35 is more significant than is usually noticed. It makes the beloved disciple a witness of John's testimony to Jesus, as well as to the beginning of Jesus' ministry, and it is certainly not accidental that the beloved disciple on his first appearance in the Gospel hears John the Baptist's testimony to Jesus as the sacrificial lamb of God (1:35, cf. 29). When the beloved disciple's own witness is explicitly highlighted at 19:35, it is his eyewitness testimony to the fulfillment of precisely these words of John the Baptist: he sees the flow of blood and water, along with the fact that no bone is broken, that show Jesus to be the true Passover lamb (19:31–37). The fact that the beloved disciple is present at the cross makes him superior to Peter, not simply as a disciple, but precisely as that disciple—the only male disciple—who witnesses the key salvific event of the whole Gospel story, the hour of Jesus' exaltation, toward which the whole story from John the Baptist's testimony onward has pointed.

If the disciple of 18:15–16 is the beloved disciple, this passage also portrays him as present at a key event: Jesus' trial before Annas, along with Peter's denials. If his entry only into the courtyard of the building makes him more obviously a witness to Peter's denials than to the trial, nevertheless his relationship to the high priest may well be intended to indicate access to information (cf. also the implications of 18:10, 26). Since it is the disciple's relationship to the high priest, rather than his relationship to Jesus, that matters for his role as witness in this context, this may account for the fact that he is not here introduced as the disciple Jesus loved. Alternatively, as we suggested above, the disciple in question may be another of the Johannine school on whose witness the Gospel has drawn at this point.

Third, the beloved disciple is portrayed as a perceptive witness, with spiritual insight into the meaning of the events of the Gospel story. However, despite his special intimacy with Jesus, it is not at all clear that this quality emerges before the resurrection. In 13:25–30, the beloved disciple witnesses, more fully than the other disciples, the way in which Jesus designates the betrayer and thus shows his awareness and willing acceptance of the fate that he must undergo as a divine destiny. The beloved disciple is given the material for a key insight into the meaning of the events that lead to Jesus' death, but it is not said that he himself at the time understands any better than the rest of the disciples (13:28). His breakthrough to understanding seems to come in 20:8–9. The narrative of the two disciples at the tomb skillfully correlates the two. The beloved disciple arrives first, but Peter goes in first. Peter has the priority as a witness to the evidence, but the beloved disciple has the superiority in perceiving its significance. This point is usually misunderstood by those who see the beloved disciple as the ideal disciple. He is not here portrayed as the model for later Christians who believe in the resurrection without seeing (20:29), since it is expressly said that "he saw and believed" (20:8). The point is that, like Peter, he provides the eyewitness testimony that later Christians need in order to believe without seeing but, unlike Peter, he already perceives the significance of what they both see. The same priority in spiritual recognition of the truth of Jesus is attributed to the beloved disciple in 21:7.

These three features of the portrayal of the beloved disciple qualify him to be the ideal witness to Jesus, his story and its meaning. These qualities are displayed to a large extent by way of contrast with Peter, but the point is not a general superiority to Peter. The beloved disciple is better qualified to be the author of a Gospel, but he is not better qualified to be the chief undershepherd of Jesus' sheep, which is Peter's mode of discipleship. It is worth noticing that, whereas in Peter's case the Gospel emphasizes his love for Jesus, in the beloved disciple's case it emphasizes Jesus' love for him. The former emphasis is appropriate for the active role of discipleship as participation in Jesus' activity of serving and sacrificing: it corresponds to Jesus' love for his disciples. The latter emphasis is appropriate for the more receptive role of discipleship as witness and corresponds to Jesus' enjoyment of his Father's love (cf. the correspondence between 13:23 and 1:18). The different, complementary roles of the two disciples shows that it is not rivalry between different branches of early Christianity (the so-called great church and the Johannine churches) that is at stake in their relationship. The Gospel acknowledges Peter's leading role in the whole church, to which its own community belongs, while claiming for the beloved disciple a role of witnessing to the truth of Jesus that is equally significant for the whole church.

Finally, on the relation between Peter and the beloved disciple, we should note that the point of their portrayal in comparison and contrast with each other is neither the way each relates to the other nor the way each relates to others within the narrative. Peter is not shown as "shepherd" to other disciples within the narrative, nor does the beloved disciple act as a witness to others within the narrative. Except at 21:7, his relation to Peter is not that of mediator to Peter of his superior insight into the truth of Jesus. Rather, he is represented as the disciple who was so related to Jesus and the events of Jesus' story that he can bear witness to the readers/hearers of the Gospel. The point of the double story of the two disciples is to show how each, through his own different way of following Jesus, relates to the church after the resurrection. Just as Peter's role in the story enables him to become the chief under-shepherd of Jesus' sheep not within the narrative but later, so the beloved disciple's role in the story enables him to witness to others not within the narrative but later. Although both can serve from time to time in the narrative as representative disciples, models for all Christians, the overwhelming emphasis is on the special roles that their personal discipleship of Jesus enables them to play in the church. In the beloved disciple's case, this is his witness as author of the Gospel.

Ideal Author

In the last section, we saw how the beloved disciple is portrayed as qualified to be the ideal witness. That this amounts to his being the ideal author of the Gospel will become clearer if we focus again on 19:35. We have already seen that, in light of 21:24 in the final form of the Gospel, 19:35 explicitly portrays the beloved disciple as author of the Gospel. But we need also to note the important connection between 19:35 and 20:30–31, which the writer of 21:24–25 also recognized in echoing both these passages. Only in these two passages are the readers/hearers of the Gospel directly addressed in the second person. Moreover, the same words are addressed to them: ἵνα καὶ ὑμεῖς πιστεύητε (19:35); ἵνα πιστεύητε (20:31). Second-person address to readers/hearers draws attention to the writer who addresses them in a way that third-person narrative usually does not. In these two passages the author addresses his readers/hearers as author in a way that is paralleled only by the unique authorial first person plural of 1:14.

Moreover, there is an important material correspondence between the two passages. John 20:30–31 speaks of the written narrative of chapters 2–20, which it concludes: the narrative of Jesus' signs, which the author has written so that his readers/hearers may believe. The seventh of these signs, the climactic and preeminently important one (cf. 2:18–19), which alone enables believing perception of Jesus' full significance, seems to be his death and resurrection. It is not the resurrection alone, which for Johannine thought is significant only in very close relation to the cross as the event of Jesus' salvific exaltation and glorification. Arguably the seventh sign itself is actually the more specific event of the flow of blood and water (19:34), which shows both the reality of Jesus' death and its significance as the sacrifice that gives life. At any rate, this is the supreme revelatory moment of the seventh sign, and it is the author's witness to this moment that 19:35 declares. John 20:30–31 does not use the vocabulary of witness: the author does not claim his own eyewitness testimony to the other signs. But at the most important moment of the whole narrative of the signs, the author addresses his readers/hearers as witness (19:35).

We should also notice that 20:30 says of the signs that are not recorded that Jesus did them "in the presence of the disciples" (ἐνώπιον τῶν μαθητῶν). Of course, this means that the signs that are recorded were also done in the presence of the disciples. This again highlights the significance of the beloved disciple as author. Only he and the women disciples were present at the cross (19:25–26). Thus in the light of the connection of 19:35 with 20:30–31, as well as in the light of the redactor's comment in 21:24, there can be no doubt that the witness of 19:35 is indeed the beloved disciple.

However, this verse is quite different in character from all the other appearances of the beloved disciple in the Gospel (including 1:35–40 and 18:15–16, and excepting only 21:24), and this difference of character is again appreciable in light of its connection with 20:30–31. Unlike all other references to the beloved disciple, 19:35 does not give him a role in the narrative. It assumes that the witness is there observing the events, and so it presupposes the presence of the beloved disciple as a character in the narrative in 19:26–27, without which the readers/hearers could not tell who the witness is. But 19:35 itself speaks of the beloved disciple's activity of bearing witness to what he then saw, an activity that takes place not within the story the Gospel tells, but beyond it. More precisely, we could say that it is the beloved disciple's activity as author of the Gospel telling this part of the story of the Gospel. Perhaps μεμαρτύρηκεν also includes the lifetime of bearing witness that preceded and was summed up in the writing of the Gospel, but it must mean primarily, as the activity of witnessing that is relevant to the readers/hearers, the writing of the Gospel. (The perfect tense μεμαρτύρηκεν is used appropriately, as in 20:31: γέγραπται; contrast 3:11, 32, which in other respects resemble the beginning of 19:35.) That the witnessing includes perceptive witness to the spiritual significance of the events is clear from καὶ ὑμεῖς ("you also"), which implies the prior belief of the witness himself, as also from the pregnant ἀληθῆ.

But it is not said that he saw the full meaning of the events at the time. It is his witness to them in writing that conveys their significance for faith.

Thus whereas the other references to the beloved disciple before 21:24 show him, by his role in the Gospel narrative, to be qualified to be the ideal author of the Gospel, in 19:35 he appears actually as the ideal author and addresses his witness directly to the readers/hearers.

The Witness That Remains

The idea of the beloved disciple as the ideal author makes the way he finally appears at the end of the narrative (21:20–22) explicable, just as the idea of him as the ideal disciple makes it inexplicable. The roles of Peter and the beloved disciple in the mission of the church (symbolized in 21:3–11) are different and the way their respective roles relate to the story told in the Gospel differs. Of Peter there is a further story to be told, concluding with the death by which he will glorify God (21:19). But of the beloved disciple there is nothing more to be said, since his role is to witness to Jesus, his story and its meaning. What the beloved disciple has to do after the events of chapter 20 is precisely to tell the story that the Gospel tells up to and including chapter 20. If he has done so orally for a lifetime, at the end of his life he does so finally as author of the Gospel. His role in the mission of the church is fulfilled with the writing of the Gospel and, strictly speaking, is fulfilled at the end of chapter 20, which concludes his witness to Jesus (and therefore looks rather too like a conclusion to the book). His role as witness to Jesus is given a place in chapter 21, at verse 7, in order to indicate its place in the mission of the church, but also to allow Peter's story then to take over the epilogue.

The beloved disciple's personal future is of no relevance to Peter (21:20–22). But it should also be of no concern to the readers/hearers. If the author himself ended his Gospel at 21:22, it was a masterly conclusion. The beloved disciple's personal fate, once the Gospel is written, is a matter for Jesus and himself alone. Like Peter, the readers/hearers are deflected from curiosity about the beloved disciple's own future and left with the summons to follow the Jesus to whom he has witnessed in the Gospel.

It might have been thought that whereas it was appropriate to Peter's mode of discipleship for him to lay down his life for the sheep, as Jesus had done, it would be appropriate for the beloved disciple's mode of discipleship for him to remain until the Parousia. As the specially privileged witness to Jesus, his survival to the Parousia would ensure the continuance of his witness to Jesus until Jesus' coming. But by the time he writes 21:20–22, this thought is no longer necessary. He has now written the Gospel in which he sums up and completes his witness. His witness can now remain until the Parousia, whether or not he personally does. So in the end the speculation about the beloved disciple's future is used as a way of emphatically saying nothing more about the beloved disciple. Although modern readers also speculate—that verse 23 presupposes the beloved disciple's death—the Gospel itself, even in its final form, actually tells us neither that he has died nor that he remains. This question is irrelevant to his witness as author. The beloved disciple has appeared in the Gospel's narrative only as its ideal author and of his activity after the events he narrates it tells us only that he wrote the Gospel.

Thus 21:20–23 brilliantly succeeds in leaving no doubt of the beloved disciple's identity (he is that disciple who, it was widely supposed, would not die) while at the same time telling us nothing whatever about him that the Gospel has not already told. The Gospel thus allows us to know him only as its ideal author. If the disciple who was expected not to die was in fact John the Elder, then it is curiously appropriate that, as scholars critical of the attribution of the Gospel to him have so often complained, we know almost nothing about John the Elder!

Anonymity

The notion of the beloved disciple as ideal author is not intended to suggest that his role in the Gospel's narrative is counterfactual. Naturally, we should assess neither this nor any other aspect of the Gospel's narrative by modern concepts of history. The historicity of the beloved disciple's role in the Gospel narrative must be assessed in the same way as the historicity of the Gospel in general, taking account of the Gospel's own characteristic conjunction of realistically told story and richly symbolic significance. But we can at least remark here that a purely ideal author could easily have been given a much more extensive role in the Gospel. He could have witnessed all the signs. Though the beloved disciple's presence in the Gospel narrative is at some of the most significant points, it is also very limited in extent. Precisely those features of his role that have convinced Hengel and many others that he is not depicted as a Galilean disciple who accompanied Jesus throughout his ministry suggest that the portrayal of the beloved disciple in the Gospel is restricted by the remembered career of the historical disciple he represents. The term "ideal author" is not meant to prejudge the degree of historicity in the portrayal of the beloved disciple. It simply means that what is said about him portrays him as the ideal author of the Gospel.

Yet we have still not asked why the ideal author should be portrayed as anonymous. This question has not often been asked in the right way, because it has usually been understood as: why is the identity of the beloved disciple concealed from the readers/hearers? Here we presuppose that in the oral context of the first readers/hearers the identity of the beloved disciple was well known. If there was any doubt it would be finally dispelled by 21:22–23. The correct question is not why the beloved disciple's identity is concealed, but why the beloved disciple, whose identity was well known to the first readers/hearers, is portrayed anonymously in the Gospel.

Probably the best answer is that anonymity is a literary device that serves to mark out the beloved disciple, who is also the author, from the other disciples in the narrative in which he appears with them. His anonymity makes him not just one named disciple among others or even the disciple closest to Jesus but, so to speak, different in kind. It gives the reader/hearer the sense that this disciple is in a different category from the others.[23] Of course, use of the first person singular (as in, for example, the Gospel of Peter) also readily distinguishes the author from other characters in the narrative. But it has the additional effect of disrupting the pastness of the narrative. The author's "I" makes the reader/hearer aware of him as the one now telling the story, and so the character in the story is at the same time acting in the narrative and addressing the reader/hearer. As we have seen, the author of the Fourth Gospel deliberately achieves this effect within the narrative only once, at 19:35, not by using the first person but by using the second person. At this point, in a parenthesis, the author wishes to speak of what he is doing in telling the story. At the point in the narrative at which his eyewitness testimony is most important, he deliberately obtrudes his authorial presence into the pastness of the narrative. But the other appearances of the beloved disciple do not have this effect. They are not appearances of the author as author addressing his readers/hearers, but only of the author as a character in the narrative, whose role in the story qualifies him to become the author. Anonymity distinguishes him without disrupting the third-person narration of the past. The literary device has, in fact, functioned in this way for all those readers—the vast majority of the Gospel's readers—to whom the identity of the beloved disciple never seemed a mystery. But for modern critics to whom the identity of the beloved disciple has become a problem, this function of his anonymity in the narrative has not been able to operate and so has not been recognized. Once we see that the identity of the beloved disciple was not intended to be concealed or even ambiguous, we can again recognize that his anonymity is that of the ideal author within his narrative.[24]

23. This understanding of the anonymity of the beloved disciple needs minor qualification if the suggestion we made above, that the anonymous disciple of 18:15–16 is not the beloved disciple but another "Johannine" disciple, is adopted. This would mean that the literary device of anonymity marks out not only the author himself, but also another personal source of the Gospel narrative, who could perhaps be regarded as, in a minor way, a coauthor.

24. This chapter was written in 1992. I have recently returned to these issues and related ones in *Jesus and the Eyewitnesses: The Gospels as Eyewitness Testimony* (Grand Rapids: Eerdmans, 2006), chapters 14–15. On one point I changed my mind: I now think the author, the beloved disciple, himself wrote the conclusion to the Gospel (21:24–25) (see *Jesus and the Eyewitnesses*, 369–83).

4

HISTORIOGRAPHICAL
CHARACTERISTICS
OF THE GOSPEL OF JOHN

Introduction

"The fourth Gospel is theology, not history" is an old dictum still to be found in Johannine scholarship. The obvious rejoinder that has been made often enough is that history and theology are not mutually exclusive. Yet for many scholars who would make such a rejoinder, theology still, as it were, gets the better of history in this case. However, it might be that history and theology combine in the Synoptic Gospels, in the case of the Gospel of John theology is considered the dominant partner, to the detriment of history. This does not, for most recent scholars, make it impossible to recover useful nuggets of reliable history from John, but their survival in this Gospel is almost accidental, so unimportant to the Gospel's purpose history is judged to be. Of course, there are still other scholars who champion the historical purpose and value of the Gospel by arguing for the historical plausibility of its account of Jesus.

However, such debate has largely taken place on the level of whether the content of the Gospel can be considered reliable history by modern historians. My question

Originally published in a slightly different form in *New Testament Studies* 53, no. 1 (2007): 17–36. Reprinted by permission of the publisher.

in this chapter is quite different. It is whether this Gospel is historiography. This is a generic question. Historiography can be reliable or unreliable, accurate in some ways, inaccurate in others, written according various different conventions of literary representation of what happened. Whether this Gospel presents itself as historiography, whether it would have appeared as historiography to competent contemporary readers, is a prior question to that of historical reliability. Without answering the generic question, we cannot even know what sort of historical reliability it might be appropriate to expect in such a work.

The generic question has largely gone unexplored because of the longstanding conviction that generically the Gospels are *sui generis*. John would have been working with the innovatory genre of a Gospel and adapting it at will. Recent work culminating in Richard Burridge's landmark study *What Are the Gospels?*[1] has convinced many, perhaps most Gospels scholars, that the Gospels belong to the broad generic category of Greco-Roman biography. Burridge finds that the criteria he developed for identifying this genre apply just as well to the Gospel of John as to the Synoptics. This is also the conclusion of Dirk Frickenschmidt in a parallel study.[2]

Biography is a form of historiography in the general sense of writing about the past, but the ancients did distinguish between biography and history.[3] History dealt with the deeds of leaders in war and politics, the affairs of states and nations, sometimes including what we might call ethnography, not with the more personal stories about eminent individuals that were the stuff of the typical *bios*.[4] Nevertheless, partly because the *bios* itself was a very flexible and developing genre, the line between biography and history was porous and moveable.[5] This was especially so in the period to which early Christianity belongs, as historiography itself developed a biographical interest[6] and some biographies, especially

1. R. A. Burridge, *What Are the Gospels? A Comparison with Graeco-Roman Biography*, SNTSMS 70 (1992; 2nd ed., Grand Rapids: Eerdmans; Dearborn, MI: Dove Booksellers, 2004). The 2004 edition contains a review and discussion of reactions to and developments of his argument since its first publication in 1992 (chapter 11).

2. D. Frickenschmidt, *Evangelium als Biographie: Die vier Evangelien im Rahmen antiker Erzählkunst*, TANZ 22 (Tübingen: Francke, 1977).

3. On Plutarch's well-known distinction, and the extent to which it needs qualification, see A. Wardman, *Plutarch's Lives* (London: Paul Elek, 1974), 2–10, and chapter 5; J. L. Moles, *Plutarch: The Life of Cicero* (Warminster: Aris and Phillips, 1988), 32–36; M. Affortunati and B. Scardigli, "Aspects of Plutarch's *Life of Publicola*," in *Plutarch and the Historical Tradition*, ed. P. A. Stadler (London/New York: Routledge, 1992), 109–31. A. Momigliano, *The Development of Greek Biography*, expanded ed. (Cambridge, MA: Harvard University Press, 1993), 12, writes: "Biography was never considered history in the classical world. The relationship between history and biography varied in different periods. We have to account both for their separation and for their changing relations" (cf. 41).

4. Momigliano, *Development*, 41, 63.

5. Burridge, *What*, 59–67; C. W. Fornara, *The Nature of History in Ancient Greece and Rome* (Berkeley: University of California Press, 1983), 34–36, 65–66; T. J. Luce, *The Greek Historians* (Leiden: Brill, 1997), 116–18.

6. See, e.g., Momigliano, *Development*, 83; C. Pelling, "Biographical History? Cassius Dio on the Early Principate," in *Portraits: Biographical Representation in the Greek and Latin Literature of the Roman*

of recent public figures, aspired to the traditional ideals of historiography. Of the Latin biographer Cornelius Nepos (ca. 99–24 BCE), Michael Grant can even write that "such was the current interest in personalities that the barrier between the two genres, if it had ever existed, had been cast down."[7]

Burridge's demonstration that all four canonical Gospels belong to the very flexible genre of ancient biography is here presupposed. But there is a further question, which he does not address: where should the Gospels be placed in relation to the wide variety of works that comprise this generic category? We still lack an adequate typology of the Greco-Roman *bios*, but one distinction that can confidently be made is that some biographies were much more like historiography than others. The authors of some biographies seem deliberately to have given their works at least some of the characteristics expected in a work of history. It would be appropriate therefore to ask about each of the Gospels, not only whether they are biographies, but also to what extent they meet the requirements of the (at least in principle) more carefully defined genre of historiography. This chapter is a first attempt to assess the Gospel of John by the features characteristic of Greco-Roman historiography.[8] Its contention is that, far from appearing the least historical of the four Gospels, to a competent contemporary reader John's Gospel will have seemed the closest to meeting the exacting demands of ancient historiography.[9]

Topography and Chronology

Topography

A good historian was expected to have a thorough knowledge of the places where the events of his history took place,[10] though it must be said that this was

---

Empire, ed. M. J. Edwards and S. Swain (Oxford: Clarendon, 1997), 117–44; Frickenschmidt, *Evangelium*, chapter 5.

7. M. Grant, *Greek and Roman Historians: Information and Misinformation* (London: Routledge, 1995), 102.

8. To my knowledge, C. S. Keener, *The Gospel of John: A Commentary* (Peabody, MA: Hendrickson, 2003), 1:11–37, is the only Johannine scholar who addresses the issue at all. Recognizing the fluidity of the generic distinction between history and biography, he considers the Gospels historical biography, and describes the characteristics of ancient historiography as well as biography. But detailed comparison with John is only implicit in his account.

9. Two of the features discussed below as characteristic of historiography might also be considered characteristic of the Greek novel (topography and narrative asides). This is not surprising in that the novel seems to have developed from historiography as, so to speak, a fictional form of it. However, the novel constituted a primarily entertaining form of literature, concerned with romance and adventure, lacking the obvious seriousness that the Gospel of John shares with historiography. Moreover, the parallels with the latter are considerably more extensive than those with the novel. However, the comparison between the Gospels and the Greek novel is a matter that deserves further study.

10. For Polybius's strong views on this matter, see, e.g., F. W. Walbank, *A Historical Commentary on Polybius* (Oxford: Clarendon, 1957), 10. Lucian, *Hist. Conscr.* 24, is scornful of historians who make geographical mistakes.

an ideal often not realized in practice. Even the much traveled Polybius, who severely criticized Timaeus for never leaving Athens (12.25d.1; 12.28a.4), makes geographical mistakes. The need for good geographical knowledge was especially related to the military matters that filled so much Greco-Roman history, but it could also be desirable for narratives of travel, a significant feature of all the Gospels. At the same time, topography was to be kept in its place. Lucian advises the historian not to indulge in unnecessarily elaborate descriptions of localities: "You will touch on them lightly for the sake of expediency and clarity, then change the subject" (*Hist. Conscr.* 57; cf. 19).

Topographical references in John's Gospel are numerous. Scholarly treatments of them have moved in two very different directions. On the one hand, those who have studied these references in detail have mostly come to the conclusion that they are accurate in general and in detail, and even that the evangelist himself must have been very familiar with the areas of Palestine in which the events of his narrative take place, including Samaria and Galilee as well as Jerusalem.[11] Challenges to John's geographical accuracy at certain points remain,[12] but the case for regarding his as the most geographically reliable of the Gospels has been very persuasively made. For our present purposes, however, this is less important than the impression the Gospel would make on contemporary readers, mostly not themselves familiar with the geography of Palestine. Does this account read *as though it is* well informed about the topography?

The other direction in which scholars have taken discussion of Johannine topography has been toward symbolic readings of it. Here there are two trends, which we can call the theological and the community-historical. The former has its roots in traditional exegesis,[13] but has also characterized the dominant modern critical trend to read this Gospel as theology *rather than* history. In recent Johannine scholar-

---

11. E.g., R. D. Potter, "Geography and Archeology in the Fourth Gospel," in *Studia Evangelica*, ed. K. Aland, F. L. Cross, J. Daniélou, H. Riesenfeld, and W. C. van Unnik, TU 73 (Berlin: Akademie-Verlag, 1959), 329–35; B. Schwank, "Efraim in Joh 11,54," in *L'Évangile de Jean: Sources, rédaction, théologie*, ed. M. de Jonge, BETL 44 (Gembloux: Duculot; Leuven: Leuven University Press, 1977), 377–83; M. Hengel, *The Johannine Question* (London: SCM, 1989), 110–11; C. Koester, "Topography and Theology in the Gospel of John," in *Fortunate the Eyes That See*, ed. A. B. Beck, A. H. Bartelt, P. R. Raabe, and C. A. Franke, D. N. Freedman FS (Grand Rapids: Eerdmans, 1995), 436; I. Broer, "Knowledge of Palestine in the Fourth Gospel?" in *Jesus in Johannine Tradition*, ed. R. T. Fortna and T. Thatcher (Louisville: Westminster John Knox, 2001), 83–90; R. E. Brown, *An Introduction to the Gospel of John*, ed. F. J. Moloney (New York: Doubleday, 2003), 92. On the other hand, M. Davies, *Rhetoric and Reference in the Fourth Gospel*, JSNTSup 69 (Sheffield: Sheffield Academic Press, 1992), 276–85, finds almost all the topographical information accurate, but derived from Scripture, the Synoptics, and historical tradition. In her view there is too little such information to suggest that the author was personally familiar with the sites. In response to this, the comment of Lucian cited above is relevant. Firsthand knowledge shows itself in accuracy rather than unnecessary prolixity.

12. E.g., Davies, *Rhetoric*, 283, finds just one topographical mistake in the Gospel: the location of Bethsaida in Galilee.

13. C. R. Koester, *Symbolism in the Fourth Gospel* (Minneapolis: Fortress, 1995), 262.

ship it comes to fruition in Thomas Brodie's commentary,[14] which offers perhaps the most comprehensive treatment of all John's precise topographical references as having *primarily* theological significance. Such an approach does not necessarily require that John has simply invented for their theological significance the geographical references that are not attested outside his Gospel.[15] It does mean that where John has retained geographical information from his sources he has done so only because he could read it symbolically. The approach recommends itself because it cannot be disputed that John's geography at least sometimes carries theological significance. For example, the fact that the meeting of Jesus with the Samaritan woman takes place at Jacob's well enables the claim that Jesus is greater than Jacob because the water he gives supplies not merely mortal but eternal life (John 4:6, 12–14). But the issue with geography, as with some other types of material in the Gospel, is whether we can convincingly read all of John's seemingly matter-of-fact details as charged with symbolic meaning. Most scholars feel that the attempt to do so produces forced or tenuous explanations in some cases. If a symbolic reading cannot be sustained comprehensively, then it is hard to maintain that the evangelist's only or even primary interest in topography is theological symbolism.

Of more recent origin than the symbolic-theological reading of Johannine geography is the community-historical reading; in other words, it is an interpretation of the geographical references in line with the so-called two-level reading of the Gospel as embodying the history of the Johannine community.[16] Here the main starting point has been an attempt to correlate the major regions of Palestine in the Gospel with stereotypical responses to Jesus: rejection in Jerusalem and Judea, acceptance in Samaria and Galilee.[17] These are then thought to reflect the

14. T. L. Brodie, *The Gospel according to John: A Literary and Theological Commentary* (New York/Oxford: Oxford University Press, 1993).

15. That some of the places in John's Gospel are fictive is maintained by N. Krieger, "Fiktive Orte der Johannes-Taufe," *ZNW* 45 (1954): 121–23 (Bethany beyond Jordan, Aenon, and Salim). But if readers are supposed to read "Salim" as "peace" (שלום), why is the word spelled Σαλείμ, rather than Σαλλουμ or Σαλλωμ, which would be accurate transliterations of the Hebrew? As a male name, שלם appears as Σαλλουμ or Σαλλωμ in LXX, Σάλλουμος in Josephus, while as a female name, very common in the New Testament period, it almost always appears as Σαλώμη.

16. E.g., W. A. Meeks, "Galilee and Judea in the Fourth Gospel," *JBL* 85 (1966): 159–69; J. M. Bassler, "The Galileans: A Neglected Factor in Johannine Community Research," *CBQ* 43 (1981): 243–57; C. H. Scobie, "Johannine Geography," *SR* 11 (1982): 80–82. K. Kundsin, *Topologische Überlieferungsstoffe im Johannes-Evangelium*, FRLANT 22 (Göttingen: Vandenhoeck & Ruprecht, 1925), was "the lone pioneer of this approach to Johannine geography," according to Scobie, "Johannine Geography," 80.

17. This is true of Meeks and Bassler, but Scobie, "Johannine Geography," 78–80, regards the attempt as unsuccessful, and distinguishes this from a reading related to the Johannine community. Cf. also R. E. Brown, *The Community of the Beloved Disciple* (New York: Paulist Press, 1979), 39–40, who also rejects the Galilee-Judea contrast as indicative of Johannine community history. Other scholars, such as Koester, "Topography," 437–38; S. Freyne, "Locality and Doctrine: Mark and John Revisited," in *The Four Gospels, 1992*, ed. F. Van Segbroeck, C. M. Tuckett, G. Van Belle, J. Verheyden, F. Neirynck FS (Leuven: Leuven University Press/Peeters, 1992), 3:1889–1900, accept the contrast as having a theological function in the Gospel, but do not associate it with Johannine community history. Against the idea of a theological contrast

experiences of groups of Johannine Christians in Palestine. Oddly, what begins as a symbolic reading ends as a literal one, except that the geography is understood literally at the level of Johannine community history rather than at the level of the history of Jesus. But can this approach be comprehensive, explaining all topographical references as referring to places with which the Johannine community was associated?[18] For example, were the pools of Bethesda and Siloam used for baptism by Johannine Christians in Jerusalem?[19] Perhaps, but then what of the Praetorium, Gabbatha, and the high priest's house? The community-history interpretation rapidly dissolves in unverifiable speculation.

Both these approaches fail to recognize precise topographical references as a characteristic feature of the Gospel in need of a comprehensive explanation. Piecemeal interpretation of this or that item of geography proves inadequate once we recognize the contours of the material as a whole. Here, as elsewhere, we still suffer the legacy of the older source criticism, which disintegrated the Gospel into sources and levels of redaction and proceeded as though the form and contents of the Gospel as we have it could be sufficiently explained by such diachronic theories. When we view the Gospel as a whole, it becomes clear that precise topography is just as much a characteristic of John as high Christology or light/darkness imagery or various other ideological features distinctive to this Gospel. That needs explanation.

Comparison of John with the Synoptic Gospels shows that the number of named or otherwise specified places,[20] indicating where an event in the Gospel occurred, is more or less the same in all four Gospels:

Table 4.1. Named Places in the Gospels

	Matthew	Mark	Luke	John*
Total	35	30	30	31
Unique to this Gospel	8	2	5	17

*These places in John (italics = unique to John), in order of first appearance, are Jerusalem; *Bethany beyond Jordan;* Galilee; Bethsaida; *Cana of Galilee;* Capernaum; temple; Judaea; *Aenon; Salim;* Jordan; Samaria; *Sychar; Joseph's field; Jacob's well;* Sheep Gate; *Bethesda (Bethzatha);* Sea of Tiberias (Galilee); *Tiberias;* Capernaum synagogue; *temple treasury; pool of Siloam;* Solomon's portico; Bethany (near Jerusalem); *Ephraim; wadi Kidron; garden;* high priest's house (with courtyard); Praetorium; *Gabbatha, the Stone Pavement;* Golgotha, the Place of the Skull.

    Other named or specified places, not used to locate an event, are: Nazareth; mountain (Gerizim); Bethlehem; Arimathea.

---

between Galilee and Jerusalem in John, see W. D. Davies, *The Gospel and the Land: Early Christianity and Jewish Territorial Doctrine* (Berkeley: University of California Press, 1974), 321–31.

    18. The only geographical material treated as alluding to Johannine community history by Brown, *Community,* is the appearance of Samaritans in chapter 4 of the Gospel (34–40). Such an arbitrary use of the Gospel's topography is common but is surely in need of substantial justification that has not been offered.

    19. This is suggested in relation to Siloam by Scobie, "Johannine Geography," 81, following Kundsin.

    20. I count, for example, instances such as Jacob's well, the synagogue in Capernaum, the high priest's house in Jerusalem, but not private houses.

However, we should note that whereas the Synoptics share the majority of their instances, in John's case half of these places are unique to John's Gospel. Many of those John does share with the Synoptics are such obvious instances as Galilee, Jerusalem, Judea, or Capernaum. So the phenomenon of precise topography is in John's case largely independent of Synoptic traditions. We must also note that John's narrative has far fewer distinct events than any of the Synoptics. John's narratives are typically much longer than Synoptic pericopes, so that, in a sense, far less happens in John. There are far fewer events to be located.

Partly for that reason, what the figures given above cannot show is that all events in John's Gospel are located, and most are located quite precisely—in a named town, village, or even more specifically. They are placed not just in Galilee, but in Cana or Capernaum; not just in Jerusalem but at the pool of Bethesda near the Sheep Gate; not just in the temple even but in Solomon's Portico. The only two significant exceptions are the feeding of the five thousand, located rather generally in the hill country east of the sea of Galilee (6:1–3), and the final appearance of the risen Jesus, which is simply "by the Sea of Tiberias" (21:1). Consequently, throughout this Gospel we always know where Jesus is, usually very precisely. The Synoptic Gospels are very different. Alongside many quite precisely located events are just as many that are placed no more specifically than in Galilee or Peraea or Samaria, or given the vaguest of settings, such as "a certain village" (Luke 10:38; 11:1), "a certain place" (Luke 11:1), "a village of the Samaritans" (Luke 9:52), in "the grainfields" (Matt. 12:1; Mark 2:23; Luke 6:1), a synagogue ("the synagogue": Luke 6:6; "their synagogue": Matt. 12:9) that could be anywhere in Galilee, several unnamed mountains or hills (Matt. 5:1; 8:1; 15:29; 17:1, 9; 28:16; Mark 3:13; 9:2; Luke 6:12; 9:28, 37). It is quite evident that the Synoptics compiled traditions that often provided no indication of place, and they often preserved this lack of location, leaving readers with only the general impression that Jesus is traveling around Galilee or on his way to Jerusalem. The broad geographical context they sketch is vague and to an informed reader might even appear confused. There is little to give readers a sense that the authors are well acquainted with the topography of their accounts, excepting perhaps Jerusalem and its immediate environs.

By comparison it is unmistakable that John's Gospel has topographical precision as a consistent characteristic. Even the two partial exceptions of the feeding miracle and the last resurrection appearance, since they are so few, could have the effect of reassuring readers that the author does not go beyond his reliable information: in these cases he cannot be more precise but elsewhere he can confidently specify. He does not indulge in unnecessarily prolix topographical descriptions; his references are concise but also precise.[21]

---

21. They correspond quite well to the category of geographical references in Josephus that Villalba i Varneda calls "simple geographical explanations": P. Villalba i Varneda, *The Historical Method of Flavius Josephus*, ALGHJ 19 (Leiden: Brill, 1986), 121–23.

The Synoptics, in this matter of topography, fall easily within the conventions of the *bios*. Intellectual biographies, those of philosophers and writers—in distinction from biographies of politicians and military leaders—often lack much geographical reference.[22] The anecdotes and reminiscences they related were often not located and did not need to be. In this respect, John's Gospel appears as a biography that is closer than many to historiographical practice. As a general feature of the Gospel, its topographical precision is not primarily a matter of symbolism but of realistic historiography.

Chronology

We can deal more briefly with the chronological precision of the Gospel of John. The chronological indications are primarily the named Jewish festivals: three Passovers (2:13; 6:4; 12:55) and the feasts of Tabernacles (7:2) and Hanukkah (10:22) between the second and third Passovers. In addition, there are the two weeks of counted days, one at the outset of Jesus' story (the week of his manifestation: 1:19–2:11), the other the last week of his story (the week of his glorification: 12:1–20:25).[23] Since a large part of the action takes place either at named temple festivals or in strict relation to the last of them,[24] a large part of the Gospel's whole narrative is very precisely dated.[25] Other events can all be placed within about six months of one of the three Passovers.[26] Moreover, John ties the whole sequence of precise dates from the first Passover onward to an absolute dating, when "the Jews" at the first Passover say, "This temple has been under construction for forty-six years" (2:20). The starting date for this calculation may be obscure to us, but it was evidently not to the author. There seems to be no explanation of the precise figure here (forty-six years) other than a claim, at least, to precise chronology.[27]

Although I think chronological precision evidently does matter in this Gospel, there is more to be said than in the case of the topographical references for

22. For example, Lucian's *Demonax* gives the impression, from its references to Athens, Athenians (11; 14; 18; 34; 57; 63; 64; cf. 30), and two specific locations within Athens (53; 54), that the philosopher rarely left Athens, but the majority of anecdotes are not localized, and there is one reference to a visit to Olympus (58) and one to an unspecified voyage (35).

23. I am leaving aside here references to the time of day (1:39; 4:6; 4:52; 9:14) (on which see N. Walker, "The Reckoning of Hours in the Fourth Gospel," *NovT* 4 [1960]: 69–73; J. E. Bruns, "The Use of Time in the Fourth Gospel," *NTS* 13 [1966–1967]: 285–90), which deserve separate treatment.

24. The whole of chapters 12–20 is precisely dated in relation to the last Passover (20:26).

25. The remaining material, placed before or after the chronologically specified points but not more precisely dated in relation to them, is 1:19–2:12; 3:22–5:47; 7:1; 10:40–11:54.

26. Cf. Thucydides' "system of relative dates attached to a few fixed points" (Fornara, *Nature of History*, 44).

27. This is not to say that there is no other explanation of the fact that "the Jews" here make a chronological statement (cf. Brodie, *Gospel*, 181), only that there seems to be no other explanation of this precise figure. In view of at least one instance of gematria in the Gospel (21:11), it is possible that forty-six has gematrial significance, but if so this has not been deciphered.

a strong symbolic significance at least in the naming of Jewish festivals, since, at least in the cases of the second Passover, Tabernacles, Hanukkah, and the last Passover, the themes of the festivals are reflected in the narratives.[28] Moreover there is one unspecified festival (5:1),[29] which John has evidently not named precisely because he does not pick up its themes in the narrative (5:2–47). In not naming it, however, he has missed an opportunity for chronological precision.

It remains the case that this Gospel dates all the events much more precisely than any of the Synoptics date any events other than those at the beginning (in Luke's case only)[30] or the end of Jesus' ministry. Luke alone provides an absolute dating for the whole narrative (3:1–2), though for modern readers this is as difficult to calculate precisely as John's is. Through the body of each Synoptic Gospel it is not difficult for readers to realize that the apparent chronological sequence is a narrative convention covering a frequently topical, rather than chronological, ordering of material. It was not uncommon for ancient biographies to deploy chronology only at their beginning and end, arranging the intervening material topically and not always with any clear principle. This was almost the rule for lives of philosophers and artists.[31] But the influence on biographies of the requirement of chronological sequence in historiography can be seen in, for example, those written by Plutarch and Tacitus, perhaps because their subjects were public figures closely involved in the political events of their times. It is notable that Philostratus, introducing his *Life of Apollonius of Tyana*, promised to provide "a true account of the man, detailing the exact times at which he said and did this or that" (2). His work does not fulfill this promise of precise dating, though he does tell his story in chronological sequence, but he must have felt the pressure of a historiographical ideal. It is surely the case that the prevalence of precise chronology in the Gospel of John would have made it look, to competent contemporary readers, more like historiography than the Synoptics. John conforms to Lucian's advice to the historian to "follow a chronological arrangement as far as he can" (49).[32]

28. Besides the commentaries, see G. A. Yee, *Jewish Feasts and the Gospel of John* (Wilmington, DE: Michael Glazier, 1989); M. L. Coloe, *God Dwells with Us: Temple Symbolism in the Fourth Gospel* (Collegeville, MN: Liturgical Press, 2001), chapters 6–7. In the case of the first Passover, the event has to be related historically to a Passover, since the tables of the moneychangers were there, in the period leading up to Passover, to enable pilgrims to change their money into the coinage required for paying their temple tax.

29. There is no good reason to identify it as a Passover. In my view it is most likely to be Purim.

30. Luke 2:1–2; 3:1–2, 23.

31. R. A. Burridge, *What Are the Gospels? A Comparison with Graeco-Roman Biography*, 2nd edition (Grand Rapids: Eerdmans; Dearborn, MI: Dove Booksellers, 2004): 135–36, 165–66.

32. Lucian is here considering an issue that occupied historians but not usually biographers: how to deal with events occurring simultaneously in different places. Cf. Dionysius of Halicarnassus, *Pomp.* 3; P. Pédech, *La Méthode Historique de Polybe* (Paris: Société d'Édition "Les Belles Lettres," 1964), chapter 10.

Topography, Chronology, and Theology

Undoubtedly, John's Gospel is not only historiography but also theology or, we might say, theological historiography. Everything in the Gospel does indeed have theological significance, but we are in a position to appreciate this only now that we have established that, in relation to topography and chronology, it is the precision characteristic of good historiography that characterizes these features of the Gospel generally.

Studies of the Gospels as biography are apt to suppose, rather naturally, that the Greco-Roman biographies that most resemble the Gospels are likely to be those of philosophers and teachers. Such biographies typically lack much topographical or chronological exactitude, whereas the biographies that do approximate such historiographical ideals are those of political and military leaders, public figures engaged in the kind of events that Thucydides and Polybius recount. The Johannine Jesus, however, is not primarily a teacher. His teaching is ancillary to his deeds. His mission is to do the works that his Father has given him to do for the salvation of the world. He is a preeminently public figure, engaged almost from the start with the leaders of the Jewish theocracy in the temple, ultimately engaged with Rome itself in the person of Pilate, and a king, though not from this world. None of the subjects of Greco-Roman biography come near to the history-making and world-changing significance of this human life. John's biography of this man aspires, in its own remarkable way, to be the universal history that Polybius and others thought the ideal kind of history.

We can go further and say that John incorporates history into metahistory. These mere two-and-half years of this-worldly history are framed by reference to the beginning of time at the outset of the Prologue, and to the end of time, in Jesus' last words in the Epilogue (21:23).[33] This cosmic metahistory is also the personal metahistory of the subject, who was at the beginning and will come at the end, who was sent from the Father in incarnation and returns to the Father through death and resurrection. But this grand metahistorical framework does not cancel the this-worldly character of the historical story the Gospel tells. The Word became flesh and lived a human life in space-time history. Nothing keeps readers more constantly aware that the story is that of the Word made *flesh* than the topographical and chronological precision of the narrative. The story can be located and dated like any other human history.

At the same time, there is a further dimension. The Word *became* flesh in order to enable those who believe in him to *transcend* flesh. He takes mortal life up into

---

33. Ancient historiographical theory stressed the need to define the most appropriate starting point and the most appropriate finishing point for a history: "a work should begin where nothing can be imagined preceding it, and end where nothing further is felt to be required" (Dionysius of Halicarnassus, *Thuc.* 10, cf. the whole of 10–12; and *Pomp.* 4). Appropriately for a truly universal history, a metahistory, John has chosen the earliest possible starting point (creation), before which quite literally no previous event could be imagined, and the latest possible end point, the one that brings all history to a fully satisfying conclusion (the Parousia).

eternal life, and becomes himself the place of God's presence and God's worship, no longer centered on Mount Zion or Mount Gerizim, but available universally.[34] This fulfillment and transcendence of holy space and holy time is enacted in Jesus' historical attendance at the festivals in the temple. Ordinary history is transcended in metahistory, but this can happen only through Jesus' real presence in ordinary history. Thus the story bears emphatically the marks of historiography at the same time as it bursts the boundaries of space and time.[35]

Some Other Historiographical Features

Selectivity

A hallmark of a good historian in the Greco-Roman world was judicious selectivity. Lucian advises the historian "to run quickly over small and less essential things, while giving adequate attention to matters of importance; indeed, a great deal should even be omitted" (*Hist. Conscr.* 56), and is scornfully critical of those "who leave out or skate over the important events, and from lack of education, taste, and knowledge of what to mention and what to ignore dwell very fully and laboriously on the most insignificant happenings" (27).[36] The historian's judgment in selecting the really important events mattered more in history than in the generally more permissive genre of biography, where trivial anecdotes might contribute interest and amusement and help to build an impression of the subject's character or attitudes. Nevertheless, even the historian could not neglect the need to retain his readers' attention,[37] and so the principle of selectivity was connected not only with the criterion of importance but also with a criterion of variety (cf. Cicero, *Fam.* 5.12). Dionysius of Halicarnassus was, rather surprisingly, critical of

34. On the spatial aspect, see D. Mollat, "Remarques sur le vocabulaire spatial du quatrième évangile," in *Studia Evangelica* [1], ed. K. Aland, F. L. Cross, J. Daniélou, H. Riesenfeld, and W. C. van Unnik, TU 73 (Berlin: Akademie-Verlag, 1959), 321–28, who distinguishes three aspects of the spatial vocabulary in John: geographical precision, theological significance, revelation and the mystical aspect. He also stresses that these different aspects are closely related.

35. I differ from Brodie in that I think the topographical references do not themselves indicate that the level of this-worldly reality needs to be transcended, whereas Brodie thinks that those geographical references he considers puzzling are deliberately such in order to work, like Johannine riddles, to challenge readers to a higher level of perception (e.g., Brodie, *The Gospel*, 201–2, 219, 264–65, 325, 558). But the references that seem puzzling to us, whether or not they are in fact geographically accurate, would not have seemed puzzling to contemporary readers of the Gospel, very few of whom would have had knowledge by which to measure John's references.

36. For evidence of this as a widespread principle of historiography, see G. Avenarius, *Lukians Schrift zur Geschichtsschreibung* (Meisenheim am Glan: Anton Hain K.G., 1956), 127–30; and, on Lucian and Polybius, see A. Georgiadou, "Lucian and Historiography: 'De Historia Conscribenda' and 'Verae Historiae,'" *ANRW* 2.34.2:1471–72. The principle goes back to Herodotus and Thucydides: Fornara, *Nature of History*, 96–97.

37. D. S. Potter, *Literary Texts and the Roman Historian* (London: Routledge, 1999), 17: "Historians had a duty not to be boring."

Thucydides for his lengthy and monotonous "description of a single war, stringing together battle after battle, armament after armament and speech after speech" (*Pomp.* 3).[38] The implication is that Thucydides would have done better to treat a few of these events at greater length, omitting more and also incorporating other types of material to avoid wearying his readers.

John's selectivity in the events he chooses to narrate is one of the factors that makes his Gospel look so different from the Synoptics. While Mark rushes breathlessly from one event to the next, John typically develops his narratives at considerable, though varying, length, often with extended dialogue or discourse. While Matthew and Luke give the impression of attempting to write comprehensive compendia of all the Jesus traditions they knew, John seems to do the opposite, rigorously selecting only what he thought of first importance. While Mark has eighteen miracle stories, Matthew twenty and Luke eighteen, John has only eight (including chapter 21), not at all because he thinks miracle stories unimportant, but because he selects the most impressive (e.g., the blind man had been blind *since birth* [9:1], Lazarus had been dead *four days* [11:17]) and those most significant in terms of their spiritual meaning as signs. The selectivity gives him space to develop the significance of the signs. The themes of Jesus' teaching are also far fewer in John than in Matthew or Luke. While John's selectivity is doubtless guided by judgments of relative importance, it also secures the desirable historiographical goal of variety. There are vivid narratives, striking miracles, dramatic actions, friendly conversations and polemical dialogues, parables and riddles, discourses and prayer.

Narrative Asides (or Parentheses)

Narrative asides are intrusions of the narrator's voice into the narrative, commenting on the story or telling about the story rather than telling the story.[39] Recent scholars, disagreeing somewhat about identifying them, variously count the number of such asides in John's Gospel as 109, 165, or 121.[40] In any event,

38. Elsewhere Dionysius accuses Thucydides of "either according too much space to unimportant matters, or skimming too nonchalantly over those requiring more thorough treatment" (*Thuc.* 13), and of making his introduction disproportionately long (19).

39. For definitions see S. M. Sheeley, *Narrative Asides in Luke-Acts*, JSNTSup 72 (Sheffield: Sheffield Academic Press, 1992), 21.

40. See the comparative lists in C. W. Hedrick, "Authorial Presence and Narrator in John: Commentary and Story," in *Gospel Origins and Christian Beginnings*, ed. J. E. Goehring, C. W. Hedrick, J. T. Sanders, and H. D. Betz, J. M. Robinson FS (Sonoma, CA: Polebridge, 1990), 77–81. The three calculations cited are those of J. J. O'Rourke, "Asides in the Gospel of John," in *The Composition of John's Gospel: Selected Studies from* Novum Testamentum, ed. D. E. Orton (Leiden: Brill, 1999), 205–14 (repr. of *NovT* 21 [1979]: 210–19); G. Van Belle, *Les parenthèses dans l'Évangile de Jean*, SNTA 11 (Leuven: Leuven University Press/Peeters, 1985); and Hedrick, "Authorial Presence." The differences reflect the fact that "the distinction between narration and commentary is a precarious one" (R. A. Culpepper, *Anatomy of the Fourth Gospel* [Philadelphia: Fortress, 1983], 17–18).

they are very numerous, and highly characteristic of John.[41] By contrast, Luke's Gospel has only eighteen.[42] John uses them for such purposes as to indicate the location or time of an event, to translate Hebrew or Aramaic words, to explain Jewish customs, to cite Old Testament passages, to clarify the inner thoughts, motivations, and feelings of characters,[43] to explain what the words of Jesus or another character mean, and to comment on the significance of events, especially with the benefit of a perspective later than that of the characters in the narrative.[44] Such parentheses, used for broadly the same range of purposes, are common in Greco-Roman historiography and biography.[45] More investigation is needed before anything more precise can be said about the similarities between the Johannine asides and those of other narrative literature, but we can at least say that in this respect the frequency and variety of the asides in John's Gospel align it more closely than the Synoptic Gospels with Greco-Roman historiography.

Eyewitness Testimony

The vital importance that was attached, in Greco-Roman historiography, to the firsthand testimony of eyewitness participants in the events, and the way in which the Gospels reflect this concern, has been highlighted recently in Samuel Byrskog's *Story as History—History as Story,*[46] and I have discussed the Gospels in

41. G. Van Belle, "Les parenthèses johanniques," in *The Four Gospels*, ed. F. Van Segbroeck, C. M. Tuckett, G. Van Belle, J. Verheyden, F. Neirynck FS (Leuven: Leuven University Press/Peeters, 1992), 3:1927, notes a wide measure of scholarly agreement on this. Van Belle, *Parenthèses*, amply demonstrated that the asides cannot be distinguished stylistically or thematically from the rest of the Gospel and should not be treated as interpolations.

42. Sheeley, *Narrative Asides*, 98–99, 186–88.

43. Modern people tend to think of the "omniscient" narrator's revelation of the inner thoughts of characters as a novelistic rather than historiographical characteristic (cf. D. Tovey, *Narrative Art and Act in the Fourth Gospel*, JSNTSup 151 [Sheffield: Sheffield Academic Press, 1997], 181–85). But Dionysius of Halicarnassus praises the historical work of Theopompus above all other historians for his "ability, in the case of every action, not only to see and to state what is obvious to most people, but to examine even the hidden reasons for actions and the motives of their agents (which most people do not find it easy to discern), and to reveal all the mysteries of apparent virtue and undetected vice" (*Pomp.* 6).

44. Scholars classify the asides somewhat differently but with a large measure of agreement: see O'Rourke, "Asides," 205–13; Van Belle, *Parenthèses*, 105–12; Hedrick, "Authorial Presence," 82; Van Belle, "Parenthèses," 1904–5 (reporting H. A. Lombard), 1908 (reporting C. A. Pourciau).

45. Sheeley, *Narrative Asides*, chapter 2, provides details and analysis of several such works, as well as three romances. He admits it is difficult to draw general conclusions about the frequency and use of such asides in the three genres (romance, history, biography) because "the narrators show remarkably individual characteristics, no matter what the genre" (95). See also C. J. Bjerkelund, *Tauta egeneto: Die Präzisierungssätze im Johannesevangelium*, WUNT 40 (Tübingen: Mohr Siebeck, 1987), 23–54, for parallels in Josephus to those Johannine asides whose function is to make statements in the narrative more precise (I have not yet been able to consult this book). It seems to me a symptom of the often isolated character of Johannine scholarship that there has been so little comparison of the functions of narrative asides in John with those in other ancient narrative literature.

46. S. Byrskog, *Story as History—History as Story: The Gospel Tradition in the Context of Ancient Oral History*, WUNT 123 (Tübingen: Mohr Siebeck, 2000; reprinted Leiden: Brill, 2002).

this light at length in my book, *Jesus and the Eyewitnesses*.[47] So a brief treatment will suffice here. The historiographical ideal, which meant that strictly speaking one could write only contemporary history, history that was still within living memory, was that the historian himself should have been a participant in many of the events and that he should have interviewed eyewitnesses of those events he could not himself have witnessed. Dionysius of Halicarnassus, for example, praises the historical work of Theopompus of Chios because "he was an eye-witness (αὐτόπτης) of many events, and conversed with many of the eminent men and generals of his day" (*Pomp.* 6). In a literary context of this kind John's Gospel would seem readily to meet the contemporary requirements of reliable historiography, probably better than the Synoptic Gospels. Its claim, whether authentic or not, is to authorship by a disciple of Jesus who notes his own presence (in the third person as was the normal historiographical convention)[48] at key events in the story he tells, and makes it plain that he belonged to a circle of other disciples from whom he could be reliably informed of other events. Widespread failure to recognize that this Gospel's claim to eyewitness testimony is *at least* a straightforward historiographical one (doubtless it has also a theological dimension) has resulted from the influence of the dictum that this Gospel is theology, not history, and the consequent isolation of it from its literary context in ancient historiography.

Discourses and Dialogues

Speeches were virtually indispensable in ancient historiography, partly because this was a highly oral and rhetorical culture in which great importance was attached to the speeches of politicians and generals as well as to those of philosophers and teachers. The historians treated speeches as historical events of significance equal to that of deeds. But speeches presented historians with two rather obvious problems. One was that of sources. For the good historian writing of events within living memory, the historian who may have heard the speeches himself or who carefully sought out and interviewed witnesses as Polybius did, more or less extensive and more or less reliable memories and notes might well be available, occasionally even something like a verbatim written report.[49] But information was not always available. Second, however, there was also the problem of how to represent a speech. Even in the rare case where a verbatim report were available, the historian could not merely transcribe it, for it would be far too long. This makes it clear that any speech in the context of a historical narrative could at best be only

47. R. Bauckham, *Jesus and the Eyewitnesses: The Gospels as Eyewitness Testimony* (Grand Rapids: Eerdmans, 2006).

48. M. J. Wheeldon, "'True Stories': The Reception of Historiography in Antiquity," in *History as Text: The Writing of Ancient History*, ed. A. Cameron (London: Duckworth, 1989), 45–47.

49. Tacitus, *Ann.* 15.63, remarks that, since the philosopher Seneca's farewell speech before his death had been published literally, the historian need not report it.

a representation of the speech actually delivered. Summarizing requires selection and almost necessarily a degree of recasting in the historian's own style.

Given these two problems, the practice of Greco-Roman historians with regard to speeches varied considerably. The strictest approach, enunciated and seemingly followed to a large extent by Polybius, considered it essential for the historian to research and to report the substance of what was said, actual arguments if not actual words. Accuracy in substance was required while freedom in style and presentation was unavoidable. Probably more widely followed than Polybius's principles was the requirement, arguably that of Thucydides, that speeches must reflect what was actually said when this could be known, but otherwise the historian should compose with appropriateness and verisimilitude, giving what the speaker in question would have said in the given circumstances.[50] Both the necessary stylistic freedom of the historian representing speeches whose substance was known and the compositional freedom to provide what would have been said allowed many historians, such as Josephus, to deploy their own rhetorical skill quite liberally.[51]

It would appear that the spectrum of contemporary historiographical practice in this matter can readily accommodate whatever view a Johannine scholar might take of the discourses and dialogues of Jesus in the Gospel of John. But we need to be more precise about the task of a Gospel writer. Jesus was undoubtedly a teacher, many of whose sayings were remembered. In such a case, complete compositional freedom to attribute speeches to him would seem inappropriate unless special justification were offered. The historian's first problem, sources, we might think should not have been a major problem: many of Jesus' sayings were remembered and available. But, second, we must remember the issue of representation. Here all the Gospel writers faced a problem that would not have arisen in the oral tradition.

As far as we can tell from the Synoptic Gospels, Jesus' words were remembered in two main forms. Some sayings were attached to short narratives, *chreiai*, or pronouncement stories. Others, the majority of them, were remembered without a narrative context, as independent aphorisms and parables. But how was the

---

50. It was certainly the view of Callisthenes (FGHist 124 F44): "The writer must compose speeches that are appropriate to the speaker as well as to the situation."

51. On speeches in Greco-Roman historiography, see F. W. Walbank, *Speeches in Greek Historians*, Third J. L. Myers Memorial Lecture (Oxford: Holywell, 1965); K. Sacks, *Polybius on the Writing of History*, University of California Publications in Classical Studies (Berkeley: University of California Press, 1981), 79–95; G. H. R. Horsley, "Speeches and Dialogues in Acts," *NTS* 32 (1986): 609–14; D. E. Aune, *The New Testament in Its Literary Environment* (Philadelphia: Westminster; Cambridge: James Clarke, 1987), 91–93; C. J. Hemer, *The Book of Acts in the Setting of Hellenistic History*, WUNT 49 (Tübingen: Mohr Siebeck, 1989), 75–79; C. Gempf, "Public Speaking and Published Accounts," in *The Book of Acts in Its Ancient Literary Setting*, ed. B. W. Winter and A. D. Clarke (Grand Rapids: Eerdmans; Carlisle: Paternoster, 1993), 259–303. The issue has been widely discussed by New Testament scholars in relation to Acts, but not, so far as I am aware, in relation to John, with the exception of Keener, *Gospel of John*, 1:68–80.

teaching of Jesus to be represented within a narrative account of his ministry? The *chreiai* presented no problem except the chronological one of where to place them in the narrative. But all three Synoptic Gospels represent Jesus as preaching to the crowds and teaching his disciples in extended teaching sessions. The way they represent what Jesus said on such occasions is mostly by means of a collection of Jesus' aphorisms and parables, sometimes with explicit thematic structuring of the material, sometimes more loosely grouped according to topic or catchword.

A point that historical Jesus scholars rarely make is that this cannot have been how Jesus actually taught. If Jesus did, as Mark represents (4:1), address the crowds from a boat on the lake of Galilee, he cannot have spoken merely the three parables Mark attributes to him on this occasion or even the larger collection of parables that Matthew provides. The issue here is not what Jesus said on a specific occasion, but the way in which Jesus generally taught. He must in fact have taught in a much more discursive and expatiating way than the Synoptic Gospels attribute to him. The aphorisms and parables were the carefully composed distillations of his teaching, put into memorable form for hearers to take away with them. They could not have been more than a small proportion of what Jesus actually said (and writers and hearers/readers of Gospels would readily understand this).[52] But not surprisingly they were what were remembered and available to the Gospel writers. It was these that they therefore used when they wished to represent Jesus engaged in teaching. The practice was quite appropriate, but we must recognize that it is also artificial. It is a particular way of *representing* the teaching of Jesus in a narrative context, not necessarily the only way.

Comparing this Synoptic practice with John, we find that in purely formal terms this Gospel differs in that it has few *chreiai* and none of the thematic collections of sayings we find in the other Gospels. Instead, it has extended conversations (such as that with the Samaritan woman), polemical dialogues, and discourses punctuated by questions and objections. Formally, this teaching or discourse material is quite varied,[53] but it has in common the negative characteristic that it does not consist of collections of the kind of aphorisms and parables the Synoptics provide.[54] Aphorisms and short parables, even sayings we also find in the Synoptics and sayings that would not have been out of place on the lips of Mark's, Matthew's, or Luke's Jesus are found, but they are scattered through the discourse material and in many cases embedded in it. The main point to be made here is that, formally speaking, Johannine discourses and dialogues could well be regarded as more realistic than the typical Synoptic presentation of Jesus' teaching. Of course they are no less representations than the Synoptic material, artificial in their own way. But they constitute a different solution to the historiographical problem of

---

52. Cf. J. A. T. Robinson, *The Priority of John*, ed. J. F. Coakley (London: SCM, 1985), 304: "It is hardly to be supposed that Jesus went around peppering his auditors with pellets of disconnected apophthegms."

53. H. W. Attridge, "Genre Bending in the Fourth Gospel," *JBL* 121 (2002): 7–11.

54. John does include some short collections of traditional sayings of Jesus: 12:24–26; 13:16–20.

representing in a narrative context the way Jesus taught. They place traditional sayings of Jesus in contexts where they serve as starting points or encapsulations of what Jesus also says in more discursive ways. Formally, this may well be much like the way such sayings actually functioned in Jesus' teaching.[55] As representations of the way Jesus taught, the conversations, dialogues, and discourses of John's Gospel are quite historically credible. Both the Synoptic and the Johannine ways of representing the way Jesus taught combine realism and artificiality. In one sense, John's presentation is more realistic than theirs, but at the same time it required much more than theirs did the putting of words into Jesus' mouth.

However, if we move beyond purely formal considerations to those of content, do the discourses of Jesus in John meet the historiographical criteria of appropriateness to speaker and situation? It is not difficult to show that they are adapted to the context in which they are spoken. For example, what Jesus says at the various temple festivals picks up the specific themes associated with each festival. But appropriateness to the speaker is another matter, and much of what is often said by scholars about the discourses would suggest that they are not appropriate to the pre-Easter Jesus. Not only are their literary style and vocabulary shared with the author of the Gospel, rather than with the Synoptic sayings of Jesus, but also they are vehicles of the Gospel writer's own theology rather than anything that could plausibly be attributed to the historical Jesus. This verdict is undoubtedly true to a significant extent, but in my view it needs to be qualified by aspects of the discourses not so often noticed that display a degree of continuity with the traditional sayings of Jesus. This continuity is not just accidental, a result of John's incorporation of some traditional Jesus material, but a matter of deliberate design. In other words, the discourses are not simply free compositions of the author, but have been designed as appropriate developments of the teaching of the pre-Easter Jesus.

The first of two main points to be noticed here is the function of the introductory formula, "Amen, amen, I say to you," by which John marks out twenty-five concise sayings of Jesus as of special significance. It seems that, in most cases, the sayings marked out by the formula are the key sayings of the discourses. Often they provide the bases for that peculiarly Johannine genre of reflection that spirals around particular ideas or statements. We might call these the "generative sayings" of the discourses. Less often the "Amen, amen" sayings function to round off a discourse or section of a discourse.[56] I have already suggested that this form of discourse may well be intended to represent the way in which the remembered

---

55. P. W. Ensor, *Jesus and His "Works": The Johannine Sayings in Historical Perspective*, WUNT 2/85 (Tübingen: Mohr Siebeck, 1996), 55–56.

56. The sayings could be classified thus: (1) "generative" sayings for discourses: 3:3, 5, 11; 5:19–20, 25; 6:26, 32, 53; 8:34–35, 51; 10:1, 7; 12:24; 14:12; 16:20, 23–24; (2) concluding encapsulations of discourse or section: 1:51; 5:24; 6:47; 8:58; 13:16, 20; (3) in conversational context: 13:21, 38; 21:28.

sayings of Jesus actually functioned in his teaching practice.[57] John's use of the "Amen, amen" formula is a way of making this characteristic of the Johannine discourses explicit, distinguishing the key saying from its development. It may be for the sake of this special function that John adapted Jesus' own characteristic formula of emphasis, as we find it in the Synoptics, by doubling the Amen.

This way of understanding the relationship between the "Amen, amen" sayings and the discourses in which they are embedded was developed especially by Barnabas Lindars,[58] who explained this formal characteristic of the discourses by understanding them to have originated as homilies preached by the Johannine author. This seems a difficult supposition in that the discourses are integrally first-person speeches in which the "I" is that of Jesus. A more plausible explanation is that the form of the discourses results, as I have suggested, from historiographical considerations. But another aspect of the argument of Lindars is important. He maintained that the "Amen, amen" sayings were in almost every case traditional sayings (even if not all authentic sayings) of Jesus.[59] Other scholars have not been convinced that all the "Amen, amen" sayings that Lindars saw as traditional can be plausibly seen as such,[60] but a case can still be made for most of them,[61] especially when allowance is made for considerable Johannine adaptation of traditional sayings. We could say that the function of the "Amen, amen" formula is to mark out the generative and encapsulating sayings in the discourses, which in most cases were versions of already known sayings of Jesus. In this sense, they help to make the continuity of the discourses with known sayings of Jesus explicit.

57. It also, of course, serves the literary purpose of enabling John's Jesus to explain and develop his ideas. This literary function need not conflict with the sense in which this form of discourse is also, in a certain sense, realistic.

58. B. Lindars, *Behind the Fourth Gospel* (London: SPCK, 1971), chapter 3; idem, *The Gospel of John*, NCB (London: Oliphants, 1972), 51–54; idem, *John*, NT Guides (Sheffield: Sheffield Academic Press, 1990), 36–37; idem, *Essays on John*, ed. C. M. Tuckett, SNTA 17 (Leuven: Leuven University Press/Peeters, 1992), chapters 7, 8, 9, 12.

59. Lindars, *Gospel of John*, 48. He excepted just four of the sayings: 6:47; 8:58; 10:7; 14:12: see ibid., 265, 336, 358, 475–76. Of these, 8:58 is the most difficult to regard as a traditional (even if not authentic) saying of Jesus.

60. R. A. Culpepper, "The AMHN, AMHN Sayings in the Gospel of John," in *Perspectives on John: Method and Interpretation in the Fourth Gospel*, ed. R. B. Sloan and M. C. Parsons (Lewiston, NY: Mellen, 1993), 57–101, examines each saying and concludes that the strongest case can be made for ten sayings that have clear parallels in the Synoptics, and a strong case for three others. This accounts for about half of all (twenty-five) of these sayings. Culpepper does not deny that a considerable number of the others could be traditional sayings, and in fact thinks some of them may well have been "maxims of the Johannine community." A shorter version of his argument is found in idem, "The Origin of the 'Amen, Amen' Sayings in the Gospel of John," in Fortna and Thatcher, eds., *Jesus in Johannine Tradition*, 253–62.

61. Note, for example, the argument of Ensor, *Jesus*, chapter 8, that 5:19–20 is an authentic saying of Jesus, developing further the well-known argument of C. H. Dodd for seeing these verses as a parable, and that of W. Sproston North, *The Lazarus Story within Johannine Tradition*, JSNTSup 212 (Sheffield: Sheffield Academic Press, 2001), chapter 3, arguing that 5:24 and 8:51–52 are Johannine versions of the saying in Mark 9:1. Lindars extended his own argument for 8:34–35 in *Essays on John*, chapter 12 (originally published in 1984).

The second point is that, although the Johannine Jesus speaks to quite a large extent Johannine language, there are also ways in which his speech uses style and terms distinctive of Jesus in the Synoptic Gospels. Despite the fact that much of the material has been composed by the Gospel writer, the composition deliberately attributes to Jesus, in these characteristics, speech appropriate to the pre-Easter Jesus. For example, there is the fact that John's Jesus, like the Jesus of all three Synoptics, never calls himself Messiah,[62] despite the importance of this title for John's Christology. Jesus does call himself Son of Man, a term unique to his usage, and especially does so in enigmatic references to his coming destiny, conforming to one category of the Synoptic Son of Man sayings. Just as in the Synoptics, when John's Jesus prays he addresses God only as "Father" (11:41; 12:27–28; 17:1, 5, 11, 21, 24, 25).

What is typical of many of the distinctive characteristics of Jesus' speech in John is that, in many cases, John adopts a usage that is rare in the Synoptic traditions and makes much more extensive use of it. Thus Jesus' frequent reference to himself as "the Son" and to God as "my Father" or "Father" is not to be understood as a postresurrection Christology inappropriately attributed to the pre-Easter Jesus, but as based on those rare occasions when this usage is found in the Synoptic traditions (Mark 13:32; Matt. 11:27; cf. 28:19). Among the other examples a particularly interesting case is that of the terms "kingdom of God" and "eternal life." It is well known that the term "kingdom of God," so frequent in the Synoptics, is used by the Johannine Jesus only twice: in 3:3 and 5, two closely parallel "Amen, amen" sayings that form the generative sayings for the ensuing discourse to Nicodemus. Thereafter John's Jesus uses instead the terms "eternal life" or "life," beginning in 3:15 and 16. What usually goes unnoticed in this connection is that if we turn to Mark's parallel to these two "Amen, amen" sayings, the only "kingdom of God" sayings in John (Mark 10:15), we also find that in the context, from Mark 9:42 to 10:31, there are several sayings that use the terms "kingdom of God" and "eternal life" or "life" in parallel and interchangeably (Mark 9:45, 47; 10:15, 17, 23, 24, 30)—in such phrases as "enter life" (9:43, 45), "enter the kingdom of God" (9:47; 10:15, 23, 24), and "inherit eternal life" (10:17, 30).[63] These Markan passages and their Synoptic parallels are almost the only occurrences of "eternal life" in Synoptic sayings (see also Matt. 25:46), but they authorize, as it were, John's adoption of this preferred usage, in place of the Synoptic "kingdom of God." A very characteristic term on the lips of the Johannine Jesus thus corresponds to a rare but real Synoptic usage. In general, in instances of this kind[64] we should see not a

62. There are two Synoptic exceptions (Mark 9:41; Matt. 23:10) and one Johannine exception (17:3), but the latter is an understandable exception in that Jesus is there addressing God.

63. Cf. H. Kvalbein, "The Kingdom of God and the Kingship of Christ in the Fourth Gospel," in *Neotestamentica et Philonica: Studies in Honor of Peder Borgen*, ed. D. E. Aune, T. Seland, and J. H. Ulrichsen (Leiden: Brill, 2003), 215–32.

64. Some other such usages that are common in John and rare, but extant in the Synoptics are: (1) Jesus as the one sent by God: Mark 9:37 (= John 13:20); Matt. 15:24; Luke 10:16; (2) Jesus as the Son sent by

departure from Synoptic usage but another instance of John's extreme selectivity. Just as he has selected a small number of events in order to give them far more extended treatment than such events receive in the Synoptics, so he has selected a small number of traditional sayings or usages of Jesus and played them out much more extensively. This is his way of meeting the historiographical requirement of speeches that are appropriate on the lips of the pre-Easter Jesus.

Conclusion

The case would not be complete without asking also the opposite question: are there ways in which the Synoptic Gospels are closer to historiography than John is? A positive answer can be given only with reference to Luke's Gospel. The preface to Luke's Gospel is arguably modeled on the conventions of prefaces to historiographical works,[65] though this has been disputed.[66] The same certainly cannot be said for the prologue to John's Gospel, though it does contain the claim that the Gospel incorporates eyewitness testimony (1:14). The special issue that arises with reference to Luke is whether, in view not only of its preface but also of its connection with Acts, it should be seen as presenting itself as a historical monograph rather than a *bios*.[67] This cannot be discussed here. But in most other respects Luke is generically indistinguishable from the other Synoptic Gospels and resembles historiography no more or less than they do.

Aside from debated implications of Luke's preface, the evidence we have examined in this study strongly suggests that to its contemporaries the Gospel of John would have looked considerably more like historiography than the Synoptic Gospels would. The historiographical characteristics discussed in the first half of this chapter align John closely with those ancient biographies that display some features typical of historiographical best practice and most closely resemble works of historiography. The discussion in the latter part of the chapter has shown that the discourses and dialogues of Jesus in John's Gospel conform to good historiographical practice at least as well as those in the Synoptics.

---

the Father: Mark 12:6; (3) Jesus' hour has (not yet) come: Mark 14:35, 41; cf. Luke 22:53; (4) to believe in Jesus: Mark 9:42 (?); Matt. 18:6; (4) the absolute "I am": Mark 6:50 (= John 6:20); cf. 14:62.

65. For recent arguments to this effect, see D. D. Schmidt, "Rhetorical Influences and Genre: Luke's Preface and the Rhetoric of Hellenistic Historiography," in *Jesus and the Heritage of Israel*, ed. D. P. Moessner (Harrisburg, PA: Trinity, 1999), 27–60; D. E. Aune, "Luke 1:1–4: Historical or Scientific *Prooimion*?," in *Paul, Luke and the Graeco-Roman World: Essays in Honour of Alexander J. M. Wedderburn*, ed. A. Christopherson, C. Claussen, J. Frey, and B. Longenecker, JSNTSup 217 (Sheffield: Sheffield Academic Press, 2002), 138–48, both responding to Alexander (see next note).

66. L. Alexander, *The Preface to Luke's Gospel*, SNTSMS 78 (Cambridge: Cambridge University Press, 1993).

67. So, e.g., Aune, *New Testament*, chapter 3.

5

THE AUDIENCE OF THE GOSPEL OF JOHN

During the last three decades many (though by no means all) important studies of the Fourth Gospel have focused much attention on the so-called "Johannine community." By this term is meant a church or small group of churches in a specific locality (though, on some theories, the community moved from one place to another in the course of its history). The Gospel is understood as in some sense a product of this community, taking shape during the course of the community's history and reflecting its experiences. Most who write about the Johannine community also assume that the Gospel was written for this community, not with the wider Christian movement in view. Indeed, it is generally assumed that the community had little or no contact with the wider Christian movement until perhaps the very latest level of redaction of the Gospel (to which chapter 21 is said to belong). In this way, the close relationship of the Gospel to an isolated and distinctive Christian group functions, among other things, as an explanation for the striking distinctiveness of this Gospel in comparison with the three Synoptic Gospels. Like the Johannine letters, the Gospel expresses both the distinctive

Originally published in a slightly different form in *Jesus in Johannine Tradition*, ed. R. T. Fortna and T. Thatcher (Louisville: Westminster John Knox, 2001), 101–11. Reprinted by permission of the publisher.

historical experience and the (closely related) distinctive theology of a particular Christian group. The distinctiveness of the Gospel, which was once attributed to the creative thought of a single Johannine author and more recently to a "Johannine school" of Christian leaders and writers who developed the particular theological terminology and outlook of the Johannine literature, has in this dominant scholarly trend come to be attributed more experientially and sociologically to the Christian community within which the writers responsible for the Fourth Gospel and the Johannine letters lived and worked. Of course, everything said about this community and its history has to be deduced from the Gospel and the Johannine letters, for there is no relevant external evidence. There are second-century traditions that attribute the Gospel to John, the beloved disciple portrayed in the Gospel, locate its writing in Ephesus, betray no awareness that its context was other than *the* Christian community in Ephesus, one of the most prominent churches within the Christian movement, and consider that the Gospel was written for all the churches, not just its community of origin. But theories about the Johannine community are rarely able to allow more than a tiny grain of truth to these traditions (the beloved disciple may have had an important role in the early history of the Johannine community) and usually dismiss them as incompatible with what can be deduced from the Gospel itself about its character, origins, and intended audience.

The prominence of the Johannine community in Johannine scholarship corresponds to the way in which, during the same period, studies of the Synoptic Gospels have increasingly focused on the Matthean, Markan, and Lukan communities, understood as the particular communities within which and for which those Gospels were written. Elsewhere I have argued against this approach to the Gospels in general.[1] That each Gospel was written for a specific church or group of churches is an assumption that has come to be widely taken for granted without ever having been established by serious argument. Most scholars treat it as virtually self-evident and have not hesitated to build increasingly sophisticated edifices of scholarly reconstruction of the various Gospel communities on it. It remains, however, an unproven assumption that needs to be tested against the other most plausible possibility: that all the Gospels were written with the intention that they should circulate around all the churches. In favor of the latter hypothesis I have argued that, according to all the evidence we have, the early Christian movement was not a scattering of relatively isolated, introverted communities, but a network of communities in constant, close communication with each other. Moreover, all the evidence we have about early Christian leaders (the kind of people who might have written a Gospel) shows them to be typically people who traveled widely and worked in more than one community

1. "For Whom Were Gospels Written?" in *The Gospels for All Christians: Rethinking the Gospel Audiences*, ed. R. Bauckham (Grand Rapids: Eerdmans; Edinburgh: T. & T. Clark, 1997), 9–48. Other essays in this volume (by Michael B. Thompson, Loveday Alexander, Richard A. Burridge, Stephen C. Barton, and Francis Watson) discuss various aspects of this issue in more detail.

at different times. Thus neither the communities nor their teachers would have been locally minded. Both would have had a strong, lively, and informed sense of participation in a worldwide movement. Even rivalry and conflict between early Christian communities took place across the general network of Christian communication: it did not produce exclusive enclaves of churches out of communication with others. In addition, the evidence we have shows that Christian literature did in fact circulate around the churches very rapidly, while some evidence shows the deliberate launching of literature produced in one major church into general circulation around other churches. That someone should write one of the most sophisticated and carefully composed of early Christian literary works—a Gospel—simply for members of the specific community in which he was then living, with its specific, local issues determining the nature of his writing, thus becomes implausible. Knowing that his work was bound very quickly to reach many other churches, the audience he would address would be the Christians in any and every church to which his Gospel might circulate. His intended readership would be not a specific community or even a defined group of communities, however large, but an open and indefinite category: any and every Christian community of his time in which Greek was understood. And if a Gospel was not addressed to a particular community, we cannot expect to learn much from it about the evangelist's own community, even if there was only one such and even if it did influence his thinking and writing. On this view of the intended audience of the Gospels, I suggested, the Matthean, Markan, Lukan, and Johannine communities can no longer play the hermeneutically significant role to which they have been elevated in the scholarship of the last three decades.

My argument was a general one, with examples drawn from and conclusions applied to the Fourth Gospel as well as the Synoptic Gospels. But there are respects in which the Fourth Gospel is a special case. Even if the Christian movement was as I have portrayed it, might there not have been a Christian group in some remote spot, out of contact with other churches, in which this Gospel originated? Johannine scholarship has increasingly tended to set the Johannine community in just such splendid isolation and may not easily be persuaded that arguments about the Christian movement in general should apply to what it has in any case regarded as a special case. Does not this Gospel bear all the marks of a "sectarian"—that is, ideologically and sociologically closed—group? Does not its very special character demand an origin apart from the rest of the Christian movement? Moreover, partly (but not only) because in this case there are the Johannine letters to complement the evidence of the Gospel, reconstructions of the Johannine community, including a series of distinct stages of its history, have been bolder and fuller than most attempts to reconstruct the communities of the Synoptic Gospels. Skeptical readers might think the attempt to reconstruct the Johannine community and its history discredited by the fact that each such reconstruction differs from the others,[2] but others may think the general hypothesis of the Johannine community supported by its fruitfulness in generating so much research. In any case, there are significant arguments in play in the Johannine case that do not have the same importance in those of the other Gospels. If my general argument about the intended audiences of the Gospels is to be sustained in the case of the Fourth Gospel, it is clearly necessary to address questions specific to Johannine scholarship. What follows is a brief account of the way I should wish to do this.

Two-Level Reading Strategy?

Much of the reconstruction of the Johannine community and its history depends on the two-level reading strategy pioneered by J. Louis Martyn.[3] This is a way of reading the Gospel as not only what it is ostensibly, the story of Jesus, but as also, at the same time, the story of the Johannine community. The community, it is suggested, would have read it as a narrative about the past history of Jesus, but as also, encoded in the same texts, its own community story. Martyn's paradigm is the story of the blind man in John 9, which he argues represents the community's own experience of being excluded from its local synagogue by the synagogue leaders, an event that most scholars who reconstruct the Johannine community's history consider the event in that history of which we can be most certain. From such a view of the Gospel's narrative it almost inevitably follows that much of the story of Jesus in the Gospel has been decisively shaped by the Johannine community's experiences. Of course, it is also rooted in the traditions about Jesus preserved in the community, but these traditions have been reshaped and developed to reflect the community's history. This is therefore the most recent of ways of explaining the origin of the peculiarities of the Johannine narrative, which are considered not to reflect early Jesus traditions. It accounts for the way that much historical interest in the Fourth Gospel, lacking any confidence in its historical value as a narrative about Jesus, displays, instead, remarkable confidence in its evidence for the history of the Johannine community.

The cornerstone of Martyn's argument was the fact that the blind man in John 9 is expelled from the synagogue (9:22; cf. also 12:42; 16:2). This is said to be inconceivable within the ministry of Jesus, but corresponds to what happened to Jewish Christians in the late first century when the *Birkat ha-Minim* (a liturgical curse against heretics) was introduced into the synagogue liturgy with this purpose. Against this particular argument, we should note: (1) The historical issue of what happened in the relationship of Jewish Christians to synagogues in the late first

2. See T. L. Brodie, *The Quest for the Origin of John's Gospel* (New York: Oxford University Press, 1993), 15–21.

3. J. L. Martyn, *History and Theology in the Fourth Gospel*, 3rd. ed. (Louisville: Westminster John Knox, 2003).

century has been much debated, and it is not at all clear that what happened to Jewish Christians in the Diaspora at that time resembled what happens to the blind man in John 9. The trend of scholarly opinion is certainly against such a resemblance. (2) If it is the case that expulsion from the synagogue is anachronistic in John 9, Martyn's two-level reading of the passage is not the obvious explanation. Anachronisms in historical writing are not uncommon, but they are not usually explained in this way.

More generally, against the two-level reading strategy, the most important point to make is that it has no basis in the literary genre of the Fourth Gospel. It is genre that generally guides readers as to the reading strategy appropriate for a particular text. What generic category would give its readers to understand that they should read the history of their own community encoded in the story of an historical individual? Recent discussion of the genre of the Gospels strongly favors the view that contemporaries would have recognized all four canonical Gospels as a special form of the Greco-Roman biography (which we should not confuse with the modern biographical genre).[4] They would certainly expect such a work to be relevant to their own community and situation, but not that it would address the very specific circumstances of one particular community, still less that it required the kind of two-level reading Martyn proposed. Moreover, the Fourth Gospel itself evinces a strong sense of the pastness of the story of Jesus it tells, temporally and geographically located in its own time and space, and not infrequently draws explicit attention to the difference between the periods before and after the cross and resurrection of Jesus (e.g., 2:22; 7:39; 12:16; 13:7). Insofar as it says anything explicit about its content and purpose, it is in terms of reference to the history of Jesus (20:30–31; 21:24–25), not to the history of the Johannine community.

We should also note that the two-level reading strategy is not at all easy to practice. It does not mean that the Gospel's narrative can be read sequentially as a story about the Johannine community. Only by placing the various parts of the Gospel in temporal order of composition could we hope to know the sequence of events and theological developments in the history of the community. Moreover, the strategy cannot be applied to every part of the narrative, nor consistently to the parts of the narrative to which it is applied. Not every character in the Gospel can plausibly represent some group in the community's history and context (Judas? Pilate? the five thousand?). Every example of the strategy in practice is riddled with arbitrariness and uncertainty. The more one realizes how complex and selective the practice of this reading strategy has to be, the less plausible it becomes.

---

4. R. A. Burridge, *What Are the Gospels? A Comparison with Graeco-Roman Biography*, 2nd ed. (Grand Rapids: Eerdmans; Dearborn, MI: dove Booksellers, 2004).

Textual Stratification?

Closely associated with the two-level reading is a view of the Gospel as a mul-tilayered work in which texts from various stages of the community's history have been preserved alongside each other. A complex history of literary redaction is treated as the key to the community's social and theological history. This is also true for reconstructions of the Johannine community that do not espouse precisely Martyn's two-level reading. The distinguishing of various sources and levels of redaction depends primarily on detecting aporias (apparent difficulties in the text) and ideological tensions between different parts of the Gospel.

In this area there are two major issues that Johannine scholarship has not yet adequately faced or resolved. One is the relationship between, on the one hand, the kind of critical approach to the text (going back to Rudolf Bultmann and beyond) that seeks discontinuities of all kinds as indications of sources and redactional layers and, on the other hand, the newer literary criticism, which treats the final form of the text as a literary and rhetorical whole. Of course, these are not mutu-ally exclusive methods, but nor are they without relevance to each other. In the light of the greater sensitivity to the literary strategies of the text, which literary criticism fosters, many of what seemed aporias to the source and redaction critics appear no longer to be so. A passage that seems awkward to the often rather prosaic mind of the source critic, whose judgment often amounts merely to observing that he or she would not have written it like that, can appear quite differently to a critic attentive to the literary dynamics of the text. Thus literary criticism of the final form of the Gospel is not just an approach that can be added to source and redaction criticism, leaving their results intact, as most Johannine scholars seem still to suppose. It must pose serious questions about the interpretation of the evidence on which the older approaches were based.

The second issue concerns assumptions about the fourth evangelist's theology. If diachronic stratification of the text too often lacks literary sensitivity, it also often displays a rather wooden and overly modern reaction to the ideological tensions and seeming conceptual contradictions between different parts of the Gospel. We need to be much more open to the possibility that tensions and even apparent contradictions belong to the character and method of this Gospel's theology. After all, the redactors who, according to the general view, put the various parts of the Gospel together were evidently content to let tensions and contradictions result when they could have edited them out. It may be at least no more difficult to read them as the deliberate theological strategies of a single author. Following this direction of thought may lead us back to an older view of the distinctiveness of the Fourth Gospel. Perhaps we are dealing, not with the product of an idiosyncratic community and its history, but with the work of a creative theologian who, in his long experience of teaching and on the basis of his rather special access to traditions about Jesus, developed a distinctive interpreta-tion of the history of Jesus.

In-Group Language?

With this topic, we reach the point where it will be possible decisively to turn the tables on those who argue for the Johannine community as the intended audience of the Gospel. The evidence here cited for this points, as we shall see, much more probably in a completely other direction.

An influential strand of Johannine scholarship has focused on the distinctive terminology and symbolism in the Gospel and identified them as the language of a sectarian community. The Gospel, it is claimed, could have been understood only by initiates, members of the community in which this language had developed as a special in-group language. Indeed, it may be added, by using everyday language with a novel sense, the Gospel actually aims to confuse outsiders and to confirm insiders in their sense of belonging and superiority, especially when characters in the Gospel, notably "the Jews," are depicted as misunderstanding Jesus' enigmatic sayings. At such points in the narrative Johannine community members, but only Johannine community members, find themselves "in the know," aligned with Jesus in radical distinction from the culpable incomprehension of outsiders (who would be identified with the non-Christian Jews of the synagogue from which the Johannine community had separated).

It should be said that this line of argument is not primarily concerned with the relationship of the Johannine community to other Christian groups or the Christian movement in general, but with its relationship to the non-Christian society (especially Jewish, but also pagan) with which it was in daily contact. It is in relation to society at large that the Johannine group is usually classified in sociological terms as sectarian. But the argument does also bear on the relationship of the Johannine community to the rest of the Christian movement, in that the in-group language of the Gospel is not treated as the common language of the Christian movement, but as the special language of the Johannine group. Perhaps non-Johannine Christians would have some advantage over non-Christians in understanding the Fourth Gospel, but the impression one gains from scholars who take this approach is that the advantage would not be very great.

Anyone who has not already become accustomed to this argument in recent Johannine scholarship may well find it surprising. In the church's historical and current experience it has often been precisely the Fourth Gospel that, among the New Testament writings, has proved most accessible both to Christians with little education in the faith and to complete outsiders who have minimal knowledge of the Christian tradition. How can this be the case, given that the characters within the Gospel so often misunderstand or are puzzled by the sayings of Jesus in it? There are at least three reasons within the literary strategy of the Gospel that explain how the Gospel's special language and symbolism prove accessible to noninitiates and that also, against the line of argument cited above, show that the Gospel is designed precisely to introduce this language to readers not already familiar with it.

First, the evangelist himself sometimes explains the meaning of figurative or enigmatic sayings of Jesus (e.g., 2:21; 6:71; 7:39; 11:13; 12:33; 13:11; cf. 11:51–52). Of these, the first example is particularly instructive. The saying of Jesus in 2:19 is the first example in the Gospel of figurative language used by Jesus. As in many later instances, what Jesus says has an obvious, literal meaning, referring to a physical reality, and a metaphorical meaning that turns the physical image into a symbol of Jesus' salvific activity or the salvation he brings. As in many later instances, "the Jews" (i.e., the Jewish leaders) understand only the literal sense and so misunderstand (2:20). Not even the disciples understood at the time (2:22). But the evangelist explains the meaning to the readers (2:21–22). He surely intends this to be an illustrative example. He will not always help them on later occasions, but he has shown them how to do it.

Second, the misunderstandings by Jesus' hearers (disciples, Jewish leaders, individuals such as the Samaritan woman) frequently have the literary function of leading Jesus to explain the image he has used or to develop it in ways that clarify its meaning (e.g., 3:3–8; 4:10–15, 31–34; 6:32–35; 8:31–36, 56–58; 10:6; 11:23–26; 14:4–6). Frequently the characters in the narrative come to understand as a result of these explanations by Jesus, sometimes they do not (e.g., 4:15; 10:6, 19), but the main point is that the readers come to understand. The dialogues teach them the Johannine language and symbolism. This is why the symbols are so often introduced and developed in dialogues, like those with Nicodemus and the Samaritan woman. Even if a symbol, at first occurrence, is as puzzling to readers as it is to characters in the Gospel, this is not because readers must already be familiar with it in order to understand it at all, but in order to stir readers into a desire to understand, which the continuing development of the dialogue then helps them to fulfill.

Read sequentially, the Gospel leads its readers and hearers progressively into a greater understanding of its themes by initiating them step by step into its symbolic world. For example, at 4:13–14, readers learn that, in Jesus' usage, the everyday language of water refers to the source of eternal life that Jesus will give. Jewish or Christian readers might well, from their knowledge of the use of water as a symbol of the Holy Spirit, see that symbolism in Jesus' words to the Samaritan woman, but readers who do not see this nevertheless learn enough to go on with. Later in the Gospel they gain the further insight that the water symbolizes the Spirit that Jesus will give, after his glorification, to those who believe in him (7:37–39). Of course, the explanations of the symbolism are never adequate, because the symbolism is not just a code that can be translated into an adequate literal description, as the sociological reduction of it to in-group language tends to suggest. The realities to which the symbols refer are transcendent realities that escape linguistic capture. This is why the symbols proliferate through the Gospel without redundancy. Each may help the reader further toward what they symbolize. But sufficient explanation of the symbols is given to point readers in the direction of their meaning.

Third, what no characters in the Gospel understand before Jesus' resurrection are his many enigmatic references to his coming death and resurrection. The evangelist makes it clear, especially in his paradigmatic explanation of the first of Jesus' figurative sayings (2:21–22), that not even Jesus' disciples understood or could have understood these references to what John calls Jesus' glorification (cf. 13:7; 12:16; 20:9). However, by pointing this out in 2:21–22, John is putting his readers in a better position than are any of the characters in the story for understanding a major theme in the words of Jesus. But the knowledge the readers have to bring to the text is not some esoteric insider information, known only within the Johannine community, but just that Jesus is going to go voluntarily to his death by crucifixion and then rise from death. Even non-Christian readers interested enough to read the Gospel would surely know that Christians believed this about Jesus.

None of this should suggest that readers of the Gospel would find it uniformly easy to understand. Jesus sometimes seems to speak in unexplained riddles (as he does also in the Synoptics). These would be more puzzling for some readers than for others, but would probably be somewhat puzzling to most first-time readers. But such riddles are part of a literary strategy that drives readers both to think about their meaning and to read on in hope of discovering their meaning. A good example is the series of three passages in which Jesus refers to his death as his being "lifted up" (3:14–15; 8:28; 12:32–34), an instance of Johannine double entendre that combines a literal use of the verb, referring to the manner of Jesus' death (lifted up on the cross), with a figurative use, referring to his exaltation. John, in fact, explains the literal meaning, leaving the paradox of its concurrence with the figurative meaning to be inferred, but it is only on the last occasion when Jesus uses the figure that he provides this explanation (12:33). On the theory that this is in-group language that Johannine Christians already know, but for other readers could and should be impenetrably opaque, the procedure is inexplicable. It makes sense if these Johannine enigmas are meant to tease initially uncomprehending readers into theological enlightenment. To those who have not managed to penetrate the meaning through the first two occurrences of the figure, John gives substantial help on its third occurrence, but he avoids depotentiating the riddle by giving too much help too soon.

One reason why scholars who read John's language as the deliberately in-group talk of a sectarian community have missed the way the Gospel seems designed, on the contrary, to introduce readers to its special language and symbolism, may be that a focus on the stratification of the Gospel in sources and redactional layers has distracted such scholars from the literary strategies of the Gospel as a text designed to be read sequentially and as a whole. Study of the Gospel's figurative language in this way has inclined me to change my mind about the Gospel's intended audience. Not only do I still think the Gospel is written for the churches in general, not just for its author's or authors' own community; I am also now inclined to think that its intended readership includes interested non-Christians.

The latter is not an alternative to the supposition that the Gospel would reach its readers through circulation around the churches, since it is unlikely that Christian literature could at that time interest or even come into the hands of outsiders other than through the mediation of Christians. Such non-Christian readers would already have been acquainted with the Christian message by Christian friends and would have to be seriously interested. But the Gospel does seem to me to be designed in such a way that it could be sufficiently understood by such seriously interested outsiders. They would doubtless miss deeper levels of meaning that would be accessible to more informed readers, but they would, I suggest, have been puzzled only enough to keep them reading.

It is noteworthy that most of the Gospel's major symbolic images come from the common experience of all people of the time: light and darkness, water, bread, vine and wine, shepherd and sheep, judgment and witness, birth and death. Many of these images also have a background in the Jewish Scriptures and Jewish tradition, which would enhance their meaning for readers who knew this background, but it is rarely the case that this kind of background is required in a way that would leave readers who lacked it simply baffled. The language would mean something to them, even though not all that it could mean to better-informed readers. For example, John's account of Jesus at the feast of tabernacles (chapters 7–8) is considerably informed by the way this festival was celebrated in the first-century Jerusalem temple (which could not be known from the Old Testament). Readers with this knowledge would certainly benefit from it in their reading of these chapters, but the chapters are nevertheless quite intelligible to readers who lack this knowledge.

It is also true that most of the major Johannine images have some place in the Synoptic teaching of Jesus and would therefore not be wholly unfamiliar to non-Johannine Christians. What is distinctive in John is the extensive development of these images. Every Christian familiar with the traditional words of Jesus at the Last Supper would recognize the "bread of life" discourse in John 6 as a further development of the same image that he or she knew in a much more concise form in the Last Supper tradition. It becomes clear that this is a Gospel designed to "work" for readers from a variety of backgrounds and to continue to work for readers who read and reread it with increasing understanding. It contains riches that only study by a scripturally informed reader could unearth, but it also speaks accessibly to a reader with only minimal prior knowledge of Christian belief. What it certainly is not is a Gospel for those who already understand everything it has to say.

Universal References

Our necessarily brief study of the way the language and imagery of the Gospel functions has taken us in precisely the opposite direction from the view that sees it as written for the Johannine community. It begins to look as though the Fourth Gospel envisages a wider readership than perhaps any other New Testament text does.

A final indication that this Gospel does not reflect an introverted and isolated group of Christians, uninterested in or even alienated from the rest of the Christian movement, can be found in its use of universal language. The Gospel's multivalent use of the word "world" includes a neutral usage in which the sense is "humanity in general." In this sense, it is the world that God loved and Jesus came to save (e.g., 3:16–17; 4:42; 6:33, 51; 17:21; and cf. 12:32). It is hard to reconcile this repeated and quite emphatic universal perspective with the outlook of a community that deliberately set itself apart from the worldwide Christian movement.

Most commentators recognize that chapter 21 is also irreconcilable with such an outlook. Here the flock that Jesus commissions Peter to tend is the universal church, not the Johannine community. The allusion to Peter's martyrdom in Rome (21:18) confirms this, if confirmation were needed. The chapter acknowledges Peter's generally recognized apostolic authority in the whole church, while asserting also the beloved disciple's less generally recognized role in relation to the whole church. This disciple's special role as a witness to Jesus, which the Gospel has already highlighted especially in 19:15, becomes a role of witness to the whole church when the beloved disciple writes his testimony (21:24) in a Gospel for the whole church to read. Thus the beloved disciple's witness, as well as Peter's apostolic pastorate, is given a role in the universal mission of the church, of which the miraculous catch of every kind of fish (21:5–11) functions as an acted parable.

The evidence of this chapter can, of course, be dismissed with the claim that it is a later addition to a Gospel that originally ended at 20:31, part of the last redaction of the Gospel by a Johannine writer attempting to integrate the Johannine community into the wider church. The alternative view, that chapter 21 is an epilogue belonging integrally, like the prologue, to the design of the Gospel, cannot be argued here,[5] but it is at least suggestive that this epilogue forms so appropriate a conclusion to the reading of the rest of the Gospel that we have explored in this chapter. Once again the issue concerns the divergence between a vertical reading of the Gospel as accumulated layers of evidence for the Johannine community's history and a horizontal reading of the Gospel as a literary whole. In the latter case, the Johannine community (in the sense of the community in which the beloved disciple lived at the end of his life) finally makes its one and only appearance in the Gospel at 21:23. This is where it belongs, leaving the rest of the Gospel free to be the narrative about Jesus that it patently claims to be.

5. But see chapter 13 below.

6

THE QUMRAN COMMUNITY AND THE GOSPEL OF JOHN

It seems to have become quite widely accepted that the parallels between the Johannine literature of the New Testament (the Gospel and Epistles of John) and those texts from Qumran that most likely express the community's own theology are probably the most impressive parallels between the New Testament and Qumran, and are so impressive as to require a historical connection closer than could be provided merely by the common Jewish milieu of late Second Temple Judaism. The hypothesis of some kind of influence from Qumran on John is widely accepted, whether this is regarded as indirect (e.g., R. E. Brown)[1] or direct (e.g.,

Originally published in a slightly different form as "Qumran and the Gospel of John: Is There a Connection?" in *The Scrolls and the Scriptures: Qumran Fifty Years After*, ed. S. E. Porter and C. A. Evans, JSPSup 26, Roehampton Institute London Papers 3 (Sheffield: Sheffield Academic Press, 1997), 267–79. Reprinted by permission of the publisher. Reprinted in a slightly different form as "The Qumran Community and the Gospel of John," in *The Dead Sea Scrolls Fifty Years after Their Discovery: Proceedings of the Jerusalem Congress, July 20–25, 1997*, ed. L. H. Schiffman, E. Tov, and J. C. VanderKam (Jerusalem: Israel Exploration Society, 2000), 105–15.

1. R. E. Brown, "The Qumran Scrolls and the Johannine Gospel and Epistles," in *New Testament Essays* (New York: Paulist, 1965), 102–31; idem, "The Dead Sea Scrolls and the New Testament," in *John and the Dead Sea Scrolls*, ed. J. H. Charlesworth (New York: Crossroad, 1990), 7–8; idem, *The Community of the Beloved Disciple* (New York: Paulist, 1979), 30–31.

K. G. Kuhn,[2] J. H. Charlesworth,[3] J. Ashton[4]). But in my view this hypothesis is mistaken. It arose from a natural enthusiasm about parallels between the Scrolls and the New Testament when the scrolls were first published,[5] but the parallels in this case have not been assessed with sufficient methodological rigor.[6] I do not think they amount to a case for influence or for any particular historical connection between John and Qumran. In this chapter, I shall focus on the evidence for a connection to which most weight is usually given: the expression of dualistic thinking in light and darkness imagery in both the Qumran texts and the Fourth Gospel,[7] and I shall add some remarks about the "spirit of truth," often regarded as the most striking terminological parallel between the Qumran texts and the Fourth Gospel.

The extent of the similarity between the dualism of the Qumran texts and the dualism of the Fourth Gospel has been debated, but even those who emphasize dissimilarities more than others seem to agree that the extensive use of light/darkness imagery to express a dualistic worldview in both cases represents a very striking similarity.[8] In assessing the hypothesis of a Qumran origin for Johannine dualism, it is therefore very useful to focus on precisely how this imagery of light and darkness is used in each case. This will enable us to avoid conducting a comparison at too high a level of abstraction from the way the theology of the texts is actually expressed in them.

2. K. G. Kuhn, "Die in Palästina gefundenen hebräischen Texte und das neue Testament," *ZTK* 47 (1950): 192–211.

3. J. H. Charlesworth, "A Critical Comparison of the Dualism in 1QS 3:13–4:26 and the 'Dualism' Contained in the Gospel of John," in Charlesworth, ed., *John and the Dead Sea Scrolls*, 76–106. He clarifies and develops his position in J. H. Charlesworth, "The Dead Sea Scrolls and the Gospel according to John," in *Exploring the Gospel of John: In Honor of D. Moody Smith*, ed. R. A. Culpepper and C. C. Black (Louisville: Westminster John Knox, 1996), 87–89, where he suggests that Essenes would have memorized 1QS 3–4, and that some entered the Johannine community after 70 CE, and so had some influence within the Johannine school.

4. J. Ashton, *Understanding the Fourth Gospel* (Oxford: Clarendon, 1991), 232–37.

5. Cf. B. Lindars, *John*, NT Guides (Sheffield: JSOT Press, 1990), 49: "Initial enthusiasm overstressed the importance of these similarities." For a minimalist view of the significance of the scrolls for understanding John, see C. K. Barrett, *The Gospel according to St. John*, 2nd ed. (London: SPCK, 1978), 34.

6. This is also true of those scholars who conclude that these same parallels show John's dependence on first-century Jewish forms of thought that Qumran exemplifies but that had wider currency (e.g., J. Painter, *The Quest for the Messiah*, 2nd ed. [Edinburgh: T. & T. Clark, 1993], 50–52). Here too there is no sufficiently careful assessment of the alleged parallels, or of the relationship of the Qumran texts, on the one hand, and of John, on the other, to comparable material in other Jewish literature.

7. For a survey of other similarities, see Brown, "Qumran Scrolls."

8. Charlesworth, "Critical Comparison," 100–101, after stressing the differences in the dualistic theologies of 1QS 3.13–4.26 and John, writes: "After full account is taken of all the dissimilarities in theological perspective, we must ask whether in the realm of symbolism and mythology there exists between John and the Rule an underlying interrelationship of conceptual framework and literary expression. We may reasonably hold that the dualistic opposition between light and darkness is not something each developed independently, but rather something that betokens John's dependence on the Rule."

The dualism of the Fourth Gospel is expressed in two different sets of images. One is the imagery of light and darkness (1:4–9; 3:19–21; 8:12; 9:4–5; 11:9–10; 12:35–36, 46; cf. 1 John 1:5–7; 2:8–11). The other is the spatial imagery that appears in the terms "from above" and "from below" (8:23), and "not from this world" and "from this world" (8:23; 18:36; cf.15:19; 17:14, 16). The two sets of images therefore are the light/darkness opposition and the above/below and God/world opposition. It is very important to notice that these two sets of images never combine or overlap in the Fourth Gospel. Each is kept distinct from the other.

Of these two sets of images, the Qumran texts provide parallels only to the light/darkness opposition, which, of course, is found also in other Jewish texts. For the distinctively Johannine use of "the world" and "this world" in a pejorative sense, and the distinctively Johannine contrast of "from above" and "from below," the Qumran texts provide no parallel at all.[9] This in itself makes implausible the view that Johannine dualism as such derives from Qumran dualism. It would surely be hard to argue that the light/darkness imagery is the primary expression of Johannine dualism and the above/below and God/world opposition a secondary development. The latter plays just as important a role in the Gospel as the former. Consequently, even if the Johannine use of light/darkness imagery derives from Qumran, this could not easily be understood to mean that Johannine dualism as such derives from Qumran.

But can the Johannine use of light/darkness imagery plausibly be held to derive from the Qumran texts? We should first recall two evident facts. First, the contrast of light and darkness is the most obvious of dualisms observable in the natural world, and has therefore acquired the metaphorical meanings of knowledge and ignorance, truth and error, good and evil, life and death, in most and perhaps all cultural traditions. Second, these metaphorical uses of the light/darkness imagery occur relatively often in the Hebrew Bible and in Second Temple Jewish literature, and so were readily available in the Jewish tradition to the authors of both the Qumran texts and Johannine literature. To establish a special connection between these it is not sufficient to point out that few of the other Jewish texts emphasize the light/darkness imagery to the extent that 1QS and the Fourth Gospel do.[10] The mere fact that both 1QS and the Fourth Gospel make more prominent use of this imagery than most Jewish texts proves very little. If the imagery was available in the Jewish tradition, it would not be especially surprising to find two authors

9. It has rarely been noticed that the best parallels to these Johannine usages are in James (1:17, 27; 3:15, 17). Since there are no other resemblances between James and the Johannine literature, these parallels are best explained by common dependence on a Jewish terminology that does not seem to have been preserved in extant Jewish texts.

10. Even in the extent to which they use the light and darkness imagery, John and the Qumran texts are not uniquely comparable. The sustained use of the metaphor of light and darkness for good and evil, truth and error through some 132 verses of the apocalypse of the clouds in 2 Baruch (chapters 53, 56–72) represents a more extensive use of the imagery than do the 16 verses of the Fourth Gospel that use the imagery.

independently developing it more extensively than most other Jewish texts do. Only if the development in the two cases exhibited extensive similarities not attributable to common roots in the common Jewish tradition would there be any reason to postulate a connection. If, however, there were extensive dissimilarities in the two developments, and if the distinctive development in each case could be plausibly explained as a development of elements in the common Jewish tradition, then to postulate a connection between the two developments would be unnecessary and implausible.

I shall argue first that the use of the light/darkness imagery in the Fourth Gospel on the one hand, and in the Qumran texts on the other, exhibits far more impressive dissimilarities than have been noticed in the scholarly enthusiasm for drawing conclusions from the comparatively unimpressive similarities. While this considerably weakens the case for influence from Qumran on John, it does not necessarily disprove it. The dissimilarities might result from John's creative adaptation of the basic motif he borrowed from the Qumran texts. In order to disprove this possibility, I shall show that the distinctively Johannine uses of the light/darkness imagery, which cannot be paralleled in the Qumran texts, can be paralleled to a significant extent in other Second Temple Jewish literature, and can very plausibly be understood as rooted in biblical texts predominantly different from the biblical texts that influenced the uses of the light/darkness imagery in the Qumran texts. Since what is distinctive in the Johannine use of the light/darkness imagery finds parallels in other Second Temple Jewish literature and sources in the Hebrew Bible, what the Johannine use has in common with the Qumran use is more plausibly attributed to common dependence on the Hebrew Bible and general Jewish tradition than to any closer relationship between John and Qumran.

Among the Qumran texts, the light/darkness dualism occurs predominantly in the *Rule of the Community* (1QS), the *War Scroll* (1QM, 4QM), and the fragmentary text known as 4QVisions of Amram (4Q543–48).[11] Since the most impressive parallels with John have been seen in the passage about the two spirits in 1QS 3.13–4.26, I shall focus on this passage, but add references to relevant material in the *War Scroll*. The passage in the *Rule of the Community* uses synonymously the three pairs of opposites: light and darkness, truth and deceit, justice and injustice. It depicts two angelic beings, the Prince of Lights and the Angel of Darkness, the spirit of truth and the spirit of deceit, who are the sources of good and evil in the world. Both were created by God, though God loves one and hates the other, and has destined the one for triumph and the other for destruction. Meanwhile,

---

11. Cf. also 4QSongs of the Sage^b (4Q511); 11QApocryphal Psalms^a (11Q11); 4QCatena^a (4Q177). The light/darkness dualism does not appear in the *Hodayot*, or in the *Damascus Rule* (though the title "the Prince of Lights" is used for Michael in CD 5.18, as in 1QS 3.20). For other significant occurrences of light/darkness imagery in the scrolls that seem more distant from the way this imagery is used in 1QS and 1QM, see 4Q462 9–10; 1QMysteries (1Q27) 1.5–6; 4QMysteries^a (4Q299) 5.1-3; 4QCryptic A (4Q298) 1.1; 4Q471 4.5.

they contend with each other in human hearts. Depending on the dominance of either, humans are divided into the sons of light, truth, or justice and the sons of deceit. The influence of the two spirits in human life is correlated with the image of the two ways drawn from the wisdom tradition: people walk either in the paths of light or in the paths of darkness. These two ways lead to different destinies at the eschatological judgment, again described partly in the imagery of light and darkness: the light of glory in eternal life, and the darkness of the nether regions in which the wicked are punished and destroyed. The *War Scroll* uses the light/darkness dualism not in this psychological and individual way, but to depict the eschatological war in which Michael, his angels, and the sons of light will defeat Belial, his angels, and the sons of darkness. The same cosmic dualism appears in different aspects in the two works.

Table 6.1. The Terminology of Light/Darkness Dualism at Qumran

Light	*Darkness*
Michael (1QM 17.6)	Belial (1QS 1.18, etc; 1QM)
Prince of Lights (1QS 3.20; CD 5.18) *Prince of Light* (1QM 13.10)	Angel of Darkness (1QS 3.20, 21)
the spirit of truth (1QS 3.19; 4.21, 23) the angel of his truth (1QS 3.24)	the spirit of deceit (1QS 3.19; 4.9, 20, 23)
all the spirits of truth (1QM 13.10)	all the spirits of his lot (1QS 3.24) *the spirits of his lot* (1QM 13.4, 12)
the men of God's lot (1QS 2,2; 1QM 1.5) *the lot of your truth* (1QM 13.12)	the men of Belial's lot (1QS 2.4–5; 1QM 1.15) *the lot of darkness* (1QM 1.11; 13.5)
the sons of light (1QS 1.9; 2.16; 3.13, 24, 25; 1QM; Luke 16:8; John 12:36; 1 Thess. 5:5; Eph. 5:8)	the sons of darkness (1QS 1.10; 1QM)
the sons of truth (1QS 4.6) *the sons of your truth* (1QM 17.8) the sons of righteousness (1QS 3.20, 22; 1QM 1.8)	the sons of deceit (1QS 3.21)
the paths of light (1QS 3.20)	the paths of darkness (1QS 3.21)
the paths of truth (1QS 4.17)	the paths of darkness and evil cunning (1QS 4.11)
the paths of righteousness and truth (1QS 4.2)	the paths of wickedness (1 QS 4.19)
wisdom (1QS 4.24)	folly (1QS 4.24)

The table focuses on terms appearing in the two-spirits passage of the *Community Rule* (1QS 3.13–4.26) but adds references to relevant material in the *War Scroll* (1QM) and (in one instance) the *Damascus Document* (CD). Terms in italics occur only in 1QM. Note that of all the terms here listed, only "the sons of light" is associated with the light/dark dualism of the Gospel of John, and it also occurs elsewhere in the New Testament. Hence it appears unlikely that the light/darkness dualism of the Gospel of John derives from Qumran.

Noteworthy differences from the use of the light/darkness imagery in the Fourth Gospel are:

1. These Qumran texts exhibit a stereotyped and elaborate dualistic terminology in which each term has its corresponding opposite: the spirit of truth and the spirit of deceit, the sons of light and the sons of darkness, the paths of light and the paths of darkness, and so on. Apart from the terms light and darkness themselves, only one of these terms—"the sons of light"—appears in those passages of the Fourth Gospel that use the light/darkness imagery (12:36). This single coincidence of terminology cannot carry much weight; while frequent in the Qumran texts we are considering,[12] it occurs only once in John, and is therefore no more characteristic of John than of Luke, Paul, and the author of Ephesians, each of whom, like John, uses the expression just once.[13] The list of terminological parallels should not be expanded to include phrases occurring in John outside the passages that use the light/darkness imagery, especially not when these are such commonplace expressions as "the Holy Spirit," "eternal life," and "the wrath of God,"[14] but not even in the case of the distinctively Johannine term "the spirit of truth," which in John has no relationship to the light/darkness imagery. (I shall return to this term later.) It is hardly credible that, if the Qumran use of the light/darkness imagery influenced John, the highly distinctive terminology that virtually constitutes the Qumran use of the light/darkness imagery should have left such minimal traces in John.[15]

12. 1QS 1.9; 2.16; 3.13, 24, 25; 1QM 1.1, 3, 9, 11, 13; 4QCatena[a] (4Q177) 2.7; 4.16; 4QFlor (4Q174) 1.8–9; 4QSongs of the Sage[a] (4Q510) 1.7; 4QDamascus Document[b] (4Q267) 1.1. The term does not seem to appear outside the Qumran texts and the New Testament, but cf. *1 Enoch* 108:11–14, where "the good who belong to the generation of light" (11) are contrasted with "those born in darkness" (11, 14), and the two groups have eschatological destinies of light and darkness respectively (12–14).

13. Luke 16:8; 1 Thess. 5:5; Eph. 5:8. Charlesworth misrepresents the matter when he claims that "the expression 'sons of light' is characteristic only of Qumran and John" ("Critical Comparison," 101).

14. The first two of these three phrases are included by Charlesworth, "Critical Comparison," 101–2, in his "four shared linguistic formulae which suggest a strong correlation between John and 1QS 3:13–4:26," while the third occurs in his "seven additional shared literary expressions." Cf. also Charlesworth, "Dead Sea Scrolls," 73–74, 82; C. A. Evans, *Word and Glory: On the Exegetical and Theological Background of John's Prologue*, JSNTSup 89 (Sheffield: Sheffield Academic Press, 1993), 147. Another such expression, listed by Evans and by Charlesworth, "Dead Sea Scrolls," 75, is "to do the truth" (1QS 1.5; 5.3; 8.2; John 3:21; 1 John 1:6), but again this is a common usage (Gen. 24:49; 32:11; 47:29; Josh. 2:14; 2 Sam. 2:6; Ezek. 18:9; Neh. 9:33; 2 Chron. 31:20; Tob. 4:6; 13:6).

15. Of the other "shared literary expressions" listed by Charlesworth, "Critical Comparison," 102, only three deserve mention as arguably instances of the light/darkness imagery : (1) "to walk in the paths of darkness" (1QS 3.21; 4.11) and "to walk in darkness" (John 8:12; 12:35; cf. 1 John 1:6; 2:11); (2) "the light of life" (1QS 3.7; John 8:12); (3) "blindness of eyes" (1QS 4:11) and "the eyes of the blind" (John 10:21; cf. John 9). On these the following comments should be made: (1) Both expressions are biblical: "to walk in the paths of darkness" (Prov. 2:13), "to walk in darkness" (Ps. 82:5; Eccles. 2:14; Isa. 9:2[1]). 1QS uses the former twice (1QS 3.21; 4.11) and the latter once (1QS 11.10), whereas John uses only the latter (John 8:12; 12:35; cf. 1 John 1:6; 2:11). The difference is significant. The usage in 1QS derives from the wisdom tradition (in 1QS 3:21; 4:11 the phrase corresponds verbatim to Prov. 2:13) and is part of the picture of the two ways. By contrast the two ways terminology makes no appearance in the Fourth

2. Conversely, expressions characterizing the Johannine use of the light/darkness imagery have no parallel in the Qumran texts: "the true light" (1:9; cf. 1 John 2:8), "the light of the world" (8:12; 9:5), "to have the light" (8:12; 12:35–36), "to come to the light" (3:20–21), "to remain in the darkness" (12:46; cf. 1 John 2:9), and the contrast of "day" and "night" (9:4; 11:9–10).

3. Important features of the way the light/darkness imagery functions in the Qumran texts are entirely absent from John. For example, essential to the Qumran usage are the two spirits of light and darkness, the Prince of Lights and the Angel of Darkness, Michael and Belial in the *War Scroll*. They do not appear in John's use of the light/darkness imagery, where Christ himself is the light, but the devil, who in other parts of the Gospel is "the ruler of this world" (12:31; 14:30; 16:11) and "the father of lies" (8:44), is never related to darkness.[16] Second, neither the conflict of light and darkness within the heart of the individual nor the conflict between the two categories of humanity, the sons of light and the sons of darkness, appears in John, where 1:5 is the only verse to make any use at all of the image of conflict between light and darkness. Third, the use of light and darkness to characterize the alternative eschatological destinies of the two classes of humanity is absent from John,[17] even though it was common in Jewish eschatological imagery (e.g. Tob. 14:10; *Pss. Sol.* 3:12; 14:9; 15:10; *1 Enoch* 1:8; 5:6–7; 46:6; 63:6; 92:3–5; 108:11–15).

4. Within the Johannine use of the light/darkness imagery, the central image is that of a great light coming into the world, shining in the darkness of the world, giving light to all people, so that they may come out of the darkness into the light, and be able to walk in this light instead of stumbling in the darkness (see 1:5, 9; 3:19; 8:12; 11:9–10; 12:35, 46). This dominant image of a great light shining in the darkness is not at all the dominant image in the Qumran texts' use of light/darkness imagery. At one point the *War Scroll* envisages the time when, following their defeat of the Kittim, the sons of light will shine in all the edges of the earth, giving light until the end of all the periods of darkness, when God's own glory will shine for eternity (1QM 1.8). But this is virtually the only instance of the image of light shining in and dispelling darkness.[18] It is subsidiary to the dominant image of conflict between light and darkness, where very often the metaphorical force

---

Gospel, whose use of light/darkness imagery seems uninfluenced by the wisdom tradition. Its use of the expression "to walk in darkness" probably derives from Isa. 9:2[1] (see below). (2) The phrase "the light of life" is a biblical expression (Job 33:30; Ps. 56:13[14]), which also occurs in later Jewish literature (*1 Enoch* 58:3). In 1QS 3.7 it derives from Job 33:30, in John 8:12 probably from Ps. 36:13[14]. (3) The phrase "blindness of eyes" (1QS 4.11) occurs in the following list: "blasphemous tongue, blindness of eyes, hardness of hearing, stiffness of neck, hardness of heart." Clearly blindness here has no particular connection with light and darkness, as it does in John 9.

16. Contrast 1 Cor. 6:14–15 and Acts 26:18, both of which are closer than John to Qumran usage.

17. In John 8.12 (cf. 12.35) "walk in darkness" refers to living in ignorance and error, not to eschatological destiny.

18. Cf. also 1QS 4.2, where the spirit of truth is said to enlighten the heart of the individual.

of the words light and darkness seems to have been largely lost and they function simply as names for opposing cosmic principles, interchangeable with truth and deceit, justice and injustice. In the Fourth Gospel the light/darkness imagery is always used to convey specific visual images of light and darkness, of which the central and dominant one, the great light shining in the darkness of the world, finds a parallel at Qumran only in one line of the *War Scroll*.[19]

5. Finally, the difference in the imagery corresponds to a difference in the meaning conveyed by the imagery. In the Fourth Gospel, the central image of the light shining in the darkness has christological and soteriological significance. Christ is the light of the world, come into the world so that people may come out of the darkness into the light. At Qumran, on the other hand, the imagery of light and darkness is used to portray a conflict between cosmic hierarchies of good and evil, which contend in the heart of the individual and on the heavenly and earthly battlefield of the eschatological war. There is no thought of people moving from "the lot of darkness" into light.

In summary, the similarity between the use of light/darkness imagery in the two cases is almost entirely limited to the basic symbolism: light and darkness symbolize truth and error operating on a cosmic scale. The particular development of this symbolism in each case diverges widely. Characteristic terminology, dominant imagery, and theological significance all differ to such an extent as to make the influence of Qumran on the Fourth Gospel unlikely.

We shall now show how the use of light/darkness imagery in the Fourth Gospel has its own sources in the Hebrew Bible and parallels in Second Temple Jewish literature, which explain precisely the ways in which it diverges from the Qumran texts' use of such imagery and make the hypothesis of influence from Qumran on John entirely redundant.

1. The opening verses of the Prologue to the Gospel are an exegesis of the opening verses of Genesis, and the first appearance of the light/darkness imagery in the Gospel (1:4–5) constitutes an interpretation of the light and darkness of the first day of the Genesis creation narrative (Gen. 1:3–5).[20] In this way, the Johannine prologue belongs to a Jewish tradition of theological exegesis of the Genesis

19. Cf. also 1QMysteries (1Q27) 1.5–6: "When those begotten of iniquity are delivered up, and wickedness is removed from before righteousness, as darkness is removed from before light, and just as smoke ceases and is no more, so wickedness will cease forever; and righteousness will be revealed as the sun throughout the measure of the world" (D. J. Harrington, trans., *Wisdom Texts from Qumran* [London: Routledge, 1996], 70). But here light and darkness appear as a simile, alongside the alternative simile of smoke, not in the way they appear in the dualistic light/darkness language of 1QS and 1QM. This text shows no other trace of light/darkness dualism. The passage in 1.5–6 is close to the imagery in *1 Enoch* 58:5–6 (and cf. 4Q541 9 1.3–5; *T. Levi* 18.2–4), and so provides general Jewish, not specifically Qumran, background to 1 John 2:8.

20. Gen. 1:3–5 may have played some part in the formation of the light/darkness dualism at Qumran. 11QApocryphal Psalms[a] (11Q11) 1.12–13 makes explicit allusion to Gen. 1:4 in connection with the light/darkness dualism. 1QS 3.25 (God "created the spirits of light and darkness") may reflect the Genesis creation account, though allusion to Isa. 45:7 is also possible. However, the other Jewish parallels to

creation narrative, which often devoted particular interest and speculation to the work of the first day and to the primordial light that appeared on that day (e.g., *4 Ezra* 6:40; *LAB* 28.8–9; 60.2; 4Q392 1.4–7; *2 Enoch* 24:4J; 25; Aristobulus, ap. Eusebius, *Praep. ev.* 13.12.9–11; Philo, *Opif.* 29–35).[21] Most instructive for our purposes is *Joseph and Aseneth* 8.9, which addresses God

> who gave life to all (things)
> and called (them) from the darkness to the light,
> and from the error to the truth,
> and from the death to the life.

This shows that to associate the contrast of light and darkness in the Genesis creation narrative with the contrasts of truth and error, life and death, as the Johannine prologue implicitly does, one did not need to be influenced by Qumran.[22]

2. The image of a great light shining in the darkness of the world in order to give light to people, which as we have seen is marginal in the Qumran texts but central and dominant in the Fourth Gospel's use of the light/darkness imagery, has several kinds of sources in the Hebrew Bible and parallels in Second Temple Jewish literature. We note first the image of a prophet or teacher as a light who by his teaching of truth gives light. For example, Samuel is described as a "light to the peoples" (*LAB* 51:6, echoing Isa. 51:4).[23] The *Aramaic Levi* text from Qumran (a pre-Qumran work, not to be attributed to the community itself)[24] depicts the teaching of the ideal priest of the future as as an eternal sun, which will shine to the ends of the earth, such that darkness will vanish from the earth (4Q541 9 1.3–5; cf. *T. Levi* 18.2–4). That John was aware of such usage is proved by his depiction of John the Baptist as "a burning and shining lamp" (5:35).[25]

3. Familiar in Jewish literature is the image of the Torah as a light that shines to give light in which people may walk. This has biblical sources (Ps. 119:105; Prov. 6:23; cf. Isa. 2:3, 5; 51:4). Two points are worth noticing about this image. First, it seems particularly prominent in Jewish literature contemporary with the Fourth Gospel (*LAB* 11.1; 19.4; 33.3; *4 Ezra* 14:20–21; *2 Bar.* 17:4; 18:2; 59:2).

John's interpretation of Gen. 1:3–5 are more impressive. Note that, unlike 1QS, John does not say that God created the darkness.

21. *Genesis Rabbah* 3.8 interprets the light and darkness of Gen. 1:3 as the deeds of the righteous and the deeds of the wicked. This later passage again shows how a Jewish exegete did not need to be influenced by Qumran in order to find good and evil symbolized by the light and darkness of the creation narrative.

22. Qumran is hardly likely to have influenced *Joseph and Aseneth*. Against alleged affinities between *Joseph and Aseneth* and the Essenes, see R. D. Chesnutt, *From Death to Life: Conversion in Joseph and Aseneth*, JSPSup 16 (Sheffield: Sheffield Academic Press, 1995), 186–95.

23. Cf. also Sir. 24:32; *2 Bar.* 18:2.

24. Cf. now R. A. Kugler, *From Patriarch to Priest: The Levi-Priestly Tradition from Aramaic Levi to Testament of Levi*, SBL Early Judaism and Its Literature 9 (Atlanta: Scholars Press, 1996).

25. The second half of this verse is strikingly similar to *2 Bar.* 18:2: "did not rejoice in the light of the lamp" (i.e., the lamp of the law, which Moses lighted).

Second Baruch, in the context of extensive use of light and darkness as symbols of good and evil, truth and error (53, 56–72), says that "the lamp of the eternal law which exists for ever and ever illuminated those who sat in darkness" (59:2), while *4 Ezra* says that without the law "the world lies in darkness, and its inhabitants are without light" (14:20). Second, when this image is used, the law is sometimes said to be a light for the world (Wis. 18:4; *LAB* 11.1; cf. Isa. 2:3, 5; 51:4). This language about the law is remarkably close to what the Fourth Gospel says about Jesus Christ as the light of the world, paralleling the central image in the Gospel's use of light/darkness imagery in a way that the Qumran texts so notably fail to do. It therefore seems likely that the Fourth Gospel deliberately claims for Jesus what the Jewish literature of its time claimed for the law. Just as Jesus is the true bread from heaven, by comparison with the bread Moses gave (6:32), and just as Jesus is the true vine, by comparison with Israel as the vine (15:1), so he is the true light (1:9), by comparison with the law given by Moses.

4. John's image of Christ as the light of the world is also, more directly, a form of messianic exegesis of prophecies in Isaiah. It reflects Isaiah 9:2[1] ("The people who walked in darkness have seen a great light; those who lived in a land of deep darkness—on them light has shined": cf. John 1:5; 8:12; 12:35), the references to the Servant of the Lord as "a light to the nations" (Isa. 42:6–7: "a light to the nations, to open the eyes that are blind, to bring out the prisoners from the dungeon, from the prison those who sit in darkness"; 49:6; cf. John 9), and the picture of the light that will rise over Zion, in the midst of the darkness that covers the earth, and attract the nations to its brightness (Isa. 60:1–3; Tob. 13:11).[26] These passages, which play no part in the light/darkness dualism of the Qumran texts, readily supply the central Johannine image of the great light shining in the darkness of the world to give light to people, as well as the christological-soteriological significance that this image bears in the Fourth Gospel.

5. In setting Jesus' declaration "I am the light of the world" (8:12) at the Feast of Tabernacles, John associates it with the light symbolism of the festival, just as Jesus' invitation to drink (7:37–39) relates to the water symbolism of the festival. The great lamps that blazed all through the night in the temple at Tabernacles (*m. Sukk.* 5:2–4) symbolized the perpetual light that God himself would be for his people in the eschatological age (Isa. 60:19–20; Zech. 14:7; cf. *1 Enoch* 58:6; Rev. 21:23–24).

In summary, the dominant picture of light and darkness in the Fourth Gospel results from a creative exegetical fusion of Jewish speculation about the primordial light of the first day of creation and messianic interpretation of the prophecies of eschatological light.[27] This understanding of the sources of the light/darkness

26. These passages are interpreted messianically and applied to Jesus in Luke 1:79; 2:32; Acts 26:23; Rev. 22:16; *Barn.* 14:6–8.

27. According to one rabbinic interpretation of Gen. 1:3, recorded in *Genesis Rabbah* 3.6, the light created on the first day is not the ordinary light of day but "has been stored away for the righteous in the

imagery in John accounts for its actual character and significance in a way that the hypothesis of influence from Qumran cannot do.

I have omitted the phrase "the spirit of truth" from this discussion of light and darkness dualism in Qumran and John because, whereas it occurs in the context of the light and darkness imagery in 1QS (3.19; 4.21, 23; cf. 4QCatenaᵃ [4Q177] 4.10), in the Johannine literature it does not. Its three occurrences, as another term for the Paraclete, in John 14–16 (14:17; 15:26; 16:13; cf. 1 John 4:6) relate rather to the courtroom language of witness and judgment (15:26–27; 16:8–11; cf. also 1 John 5:6–9), which is prominent in John but absent from 1QS 3–4. Nor is the context in John especially dualistic. The devil is mentioned (16:8), but in the political image of "the ruler of this world," not as an evil counterpart of the spirit of truth. Only in chapter 8 is he called "the father of lies" in whom there is "no truth" (8:44), but here the contrast is not with the spirit of truth but with Jesus as the one who speaks truth (8:45–46).

There is therefore little except the term "spirit of truth" itself to suggest a connection between its occurrences in 1QS and its occurrences in John. The coincidence of terminology is far less remarkable when we remember that genitival phrases connecting the term "spirit" with an abstract noun are common in the Old Testament, early Jewish literature, and the New Testament. Among the more common expressions are "spirit of power" (Isa. 11:2; Sir. 48:24; *LAB* 27.10; *1 Enoch* 49:3; 71:11; 2 Tim. 1:7) and "spirit of wisdom" (Deut. 34:9; Isa. 11:2; *1 Enoch* 49:3; 61:11; Wis. 7:7; Eph. 1:17). But there are many others (cf. Num. 5:14, 30; Isa. 28:6; Zech. 12:10; Sir. 39:6; 1 Pet. 4:14; Rom. 8:2, 15; 2 Cor. 4:13; Heb. 10:29; and the lists in Isa. 11:2; 1QSb 5.25; *1 Enoch* 49:2–3; 61:11; 1QS 4.3–4; 2 Tim. 1:7). Such expressions can be used of a human disposition, especially as God-given, and in Qumran usage they can designate angels (1QM 13.11–12; 1QH 11.22; 4QShirShabbᶠ [4Q404] 17.3), but they can also designate the Spirit of God with reference to a particular aspect or effect of the divine activity.

The phrase "spirit of truth" is therefore a natural formation within this general terminological phenomenon. In fact, it occurs twice in early Jewish literature outside the Qumran texts. In *Jubilees* 25.14, when Rebecca is about to give her blessing to Jacob, we are told that "a spirit of truth descended upon her mouth." In *Joseph and Aseneth* 19.11, Joseph kisses Aseneth three times, imparting to her first "a spirit of life," second "a spirit of wisdom," and third "a spirit of truth." The meaning is probably that he conveys to her the divine Spirit in three of its effects (cf. John 20:22).

The explanation of the coincidence of terminology between 1QS and John is therefore that "truth" is a key concept and term in both, and "spirit of truth" a natural formation in a Jewish context. We need no elaborate explanations of the way the term borrowed from Qumran usage could come to be used in a different

---

age to come" (with reference to Isa. 30:26). This shows another Jewish exegete connecting the primordial and eschatological light as John did.

way in John.[28] It is much easier to suppose that the term was formed independently in the two cases.

In conclusion, there is a curious irony to be observed. It was the publication of Qumran texts that effected a shift in Johannine scholarship toward recognizing the thoroughly Jewish character of Johannine theology. In retrospect this appears to have been a case of drawing the correct conclusion from the wrong evidence. There is no need to appeal to the Qumran texts in order to demonstrate the Jewishness of the Fourth Gospel's light/darkness imagery. This can be done more convincingly by comparison with other Jewish sources, which were already available long before the discovery of the Dead Sea Scrolls.

28. The proposals of H. D. Betz (*Der Paraklet* [Leiden: Brill, 1963]) and G. Johnston (*The Spirit/ Paraclete in the Gospel of John*, SNTSMS 12 [Cambridge: Cambridge University Press, 1970]) are summarized and critiqued in G. M. Burge, *The Anointed Community: The Holy Spirit in the Johannine Tradition* (Grand Rapids: Eerdmans, 1987), 16–23.

7

NICODEMUS
AND THE GURION FAMILY

I. Introduction

Most commentators on the reference to Nicodemus in John 3:1 draw attention to the rabbinic traditions about a wealthy Jerusalem aristocrat called Naqdimon (Nicodemus) ben Gurion, and quickly conclude either that there can be no connection between the two or that it is impossible to know whether there was.[1] But occasionally the two have been identified,[2] while the latest significant discussion, by J. A. T. Robinson, suggests that John's Nicodemus was the grandfather of the rabbis' Naqdimon.[3] A few scholars have also discussed occurrences in Josephus of the names Nicodemus and Gurion, borne by prominent Jerusalem citizens, and the possibility that some or all of these were members of the same family as

Originally published in a slightly different form in *JTS* 47 (1996): 1–37. Reprinted by permission of the publisher. The present version is revised in light of recently published material.

1. Besides the commentaries, see also H. L. Strack and P. Billerbeck, *Kommentar zum Neuen Testament aus Talmud und Midrasch* (Munich: Beck, 1922–1928), 2:412–17; S. Mendner, "Nikodemus," *JBL* 77 (1958): 294–96; J. Jeremias, *Jerusalem in the Time of Jesus*, trans. F. H. and C. H. Cave (London: SCM, 1969), 96 n. 27.

2. Most recently D. Flusser, *Jesus in Selbstzeugnissen und Bilddokumenten* (Hamburg: Rowohlt, 1968), 122; T. Rajak, *Josephus: The Historian and His Society* (London: Duckworth, 1983), 25.

3. J. A. T. Robinson, *The Priority of John*, ed. J. F. Coakley (London: SCM, 1985), 284–87.

Naqdimon ben Gurion.[4] Finally, commentators on John sometimes also refer to
the puzzling rabbinic tradition of the five disciples of Jesus, which seems, in a way
that has never been satisfactorily explained, to link the Johannine Nicodemus
and the rabbinic Naqdimon.[5] The latter was also known as Buni, and the five
disciples of Jesus include both Naqqai (which could be short for Nicodemus/
Naqdimon) and Buni.

These issues merit a much more thorough investigation. In the course of an
examination of all the relevant material in Josephus and rabbinic traditions—
important parts of which have not previously been noticed as relevant—we shall
show that there was in the first century CE a very prominent Jerusalem family in
which the names Gurion and Nicodemus were repeated as characteristic family
names. This argument will make a contribution to our knowledge of the ruling
elite in pre-70 Jerusalem, which is of interest and significance quite apart from
its relevance to the Fourth Gospel. We shall also argue that John's Nicodemus
must have belonged to this family, and, in the light of this, we shall offer a new
solution to the hitherto unsolved riddle of the five disciples of Jesus.

II. Naqdimon ben Gurion in Rabbinic Traditions

In this section we examine all the rabbinic traditions about Naqdimon ben
Gurion, with a view to determining what can be known about him with reasonable historical probability.

II.1. The Three Wealthy Men during the Siege of Jerusalem

There are four versions of this tradition.

II.1.1. The first version is in b. Git. 56a:

He [the emperor] sent against them Vespasian the Caesar who came and besieged
Jerusalem for three years. There were in it three men of great wealth, Naqdimon
ben Gurion, Ben Kalba Shevua', and Ben Ṣiṣit Hakkeset. . . .[6] One of these said
to the people of Jerusalem, I will keep them in wheat and barley. A second said, I
will keep them in wine, oil and salt. The third said, I will keep them in wood. The
Rabbis considered the offer of wood the most generous, since R. Ḥisda used to say,

4. A. Schlatter, *Der Evangelist Johannes*, 2nd ed. (Stuttgart: Calwer, 1948), 84; Flusser, *Jesus*,
120–22; Robinson, *Priority*, 284–85.

5. Besides the commentaries, note M. Hengel, *Die johanneische Frage* (Tübingen: Mohr Siebeck,
1993), 307 n. 144. For literature on the five disciples, see the references in J. Maier, *Jesus von Nazareth
in der talmudischen Überlieferung*, Erträge der Forschung 82 (Darmstadt: Wissenschaftliche Buchge-
sellschaft, 1978), 232–35.

6. The separate tradition explaining the names of the three, given below in section II.2, is inserted
here.

A storehouse of wheat requires sixty stores of wood [for fuel]. These men were in a position to keep the city for twenty-one years.[7]

This account occurs in a collection of traditions about the siege and destruction of Jerusalem, which have been arranged in a chronologically appropriate order, thus: (a) Bar Qamṣa causes the emperor's offering to be refused in the temple; (b) the emperor sends Nero against Jerusalem, but he becomes a proselyte; (c) the emperor sends Vespasian, who besieges Jerusalem for three years, and the three wealthy men offer to keep the city supplied with necessities; (d) the *baryônê*[8] burn the stores of wheat and barley, and famine ensues; (e) Martha the daughter of Boethius dies in the famine; (f) Yoḥanan ben Zakkai escapes from Jerusalem.

Our tradition, referring among other things to the stores of wheat and barley available in the city, is appropriately placed before the tradition that recounts how the *baryônê* burned the stores of wheat and barley. This does not mean, however, that these two traditions originally belonged together. They are distinct traditions that have been brought together in the collection.

There are clearly historical memories behind many of the traditions in this collection. Thus tradition (a) reflects the fact that the sacrifices offered on behalf of the emperor were rejected at the outbreak of the revolt (Josephus, *BJ* 2.409),[9] while tradition (d) corresponds to Josephus's account of the burning of the corn stores by the followers of John of Gischala and those of Simon bar Giora[10] during the faction fighting in Jerusalem (*BJ* 5.24; cf. also Tacitus, *Hist.* 5.12). But this cannot in itself guarantee the historical value of our tradition (c), as Robinson supposed.[11]

Our tradition is folkloric in form, but this need not negate a historical basis, which it most probably has. The three highly unusual names—attested also in other traditions[12]—were evidently remembered as those of the wealthiest members of the Jerusalem aristocracy at the time of the siege. The allocation of a different type of produce to each of the three is artificial, and is probably a secondary

---

7. Soncino translation. Transliteration of the names has been altered.

8. On this term, see M. Hengel, *The Zealots*, trans. D. Smith (Edinburgh: T. & T. Clark, 1989), 53–56.

9. Cf. Hengel, *Zealots*, 360–61.

10. Not by the Zealots, as is usually said (e.g., Robinson, *Priority*, 286; Hengel, *Zealots*, 367). In other versions of the same rabbinic tradition the action is attributed to the Zealots (*qannāʾîm*) or to the Sicarii (*sîqārîn*): see Hengel, *Zealots*, 50, 394.

11. Robinson, *Priority*, 286.

12. In addition to the rest of the traditions discussed in this section, which refer either to all three men or to Naqdimon alone, Ben Ṣiṣit Hakkeset and Ben Kalba Shevua' appear in the following rabbinic traditions: (1) R. Aqiva married the daughter of Ben Kalba Shevua' (b. Ned. 50a); (2) the "genealogical scroll found in Jerusalem" includes the house of Kalba Shevua' and the house of Ṣiṣit Hakkeset (*y. Ta 'an.* 4.2; *Gen. R.* 98.8; see Jeremias, *Jerusalem in the Time of Jesus*, 284–85). The peculiar names Ben Kalba Shevua' and Ben Ṣiṣit Hakkeset may be family nicknames, rather than true personal names. Cf. the "Goliath" family of Jericho: R. Hachlili, "The Goliath Family in Jericho: Funerary Inscriptions from a First Century CE Jewish Monumental Tomb," *BASOR* 235 (1979): 52.

development. The figure of twenty-one years probably originally meant that each of the three had sufficient produce to supply the city for seven years.[13] Thus it is a mistake to think of them as merchants dealing respectively in the type of supplies assigned to each by the tradition.[14] The wealthiest men in Jerusalem will not have been merchants, but owners of vast estates.[15]

II.1.2. A second version appears in *Lam. R.* 1.5.31:

> In Jerusalem there were four councillors, viz. Ben Ṣiṣit, Ben Gurion, Ben Naqdimon, Ben Kalba Shevua'. Each of them was capable of supplying food for the city for ten years.[16]

—and a third in *Eccles. R.* 7.12.1:

> Three councillors were in Jerusalem, viz. Ben Ṣiṣit Hakkeset, Naqdimon ben Gurion and Ben Kalba Shevua', each of whom was capable of supplying food for the city for ten years.[17]

Ecclesiastes Rabbah is probably dependent on *Lamentations Rabbah*,[18] but shows that the latter originally spoke of three councillors, not four. (The expansion to four results from standardizing the "Ben-" form.) The tradition again occurs in a collection of traditions about the siege and destruction of Jerusalem, but all except this one concern Yoḥanan ben Zakkai. Some of the stories about Yoḥanan ben Zakkai are divergent versions of ones in *b. Giṭ.* 56a. The compilation of traditions is certainly late,[19] but we cannot be sure whether the tradition about the three wealthy men is dependent on *b. Giṭ.* 56a or an independent version of the same tradition. Its less developed form, as well as the fact that the separate tradition about the origin of the names of the three, which has been inserted into the tradition in *b. Giṭ.* 56a, does not appear here, suggests the latter. It is therefore quite possible that the information that the three were "councillors" (בול וטס = βουλευτής) has historical value. It is in any case extremely probable that the three wealthiest citizens of Jerusalem would have been members of the council.

---

13. In this respect, the version in *Lam. R.* 5.1.31 ("Each of them was capable of supplying food for the city for ten years") may be more original.

14. Jeremias, *Jerusalem in the Time of Jesus*, 38–39, 95–96.

15. D. Fiensy, *The Social History of Palestine in the Herodian Period* (Lewiston/Queenston/Lampeter: Edwin Mellen, 1991), 49–55.

16. Soncino translation. Transliteration of the names has been altered.

17. Soncino translation. Transliteration of the names has been altered.

18. J. Neusner, *Development of a Legend: Studies on the Traditions concerning Yoḥanan ben Zakkai*, SPB 16 (Leiden: Brill, 1970), 175.

19. Neusner, *Development*, 165–66.

II.1.3. A fourth version, in *ARN* A6, is very probably dependent on *b. Giṭ.* 56a. The story has been elaborated and combined with the story of the burning of the stores. It has also been turned into a story about Ben Kalba Shevua' alone. This is because of the structure of the passage, which takes each of the three in turn, explains the origin of the name, and tells a story about him. *ARN* B13 has a much more summary form of the tradition in *ARN* A6.

II.2. The Explanations of the Names of the Three

II.2.1. An explanation of the names of the three councillors is given in *b. Giṭ.* 56a:

> Naqdimon ben Gurion was so called because the sun continued to shine [נקדה] for his sake. Ben Kalba Shevua' was so called because one would go into his house hungry as a dog [כלב] and come out full [שבע]. Ben Ṣiṣit Hakkeset was so called because his fringes [ציצית] used to trail on cushions [כסת]. Others say he derived the name from the fact that his seat [כסא] was among those of the nobility of Rome.[20]

II.2.2. Explanations of the three names also occur in *ARN* A6, where the explanation of Ben Ṣiṣit Hakkeset is different (connecting the name with כסף [silver], as well as apparently also with כסת [cushion], which suggests reclining): "Because he used to recline on a silver couch at the head of all the great ones of Israel."[21] *ARN* B13 explains only Ben Ṣiṣit Hakkeset,[22] in the same way as *ARN* A6.

The punning explanations of the names are probably not an original part of the tradition in section II.1 above. In *ARN* they are attached rather to the tradition discussed in section II.4 below. The explanations are, of course, examples of the folk etymologies common in rabbinic literature. In the case of Ben Kalba Shevua' and Ben Ṣiṣit Hakkeset, the explanations relate to what was certainly known about these persons: their enormous wealth.[23] In the case of Naqdimon, the explanation presupposes the story in section II.3, which is attached to it in *ARN* A6.

II.3. How Naqdimon Got His Name

The following story is found in *b. Taʿan.* 19b–20a:

20. Soncino translation. Transliteration of the names has been altered.

21. Translation from J. Goldin, *The Fathers according to Rabbi Nathan*, Yale Judaica Series 10 (New Haven/London: Yale University Press, 1955), 44.

22. Here the name is in the form Hakkesef, to conform to the explanation, though it may be the original text also in *b. Giṭ.* 56a and *ARN* A6: see A. J. Saldarini, *The Fathers according to Rabbi Nathan (Abot de Rabbi Nathan) Version B*, SJLA 11 (Leiden: Brill, 1975), 101 n. 20.

23. Perhaps the second explanation of the name Ben Ṣiṣit Hakkeset in *b. Giṭ.* 56a preserves a memory that the family moved to Rome after 70 CE.

Our Rabbis have taught: Once it happened when all Israel came up on pilgrimage to Jerusalem that there was no water available for drinking. Thereupon Naqdimon ben Gurion approached a certain [heathen] lord and said to him: Loan me twelve wells of water for the Pilgrims and I will repay you twelve wells of water; and if I do not, I will give you instead twelve talents of silver, and he fixed a time limit [for repayment]. When the time came [for repayment] and no rain had yet fallen the lord sent a message to him in the morning: Return to me either the water or the money that you owe me. Naqdimon replied: I have still time, the whole day is mine. At midday he [again] sent to him a message, Return to me either the water or the money that you owe me. Naqdimon replied: I have still time today. In the afternoon he [again] sent to him a message, Return to me either the water or the money that you owe me. Naqdimon replied: I have still time today. Thereupon the lord sneeringly said to him, Seeing that no rain has fallen throughout the whole year, will it then rain now? Thereupon he repaired in a happy mood to the baths. Meanwhile, whilst the lord had gone gleefully to the baths, Naqdimon entered the Temple depressed. He wrapped himself in his cloak and stood up to pray. He said, "Master of the universe! It is revealed and known before Thee that I have not done this for my honour nor for the honour of my father's house, but for Thine honour have I done this in order that water be available for the Pilgrims." Immediately the sky became covered with clouds and rain fell until the twelve wells were filled with water and there was much over. As the lord came out of the baths Naqdimon ben Gurion came out from the Temple and the two met, and Naqdimon said to the lord, Give me the money for the extra water that you have received. The latter replied, I know that the Holy One, blessed be He, disturbed the world but for your sake, yet my claim against you for the money still holds good, for the sun had already set and consequently the rain fell in my possession. Naqdimon thereupon again entered the Temple and wrapped himself in his cloak and stood up to pray and said, "Master of the universe! Make it known that Thou hast beloved ones in the world." Immediately the clouds dispersed and the sun broke through. Thereupon the lord said to him, Had not the sun broken through I would still have had a claim against you entitling me to exact my money from you. It has been taught: His name was not Naqdimon but Buni and he was called Naqdimon because the sun had broken through [נקדה][24] on his behalf.

The Rabbis have taught: For the sake of three the sun broke through [נקדה],[25] Moses, Joshua and Naqdimon ben Gurion. Now of Naqdimon we know from the above tradition. . . .[26]

There is a parallel in *ARN* A6, and the final baraita occurs also in *b. 'Abod. Zar.* 25a. Probably the story originated as an explanation of the name Naqdimon,[27] though it may reflect Naqdimon's reputation for wealth, piety, and charity, as well as the fact that he lived before the fall of Jerusalem.

24. So MS. M. The corrected reading נקדדרה supposes the verb to be קדר, but Jastrow (931) accepts נקדה as from the verb נקד (to sting, point, puncture).

25. Jastrow (931) corrects to עמדה (stood still), as in *b. 'Abod. Zar.* 25a.

26. Soncino translation. Transliteration of the names has been altered.

27. Robinson, *Priority*, 285–86, seems to accept it as historical.

The point of most interest is the baraita: "His name was not Naqdimon but Buni . . ." The story, of course, requires that Naqdimon was not given the name Naqdimon at birth but acquired it, and so that he already had another name. But this does not show that the name Buni was invented for the sake of the story. The parallel in *ARN* A6 tells the story quite adequately as an explanation of the name Naqdimon without reporting his previous name. The explanations of the names Ben Kalba Shevua' and Ben Ṣiṣit Hakkeset (*b. Giṭ.* 56a) also explain these names as acquired names, but no previous names are ascribed to these persons. It is therefore likely that the baraita preserves knowledge, originally independent of the explanation of the name Naqdimon, that Naqdimon was also called Buni.

This information is credible, because it would not be surprising for an aristocratic Palestinian Jew bearing a Greek name (נקדימון = Νικόδημος) also to have had a Hebrew name.[28] Greek (or Latin) names were sometimes chosen because they sounded similar to Hebrew names (Simon/Simeon, Jason/Joshua, Paul/Saul, Justus/Joseph, Rufus/Reuben)[29] or because they were translations of the Hebrew names (e.g., Theodotus, Dositheus, etc., for Nathan, Nathanael, Mattithiah, etc.; Justus for Zadok).[30] Although Nicodemus is not a translation of Buni, it may be that it was considered an appropriate Greek equivalent to Buni, for a reason we shall shortly see.

The name Buni (בוני) is found once in the Hebrew Bible (Neh. 11:15), but the text is probably corrupt.[31] Otherwise it is known only as the name of Naqdimon's father and as the name of one of Jesus' disciples in the rabbinic tradition of the five disciples of Jesus (see section V below). But it is probably an abbreviation of the name Benaiah (בניהו or בניה), a name which was certainly in use among Palestinian Jews in the first century CE.[32] We might have expected, by analogy with

28. Compare, e.g., the members of the Hasmonean dynasty: John Hyrcanus, Judah Aristobulus, Alexander Jannaeus, Salome Alexandra, Mattathias Antigonus. For some other examples, see G. R. H. Horsley, "Names, Double," *ABD* 4:1015.

29. Cf. G. Mussies, "Jewish Personal Names in Some Non-Literary Sources," in *Studies in Early Jewish Epigraphy*, ed. J. W. van Henten and P. W. van der Horst, AGAJU 21 (Leiden: Brill, 1994), 249, 273; N. G. Cohen, "Jewish Cultural Indicators in Antiquity," *JSJ* 7 (1976): 112–28.

30. Mussies, "Jewish Personal Names," 244–45; S. Klein, *Jüdisch-palästinisches Corpus Inscriptionum* (Vienna/Berlin: R. Löwit, 1920), 102; Hachlili, "The Goliath Family in Jericho," 49. See also Horsley, "Names, Double," 1016.

31. Cf. the parallel in 1 Chron. 9:14, and the much abbreviated LXX text, which lacks it.

32. It occurs on Masada ostracon §423 (Y. Yadin and J. Naveh, *The Aramaic and Hebrew Ostraca and Jar Inscriptions*, in *Masada I: The Yigael Yadin Excavations, 1963–1965: Final Reports* [Jerusalem: Israel Exploration Society/Hebrew University, 1989], 26) and on an ossuary (Tal Ilan, *Lexicon of Jewish Names from Late Antiquity*, part 1, *Palestine 330 BCE–200 CE*, TSAJ 91 [Tübingen: Mohr Siebeck, 2002], 81 [no.7]). It is also found in a writing exercise which lists names ending in יה: E. Puech, "Abécédaire et liste alphabétique de noms hébreux du début du IIe s. A.D.," *RB* 87 (1980): 118–19. (Fragments of the same list are found on Masada ostraca §608, §609, but not attesting attesting בניה.) The Aramaized form בניא occurs on an ostracon from Masada as the second name of a man called Simon (Ilan, *Lexicon*, 81, no. 11). Anyone with that most common of all first-century Palestinian Jewish names, Simon, needed a second name. In this case, בניא may mean that "builder" was his profession and therefore also nickname.

many similar names, the hypocoristic form of Benaiah to be Bannai (בנאי or בני).
In fact, this form seems to be found only as the name of a fifth-generation Tanna,
Rabbi Banna'ah (בנאה), Bannai (בנאי) or Bannayah (בנייה), which are probably
not forms of Benaiah, but the Hebrew and Aramaic words for "builder."[33] The fact
that Bannai means "builder" may have inhibited its use as a form of Benaiah. But
other hypocoristic forms of Benaiah are known. In the early post-exilic period,
when the name was very popular, perhaps because its meaning ("YHWH has
built") had an obvious appeal to the returning exiles, the two forms Bani (בני)
and Binnui (בנוי) were common.[34] We might be tempted to vocalize the former
as Bannai (בַּנַּי), but the Masoretic pointing (בָּנִי) is supported by the LXX of Ezra,
Nehemiah and 1 Esdras (usually Βανι, sometimes Βααυι). Many who bore this name
were Levites, but Bani was also one of the lay clans to which many of the returning
exiles belonged.[35] After the Persian period, the form Bani is much less common,[36]
while there may be just one known instance of Binnui in the first century CE. It
was probably the Hebrew name of Josephus' religious mentor Bannus (Βαννους,
Vita 11).[37] Perhaps Buni replaced Bani in common use, or perhaps Buni was an
unusual hypocoristic, distinctive of the family to which Naqdimon belonged.[38]

The name Benaiah was best known as that of a famous hero among David's
military commanders (2 Sam. 23:20–23; 1 Chron. 11:22–25; 27:5–6), who also
became, following his execution of Joab, Solomon's commander in chief (2 Kings
2:28–35; 4:4). Since Nicodemus, like Nicolaus, means "conqueror of the people,"

33. W. Bacher, *Die Agada der Tannaiten* (Strasbourg: Trübner, 1890–1903), 2:539 n.3.

34. Benaiah: Ezra 10:25, 30, 35, 43. Bani (בני): Ezra 2:10; 10:29, 34; Neh. 8:7; 9:4–5; 11:22; 10:14[13],
15[14]. (In addition, the name should be restored in Ezra 8:10, following 1 Esd 8:36. In Ezra 10:38, the
text is corrupt and Bani should not be read.) Binnui (בנוי): Ezra 8:33; 10:30, 38; Neh. 3:18 (cf. LXX),
24; 7:15; 10:10[9]; 12:8. Also the name Bunni (MT בֻּנִּי) is found in Neh. 9:4; 10:16[15], but in both
cases this vocalization is presumably used only because Bani (בָּנִי) also occurs in the same list of names.
Whether it is really a distinct form seems dubious. Variation between Bani and Binnui in parallel passages
(e.g., Ezra 2:10; 1 Esd. 5:12; Neh. 7:15) and in LXX and MT of the same passages may indicate that they
were treated as interchangeable forms, but they were easily confused by scribes and translators, who also
easily confused בְּנֵי with בְּנֵי ("sons of").

35. Ezra 2:10; 8:10; 10: 29, 34 (but one of these two occurrences in Ezra 10 must be corrupt); Neh.
10:15[14] (where the names are of clans, not individuals). Where Ezra 2:10 has Bani (so also 1 Esd. 5:12,
but LXX Βανουι = Binnui), the parallel in Neh. 7:15 has Binnui. But the occurrences of both Bani (10:29,
34) and Binnui (10:38) in the list of clans in Ezra 10 may suggest that there were in fact two clans: Bani
and Binnui. Possibly the family of Naqdimon ben Gurion was a prominent family in the Bani clan. (That
the clans of the early postexilic period survived into the late Second Temple period is probably shown
by *m. Ta'an.* 4:5, which is not dependent on Ezra-Nehemiah but seems to preserve a genuine tradition
from Second Temple times.)

36. The name Bani (בני) occurs on an ostracon from Masada and once in the Babatha archive (P Yadin
36) (Ilan, *Lexicon,* 81, nos. 8, 10). The name Βανέας in *Letter of Aristeas* 50 may represent Bani (בני)
rather than the Iranian name Vanya (cf. Ezra 10:36); cf. N. G. Cohen, "The Names of the Translators in
the Letter of Aristeas: A Study in the Dynamics of Cultural Transition," *JSJ* 15 (1984): 57–58.

37. Binnui (בנוי) is usually in LXX Βανουι, but 1 Esd. 9:34 has Βαννους.

38. We shall argue in section V below that the instance of Buni as the name of a disciple of Jesus is
to be explained from usage in the same family as Naqdimon's.

it could easily have been thought a suitable Greek equivalent to Benaiah. We shall return to the significance of these names below (section III). For the moment we conclude that it is historically credible that Naqdimon also bore the Hebrew name Benaiah/Buni.

II. 4. The Young Eliezer ben Hyrcanus Lectures the Three Great Men

A story of R. Eliezer's youth includes:

> After some days his father came up to disinherit him from his property, and he found him sitting and expounding a lesson with the great figures of the realm in session before him, namely, Ben Ṣiṣit Hakkeset, Naqdimon ben Gurion, and Ben Kalba Shevua'[39] (*Gen. R.* 42.1; cf. parallels in *ARN* A6; *ARN* B13; *PRE* 2; *Midrash Tanhuma* [Buber] Lekh Lekha 10).[40]

The inclusion of the three in this story might be dependent on *b. Git.* 56a, but the names occur in a different order and they are differently described, as "the great ones" of the land. So the tradition, while not as such historical, may preserve an independent memory of these three names as those of the most prominent aristocrats in Jerusalem before 70, the period of Eliezer's youth. The story presupposes that they are of Pharisaic allegiance, but cannot be treated as reliable evidence of this.

II.5. The Widow's Allowance of Naqdimon's Daughter

The story of Naqdimon's daughter's allowance is given in *b. Ket.* 66b:

> Rab Judah related in the name of Rab: It once happened that the daughter of Naqdimon ben Gurion was granted by the Sages an allowance of four hundred gold coins in respect of her perfume basket for that particular day, and she said to them, "May you grant such allowances to your own daughters!" and they answered after her: Amen.[41]

There are four parallels (*y. Ket.* 5.11; *t. Ket.* 5.9; *Lam. R.* 1.16.48; *Pesiqta Rabbati* 29/30; cf. also an allusion to the tradition in *ARN* A6), in three of which the daughter is called Miriam (*y. Ket.* 5.11;[42] *Lam. R.* 1.16.48; *Pesiqta Rabbati* 29/30), in three of which the allowance is 500 gold dinars (*y. Ket.* 5.11; *t. Ket.* 5.9;

---

39. Translation from J. Neusner, *Genesis Rabbah: A New American Translation*, Brown Judaic Studies 105 (Atlanta: Scholars Press, 1985), 2:99. Transliteration of the names has been altered.

40. The tradition in its various versions is discussed by Neusner, *Development*, 242–47; idem, *Eliezer ben Hyrcanus: The Tradition and the Man*, SJLA 3–4 (Leiden: Brill 1973), 445–46; Z. Kagan, "Divergent Tendencies and Their Literary Moulding in the Aggadah," *Scripta Hierosolymitana* 22 (1971): 151–70.

41. Soncino translation.

42. In *y. Ket.* 5.11, she is called Miriam the daughter of Simon ben Gorion.

Lam. R. 1.16.48),[43] three of which explain that she was a widow awaiting levirate marriage to her brother-in-law (*y. Ket.* 5.11; *t. Ket.* 5:9; *Pesiqta Rabbati* 29/30), and two of which cite the authority of R. Aḥa for the sages' final Amen (*y. Ket.* 5.11; *Lam. R.* 1.16.48). The allowance was made out of her husband's estate pending her remarriage. The considerable sum of money and her anger at being granted so little illustrate the fabulous wealth for which the family was remembered. The connection of this tradition with a story of Naqdimon's daughter reduced to poverty after the fall of Jerusalem (see section II.6 below), which follows it in all five versions but which also exists independently, is secondary.

In *y. Ket.* 5.11; *Lam. R.* 1.16.47–48, the tradition is preceded by a tradition that Martha the daughter of Boethus (another extremely wealthy woman who lived at the time of the fall of Jerusalem), when widowed, was granted an allowance of two *se'ah* of wine daily. The traditions must have been originally independent (and are collected as two examples of rich widows' allowances), but have been assimilated in *y. Ket.* 5:11, which adds that Martha cursed the sages in the same terms as Miriam used, and that, according to R. Aḥa, they responded, "Amen."

II.6. Naqdimon's Daughter Gathers Barley

The story exists in three main forms.

II.6.1. In the first, R. Yoḥanan ben Zakkai, on his way to Emmaus, sees a girl picking barley out of horse dung. On asking his disciples, he is told that the girl is Jewish and the horse belongs to an Arab. He realizes the full meaning of Song 1:8: "You were unwilling to be subject to God, behold now you are subjected to the most inferior of the nations, the Arabs" (*Mekilta R. Ishmael* Bahodesh 1).[44]

II.6.2. The second occurs in *b. Ket.* 67a:

It was taught: R. Eleazar the son of R. Zadok said, "May I [not] behold the consolation [of Zion] if I have not seen her [the daughter of Naqdimon ben Gurion] picking barley grains among the horses' hoofs at Acco. [On seeing her plight] I applied to her this Scriptural text [Song 1:8]."[45]

The same tradition appears in *b. Ket.* 66b; *t. Ket.* 5.10; *y. Ket.* 5.11;[46] *Lam. R.* 1.16.18. The distinctive version in *Pesiqta Rabbati* 29/30 (where the rabbi is

---

43. According to *Pesiqta Rabbati* 29/30, she was granted 25 *libra* of silver for cosmetics and two *se'ah* of wine: the latter is borrowed from the similar story of Martha the daughter of Boethus (*y. Ket.* 5.11). On the confusion between the two women in some rabbinic traditions, see Tal Ilan, *Mine and Yours Are Hers: Retrieving Women's History from Rabbinic Literature* (Leiden: Brill, 1997), 94–95.

44. Translation from Neusner, *Development*, 15–16.

45. Soncino translation.

46. In *y. Ket.* 5.11 this story is told of Martha the daughter of Boethus, and another story, also featuring R. Eleazar ben Zadok, but in which the woman is tied by her hair to the tail of a horse, is told

R. Zadok and he encounters both Naqdimon and his daughter in the marketplace) is closest to this form of the tradition.

II.6.3. R. Yoḥanan ben Zakkai sees a girl picking barley from under the feet of Arab cattle. When asked, she tells him she is the daughter of Naqdimon ben Gurion, and reminds him that he signed her marriage contract. Yoḥanan ben Zakkai remembers it and tells his disciples that it specified a million gold dinar. He reflects that when Israel does not obey the will of God, he subjects them to the meanest of nations and to their cattle (*b. Ket.* 66b; *ARN* A17; *Sifre Deut.* 305). Two of these texts say that Yoḥanan saw the girl in the marketplace (*ARN* A17; *Sifre Deut.* 305), the other that he was riding his ass. Two of them have Yoḥanan, when he hears who she is, cite a proverb to the effect that wealth is preserved when it is given away in charity (*b. Ket.* 66b; *ARN* A17). Two of them add to his statement about the marriage contract this further evidence of the family's great wealth before the fall of Jerusalem: "They did not go from their home to the Temple unless woolen carpets were laid for them to walk on" (*ARN* A17;[47] cf. *Sifre Deut.* 305), while in *b. Ket.* 66b this information forms part of a further tradition, which follows (see section II.7 below). Two of the texts (*ARN* A17; *Sifre Deut.* 305), like all other versions of the tradition, have Yoḥanan realize the meaning of Song 1:8.

It is impossible to reconstruct the tradition-history with confidence.[48] Perhaps the same story (a rabbi finds a Jewish girl picking barley from Arab horses' dung/hooves, and realizes the meaning of Song 1:8) was told both of Yoḥanan ben Zakkai with an anonymous Jewish girl (II.6.1), and of Eleazar ben Zadok with the daughter of Naqdimon (II.6.2). The latter story then influenced the former, so that Yoḥanan ben Zakkai's interlocutor was identified as the daughter of Naqdimon. Further details about the wealth of the family (which may have been known from other traditions) were then added to this form of the story (II.6.3).

It is therefore impossible to conclude with confidence that the tradition preserves a reliable historical memory to the effect that Naqdimon's family lost all its wealth in the fall of Jerusalem.[49] Knowledge that Naqdimon was fabulously wealthy and had a daughter (II.5) would be sufficient to make her a suitable figure for this story. Similarly, the implication that Naqdimon's family did not practice charity (II.6.3) is required in order to make the fate of his daughter a suitable illustration of the conclusion Yoḥanan draws: that Israel's humiliating condition is the result of her disobedience to God. It has no historical value. This tradition corroborates the fact that Naqdimon was remembered in rabbinic tradition as enormously wealthy, but adds nothing else of historical significance.

---

of Miriam the daughter of Simon ben Gorion. But *Lam. R.* 1.16.47–48 has these two traditions in the reverse order: the latter referred to Miriam the daughter of Naqdimon ben Gorion, the former to Martha the daughter of Boethus.

47. Translation from Goldin, *Fathers according to Rabbi Nathan*, 89.

48. Cf. the discussion in Neusner, *Development*, 235–38.

49. As Robinson does (*Priority*, 286).

II.7. Naqdimon's Charity

The following account of Naqdimon's charity is given in *b. Ket.* 66b–67a:

> Did not Naqdimon ben Gurion, however, practice charity? Surely it was taught:
> It was said of Naqdimon ben Gurion that, when he walked from his house to the
> house of study, woollen clothes were spread beneath his feet and the poor followed
> behind him and rolled them up! [i.e., taking them away]—If you wish I might
> reply: He did it for his own glorification. And if you prefer I might reply: He did
> not act as he should have done [i.e., he did not give in accordance with his means],
> as people say, "In accordance with the camel is the burden."[50]

Here the basic tradition (about the woollen clothes) concerns Naqdimon's charity
and is a variant of the tradition incorporated in section II.6.3, that uses similar
information merely to illustrate his wealth. The question and the suggested answers
arise from bringing this tradition into confrontation with the tradition that has
just been recounted (section II.6.3), in which Yoḥanan ben Zakkai's quotation
of a proverb implies that Naqdimon's daughter found herself destitute because
the family had not practiced charity. The present passage is simply an attempt to
reconcile these two apparently conflicting traditions by suggesting that Naqdimon's
charity was not sincere or was not sufficient.

Since the idea that Naqdimon did not practice charity originated purely from
the requirements of the story in section II.6.3, where it had no historical basis, the
present passage is not evidence that Naqdimon was remembered critically in rabbinic
tradition.[51] On the contrary, if the present passage has any historical contribution to
make, it is to confirm the previously cited evidence that Naqdimon was remembered
not only for his immense wealth[52] but for correspondingly generous charity. Doubts
about this were a secondary, quite artificial development in the tradition.

III. The Gurion Family in Josephus and Rabbinic Traditions

In this section we shall argue that several individuals named by Josephus and
rabbinic literature can be identified as members of the same, very wealthy, lay

---

50. Soncino translation.

51. Cf. Robinson, *Priority*, 286: "Nakdimon's obituary reads ambiguously" (referring to *b. Ket.*
66b–67a).

52. Two minor pieces of tradition are further evidence of this: *ARN* A6: "It is told of the daughter
of Naqdimon ben Gorion that her couch was overlaid with a spread worth twelve thousand golden denar,
that she would spend a Tyrian gold denar every single Sabbath eve for spice puddings, and that she was
awaiting a levirate marriage" (trans. Goldin, *Fathers according to Rabbi Nathan*, 44; with the last point
here, cf. section II.5 above, but the position of this collection of statements in the sequence of *ARN* A6
really requires a passage about the daughter of Ben Ṣiṣit Hakkeset); *ARN* B13: "It was told of Naqdimon
ben Gorion that he had in his house forty kors of gardens made of gold" (trans. Saldarini, *Fathers according
to Rabbi Nathan*, 101–2; for the meaning, see his n. 21).

Table 7.1. The Family of Josephus

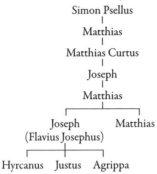

Simon Psellus
|
Matthias
|
Matthias Curtus
|
Joseph
|
Matthias
|
Joseph   Matthias
(Flavius Josephus)
|
Hyrcanus   Justus   Agrippa

aristocratic family as that of which Naqdimon ben Gurion was one of the best remembered members.

An important aid to this process of reconstructing the family is our knowledge of the way male names[53] were repeated across generations in upper-class Jewish families of this period. Fortunately, a number of genealogies of such families are known or can be reconstructed. Those given in the tables are of four Jerusalem priestly families (tables 7.1, 7.3, 7.5, 7.6), one family in Jericho which may well have been priestly (table 7.4), and one Jerusalem family that was among the foremost of the lay aristocracy in Jerusalem before 70 CE (table 7.2). The genealogy of Josephus,[54] stretching from the early second century BCE to the end of the first century CE, and the genealogy of the Gamaliel family, which can be

Table 7.2. The Gamaliel Family

Gamaliel I
|
Simeon
|
Gamaliel II
|
Simeon II
|
Judah ha-Nasi
|
Gamaliel III
|
Judah II

53. The evidence discussed in this section includes no female members of the Gorion family, and so the question whether female names were similarly repeated in a family is not important here. Women have therefore been omitted from the genealogies in tables 7.1–7.5. There does not seem to be any evidence of the naming of sons after maternal grandfathers or uncles, though we do not have enough evidence to know that this did not happen.

54. From Josephus, *Vita* 1–6. The accuracy of Josephus's account of his descent has been questioned, but there is no serious reason to doubt it, as Rajak, *Josephus*, 16–17, shows. If Josephus omitted a generation or two, as is not uncommon in genealogies, its value for our purposes would not be affected.

Table 7.3. The High Priestly Family of Annas

traced from the early first century CE[55] and became the most illustrious dynasty of Palestinian rabbis,[56] are rare examples of lines that can be traced over many generations. They show the way in which the same names were repeated across the generations. The other four genealogies cover only four generations each,[57] but include more collateral lines, and so enable us to see the pattern of repeated names among several members of the same and contiguous generations. The genealogies of the Goliath (table 7.4) and Kallon (table 7.5) families have been reconstructed from ossuary inscriptions by Hachlili and Smith[58] and by Klein,[59] respectively: the reconstructions are not certain at every point, but the evidence of repeated names is clear enough.

Table 7.4. The Goliath Family of Jericho

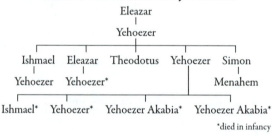

*died in infancy

55. Gamaliel I, "the elder," was the teacher of the apostle Paul (Acts 22:3) and a member of the Sanhedrin (Acts 5:34–39). His son Simeon was prominent among the lay aristocracy of Jerusalem during the Jewish War (Josephus, *BJ* 4.159; *Vita* 190–96, 216, 309). Both were Pharisees. Later rabbinic tradition made Gamaliel I the son of Simeon and the grandson of Hillel, but this is dubious.

56. From the time of Judah ha-Nasi, it is the line of the hereditary patriarchate, which continued until the fifth century. In table 7.2 the line is given only as far as the early third century.

57. The information from which table 7.3 was compiled can be found in E. Schürer, *The History of the Jewish People in the Age of Jesus Christ (175 B.C.–A.D. 135)*, revised by G. Vermes, F. Millar, and M. Black (Edinburgh: T. & T. Clark, 1979), 2:229–32. All the persons in the genealogy held office as high priest, except Sethi. The information in table 7.6 is from the inscription on the tomb of the Benê Hezîr in the Kidron Valley, as read by N. Avigad, *Ancient Monuments in the Kidron Valley* (Jerusalem: Bialik Institute, 1954), 60.

58. R. Hachlili and P. Smith, "The Genealogy of the Goliath Family," *BASOR* 235 (1979): 66–73. I have included, without distinction, the identifications they regard as "positive" and "probable," and omitted the part of the reconstruction they regard as only "possible."

59. Klein, *Jüdisch-palästinisches Corpus Inscriptionum*, 11. The ossuary inscriptions on which his reconstruction is based are *CIJ* nos. 1350–55.

Table 7.5. The Kallon Family

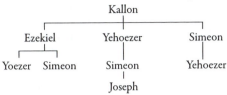

Sons were sometimes named after their fathers (examples in tables 7.1, 7.3, 7.4),[60] but this does not seem to have been especially common. Such evidence as there is suggests that when this practice was employed, it was not the eldest but a younger son who was named after his father.[61] The relative rarity of the practice is no doubt due to the potential confusion if a man and his son were both known as Jacob ben Jacob.[62] Naming sons after fathers sometimes, but not in every generation, would avoid such confusion. Apparently more common were the practices of naming a son after his grandfather (examples in tables 7.1, 7.2, 7.4, 7.6)[63] or his uncle (examples in tables 7.3, 7.4, 7.5, 7.6). These practices produce patterns of names in which, although the same names recur in a family, two individuals with the same name and the same patronymic are not very likely to be contemporaries. It may be that names were so chosen as to avoid this possibility. Thus although both Josephus and his grandfather were Joseph ben Matthias, we know that Josephus's grandfather was no longer alive when Josephus was born.[64]

Table 7.6. The Bene Hezir

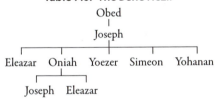

60. For some other evidence, see Hachlili, "Goliath Family in Jericho," 53, who gives four examples from Josephus, but notes that at the time of writing only one example from ossuary inscriptions was known, besides those of the Goliath family.

61. Jesus' brother Joseph/Joses was not the eldest son of his father Joseph (Matt. 13:55; Mark 6:3).

62. Other ways of avoiding confusion were to give an individual two names (Yehoezer Akabia in table 7.4) or to use different forms of the same name for father and son. See E. L. Sukenik, "A Jewish Hypogeum near Jerusalem," *Journal of the Palestine Oriental Society* 8 (1928): 121, for a family in which grandfather, father, and son are called Dositheus (Greek equivalent of Mattathias), Mattathias, and Mattathias. One of Jesus' brothers was known as Joses, the abbreviated form of Joseph, no doubt to distinguish him from his father (Mark 6:3).

63. Among other evidence for naming sons after grandfathers, see, e.g., N. Avigad, "The Burial-Vault of a Nazirite Family on Mount Scopus," *IEJ* 21 (1971): 198–99 (ossuary no. 16): אשוני (unknown name) son of Simeon son of אשוני.

64. If we accept the chronology in *Vita* 4–5, Josephus's grandfather Joseph was about seventy-five when his son Matthias was born, and Matthias was about thirty-two when his son Joseph (Josephus) was born.

The repetition of names within a family was a way in which, in an age without surnames, a distinguished family could sustain its distinctive identity. This would be especially the case if some of the names were unusual. Thus whereas Simeon was the commonest male name in this period, Gamaliel was very unusual. To be called Simeon ben Gamaliel would proclaim his membership of the well-known aristocratic family, as would not be the case were he called Simeon ben Judas. We shall argue that Naqdimon ben Gurion's name and patronymic were both unusual names, distinctive of and repeated in the prominent Jerusalem family to which he belonged.

Despite assertions made in some of the commentaries on John,[65] Nicodemus was a very unusual name among Jews. Besides Naqdimon ben Gurion, only three Palestinian Jews by the name of Nicodemus are known: two in Josephus (*BJ* 2.451; *Ant.* 14.37) and one in the Gospel of John. We shall argue below that all these belonged to the same family as Naqdimon ben Gurion. In the Diaspora, only two Jews bearing the name Nicodemus are known, one in Alexandria (first century BCE),[66] the other in Rome (fourth-fifth century CE?).[67] The abbreviated form Naqqai (נקי or נקאי), which could equally well be an abbreviation of Nicandrus, Nicanor, Nicharchus, Nicetas, Nicolaus, Nicomachus, Nicomedes or Nicostratus,[68] is found as the name of a disciple of Jesus in the rabbinic tradition

---

65. Rudolf Bultmann, *The Gospel of John: A Commentary*, trans. G. R. Beasley-Murray (Oxford: Blackwell, 1971), 133 n. 3 ("occurs frequently among Jews"); Raymond E. Brown, *The Gospel according to John (I–XII)*, AB29 (New York: Doubleday, 1966), 129 ("not unusual among Jews"); Craig S. Keener, *The Gospel of John: A Commentary* (Peabody, MA: Hendrickson, 2003) 1:535 ("not ... an unusual name among Greek-speaking Jews"). Outside the Gospel of John, and if my identification of Naqdimon ben Gurion with a Nicodemus in Josephus is not accepted, just *five* individuals bearing the name are known, two in the Diaspora (see next two notes) and three in Palestine (Naqdimon ben Gurion; Josephus *BJ* 2.451; *Ant.* 14.37). Five occurrences, when several thousands of named individual Jews in the period 300 BCE–400 CE are known in literature, documentary papyri, and inscriptions, hardly justify the judgment "not unusual." A more appropriate judgment would be "very unusual." Ilan, *Lexicon*, catalogues about three thousand named individuals. For Nicodemus, she lists only four instances (Naqdimon ben Gurion, John's Nicodemus, and Josephus *BJ* 2.451; *Ant.* 14.37) (298–99).

66. V. A. Tcherikover and A. Fuks, *Corpus Papyrorum Judaicorum [CPJ]* (Cambridge, MA: Harvard University Press, 1960–1964) 1:6 §142; 9 §143.

67. David Noy, *Jewish Inscriptions of Western Europe*, vol. 2, *The City of Rome* (Cambridge: Cambridge University Press, 1995), 440–41 §557 (= *CIJ* 1:295 §380).

68. Evidence of these names borne by Jews:

Νικάνδρος: Ilan, *Lexicon*, 297;

Νικάνωρ: Ilan, *Lexicon*, 297–8; Acts 6:5; *CIJ* 2 §1256; *CPJ* 1 §24; *CPJ* 3, Inscr. 1491; W. Horbury and D. Noy, *Jewish Inscriptions of Graeco-Roman Egypt* (Cambridge: Cambridge University Press, 1992) § 67, §153; Walter Ameling, ed., *Inscriptiones Judaicae Orientis*, vol. 2, *Klein Asien*, TSAJ 99 (Tübingen: Mohr Siebeck, 2004) §192; J. P. Kane, "The Ossuary Inscriptions of Jerusalem," *JSS* 23 (1978) 279–82;

Νίκαρχος: Ilan, *Lexicon*, 298;

Νικήτας: Ilan, *Lexicon*, 298; *CIJ* 2 §749; Ameling, ed., *Inscriptiones Judaicae Orientis*, vol. 2, §21;

Νικόλαυς: Ilan, *Lexicon*, 297; Acts 6:5; *CPJ* 3, Inscr. 1531, 1509; Horbury and Noy, *Jewish Inscriptions*, §32, §115; David Noy, Alexander Panayotov, and Hanswulf Bloedhorn, eds., *Inscriptiones Judaicae Orientis*, vol. 1, *Eastern Europe*, TSAJ 101 (Tübingen: Mohr Siebeck, 2004) §Ach12 (= *CIJ* §707);

Νικόμαχος: Ameling, ed., *Inscriptiones Judaicae Orientis*, vol. 2, §22; *y. Sanh.* 23d,58;

of the five disciples of Jesus (discussed in section V below), and also as the name of a scribe who lived in Magdala in the early second century CE, who appears in rabbinic traditions.[69] I know of no other literary or epigraphic evidence for the name Nicodemus among Palestinian Jews. The name Gurion (גוריון) or Guria (גוריה, גוריא) is attested only in Josephus and rabbinic literature, and all instances I know, except three rabbis of the name and the father of two rabbis who lived in the period from the second to the fourth centuries CE,[70] will be discussed in this section.

Nicodemus and Gurion were not common Palestinian Jewish names. If they are found among other members of the Jerusalem lay aristocracy, it is probable that they were characteristic of the family to which Naqdimon ben Gurion and others who bore these names belonged.

III.1. Gorion Son of Nicodemus (BJ 2.451)

In 66 CE, when the Jewish rebels, led by Eleazar the captain of the temple, had besieged the Roman garrison in Herod's palace and the commander of the garrison had offered to surrender, the besiegers sent three representatives of the people of Jerusalem to receive the surrender: Gorion son of Nicomedes (Γωρίονά τε Νικομήδους υἱόν), Ananias son of Zadok, and Judas son of Jonathan (Josephus, BJ 2.451). In place of Νικομήδους, the Latin has *Nicodemi*, which should probably be preferred.[71] Clearly these three are prominent citizens: "evidently the kind of rich Jews the Romans

---

Νικομήδης: *CPJ* 3, Inscr. 1497; Horbury and Noy, *Jewish Inscriptions*, §73;

Νικόστρατος: Noy, Panayotov, and Bloedhorn, eds., *Inscriptiones Judaicae Orientis*, vol. 1, §Mac12.

69. The texts are collected in F. Manns, "Magdala dans les sources littéraires," in *Studia Hierosolymitana*, vol. 1, *Studi archeologici*, B. Bagatti FS, SBF Collectio Maior 22 (Jerusalem: Franciscan Printing Press, 1976), 323–25. Ilan, *Lexicon*, 297, identifies, in the same texts, two such scribes called נקיר, but regards one as fictitious.

70. These are: (1) Abba Gurion (גוריון) of Sidon (*m. Qidd.* 4:14; *Lam. R.* Proem 9; and see Bacher, *Agada*, 1:90–91) (second century CE); (2) R. Gurion of Asporaq, an unidentified place in the eastern diaspora (*b. B. Qam.* 65b, 94a; *b. Tem.* 30b; see A. Oppenheimer, *Babylonia Judaica in the Talmudic Period*, Beihefte zum Tübinger Atlas des vorderen Orients B47 [Wiesbaden: L. Reichert, 1983], 467) (second century CE?) ; (3) R. Gurion, a Palestinian rabbi of the fourth century CE (*y. Mo'ed Qat.* 82d,54; *y. Pe'a* 17d,70; *Gen R.* 100.7 etc.); (4) Isi ben Guria (*b. Pes.* 113b; *b. Yoma* 52b) (2nd century CE?); (5) R. Hama ben Gurion (*y. Shabb.* 11d; *y. 'Abod. Zar.* 43d) or Guria (גוריא: *y. Meg.* 73b; *y. Yebam.* 6c; *Pesiqta de Rab Kahana* 28:3) (3rd century CE).

In addition, *m. Qidd.* 4:14, in the Babylonian text, refers to a rabbi Abba Guria: "Abba Gurion (גוריון) of Sidon says in the name of Abba Guria (גוריא)." But the text in the Palestinian Talmud, which has שאול for גוריא, referring to the third-generation Tanna Abba Saul, should be preferred (so Bacher, *Agada* 2:368 n.2). Finally, the name Giriya (גיריא) may be another variant: it is found in references to R. Yudan ben Giria (*y. Sheb.* 33d; *y. Ta'an.* 66d).

Guria (גוריא) is perhaps used as a female name in *b. 'Erub.* 63a (Munich MS): see Tal Ilan, *Mine and Yours*, 75–76; idem, *Lexicon*, 420.

71. The two names were easily confused in transcription. In *Ant.* 14.37, the textual situation is the reverse: Greek Νικόδημος, Latin *Nicomedes*. On the phenomenon of letter displacement in names, see Ilan, *Lexicon*, 30.

were accustomed to find co-operating with them in peaceful times."[72] Ananias son of Zadok was a Pharisee (*Vita* 197) and was later one of a group of four "distinguished" (ἐπιφανῶν) men (*BJ* 2.628) sent to Galilee to relieve Josephus of his command.[73] Since Josephus in the *Bellum* refrains from identifying as Pharisees the leading citizens during the revolt whom in the *Vita* he does identify as Pharisees,[74] it is likely that Gorion, mentioned only in the *Bellum*, was also, like Ananias, a Pharisee.

If Gorion son of Nicodemus was a prominent Jerusalem citizen in 66, he can hardly be unconnected with Nicodemus (Naqdimon) son of Gurion, one of the three wealthiest men in Jerusalem at the time of the Jewish War, according to rabbinic tradition. Three proposals for connecting the two have been made: (1) They are the same person, and Josephus has the name wrong.[75] In view of the phenomenon of repeated names in aristocratic families, this imputes error quite unnecessarily. (2) The Rabbis' Naqdimon ben Gurion was the son of Josephus's Gorion son of Nicodemus.[76] This is improbable because if the father of Naqdimon ben Gurion was still alive at the time remembered in the rabbinic traditions, Naqdimon himself would not yet have inherited the fortune and it is hard to see why he, not his father, would be remembered as one of the three wealthiest citizens. Gorion son of Nicodemus could have died soon after the event narrated by Josephus and his son could therefore have inherited the family estates by the time of the siege, but it is most likely that the strong impression left by Naqdimon ben Gurion on people's memories, reflected in the various rabbinic traditions, presupposes that he was one of the very wealthiest men in Jerusalem for some time, not merely during the siege. (3) Josephus's Gorion son of Nicodemus was the son of the rabbis' Naqdimon ben Gurion.[77] This seems the obvious solution. If Naqdimon ben Gurion was an elderly man in 66, he would be remembered as the head of the family and owner of its wealth, but his son could already be prominent in public affairs.

This would give three generations (Gorion—Nicodemus—Gorion), which conforms to the common pattern of a son bearing the same name as his grandfather. Because this was not the only way in which names were repeated in families, other

72. Martin Goodman, *The Ruling Class of Judaea: The Origins of the Jewish Revolt against Rome A.D. 66–70* (Cambridge: Cambridge University Press, 1987), 159.

73. According to *BJ* 2.628, Judas the son of Jonathan was also one of this group of four, but in *Vita* 197 his place is taken by Jonathan, a Pharisee. The latter cannot be a textual error, since Jonathan is then repeatedly mentioned. There may be a textual error in *BJ* 2.628, influenced by 2.451. On the problem, see Goodman, *Ruling Class of Judaea*, 185 n. 7; Tal Ilan and Jonathan J. Price, "Seven Onomastic Problems in Josephus' *Bellum Judaicum*," *JQR* 84 (1993): 189–208, here 192–94.

74. S. Schwartz, *Josephus and Judean Politics*, Columbia Studies in the Classical Tradition 18 (Leiden: Brill, 1990), 172 n. 6.

75. Hengel, *Zealots*, 367. Hengel claims: "Changes of this kind often appear in Josephus' work; see, for example, *Bell* 2,563 and 4,159" (367 n. 267). But these last two references are, as we shall see, references to two different members of the Gorion family: Joseph son of Gorion and Gorion son of Joseph. Josephus does sometimes confuse names, but he knew the Jerusalem aristocracy well.

76. Robinson, *Priority*, 287.

77. Schlatter, *Der Evangelist Johannes*, 84; Flusser, *Jesus*, 120.

relationships between Naqdimon ben Gurion and Gorion son of Nicodemus are conceivable, but this one seems the most plausible as a working hypothesis.

III.2. Joseph Son of Gorion (BJ 2.563) and Gorion Son of Joseph (BJ 4.159, 358)

In late 66, Joseph son of Gorion[78] and the ex-high priest Ananus (II) were elected by the assembly of the people to supreme military command in Jerusalem with the task especially of improving the city's defenses (Josephus, *BJ* 2.563). Since we shall later have reason to wonder whether the Gurion family was a family with a military tradition, it is worth noting Goodman's conjecture that, because Ananus is unlikely to have had military experience, Joseph "was retained primarily as a general because of his military expertise."[79] In any case, he was clearly a leading citizen. Like Ananus, he is more likely to have been a senior person than a young man, and so the Gorion son of Joseph who appears in *Bellum judaicum* 4.159 is more likely his son than his father.

In December 67, this Gorion, along with the leading Pharisaic aristocrat Simon son of Gamaliel, in alliance with the chief priests Jesus son of Gamalas and Ananus II, tried to organize popular opposition to the Zealots by public addresses in the assembly and private visits to individuals. This grouping of leading citizens probably indicates that Gorion, like Simon, was a Pharisee:[80] the alliance would be between leading Pharisaic lay aristocrats and leading members of the priestly aristocracy. This Gorion is no doubt the Gurion (Γουρίων)[81] who in 68 was put to death by the Zealots (*BJ* 4.358). He was important enough to be one of the two instances Josephus gives of the many members of the nobility put to death by the Zealots at this time. He calls him "a person of exalted rank and birth, but also a democrat"; that is, like other members of the elite who were politically active during the war, he claimed to represent the will of the people and depended on their support in the assembly.

These two men therefore provide another chain of three generations: Gorion—Joseph—Gorion. The three generations are contemporary with those we deduced above: Gorion—Nicodemus—Gorion. The repetition of the name Gorion in both

78. The medieval Hebrew adaptation of Josephus *(Josippon)* is attributed to Joseph ben Gorion, because the author thought this Joseph was Josephus himself. He did not know the parts of Josephus's works in which he refers to his father Matthias, but used the Latin Josephus (Hegesippus), which refers to "Josephus Gorione genitus" (3.3.2 = *BJ* 2.563). The modern Israeli politician David ben Gurion took his name from the title of *Josippon*. See D. Flusser, "Der lateinische Josephus und der hebräische Josippon," in *Josephus-Studien*, ed. O. Betz, K. Haacker, and M. Hengel, O. Michel FS (Göttingen: Vandenhoeck & Ruprecht, 1974), 131–32.

79. Goodman, *Ruling Class of Judaea*, 164 n. 11.

80. Josephus's failure to say so is in accordance with his policy in the *Bellum*, as already noted above in section III.1. Ilan and Price, "Seven Onomastic Problems," 202, are uncertain: "Gorion may or may not have had a factional link to Simon ben Gamaliel."

81. The forms of the name in Josephus are: Γωριονα or Γωριωνα (*BJ* 2.451); Γωριονος or Γωριωνος (*BJ* 2.563); Γωριων (*BJ* 4.159); Γουριων (*BJ* 4.358).

cases, among members of the wealthy lay aristocracy of Jerusalem (not a very large group), indicates that this is one family.[82] Very plausibly the elder Gorion in each case is the same person, and Nicodemus and Joseph were brothers.

III.3. Nicodemus (Ant. 14.37)

In 64 BCE Aristobulus II sent (from Jerusalem) an envoy called Nicodemus[83] to Pompey (Josephus, *Ant.* 14.37). Such a person must have been a leading citizen, who took the side of Aristobulus against Hyrcanus II. He may well have been an ancestor of Naqdimon ben Gurion.[84]

III.4. Guria's House in Jericho

A tradition preserved in *t. Sotah* 13.3:

> The story is told that sages entered the house of Gurio [*v.l.* the upper room of Ben Gurio] in Jericho and heard an echo saying, "There is here a man who is worthy of the Holy Spirit, but his generation is not sufficiently righteous," and they set their eyes on Hillel the Elder. And when he died, they said concerning him, "Oh the modest [man], the pious [man], disciple of Ezra."[85]

The same tradition appears in *y. Sotah* 9.13; *b. Sotah* 48b; *b. Sanh.* 11a; *y. 'Abod. Zar.* 3.1; *y. Hor.* 3.5. The last four of these texts specify that the sages were reclining in the upper room of the house.

The name of the owner of the house varies as follows: גוריי (*t. Sotah* 13.3), גוריה (*b. Sanh.* 11a), גוריא (*b. Sotah* 48b), גדייא (*y. 'Abod. Zar.* 3.1; *y. Hor.* 3.5), גדיא (*y. Sotah* 9.13). The forms with ד no doubt result from transcriptional error.[86] The original form of the name in this tradition may be גוריא, which in Aramaic (like גור in Hebrew and Aramaic) means "young animal," especially "lion's whelp." גור or גוריא is presumably also the source of the name Gurion (גוריון), which conforms to a standard form of name ending in ון (cf. עבדון, אבטליון, נקדימון, גדעון, שמעון, קלון, cf. Greek names ending -ων).[87] Guria and Gurion are therefore variants of the same name.[88] It is possible that the odd form גוריי (*t. Sotah* 13.3) indicates that גורין was the original form in the tradition.

---

82. This is recognized by Flusser, *Jesus*, 120, 122.

83. The Latin text here has *Nicomedes*.

84. So Schlatter, *Der Evangelist Johannes*, 84.

85. Translation from Jacob Neusner, *The Rabbinic Traditions about the Pharisees before 70* (Leiden: Brill, 1971), 1:237–38. Neusner's transliteration "Guryo" has been changed to "Gurio."

86. גדיא, though found elsewhere as a name (see Jastrow, s.v.), is perhaps always a corruption of גוריא. Ilan, *Lexicon*, 366, thinks that גריא is the original form (cf. Γαδία in Josephus, *Ant.* 15.252)

87. Cf. Ilan, *Lexicon*, 27.

88. Thus the name of the father of the third-century Rabbi Ḥama occurs both as Gurion (גוריון: *y. Shabb.* 11d; *y. 'Abod. Zar.* 43d) and as Guria (גוריא: *y. Meg.* 73b; *y. Yebam.* 6c).

The tradition seems to go back at least to the first half of the second century.[89] The story as such is hardly likely to be historical, but the reference to Guria's house in Jericho is inexplicable except as a historical memory. In other words, it was well known that in the time of Hillel the Pharisees used to meet in Guria's house in Jericho. To host such gatherings a large house would be required. Guria could well have been a Jerusalem aristocrat wealthy enough to have (as Herod did) a winter residence in the warmer climate of Jericho.

Although we have so far found no evidence that proves conclusively that the Gurion family were of Pharisaic allegiance, we have found strong indications that they may well have been. Naqdimon ben Gurion was well remembered in rabbinic circles as not only wealthy but also pious. Gorion son of Nicodemus appears in Josephus in company with the Pharisee Ananias son of Zadok (*BJ* 2.451), and Gorion son of Joseph is closely associated with the leading Pharisee Simeon son of Gamaliel (*BJ* 4.159). At least this evidence is consistent with the possibility that Guria the patron of the Pharisees in the time of Hillel was a member of the same family.

As a contemporary of Hillel, Guria would belong to the same generation of the family as Gurion the father of Nicodemus and Joseph. He may well be the same person.

II.5. Hananiah ben Hezekiah ben Gurion

III.5.1. Here is a tradition preserved in *m. Shabb.* 1:4:

> These are among the rulings which the Sages enjoined while in the upper room of Hananiah [חנניה, *v.l.* חנינא] ben Hezekiah ben Gurion [גוריון, *v.l.* גרון]. When they went up to visit him they voted, and they of the School of Shammai outnumbered them of the School of Hillel; and eighteen things did they decree on that day.[90] (cf. *t. Shabb.* 1.17–19)

This event seems to have taken place around the time of the outbreak of the revolt in 66, when, in a growing climate of anti-Roman feeling, eighteen decrees aimed at rigorously separating Jews from Gentiles and at purifying the land of idolatry were passed on the initiative of the house of Shammai.[91] For our purposes, what matters is that the place of this famous occasion was remembered. Neusner finds the correspondence with the tradition cited above (section III.4: upper room,

89. See Neusner, *Rabbinic Traditions*, 1:238–40.

90. Translation from Danby.

91. See A. Guttmann, *Rabbinic Judaism in the Making* (Detroit: Wayne State University Press, 1970), 102–4; Hengel, *Zealots*, 200–206; Goodman, *Ruling Class of Judaea*, 107–8; A. Kasher, *Jews and Hellenistic Cities in Eretz-Israel*, TSAJ 21 (Tübingen: Mohr Siebeck, 1990), 266–67. Neusner, *Rabbinic Traditions*, 2:121–23, is far too skeptical about the historicity of this tradition. It was evidently a famous occasion, well remembered, even if tradition did not accurately transmit what the eighteen decrees were.

Gurio/Gurion or his grandson) suspicious,[92] but this is to think in purely literary, rather than historical terms. The large upper room of a wealthy person's house, available for entertaining a large number of guests, is precisely where a large gathering of this kind would have to meet (cf. Mark 1:15; Luke 22:12; Acts 1:13).[93] Hananiah ben Hezekiah ben Gurion is called by his papponymic as well as his patronymic—a relatively rare practice—because it is the name Gurion that reveals his membership of an illustrious Jerusalem family. Probably it was his grandfather who had played host to gatherings of Pharisees in the time of Hillel.

III.5.2. According to the following traditions, Hananiah was more than a rich patron of the Pharisees. He was himself a learned Pharisaic scholar.

> Our rabbis taught, Who wrote *Megillat Ta'anit?* They said, Hananiah ben Hezekiah and his companions, who cherished their troubles. . . ."
> Rav Judah in Rav's name said: "Verily that man, Hananiah ben Hezekiah is his name, is to be remembered for blessing, for, but for him, the book of Ezekiel would have been hidden, for its words contradicted the Torah. What did he do? Three hundred barrels of oil were taken up to him, and he sat in an upper chamber[94] and reconciled them." (*b. Shabb.* 13b; the second paragraph also appears in *b. Menah.* 45a; *b. Hag.* 13a).

> Our rabbis taught: There was once a child who was reading at his teacher's house the book of Ezekiel, and he apprehended what *Hashmal* was, whereupon a fire went forth from *Hashmal* and consumed him. So they sought to suppress the book of Ezekiel, but Hananiah ben Hezekiah said to them, "If he was a sage, all are sages."[95] (*b. Hag.* 13a)

Megillat Ta'anit (the Scroll of Fasts)[96] is a list of the days on which fasting is forbidden, because of the joyful events (especially the Maccabaean victories) commemorated on them. The compilation of the list has been plausibly assigned to the

92. Neusner, *Rabbinic Traditions*, 2:122–23.
93. Cf. also *Sifre Num.* 115: "Once the elders of the School of Shammai and the elders of the School of Hillel went into the upper chamber of Jonathan ben Bathyra" (parallel in *b. Menah.* 41b). The Bathyra family was a priestly aristocratic Jerusalem family—again precisely the kind of family who would have a large upper room available for entertaining this number of guests. For later meetings of rabbis in upper rooms of houses in Lydda, see *y. Pes.* 30b, 41; *y. Sanh.* 21b, 9; *b. Sanh.* 74a.
94. Here the upper room is not the kind of large upper room used for large gatherings to which the tradition in section III.5.1 refers, but the small room on the roof of an ordinary house, which, secluded from the rest of the house, was suitable for study or prayer (*b. Ber.* 34b).
95. Translations from Neusner, *Rabbinic Traditions*, 1:416.
96. Edition (with the later scholion) in H. Lichtenstein, "Die Fastenrolle: Eine Untersuchung zur jüdische-hellenistischen Geschichte," *HUCA* 8–9 (1931–1932): 257–351; note the strictures on this edition in S. Z. Leiman, "The Scroll of Fasts: The Ninth of Tebeth," *JQR* 74 (1983): 174 n. 2. (Leiman's article is about not this Aramaic *Megillat Ta'anit*, but the quite different Hebrew *Megillat Ta'anit*.)

beginning of the revolt, its purpose being to inspire those fighting the Romans.[97] Its ascription to a group around Hananiah ben Hezekiah ben Gurion is therefore plausible, and would suggest that he himself favored the (Shammaite) majority who voted for the eighteen decrees at the gathering in his house. But the scholion to the work ascribes it to the colleagues of "Rabbi Eliezer ben Hanina ben Hezekiah, a man of Guron (איש גורון)."[98] The last phrase is interesting, in that it treats Gurion as the name of the family rather than the father of Hezekiah (see also section III.6 below). Whether Hananiah or his son is correctly associated with the Scroll, it is impossible to be sure. Perhaps in the talmudic tradition Eliezer (or Eleazar, see section III.5.3 below) ben Hananiah became his better-known father.

III.5.3. The son appears, as Eleazar ben Hananiah ben Hezekiah ben Garon, in one other tradition (*Sifre Deut.* 294; *Mek. Bahodesh* 7:66) in which a saying about the Sabbath, elsewhere ascribed to Shammai (*b. Besah* 16a), is attributed to him.[99] If this has any historical value, it confirms (this branch of) the family's allegiance to the school of Shammai.

III.6. The Household of Gurion in Rumah

The following story of the household of Gurion is given in *t. 'Erub.* 3.17:

> Said R. Judah, "The story is told that in the household (בית) of Mammal and in the household (בית) of Gurion in Rumah (רומא), they would hand out dried figs to the poor in time of famine. And the poor people of Shiḥin went out and made an *'erub* with their feet, so that they could go into the other town and eat the figs once it got dark."[100]

---

97. Lichtenstein, "Die Fastenrolle," 257–58; S. Zeitlin, "Megillat Taanit as a Source for Jewish Chronology and History in the Hellenistic and Roman Periods," *JQR* 9 (1918–1919): 73; W. R. Farmer, *Maccabees, Zealots and Josephus* (New York: Columbia University Press, 1956), 157–58; Hengel, *Zealots*, 19; Kasher, *Jews and Hellenistic Cities*, 267–68.

98. Lichtenstein, "Die Fastenrolle," 351.

99. See Neusner, *Rabbinic Traditions*, 1:416–17; Bacher, *Agada*, 1:19 n. 5; E. E. Urbach, *The Sages: Their Concepts and Beliefs*, trans. I. Abrahams (Jerusalem: Magnes, 1979), 959 n. 27. Urbach, *Sages*, 595–96, following H. Graetz, identifies him with Eleazar the captain of the temple, son of the high priest Ananias, who initiated the revolt by stopping the sacrifices for the emperor (*BJ* 2.409–10, 424, 443, 445, 450, 453; *Ant.* 20.121), but this is impossible, if only because the father of this Ananias was Nedebaius, not Hezekiah. Cf. Hengel, *Zealots*, 359–60. Urbach further takes our Eleazar to be Eleazar son of the high priest Neus (*BJ* 2.566). The emendation of Νέου to Ἀνανίου in this passage is plausible, but the most likely identification is then with Eleazar son of Ananias son of Nedebaius.

100. Translation from J. Neusner, *The Tosefta: Second Division: Moed* (New York: Ktav, 1981), 85. Transliteration of the names has been altered. Neusner incomprehensibly renders רומא as "Rome," which is its usual meaning, but is impossible here, because of the relationship with Shiḥin. Cf. parallel in *y. 'Erub.* 22a, which has: "the family of the household of Gurion (בית משפחת גוריון)". The phrase "family of the household" is biblical; cf. Judg. 9:1; 2 Sam. 16:5.

The point is that the people of Shiḥin, by making an *'erub*, were able to walk to the neighboring town of Rumah on the evening of the Sabbath. Rumah must have been more than 2000 cubits, the Sabbath limit, but no more than 4000 cubits (less than 4 kilometers) from Shiḥin. Since Shiḥin (שׁיחין = Ἄσωχις in Josephus, *BJ* 1.86; *Ant.* 13.337; *Vita* 207, 233, 384)[101] was north of Sepphoris, in the Bet Netofa valley between Jotapata and Sepphoris, רומא must be the Galilean village of that name (2 Kings 23:36: רומה; Josephus, *BJ* 3.233: Ῥοῦμα), probably modern Khirbet er-Rumeh,[102] about 3 kilometers north of Sepphoris.

This tradition is clear evidence that there were not only individuals called Gurion, but a family named after its prominent ancestor Gurion (who *may* be the Guria of section III.4 and the father of Nicodemus and Joseph, though it is also quite possible that he was an earlier ancestor). The period remembered in the tradition is likely to be after 70 CE. Presumably the Gurion family were among those Jerusalem aristocratic families who moved to Galilee after the fall of Jerusalem.[103] They owned an estate in the area of Rumah and presumably lived in Sepphoris. But it is not unlikely that the estate at Rumah already belonged to the family in the pre-70 period.[104] To be one of the richest Jerusalem families they must have owned very extensive estates, and it was not unknown for landowners to live in Jerusalem and own estates in very distant parts of the country.[105]

III.7. Conclusions

Table 7.7 offers a plausible reconstruction of the genealogy of the Gurion family. It is a reconstruction that takes account of all the evidence. All known Palestinian Jews called Gurion or Nicodemus (except the Nicodemus of the Fourth Gospel), who lived before 100 CE, are included.[106] The identifications proposed involve no chronological or other problems. But, of course, other reconstructions are possible. In particular, the four Gurions who have been identified (the father of Naqdimon/Nicodemus, the father of Hezekiah [section III.5.1 above], the father of Joseph [III.2], and Guria the patron of the Pharisees in Hillel's time

101. M. Avi-Yonah, *Gazetteer of Roman Palestine*, Qedem 5 (Jerusalem: Institute of Archaeology, Hebrew University/CARTA, 1976), 33.

102. Avi-Yonah, *Gazetteer*, 91.

103. Cf. S. Freyne, *Galilee from Alexander to Hadrian* (Wilmington, DE: Glazier, 1980), 127. For the possibilities of the landed aristocracy who had been involved in the revolt retaining or recovering their property after 70, see Josephus, *BJ* 6.113–16; and Schwartz, *Josephus and Judaean Politics*, 77–82.

104. So Z. Safrai, *The Economy of Roman Palestine* (London: Routledge, 1994), 379. Since Rumah is in the vicinity of Nazareth and Cana, it is tempting—but futile—to speculate that the Nicodemus of the Fourth Gospel (who, we shall argue, belonged to the Gurion family) may have encountered or heard of Jesus in Galilee as well as in Jerusalem.

105. Cf. Freyne, *Galilee*, 165; Fiensy, *The Social History of Palestine*, 52, 54–55; Safrai, *Economy of Roman Palestine*, 379.

106. It is quite possible that later rabbis called Gurion were also descendants of the same family, but this can be only a guess.

Table 7.7. The Gurion Family: A Possible Reconstruction

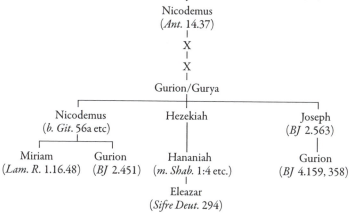

Nicodemus
(*Ant.* 14.37)
|
X
|
X
|
Gurion/Gurya

Nicodemus (*b. Git.* 56a etc)	Hezekiah	Joseph (*BJ* 2.563)

Miriam (*Lam. R.* 1.16.48)	Gurion (*BJ* 2.451)	Hananiah (*m. Shab.* 1:4 etc.)	Gurion (*BJ* 4.159, 358)

Eleazar
(*Sifre Deut.* 294)

[III.4]) may not have been one man, but two or more contemporary members of the same family, related as cousins or as uncle(s) and nephew(s). In that case, the name Gurion would go back further into the family history, whereas if the reconstruction is correct, this Gurion may have been the first of the name. But the real value of the reconstruction is to demonstrate that the data can easily be interpreted as referring to a single, very wealthy, very prominent Jerusalem family of Pharisaic allegiance.

Finally we return to the significance of the characteristic family name Gurion. We have already observed (II.3) that the name Nicodemus ("conqueror of the people") may have been used as equivalent to Buni/Benaiah because its military meaning could relate to the reputation of Benaiah as the great military commander of the time of David and Solomon. Gurion may also have been chosen for its military significance. The word גור, from which it most probably derives, usually in the Hebrew Bible means "lion's cub."[107] From its use in Genesis 49:9, it—and the lion image in general—came to be associated with the royal house of Judah (in Ezek. 19:2, 3, 5, it refers to the royal princes) and the hope of the Messiah of David (cf. 1QSb 5.29; 4 Ezra 12:31–33). But it was also an image of military prowess and victory:[108] the lion's whelp devours its prey (Gen. 49:9; Ezek. 19:3, 6–7). In this sense the image is used in the song of praise for Judas Maccabeus's military victories:

107. Six times (Gen. 49:9; Deut. 33:22; Ezek. 19:2, 3, 5; Nah. 2:12); once of the young of the jackal (Lam. 4:3). Cf. also גור (Jer. 51:38; Nah. 2:13).

108. In fact, this was the main point when the lion image was used of the Davidic Messiah: see R. Bauckham, *The Climax of Prophecy: Studies on the Book of Revelation* (Edinburgh: T. & T. Clark, 1993), 181–82. For the lion as a symbol of victory in the ancient Mediterranean world, see also D. Frankfurter, *Elijah in Upper Egypt: The Apocalypse of Elijah and Early Egyptian Christianity* (Minneapolis: Fortress, 1993), 212–13.

He was like a lion in his deeds,
like a lion's cub (σκύμνος) roaring for the prey. (1 Macc. 3:4)

(In the LXX, σκύμνος translates both גוּר and the synonymous גּוּר at every occurrence of these words.)

The family's unusual and distinctive names are those appropriate to military
heroes. So it may be that the first Gurion or the first Benaiah/Buni/Nicodemus
was a successful general in the Hasmonean period, won the name in the first
place as a laudatory nickname, and received landed estates as reward for his distinguished service.

IV. Nicodemus in the Fourth Gospel

Only now that we have assessed all the evidence for the Gurion family outside
the New Testament are we in a position to answer the question of the relationship
of the Fourth Gospel's Nicodemus to it. We have already established that the name
Nicodemus is sufficiently rare among Palestinian Jews of the period for this to be
a very appropriate question to ask. We shall proceed by noticing the main features
of the portrayal of Nicodemus in the Fourth Gospel and the extent to which they
correlate with reliable information about the Gurion family.

1. The Nicodemus of the Fourth Gospel belongs to the Jewish ruling elite,
whom John calls οἱ ἄρχοντες (3:1; 7:26, 48; 12:42). He probably uses this term
in the same way as Josephus, who distinguishes them from the council (βουλή:
Ant. 20.11; βουλευταί: *BJ* 2.405), though probably they were also included in
the latter. They comprise[109] both the chief priests and the leading citizens whom
Josephus usually calls "the powerful men" (οἱ δυνατοί: *BJ* 2.199, 274, 287, 301,
316, 336, 411, 428) or "the distinguished men" (οἱ γνώριμοι: *BJ* 2.240, 243, 318,
322, 410, cf. 301). How formally constituted a group they were, we do not know,
but it is clear that they, acting either with or without the formal council (to which
John 11:47 probably refers), were the effective Jewish government.[110] Since there
is no indication that Nicodemus was a priest, he must belong to one of the small
number of lay aristocratic families who, together with the chief priests, composed
the ruling group. Since the Gurion family was one of the very wealthiest families

109. Compare *BJ* 2.336 with *BJ* 2.405; *Ant.* 20.11. At *BJ* 2.333 οἱ τῶν Ἱεροσολύμων ἄρχοντες are
most naturally understood to be the chief priests and the leading citizens to whom the preceding narrative has referred (*BJ* 2.301, 316, 318). See also *BJ* 2.234, 237, where οἱ ἄρχοντες are distinguished from
the ordinary people attending the festival (τὰ πλήθη), and seem to be the same group as οἱ γνώριμοι τῶν
Ἰουδαίων καὶ ὁ ἀρχιερεὺς Ἰωνάθης (*BJ* 2.240).

110. For recent discussions (which differ but also have much in common) of the ruling Jewish group
and the problem of the Sanhedrin, see Goodman, *Ruling Class of Judaea*, 113–17; E. P. Sanders, *Judaism: Practice and Belief, 63 BCE–66 CE* (London: SCM, 1992), 472–90; A. J. Saldarini, "Sanhedrin,"
ABD 5:975–80.

in Jerusalem, there can be no doubt that they also will have belonged to this lay aristocratic elite.

2. Nicodemus is a Pharisee (John 3:1). The Pharisees in the Fourth Gospel are not usually the Pharisees in general, but the small number of wealthy aristocratic Pharisees who belonged to the ruling elite. Because they formed the one identifiable party other than the chief priests,[111] John can refer to the ruling group as "the chief priests and the Pharisees" (7:32, 45; 11:47, 57; 18:3), ignoring other members of the lay nobility. Josephus, when he takes the trouble to distinguish these Pharisees from the other leading lay citizens, refers to "the powerful" (οἱ δυνατοί) meeting with the chief priests and "the distinguished men of the Pharisees" (τοῖς τῶν Φαρισαίων γνωρίμοις: *BJ* 2.411; cf. also *Ant.* 20.201–2),[112] but on one occasion Josephus also, like the Fourth Gospel, refers to the ruling elite as "the chief priests and the leading men of the Pharisees" (τοῖς πρώτοις τῶν Φαρισαίων: *Vita* 21). Gamaliel (Acts 5:34) and his son Simeon (*BJ* 4.159; *Vita* 190–96, 216, 309) belonged to this group of aristocratic Pharisees. The Gurion family is probably the only other known family that can be confidently assigned to it (see sections III.1, III.4, III.5 above).

3. Nicodemus is a teacher of the law (John 3:10; cf. 7:51). Not all Pharisaic aristocrats were rabbis, but Gamaliel (Acts 5:34; 22:3) and his son Simeon were,[113] and so were two members of the Gurion family (see sections III.5.2, III.5.3).

4. Nicodemus is portrayed as an extremely rich man (John 19:39). Whatever further significance the evangelist may have seen in the vast quantity (65.45 lbs.) of very expensive spices, his narrative is in the first place an anecdote about a fabulously wealthy man. If the figure is exaggerated, it is precisely the kind of hyperbole in which the rabbinic traditions about Naqdimon ben Gurion and his daughter delightedly indulged: that his stores were sufficient to feed the whole population of Jerusalem for ten years (III.1.2), that his daughter's marriage portion was a million gold dinars (III.6.3), that her widow's allowance for perfume was 400 gold dinars a day (II.5) (cf. also II.3, II.7).

5. The Fourth Gospel leaves us to infer that Nicodemus became a Christian. This point is the most controversial and must therefore be discussed at some length. The usual view has been that in chapters 3 and 7 Nicodemus is portrayed as sympathetic to Jesus but unable to understand Jesus' real significance and unwilling to

111. If there were lay Sadducees, which is not certain, they were allied with the chief priests.

112. Cf. A. J. Saldarini, *Pharisees, Scribes and Sadducees in Palestinian Society* (Edinburgh: T. & T. Clark, 1989), 102: "The notables among the Pharisees were consulted but the basis for their status is not clear. They may have come from hereditary families which had aristocratic position in the city or they may have been powerful by virtue of their leadership of the Pharisees." But strongly in favor of the former option is Josephus's use of the word γνώριμοι, which elsewhere refers to the aristocracy: τοῖς τῶν Φαρισαίων γνωρίμοις means the aristocratic members of the ruling elite who belonged to the Pharisaic party. See also Josephus's account of Simeon son of Gamaliel (*Vita* 191). Cf. also Schwartz, *Josephus and Judaean Politics*, 63 n. 27.

113. Rabbinic traditions about them are collected in Neusner, *Rabbinic Traditions*, vol. 1, chapters 11–12.

commit himself fully, but that in 19:39–40 he is portrayed as a devoted disciple of Jesus who here makes his faith in Jesus public.[114] This has been challenged more recently by those who see him in 19:39–40 as still a secret disciple,[115] who in fact so fails to understand Jesus that his action at the burial of Jesus is actually "an act of unbelief."[116] His lavish attention to the corpse of Jesus shows that he has no expectation of his resurrection[117] and "finds no life in Jesus' death."[118] The issue is not unconnected with the fashion for seeing the figure of Nicodemus as representative of a group in the context of the Johannine community: "crypto-Christians" who remained in the synagogue (even as "rulers" of the synagogue), who held a christologically inadequate view of Jesus, in the evangelist's view, and who lacked the courage to break with synagogue Judaism and openly to join the Christian community.[119]

Two questions about the portrayal of Nicodemus in 19:39–40 should be distinguished, though they are often confused: (1) Does he remain a secret disciple? (2) Is his faith in Jesus adequate? On the first point, it can be questioned whether Nicodemus is portrayed as keeping his attitude to Jesus secret at any point in the

---

114. For a recent extended argument for this position, see J.-M. Auwers, "La nuit de Nicodème (*Jean* 3,2; 19, 39) ou l'ombre du langage," *RB* 97 (1990): 481–503, who sees a progress from immature to full faith. J. M. Bassler, "Mixed Signals: Nicodemus in the Fourth Gospel," *JBL* 108 (1989): 635–46, sees Nicodemus as a deliberately ambiguous figure, as does Gabi Renz, "Nicodemus: An Ambiguous Disciple? A Narrative Sensitive Investigation," in John Lierman, ed., *Challenging Perspectives on the Gospel of John*, WUNT 2/219 (Tübingen: Mohr Siebeck, 2006), 255–82. Renz provides an overview of recent scholarly attitudes to the figure of Nicodemus (255–58).

115. J. L. Martyn, *History and Theology in the Fourth Gospel*, 2nd ed. (Nashville: Abingdon, 1979), 87; R. A. Culpepper, *Anatomy of the Fourth Gospel* (Philadelphia: Fortress, 1983), 136.

116. D. Rensberger, *Overcoming the World: Politics and Community in the Gospel of John* (London: SPCK, 1988), 40.

117. M. de Jonge, "Nicodemus and Jesus: Some Observations on Misunderstanding and Understanding in the Fourth Gospel," *BJRL* 53 (1971): 343; W. A. Meeks, "The Man from Heaven in Johannine Sectarianism," *JBL* 91 (1972): 55 n. 39; D. B. Sylva, "Nicodemus and His Spices (John 19,39)," *NTS* 34 (1988): 148–51.

118. Culpepper, *Anatomy of the Fourth Gospel*, 136.

119. De Jonge, "Nicodemus and Jesus"; Martyn, *History and Theology in the Fourth Gospel*, 86–88; Rensberger, *Overcoming the World*, 37–41. R. E. Brown, *The Gospel according to John (XIII–XXI)*, AB 29A (London: G. Chapman, 1971), 959–60, sees Nicodemus, like Joseph, as a secret believer who makes his faith public in 19:39–40: "John may be hinting that crypto-believers in the Synagogue of his own time should follow the example of Joseph and Nicodemus." But in *The Community of the Beloved Disciple* (New York: Paulist Press, 1979), 72 n. 128, reacting against de Jonge and others, while firmly believing there were "crypto-Christians" in the Johannine context, he denies that the figure of Nicodemus is intended to represent them or any contemporary group in the Johannine community's context. For a trenchant, though all too brief, attack on the whole method of finding the Johannine community and the groups in its context depicted in the Gospel, see F. Wisse, "Historical Method and the Johannine Community," *Arc* 20 (1992): 35–42. With regard to Nicodemus, it is hard to see how his role in 7:50–52 contributes to his supposedly representative function in the Gospel, while the form of chapter 3 should raise considerable doubts about whether he is there intended to function as a representative character. Once his misunderstandings have provided the occasion for Jesus' teaching, Nicodemus himself drops completely out of view: readers are expected to have lost interest in him.

Gospel. His coming to Jesus "at night" (3:1; 19:39)—that is, after sunset—need not mean that he fears his meeting with Jesus becoming known. Whatever its further meaning at the level of the Johannine symbolism of light and darkness, at the literal level of Nicodemus's intention, it is at least as likely to mean that he seeks an uninterrupted, lengthy discussion with Jesus.[120] If, as seems likely, the narrative takes for granted that Nicodemus, an eminent rabbi, is accompanied by disciples (who are more appropriately the subjects, with Nicodemus, of οἴδαμεν [3:2] than are the rest of the Pharisees or the rest of the ἄρχοντες),[121] secrecy seems improbable. So it is not at all clear that Nicodemus is among the ἄρχοντες who, according to 12:42, believed but did not dare confess. But even if he is, as Joseph of Arimathea is (19:38), there cannot be any doubt that 19:39–40 makes his allegiance to Jesus highly public. He treats with immense honor the body of the man condemned and repudiated by the ἄρχοντες as a criminal. He does so in broad daylight, before the Sabbath, which began at sunset (cf. 19:42), so that if his coming to Jesus by night had been for the sake of secrecy, his action now is in stark contrast. No first-century reader would have imagined he carried the spices himself. Numerous servants would be assisting him and Joseph. Nothing could be more public. On the second point, it is relevant to ask what sort of faith the evangelist would expect of a disciple of Jesus at this point in the narrative.[122] None of the disciples of Jesus expect his resurrection (20:2, 9). Even the beloved disciple, who is the first to believe, does not do so until he sees the empty tomb and, unlike Peter, grasps its significance (20:8).

John's account of the burial of Jesus should be seen as the conclusion of his passion narrative, and of two of its dominant themes: the paradox that Jesus' messianic kingship is revealed in his suffering and death, and the rejection of Jesus as king by the official leaders of the Jewish theocracy (19:15). Just as Jesus' kingship is proclaimed in the very process of his condemnation (19:2–3) and crucifixion (19:19–22), so that the events that seem to confirm the Jewish rulers' repudiation of his kingship in fact reveal him to be the king of the Jews, so even at his death he receives a burial appropriate to a king. At the same time, the theme of the rejection of Jesus' kingship by the ἄρχοντες (19:15) is nuanced by the conclusion in which two of the ἄρχοντες themselves publicly dissent from this verdict and give him the extravagant honor due to the messianic king (19:38–41). Nicodemus's vast provision of spices is not in the least "ludicrous."[123] It is the culturally recognized

120. So, e.g., Bultmann, *Gospel of John*, 133 n. 5; G. R. Beasley-Murray, *John*, WBC 36 (Waco: Word, 1987), 47. Discussion of the law late into the night was evidently known to later rabbinic tradition, which attributed it to early Pharisees (*b. Yoma* 35b). Cf. also 1QS 6.7.

121. F. P. Cotterell, "The Nicodemus Conversation: A Fresh Appraisal," *ExpTim* 96 (1984–1985): 238.

122. D. A. Carson, "Understanding Misunderstandings in the Fourth Gospel," *TynBul* 33 (1982): 59–91, is relevant here, in showing conclusively that misunderstandings and failures to understand in the Fourth Gospel cannot be correlated with the distinction between insiders and outsiders in the contemporary context of the Johannine community.

123. Meeks, "Man from Heaven," 55 n. 39.

way of appropriately honoring a very eminent person.[124]Although it is not the evangelist's purpose to tell us what happened to Nicodemus thereafter, the natural implication is that his acknowledgment of Jesus before the resurrection became, like the faith of the other disciples, full Christian faith afterward.

Of the five features of the portrayal of Nicodemus in the Fourth Gospel, we have seen that all except the fifth correspond exactly to what we have learned of the Gurion family in sections II and III. Not just the coincidence of a very rare name, but this coincidence within the small circle of very wealthy Pharisaic families who belonged to the Jewish governing elite in the period before 70 CE, leads us to conclude that there is a very high degree of probability that the Nicodemus of the Fourth Gospel belonged to the Gurion family. Any early reader of the Gospel who knew pre-70 Jerusalem would readily recognize this. If John invented the character of Nicodemus, we should have to say not merely, with Lindars, that he chose "the name as a typical one for a Jewish ruler,"[125] but that he invented a fictional member of the Gurion family. It is easier to suppose that the character has a historical prototype.

Was this historical prototype actually the Naqdimon ben Gurion who is remembered in rabbinic tradition? The identification has occasionally been made,[126] but there are serious difficulties. First, that Naqdimon ben Gurion was alive in the period immediately before the fall of Jerusalem is required by some rabbinic traditions (II.1 above; cf. also II.6.2, II.6.3). The traditions could be unreliable in this respect, but if they are correct, Naqdimon could hardly have been much more than thirty at the time of Jesus' ministry. John 3:4 is not, as some think,[127] a problem in this case: "Nicodemus need not be thinking of himself; the extreme case of the aged makes flagrantly clear what is true of every age, that there is only one birth."[128] But it is not easy to think of such a young man as one of the ruling elite and an eminent Pharisaic teacher.

---

124. Most of the commentaries appropriately cite Josephus, *Ant.* 17.199 (the funeral procession of Herod the Great included 500 servants carrying spices) and *b. Sem.* 47a (the proselyte Onqelos burned more than eighty pounds of spices at the funeral of R. Gamaliel I), though the number of commentators who seem unquestioningly to accept the latter as a simple historical fact is remarkable. Some also refer to 2 Chron. 16:14; Josephus, *Ant.* 15.61. Also relevant is Pliny the Elder, *Nat.* 12.82–83, where the story that Nero burned more perfumes at the funeral of Poppaea than Arabia produces in a whole year is the most outrageous example illustrating Pliny's general complaint against this extravagance of the rich: that "the perfumes such as are given to the gods a grain at a time . . . are piled up in heaps to the honour of dead bodies." Cf. also the observation on this theme in Latin literature of the period by E. H. Warmington, *The Commerce between the Roman Empire and India*, 2nd ed. (London: Curzon, 1974), 90: "So great was the use of aromatics at funerals that the death of any living thing tended to call forth from the poets reference to Indian and Arabian perfumes."

125. B. Lindars, *The Gospel of John*, NCB (London: Oliphants, 1972), 149.

126. Flusser, *Jesus*, 122; cf. also Ilan, *Lexicon*, 299, citing an unpublished lecture by Z. Safrai.

127. Robinson, *Priority*, 287; D. A. Carson, *The Gospel according to John* (Grand Rapids: Eerdmans, 1991), 186.

128. Schnackenburg, *Gospel according to St. John*, 1:368.

Second, there is not the slightest hint in the rabbinic traditions that Naqdimon ben Gurion was a rabbi. However, a Pharisaic teacher who became a Christian would probably not be remembered as a rabbi in rabbinic traditions. His earlier reputation would be eclipsed in the tradition by his later Christian allegiance. This leads at once to the final problem.

Third, Naqdimon ben Gurion is remembered entirely favorably in the rabbinic traditions (with the exception of the artificial, secondary criticism implied in section II.6.3 above and expressed in II.7). His piety and charity are praised. While it is not impossible that a Jerusalem Christian before 70 maintained good relations with the Pharisees (cf. Josephus, *Ant.* 20.201), it is unlikely he would be remembered so entirely favorably in later rabbinic tradition.

It is therefore unlikely that John's Nicodemus and the rabbis' Naqdimon ben Gurion are the same person. Robinson's proposal that John's Nicodemus was the grandfather of the rabbis' Naqdimon ben Gurion[129] we have already rendered chronologically impossible by concluding that Gorion son of Nicodemus (Josephus, *BJ* 2.451) was the son, not, as Robinson thought, the father of Naqdimon ben Gurion (see section III.1 above). But, as we have seen, sons were named not only after grandfathers, but also after fathers and uncles. There are therefore other possible relationships in which John's Nicodemus could have stood to the other family members we know. The most obvious possibility is that he was the uncle of Naqdimon ben Gurion and (if our reconstruction of the genealogy is correct) brother of the famous Guria/Gurion at whose house in Jericho the Pharisees met.

V. Naqqai and Buni among the Five Disciples of Jesus

Since we have concluded that Naqdimon ben Gurion, also called Buni, remembered in rabbinic traditions, was not the same person as the Nicodemus of the Fourth Gospel, though he was related to him, we must finally consider the remarkable fact that the rabbinic tradition of the five disciples of Jesus includes both Naqqai (which could be the hypocoristic form of Nicodemus/Naqdimon) and Buni.

> Our Rabbis taught: Yeshu had five disciples, Mattai (מתאי), Naqqai (נקאי), Neṣer (נצר), Buni (בוני) and Todah (תודה).[130]
> When Mattai was brought [before the court], he said to them [the judges]: Shall Mattai be executed? Is it not written, *Mattai* [מתי = when] *shall I come and appear before God?* [Ps. 42:3] Thereupon they retorted: Yes, Mattai shall be executed, since it is written, *Mattai* [מתי = when] *shall [he] die and his name perish?* [Ps. 41:6].

129. Robinson, *Priority*, 287.
130. For these names in the Toledot Yeshu literature, see E. Bammel, "What Is Thy Name?" *NovT* 12 (1970): 223–28.

When Naqqai was brought in, he said to them: Shall Naqqai be executed? Is it not written, *Naqqai* [נקי = the innocent] *and the righteous slay thou not* [Ex. 23:7]? Yes, was the answer, Naqqai shall be executed, since it is written, *In secret places he slays Naqqai* [נקי = the innocent] [Ps. 10:8].

When Neṣer was brought in, he said: Shall Neṣer be executed? Is it not written, *And Neṣer* [a branch] *shall grow forth out of his roots* [Isa. 11:1]? Yes, they said, Neṣer shall be executed, since it is written, *But thou art cast forth from the grave like Neṣer* [an untimely birth] [Isa. 14:19].

But when Buni was brought in, he said: Shall Buni be executed? Is it not written, *Beni* [בני = my son], *my first-born* [Ex. 4:22]? Yes, they said, Buni shall be executed, since it is written, *Behold I will slay Bine-ka* [בנך = thy son], *thy first-born* [Ex. 4:23]?

And when Todah was brought in, he said to them: Shall Todah be executed? Is it not written, *A psalm for Todah* [thanksgiving] [Ps. 100:1]? Yes, they answered, Todah shall be executed, since it is written, *Whoso offereth the sacrifice of Todah* [thanksgiving] *honoreth me* [Ps. 50:23].[131] (*b. Sanh.* 43a)

Despite much ingenious speculation about the five names,[132] no satisfactory explanation of the set of five has been found before now. It is important, in the first place, to recognize that the account of the trials of the five disciples is wholly secondary to the list. It is created entirely by the kind of wordplay involving names and scriptural texts that is common enough in Jewish exegetical traditions. An existing list of five names has inspired the discovery of texts including words understood as puns on the names—for each disciple one text against his execution, one in favor. In each case, the second text is more decisive. However, in at least one case, as is generally acknowledged, the pun has affected the name itself in the list of five. The last name must originally have been Taddai (תדי), that is, Thaddaeus (Matt. 10:3; Mark 3:18). But the scriptural pun on his name (תודה) has replaced his name in the list.

This example should alert us to the possibility that the same thing has happened in another case. Like Todah, Neṣer is not a name. Like Todah, it is the actual word used in the texts cited, not a name for which the texts then provide a punning equivalent. It too should be a substitute for a name that originally stood in the list. The name must have been Nittai (נתאי or נתי),[133] the hypocoristic form of

---

131. Translation from J. Neusner, *The Talmud of Babylonia: An American Translation*, vol. 23B, *Tractate Sanhedrin, Chapters 4–8*, Brown Judaic Studies 84 (Chico, CA: Scholars Press, 1984), 74–75, with minor alterations.

132. For a catalog of most noteworthy suggestions, see Maier, *Jesus von Nazareth in der talmudischen Überlieferung*, 233–34. Peter Schäfer, *Jesus in the Talmud* (Princeton: Princeton University Press, 2007), chapter 7, argues that the scriptural puns on the names are ingenious polemic against Jesus himself.

133. Nittai occurs (1) in *Letter of Aristeas* 49 (Ναtθαῖος; cf. Cohen, "Names of the Translators in the Letter of Aristeas," 52–53; despite the comments of Ilan, *Lexicon*, 199, this is very likely a Greek form of נתאי); (2) the early Pharisaic sage Nittai (נתאי) the Arbelite (*m. 'Abot* 1:6–7; *m. Ḥag.* 2:2); (3) Nittai (נתאי) of Tekoa, mentioned in *m. Hall.* 4:10; (4) as נתי on an ossuary inscription: E. Puech, "Inscriptions funéraires palestiniennes: Tombeau de Jason et ossuaires," *RB* 90 (1983) 500 (§2 = *CIJ* 1304); (5) as נתי

Nathanael (נתנאל). Not only is Nathanael the only known disciple of Jesus (John 1:25; 21:2), other than Nicodemus, whose name begins with נ; the name Nittai also conforms to the pattern of hypocoristic names in the rest of the list.[134] It is quite intelligible that only the two names Nittai and Taddai should have been suppressed in favor of their punning substitutes from the scriptural texts. The other three names are very close to the word in the scriptural text that is used as the pun, but Nittai and Taddai are relatively distant from it.

Thus the original list read: Mattai, Naqqai, Nittai, Buni, Taddai. Since Buni can be vocalized as Bunai (בוני), it is a list of rhyming hypocoristics. This helps us to see how the list has been compiled. Probably the number five is a conventional number for the students of a teacher. Just as Yohanan ben Zakkai had five disciples (m. 'Abot 2:8; b. Sanh. 43a) and R. Aqiva had five disciples (b. 'Abod. Zar. 8b), so Jesus must have had five disciples.[135] Given this number, the compiler selected those disciples of Jesus known to him whose names could be reduced to hypo-coristics ending in -ai, in order to make a rhyming set. But given this principle of selection, it is still surprising that he did not include Yannai (ינאי), for John, or Andrai (אנדראי). Certainly, to a Christian or to a Jew working from Christian sources, these would be more obvious choices than most of those included. We must suppose that the compiler's information about disciples of Jesus came from Jewish traditions now unknown to us.

Naqqai must, as many scholars have agreed, be Nicodemus.[136] But the most puzzling name in the list is still Buni. Most suggestions (other than those that appeal to b. Ta'an. 20a) fail to recognize that Buni is a name, though otherwise only attested as the original name of Naqdimon ben Gurion (see b. Ta'an. 20a in section II.3 above). There is no need to explain it as a corruption of some other name,[137] and it should certainly not be explained as something other than a real name.[138] Rather than resort to these devices, it would be more in keeping with the character of the rest of the list to suppose that Jesus had a disciple called Buni, who featured in Jewish traditions but not in surviving Christian traditions. Yet there

on a jar from Masada: Yadin and Naveh, *Aramaic and Hebrew Ostraca and Jar Inscriptions*, 41 (§475). Ilan, *Lexicon*, 198–99, treats Nittai as a form of Nathan. It could have been used as an abbreviated form of either Nathan or Nathanel.

134. This is not to say that the resemblance between נצר and נוצרי (Nazarene, Christian), and even the Christian use of Isa. 11:1 with reference to Jesus, may have played some part in the choice of texts. But analogy with the rest of the list shows that a real name must originally have stood in place of נצר.

135. W. Bacher, "R. Travers Herford's 'Christianity in Talmud and Midrash," *JQR* 17 (1905): 180.

136. Other suggestions (in Maier, *Jesus von Nazareth in der talmudischen Überlieferung*, 234) require a reference to someone who was not an actual disciple of Jesus (Nicanor, Nicolaus, Luke). Since a disciple of Jesus whose name was Naqqai (Nicodemus) is available, we should prefer this obvious identification, especially as other names in the list are of actual disciples of Jesus.

137. E.g., J. Klausner, *Jesus of Nazareth*, trans. H. Danby (London: Allen & Unwin, 1925), 30 (corruption of Yohanni, i.e., John).

138. R. T. Herford, *Christianity in Talmud and Midrash* (London: Williams & Norgate, 1903), 93–94 ("Son of God" title for Jesus); Schäfer, *Jesus*, 79–80 (Jesus as God's firstborn son).

is the intriguing fact that in its only other known occurrence, Buni is the Hebrew name of Naqdimon ben Gurion, while here the name Buni appears alongside the name Naqqai, used as the shortened form of Naqdimon. It should be apparent that the two traditions must be independent of each other. If a compiler or editor of the list of Jesus' five disciples were influenced by the tradition that Naqdimon ben Gurion was also called Buni, he probably would not have added Buni to a list that also included Naqqai, or Naqqai to a list that also included Buni. Nor is influence from this list on the tradition in *b. Ta'an.* 20a conceivable.

The probable explanation is as follows. The use of both the Hebrew name Buni and the Greek name Nicodemus would not have been peculiar to Naqdimon ben Gurion. Just as Nicodemus was a name repeated in the family, so Buni was its Hebrew equivalent in family usage. Thus Nicodemus the disciple of Jesus would also have been called Buni. The compiler of the list of the five disciples, who worked from a number of disparate Jewish traditions about disciples of Jesus, in which different disciples occurred in different traditions, knew a tradition in which Nicodemus was named and a tradition in which Buni was named. He did not know they were the same person.

This strongly confirms our argument that Nicodemus the disciple of Jesus belonged to the same family as Naqdimon ben Gurion. It also allows us to conclude that Nicodemus the disciple of Jesus featured in Jewish traditions about Jesus quite independent of the Fourth Gospel. The more general conclusion of interest is that there were numerous Jewish traditions about disciples of Jesus that have not survived.

VI. General Conclusions

In the first place, this essay is a contribution to the prosopography of pre-70 Jerusalem. Alongside other powerful aristocratic families that are well known to historians, such as the high priestly families and the Gamaliel family, the Gurion family can now take its place as one of the wealthiest and most powerful of the lay aristocratic families represented on the governing high priest's council. Like the Gamaliel family, they were Pharisaic in allegiance, the only other such family known to us by name. They belonged to the Pharisaic minority that shared power with the Sadducean priestly aristocracy. From Josephus and the rabbinic traditions we know the names of nine male members of the family and one female whose name is not certain.[139]

Every Palestinian Jew known to us, from Josephus and rabbinic traditions, who bore the names Gurion (Guria) or Nicodemus, can be very plausibly identified as a member of this family. In a society without formal surnames, it was common

---

139. In most of the rabbinic traditions she is anonymous, and so the name Miriam, given her in just three passages, may not be reliable.

practice among the Jewish aristocracy to maintain the family's identity onomastically by repeating one or two very unusual names, distinctive to the family, across the generations, with the result that most male members of the family would bear one of these distinctive names either as his own or as his patronymic. To maintain this pattern, individuals were more often named after their grandfather or their uncle than after their father. This practice means that, while our evidence does not allow us to be certain of the precise family relationships between all of the ten individuals known to us, we can be much more sure that all belonged to the same family. The genealogy offered in table 7.7 is thus partly conjectural but shows that it is not difficult to posit a plausible set of relationships that do full justice to all the evidence.

Josephus provides us with a few glimpses of the political activities of the family over the period from the mid-first century BCE to 70 CE. During the revolt against Rome they were evidently among the moderate leading citizens who opposed the excesses of the Zealots. Gurion ben Nicodemus was one of the group of leading citizens who negotiated the surrender of the Roman garrison in Jerusalem in 66. Also in 66, Joseph ben Gurion (perhaps his uncle) was appointed, along with the ex–high priest Ananus II, to supreme command in Jerusalem, while Gurion ben Joseph, probably his son, was one of group of moderate leading citizens who, along with the Pharisaic aristocrat Simon ben Gamaliel and two of the chief priests, tried to organize popular opposition to the Zealots and was put to death by the Zealots in 68.

The rabbinic traditions must be treated with more caution. Most of the stories about the Nicodemus they remember (Naqdimon) and his daughter are doubtless legendary as such, but they are numerous enough to make it very probable that they do preserve the memory of a man who was remembered as one of the wealthiest of the pre-70 Jerusalem aristocracy, indeed a fabulously wealthy individual, and of a daughter left destitute by the Roman conquest of the city. He was also, no doubt reliably, remembered for his Pharisaic piety and his generous charity. At least some of the family's estates, to which it owed its prosperity, were at Rumah in Galilee, and, like other wealthy Jerusalem families, the Gurion family had a winter residence in Jericho. The family's patronage of the Pharisees was remembered in the tradition that their house in Jericho was a meeting place for large gatherings of Pharisees, while the famous occasion at the outbreak of the revolt in 66 when a gathering of Pharisees passed the eighteen decrees took place in the large upper room of the family house in, presumably, Jerusalem. One family member, Hananiah ben Hezekiah ben Gurion, who lived around the time of the Jewish revolt, was remembered in the rabbinic traditions as himself a rabbi, as was, it appears, his son Eleazar. Either Hananiah or his son was credited with the composition of *Megillat Ta'anit*, probably early in the revolt.

Nicodemus was a rare name among Jews. Even in the diaspora only two instances are known. The few instances among Palestinian Jews, known from Josephus and rabbinic traditions, can all be confidently assigned to the Gurion family, like all instances of Gurion or Guria before the second century. This was precisely the point of the use of such unusual names among the Jerusalem aristocracy: they were utterly distinctive of a particular family and so unmistakably identified members of that family. The name Gamaliel is another well-known instance. Therefore, to anyone who knew anything about pre-70 Jerusalem, the character of Nicodemus in John's Gospel would have had to be a member of the Gurion family. Either he was a historical person, an actual member of the family, or, if John invented him, he must have intended him to be a fictional member of the well-known family.

This argument from the name alone can be supported also by the other characteristics that John's Nicodemus shares with the Gurion family. He is a Pharisee belonging to the ruling elite and extremely wealthy. That he is also a teacher of Torah is not, naturally, something he would have in common with the rest of his family, but some members of the Gurion family were also rabbis. An important point to notice is that, although John's Gospel has often been charged with giving an unhistorical picture of the Jewish ruling elite by imagining the Pharisees sharing power with the chief priests, in fact it accurately represents the situation in which a few members of the high priest's council belonged to the aristocratic families who favoured the Pharisees and were too prominent to be excluded. This is how Josephus portrays the situation. John's Pharisees are neither the rank-and-file Pharisees who feature in the Synoptics nor, for the most part, one must suppose, teachers, but precisely that aristocratic group who belonged to the council and did therefore have some power and influence. That John's Nicodemus belongs to "the rulers" coheres very well with the status of the Gurion family as we can ascertain it from Josephus and rabbinic traditions.

That the Nicodemus remembered by the rabbis was also, as they claim, known as Buni is entirely credible because it was normal for a Palestinian Jew bearing a Greek name to have also a Semitic one. It is likely that other members of the family called Nicodemus would similarly have been called Buni. That this name is otherwise known only in the rabbinic tradition about the five disciples of Jesus is therefore very striking. That the five also include Naqqai, the abbreviated form of Nicodemus, seems to suggest some kind of confusion in the list, the same disciple appearing twice under different names. Whatever the explanation, it seems probable that there is a connection with both John's Nicodemus and the rabbinic tradition about the second name of the most famous Nicodemus.

8

THE BETHANY FAMILY
IN JOHN 11–12:
HISTORY OR FICTION?

According to the Gospel of John, Jesus counted among his close friends three siblings: Lazarus and his sisters Martha and Mary, who lived in the village of Bethany near Jerusalem. This chapter is primarily concerned with the historicity of this family, but this can scarcely be separated from the historicity of the events in which they are involved in John's narrative: the resuscitation of Lazarus by Jesus, and the anointing of Jesus by Mary. It is true that the historicity of these events could be defended, while regarding the family as a Johannine invention. John, it might be argued, has a habit of identifying characters who were anonymous in the tradition with known disciples of Jesus: the generalized "disciples" of Mark 6:35–38 are identified as Philip and Andrew in John 6:5–8; the man who injured the high priest's servant in Gethsemane, anonymous in the Synoptics (Matt. 26:52; Mark 14:47; Luke 22:50), is identified as Peter in John 18:10–11. Perhaps he has done the same in the story of the anointing of Jesus by a woman who is anonymous in Matthew (26:7) and Mark (14:3).[1] Perhaps he knew a story in which Jesus raised an anonymous man from death and has identified this man as Lazarus. But in that case we should know nothing about the Bethany family

---

1. In my view, Luke 7:36–50 narrates a different story (many think the four anointing stories in the four Gospels all derive from one event), but here too the woman is anonymous.

(except perhaps Luke's story about Martha and Mary [Luke 10:38–42]). It would be very hard to tell whether John knew of their existence apart from the stories he tells of them, or whether he borrowed the sisters from Luke's narrative and invented their brother, Lazarus. In this study, I shall consider the historicity of the Bethany family along with the events in which the Gospel of John portrays them as major participants.

The Personal Names

Many scholars have been much too impressed by the fact that the name Lazarus occurs not only in John 11–12 but also in Luke's parable of the rich man and Lazarus (Luke 16:19–31). But we now know that the name Lazarus (Eleazar)[2] was the third most popular male name among Palestinian Jews (Simon and Joseph were respectively the first and second): 6.32 percent of Jewish men bore the name (166 occurrences in a database of 2,625).[3] If anything, what is surprising is that only two persons in the Gospels bear this name,[4] not that as many as two do. The coincidence of name between John's character and the poor man in the Lukan parable, supposed by so many scholars to be significant,[5] is therefore not in the least remarkable. Nor is the alleged thematic connection between the two convincing. The proposed return of Lazarus in the parable is not a return to earthly life after temporary death, but a temporary visit by the dead Lazarus as a ghost or in a dream.[6] His visit is not regarded as a sign that the rich man's brothers need in order to believe. The point is rather that Lazarus will be able to tell them about the fate that is awaiting them in the afterlife unless they reform. None of this is at all like the resuscitation of Lazarus in John 11.[7] It is true that

2. The form Λάζαρος is a colloquial form (also found in Greek in Josephus, *BJ* 5.567; cf. Λαζαρ on an ostracon from Masada; whereas elsewhere Josephus has Ἐλεάζαρος). "The Palestinian Hebrew/Aramaic dialect tended to drop the א prefix" (Tal Ilan, *Lexicon of Jewish Names in Late Antiquity*, part 1, *Palestine 330 BCE–200 CE*, TSAJ 91 [Tübingen: Mohr Siebeck, 2002], 29). This is an example of how the New Testament "often preserves less official orthography which coincides with the common pronunciation rather than the traditional or official spelling found in Josephus" (Ilan, *Lexicon*, 18).

3. I am using the tables of names in order of popularity in Richard Bauckham, *Jesus and the Eyewitnesses: The Gospels as Eyewitness Testimony* (Grand Rapids: Eerdmans, 2006), 85–92. These were compiled from the data in Ilan, *Lexicon*, an invaluable reference work. My statistics are a little different from hers because I have differed from her in a few aspects of the criteria used for calculating statistics (see Bauckham, *Jesus*, 68–83). Consequently, whereas I put Eleazar third and Judah fourth in order of popularity, Ilan puts Judah third and Eleazar fourth. But both calculations put them very close together (Bauckham: Eleazar 166 occurrences, Judah 164; Ilan: Judah 179, Eleazar 177).

4. There are eight Simons and six Josephs in the Gospels and Acts.

5. E.g., most recently, Andrew T. Lincoln, *The Gospel according to St. John*, BNTC 4 (London: Continuum, 2005), 42.

6. The reading ἀπελθῇ should be preferred to ἀναστῇ in Luke 16:31: see V. Tanghe, "Abraham, son fils et son envoyé (Luc 16,19–31)," *RB* 91 (1984): 557–77.

7. So also George R. Beasley-Murray, *John*, WBC 36 (Waco: Word, 1987), 200.

Lazarus in the parable is the only occurrence of a personal name in any Gospel parable, but there are other explanations more plausible than that it has been borrowed from John 11 or from a story lying behind John 11.[8] So there is no reason either to suppose that John borrowed the name from the parable or that an early tradition about Jesus' resuscitation of a man called Lazarus lies behind the parable. Sometimes adequate information renders banal what might otherwise seem significant coincidences.

Mary was the most common female name among Palestinian Jews: 21.34 percent of Jewish women were called Mary (70 occurrences in a database of 328). Martha was the fourth most common:[9] 6.10 percent of Jewish women were called Martha (20 out of 326). These statistics have some relevance to the relationship of the Bethany family in John to the story of Martha and Mary in Luke (10:38–42). It would not be at all surprising if there were more than one pair of sisters called Mary and Martha in Jewish Palestine at this time. But it would be more surprising if two such pairs of sisters were both nonitinerant disciples of Jesus and, moreover, lived as adults in the same home. What makes the identity of the sisters in Luke with those in John undeniable is the correspondences in the characterization of them, to be discussed below.

Our evidence for naming practices among Palestinian Jews of this period enables us to rule out one suggestion for harmonizing John and Mark: that "Lazarus was a former leper also known as Simon (double names were not uncommon)."[10] Double names were certainly common, but they fall into two categories. Many Palestinian Jews used a Greek or (less commonly) Latin name as well as their Semitic name. Second, since a small number of names were very common, a patronymic or a nickname of some kind was often used with or instead of a very common name. In some families, a family nickname became virtually a surname. But Simon was the most common Jewish male name and Lazarus the third most common, and there is no reliable evidence of the use of two common names for the same person.[11] The practice would serve no purpose.

8. There may be a purely narratological reason. The theme of reversal of fortune would make it misleading to call the character "the poor man" poor after his death. The story is easier to tell if the man has a name. However, it is also relevant to notice that in popular stories about the return of a dead person, the sort of stories of which this parable is an example, he or she is almost always named, since they either purport to be true anecdotes about known people or else are fictional imitations of such true anecdotes. Giving the poor man a name may therefore belong to the genre of this kind of story (see Richard Bauckham, *The Fate of the Dead: Studies on the Jewish and Christian Apocalypses*, NovTSup 93 [Leiden: Brill, 1998], 115–16).

9. Salome (fifty-eight occurrences) and Shelamzion (twenty-four occurrences) are second and third. Since the database for women's names is much smaller than that for men's, the proportions are somewhat less certainly indicative of those in the whole population.

10. Craig S. Keener, *The Gospel of John: A Commentary* (Peabody, MA: Hendrickson, 2003), 2:861. In the medieval period this identification led to the common belief that Lazarus was a leper (Percy Gardner-Smith, *Saint John and the Synoptic Gospels* [Cambridge: Cambridge University Press, 1938], 46).

11. Bauckham, *Jesus and the Eyewitnesses: The Gospels as Eyewitness*, 108–10.

Throughout the four Gospels, the recipients of Jesus' healings and exorcisms in stories of those events are not usually named. In the Synoptics, the only exceptions are Jairus (Mark 5:22; Luke 8:41)[12] and Bartimaeus (Mark 10:46).[13] John's Gospel fits the same pattern: he does not name the steward or the groom at the wedding, the royal official or his son, the lame man healed by Jesus or the blind man healed by Jesus. Lazarus, Mary, and Martha are the only exception (the two sisters count as recipients of the miracle because they had their brother restored to them). It should be noted that these examples of naming and not naming certainly do not support a claim that adding names was a tendency of the Gospel traditions. The evidence in general shows that sometimes names are added, sometimes they are omitted: there is no consistent tendency.[14] Moreover, it is not plausible that John has given Lazarus, Mary, and Martha their names only because they are relatively individualized characters in a relatively long narrative. The same is true of the blind man in chapter 9.

I have argued elsewhere that the occurrence and nonoccurrence of names in stories in the Gospels may be partially explained by supposing that the named characters were members of the early Christian communities and themselves told the stories of the events in which they had been participants. So long as they were known figures, their names remained attached to their stories as indications of the eyewitness sources of these stories.[15] The same explanation easily fits the case of Lazarus, Martha, and Mary.

If we take broader account of the occurrence and nonoccurrence of personal names in John, we find that, apart from publicly known persons (John the Baptist, Caiaphas, Annas, Pilate, Barabbas), almost all the named characters are disciples of Jesus. The only exception is Malchus (18:10).[16] A closer look at the disciples (itinerant and nonitinerant) shows that only three of those who are prominent in John are also prominent in the Synoptics: Peter and Mary Magdalene, who seem to have been universally treated as the most prominent of Jesus' male and female disciples respectively, and Judas Iscariot, for obvious reasons. In John, disciples who appear only in the lists of the Twelve in the Synoptics acquire prominent roles: Philip (1:43–46; 6:7; 12:21–22; 14:8), Thomas (11:16; 14:5; 20:24–29; 21:2) and the other Judas (14:22; cf. Luke 6:16). Also prominent is Andrew (1:40; 6:7; 12:22), mostly detached from his brother Peter, with whom he is always found in the Synoptics. By contrast, the sons of Zebedee, so prominent in the Synoptics, appear only once in John (21:2). But then there are the disciples peculiar to John: Nathanael, Nicodemus, Mary of Clopas, and Lazarus. These differences from the Synoptics suggest that the sources of the Johannine traditions come from a circle or circles of disciples of Jesus different from the circles from

12. I count Jairus as a recipient because his daughter was restored to him.
13. According to Luke 8:3, Jesus cast demons out of Mary Magdalene, but the story is not told.
14. Bauckham, *Jesus*, 42–45.
15. Ibid., chapter 3.
16. It is possible that Malchus became a member of the early Jerusalem church.

which the Synoptic traditions derive (especially the inner three of the Twelve: Peter, James, and John).[17] These would be the circles in which the beloved disciple moved and acquired those traditions of which he was not himself a direct witness. Finally, we should note that four of the disciples peculiar to John or appearing only once in the Synoptics were nonitinerant disciples resident in the Jerusalem area: Nicodemus, Lazarus, Martha, and Mary. If we accept the now quite widely held view that the beloved disciple himself was a Jerusalem resident, his personal knowledge of those four disciples makes very good sense. Perhaps we should add that, if he was the owner of the house where the last supper took place, he must have belonged to at least a moderately wealthy family, as must also have been true of Nicodemus, Lazarus, Martha, and Mary.[18] Thus the Bethany family members fit very well into the pattern of John's use of personal names.

Relationships with Luke and Mark

A common view is that John borrowed Martha and Mary from Luke, invented Lazarus or at least gave him a name, used Mark alone as his source for the anointing, embellishing Mark's story by naming the anonymous woman Mary, and finally, located the family in Bethany because Mark located the anointing there.[19] We must tackle these possibilities by examining the relationships of the two Johannine narratives—the raising of Lazarus and the anointing—to Luke's story of Martha and Mary and Mark's story of the anointing. The aim here is not to prove that John's narratives are reliable, but to establish that their relationships with the Synoptic narratives are not obstacles to considering them basically reliable.

Martha and Mary in Luke and John

Whereas John locates the home of the sisters and their brother in Bethany, Luke refers only to "a certain village" in a context that gives no indication that it is near Jerusalem (10:38). This merely shows that the tradition Luke knew gave no specific location for the story. The difference does establish that Luke's story is not dependent on John, for Luke is not likely to have ignored John's specific location of the family in Bethany.

17. A parallel that may merit some attention is the way different early accounts of Francis of Assisi derive from different circles of his disciples.

18. For the Bethany family, note the extreme value of Mary's perfume (12:3). Other evidence for their relatively high social status is given by Ben Witherington, *John's Wisdom* (Louisville: Westminster John Knox, 1995), 200, though his argument that their house could accommodate a banquet for at least fifteen people assumes, perhaps incorrectly (see below), that the dinner in John 12:2 is located in their house.

19. E.g., Barnabas Lindars, *The Gospel of John*, NCB (London: Marshall, Morgan & Scott, 1972), 384–86. He thinks the name Lazarus may have been in the miracle story John used. For a different account of how John created the story of the raising of Lazarus out of Synoptic elements, see Thomas L. Brodie, *The Quest for the Origin of John's Gospel* (New York/Oxford: Oxford University Press, 1993), 86–88.

That Lazarus does not appear in Luke's story of the sisters (where Martha "received him as a guest" [10:38])[20] is not at all a plausible argument against his historicity.[21] In Gospel pericopes as brief and focussed as Luke 10:38–42, extraneous details unnecessary to the story are not to be expected.

There are no convincing verbal contacts between Luke's story and John 11–12, though two have been suggested:[22] (1) In Luke 10:39 Mary "sat at the feet" of Jesus, while in John 11:32 Mary "fell at the feet" of Jesus. But these are different idioms with quite different meanings: to sit at someone's feet is to listen their teaching (so also Luke 8:35; Acts 22:3), while to fall at someone's feet is an expression of humility and devotion (so also Mark 5:22; 7:25; Luke 8:41; 17:16; Acts 5:10; 10:25). Both are common. (2) In Luke 10:40 Martha "was distracted with much serving (διακονίαν)," while in John 12:2 Martha "served (διηκόνει)." These words are so common in the general sense of domestic work or, more especially, preparing a meal that the *verbal* coincidence is unremarkable. The *substantive* resemblance is more remarkable (see below).

Most commentators have noticed the consistency of characterization of the two sisters in the two Gospels, but are sharply divided on the significance of this. Whereas some scholars take it to be strong evidence of the historicity of John's portrayal of the sisters,[23] others think it shows that John borrowed them from Luke.[24] The case is similar, on a smaller scale, to the strikingly consistent portrayal of Peter across all four Gospels. In assessing this issue, we should take care to avoid allowing our reading of the characterization in one Gospel to affect our reading of the characterization in the other Gospel. A composite picture of the two sisters based on both Gospels can easily mislead.[25] In fact, the commonality between the two Gospels in this respect is striking but limited. It seems clear in both Gospels that Martha is the elder sister, since in Luke Martha appears first

20. Many manuscripts add εἰς τὴν οἰκίαν, with or without αὐτῆς, or εἰς τὸν οἶκον αὐτῆς, but the shorter reading is preferable (Bruce M. Metzger, *A Textual Commentary on the Greek New Testament* [Stuttgart: UBS, 1975], 153, though other scholars disagree) and does not necessarily suggest that the house was hers in any exclusive sense.

21. *Contra* Philip F. Esler and Ronald Piper, *Lazarus, Mary and Martha: Social Scientific Approaches to the Gospel of John* (Minneapolis: Fortress, 2006), 76.

22. Raymond E. Brown, *The Gospel according to John (I–XII)*, AB29 (New York: Doubleday, 1966), 433; Lindars, *Gospel of John*, 385; C. Kingsley Barrett, *The Gospel according to St. John*, 2nd ed. (London: SPCK, 1978), 411.

23. E.g., Ethelbert Stauffer, *Jesus and His Story*, trans. R. and C. Winston (New York: Knopf, 1974), 223–24, quoted in Ben Witherington, *Women in the Ministry of Jesus*, SNTSMS 51 (Cambridge: Cambridge University Press, 1984), 115; Mark W. G. Stibbe, *John's Gospel*, NT Readings (London/New York: Routledge, 1994), 101; Graham H. Twelftree, *Jesus: The Miracle Worker* (Downers Grove, IL: InterVarsity, 1999), 309–10.

24. E.g., Lincoln, *Gospel*, 333, 340.

25. Thus it would be easy to parallel Martha's outspoken complaint to Jesus in Luke 10:40 with her complaint to Jesus in John 11:21 (cf. 11:39), but this would overlook the fact that in John Mary makes identically the same complaint as her sister (11:32). This mistake is made, e.g., by C. J. Wright, quoted in Leon Morris, *Studies in the Fourth Gospel* (Exeter: Paternoster, 1969), 170–71.

and Mary is then introduced as her sister (Luke 10:38–39), while in John references to both sisters usually place Martha before Mary (John 11:5, 19).[26] She may well be considerably older. In both Gospels she takes responsibility for domestic work, especially preparing meals for guests (Luke 10:40; John 12:2). The fact that in John she goes out to meet Jesus, whereas Mary stays at home (11:20), may be due to her responsibility, as elder sister, for managing the household and its affairs (especially now that her brother has died), as may also her words in John 11:39.[27] In John, at least, there is no suggestion that she is less devoted to Jesus than her sister is, but in both Gospels Mary, unlike Martha, expresses her devotion to Jesus in overt ways other than domestic work (listening to him teaching [Luke 10:39], falling at his feet [John 11:32], anointing him with the expensive perfume [12:3]) and Jesus defends her unconventional expressions of devotion (Luke 10:42; John 12:7).[28]

It is important to note that, as usually in ancient narrative, the character of the sisters is portrayed by their actions and words, not by explicit character description. What is common to both Gospels in Martha's case really comes down to her responsibility for the household, while what is characteristic of Mary is her two rather unconventional acts of devotion (sitting like a disciple at the feet of her teacher, anointing him with costly perfume). These acts of Mary were central to the two narratives in which they occur, and so the consistent characterization of Mary would have been embodied in the tradition of the two stories quite independently of each other. That Martha was the older sister and the one with domestic responsibility is similarly integral to Luke's story and it is important, if not wholly necessary, to John's narrative of the raising of Lazarus.[29] There is nothing very subtle about this characterization of Martha. It could easily correspond to historical reality and it could easily have belonged to both stories quite independently of each other. We may conclude that what is common to the characterization of the two sisters in the two Gospels does not at all require that John borrowed this characterization from Luke.

---

26. John 11:1–2 is an exception because the author evidently expects his readers to know of Mary already (even if not by name, if they knew her from Mark) but not Martha.

27. Another feature of the characterization of Martha in John, her "discerning faith" (R. Alan Culpepper, *Anatomy of the Fourth Gospel* [Philadelphia: Fortress, 1983], 141–42), does not appear in Luke.

28. The commonly expressed view that in both Gospels Martha is the more active, Mary the more passive figure, neglects the anointing, where Mary on her own initiative performs a bold and unconventional act.

29. A number of scholars have argued for an original (pre-Johannine) form of this story in which Martha did not appear (e.g., Robert T. Fortna, *The Fourth Gospel and Its Predecessors* [Edinburgh: T. & T. Clark, 1988], 94–108; René Latourelle, *The Miracles of Jesus and the Theology of Miracles*, trans. Matthew J. O'Connell [New York: Paulist, 1988], 233–34; John P. Meier, *A Marginal Jew: Rethinking the Historical Jesus*, vol. 2, *Mentor, Message and Miracles* [New York: Doubleday, 1994], 819–22), though Mary did. I think attempts to reconstruct an original story are hopelessly speculative. See the survey and critique in Alain Marchadour, *Lazare: Histoire d'un récit; Récits d'une histoire*, LD 132 (Paris: L'Éditions du Cerf, 1988), chapter 2.

Timing and Location of the Anointing in John and Mark

There is enough verbal agreement between John 12:1–8 and Mark 14:3–9 to make it more probable that John knew Mark's account (see especially John 12:3a and Mark 14:3b) than that both depend on a common oral source.[30] This does not, however, preclude the possibility that John also had independent knowledge of the event. But in that case we must consider two respects in which John is supposed to contradict Mark. First, whereas Mark seems to date the event two days before Passover (14:1), John dates it six days before Passover (12:1). Second, whereas Mark places the event in the house of Simon the leper (14:3), John appears to place it in the house of Lazarus and his sisters. Of course, it is quite possible that John corrected Mark's account from what he considered better information. But in fact the contradictions, when more closely examined, turn out not to be real contradictions at all.

In the first place, Mark makes the supper at Bethany the "filling" in a typical Markan "sandwich" (an ABA pattern, thus: 14:1–2 + 14:3–9 + 14:10–11). He frames the event with the two stages of the plot against Jesus: (1) the authorities determine to put Jesus to death, but hesitate to provoke the people to riot (14:1–3); (2) Judas offers to betray Jesus, thus enabling the authorities to arrest him secretly, away from the crowds (14:10–11). Markan sandwiches are contrived for thematic rather than chronological reasons. Thus, for example, the sandwiching of Jesus' demonstration in the temple (11:15–19) between the two-stage narrative of the cursing of the fig tree makes the fig tree a symbol of the temple, which would not be at all evident otherwise. Similarly the sandwich in 14:1–11 creates a thematic rather than chronological link between the anointing and the plot against Jesus (exactly what this link is will be discussed in the next section). Recognizing that Mark's apparent chronology here is artificial makes it entirely possible that John is historically correct in placing the anointing prior to the triumphal entry. It is an example of John's habitual precision in chronological and geographical matters, a precision that distinguishes John markedly from the Synoptics.[31]

Second, John does not locate the supper in the house of Lazarus and his sisters. He certainly places it in Bethany (John 12:1–2), as does Mark, but the house is unmentioned. That "Lazarus was one of those at the table with" Jesus (12:2) indicates, if anything, that Lazarus was not the host.[32] The impression that the house is that of Lazarus and his sisters has probably been produced primarily by the statement that "Martha served" (12:2). But we must envisage a quite major

---

30. Gardner-Smith's case (*Saint John*, 42–50) is probably the least convincing part of his argument for John's complete independence of Mark. Both his argument and that of Charles H. Dodd, *Historical Tradition in the Fourth Gospel* (Cambridge: Cambridge University Press, 1963), 162–73, are in reality strong arguments for the view that John's account is not solely dependent on Mark's, rather than the view that John had no knowledge of Mark whatever.

31. See chap. 4 above.

32. Brown, *Gospel*, 1:448; Craig L. Blomberg, *The Historical Reliability of John's Gospel* (Downers Grove, IL: InterVarsity, 2001), 176.

social occasion, which the house of Lazarus and his sisters may not have been large enough to accommodate. We can easily imagine Martha helping to prepare or even taking charge of preparing the meal even though it was held in a neighbor's house.[33] Finally, and perhaps most tellingly, the subject of "made (ἐποίησαν) a meal for him" (12:2) cannot be Martha and Lazarus, since at this point only Lazarus has been mentioned (12:1). The plural verb has an indefinite subject, indicating that the dinner was arranged and Jesus was invited by Bethany villagers, not exclusively Lazarus and his sisters.[34] Thus, if John knew Mark's account, it is not necessary to suppose that he deliberately contradicted Mark in this respect.

The Silence of the Synoptics

The weightiest argument against the historicity of the raising of Lazarus (apart from naturalistic objections to the miraculous) has always been its absence from the Synoptics.[35] There are a number of commonly deployed responses to this argument. It is rightly pointed out that the presence of a tradition in only one Gospel is no necessary argument against its historical value.[36] More specifically, the Synoptic Gospels focus on the Galilean ministry,[37] whereas the raising of Lazarus belongs to the Gospel of John's greater attention to events in Jerusalem and Judaea. Moreover, the Synoptic Gospels locate only one specific miracle in the vicinity of Jerusalem: the healing of the blind man (Bartimaeus in Mark) or men near Jericho (Mark 10:46–52; Luke 18:45–53; Matt. 20:29–34). It seems to have been Mark's compositional decision (followed by Matthew and Luke) to limit the narration of miracles to the earlier stages of Jesus' ministry (up to 9:29), breaking this rule only in the case of Bartimaeus for a specific reason: to introduce the theme of Jesus' Davidic kingship that features prominently in Mark's passion narrative. Since Matthew and Mark do have one resuscitation miracle (Jairus's daughter) and Luke two (Jairus's daughter and the son of the widow of Nain), they may not have wished to include another.[38]

However, although these arguments carry some weight, they do not reckon fully with the fact that John portrays the raising of Lazarus as an especially impressive miracle and also gives it a key role in the sequence of events that led to Jesus' death. Many scholars think that John has exaggerated the miracle

33. Cf. Donald A. Carson, *The Gospel according to John* (Grand Rapids: Eerdmans, 1991), 428: "A village dinner honoring a celebrated guest might well draw in several families to do the work, and the presence of Lazarus at any Bethany dinner designed to honor Jesus would scarcely be surprising."

34. J. H. Bernard, *A Critical and Exegetical Commentary on the Gospel according to St. John*, ICC (Edinburgh: T. & T. Clark, 1928), 2:415.

35. E.g., recently, Maurice Casey, *Is John's Gospel True?* (London: Routledge, 1996), 55.

36. E.g., Latourelle, *Miracles*, 230–31.

37. E.g., Witherington, *Women*, 104; Stibbe, *John's Gospel*, 103; Blomberg, *Historical Reliability*, 55.

38. E.g., Twelftree, *Jesus*, 309.

he found in the tradition and has given it a role in his overall narrative that it did not have in pre-Johannine tradition.[39] In that case, its nonappearance in the Synoptics could be adequately explained by the arguments adduced above. But if the miracle was as dramatic and crucial to the course of events as John represents it, the silence of the Synoptics is less intelligible. Ben Witherington puts the issue thus:

> If . . . this story was but one of a number of stories of Jesus' raising the dead that were told and retold in the early church as self-contained narratives, there is no compelling reason why the Synoptic writers would have had to include the Lazarus story if they knew it. If, on the other hand, the Lazarus narrative was known to other evangelists and this episode was the event that triggered the events that led to Jesus' death and resurrection, it is very difficult to see how the Synoptic writers could possibly have afforded to omit the story.[40]

If, as we have suggested, John's knowledge of the events involving the Bethany family derives from the Beloved Disciple's own familiarity with the family, it is not so easy to leave aside the place that the raising of Lazarus has in the Gospel's account of the development of events. It will not do to put this down to John's alleged concern with theology rather than history. Caiaphas's words in 11:50 are instructive: at one level they make good sense as a statement of political expediency provoked by the fear that Jesus' popularity will lead to popular revolt, and it is only on a second, ironic level that they also express the divinely ordained reason why Jesus had to die. John is deeply concerned with the theological reasons for Jesus' death, but he evidently purports also to provide a straightforwardly historical explanation, in the sense of an account of how one thing led to another. His Gospel portrays the opposition of the Jewish authorities to Jesus, first aroused by his demonstration in the temple (2:18–20), mounting during a series of clashes on Jesus' periodic visits to Jerusalem. The report of the raising of Lazarus is, so to speak, the last straw because it is no longer simply a matter of the Jewish leaders' theological objections to Jesus' actions and claims but now also of the specter of popular revolt aroused by the huge following in Jerusalem that the reports of the raising of Lazarus have created for him. Dealing with Jesus thus becomes a matter of urgency, the more so when Passover approaches and Jesus returns to the Jerusalem area. This account does not make everything hang on the raising of Lazarus. In 11:47 the assembled Jewish leaders refer to

39. Some argue that the story was added in a second edition of the Gospel to a narrative that originally had the same sequence as Mark: the triumphal entry, the cleansing of the temple, and the chief priests' plot. Only in the second edition did the raising of Lazarus acquire the key role in leading to the chief priests' plan to put Jesus to death: Brown, *Gospel*, 1:429–30; Lindars, *Gospel*, 379–82; Witherington, *Women*, 104–5.

40. Witherington, *John's Wisdom*, 196.

Jesus' "many signs," not only that of Lazarus.[41] But the raising of Lazarus was a focus of popular attention, especially as it was possible to see the recently dead man now alive and well (12:9).

While not all scholars find this a convincing historical account of how the Jewish authorities became determined to put Jesus to death,[42] there can be no doubt that it does offer a *historical* form of explanation, which is arguably more convincing than Mark's, in which it seems to be Jesus' demonstration in the temple alone that provokes the authorities to plot his death (Mark 11:18). John's account, by explaining the enthusiasm for Jesus that gripped not only pilgrims from Galilee but also the people of Jerusalem at the approach of Passover, plausibly shows how the authorities could have viewed Jesus as a danger and have expected to convince Pilate that he was. Moreover, since John's account of the raising of Lazarus and the subsequent decision of the authorities makes Jesus already a wanted man as soon as he arrives in the Jerusalem area, the atmosphere of danger and subterfuge that, in Mark's account, already attends Jesus' preparations for the triumphal entry (Mark 11:1–6) actually becomes more intelligible if we assume some historical substance to the narrative of John 11:1–54.[43] But in that case why did Mark himself not tell that story?

Protective Strategies in Gospel Passion Narratives

In a significant essay on the Markan passion narrative, which he argues took shape in the Jerusalem church in the 40s CE, Gerd Theissen makes use of the notion of "protective anonymity."[44] He applies this primarily to two anonymous characters in Mark's account of the arrest of Jesus in Gethsemane (Mark 14:43–52): "one of the bystanders" who cut off the ear of the high priest's servant (14:47) and "a certain young man" who escaped arrest by fleeing naked (14:51–52). Theissen points out how difficult it is to tell whether either or both of these are disciples of Jesus. He offers an explanation of why they are anonymous and also why their relationship to Jesus is left so unclear:

> It seems to me that the narrative motive for this anonymity is not hard to guess: both of them [had] run afoul of the "police." The one who draws his sword commits no minor offense when he cuts off someone's ear. Had the blow fallen only

41. Where John says the crowd at the triumphal entry went to see Jesus because they had heard of the raising of Lazarus (John 12:18), Luke has them praising God "for all the deeds of power they had seen" (Luke 19:37).

42. See, e.g., Lindars, *Gospel*, 380–82.

43. Cf. John A. T. Robinson, *The Priority of John*, ed. J. F. Coakley (London: SCM, 1985), 222–23, which takes this argument further.

44. Gerd Theissen, "A Major Narrative Unit (the Passion Story) and the Jerusalem Community in the Years 40–50 C.E." in *The Gospels in Context*, trans. L. M. Maloney (Minneapolis: Fortress, 1991), chap. 4.

slightly awry, he could have wounded the man in the head or throat. This blow with a sword is violence with possibly mortal consequences. The anonymous young man has also offered resistance. In the struggle, his clothes are torn off, so that he has to run away naked. Both these people were in danger in the aftermath. As long as the high priest's slave was alive (and as long as the scar from the sword cut was visible) it would have been inopportune to mention names; it would not even have been wise to identify them as members of the early Christian community. Their anonymity is for their protection, and the obscurity of their positive relationship with Jesus is a strategy of caution. Both the teller and the hearers know more about these two people.[45]

This argument, among others, suggests to Theissen that the tradition has its origin in Jerusalem during the lifetime of these two persons: "Only in Jerusalem was there reason to draw a cloak of anonymity over followers of Jesus who had endangered themselves by their actions."[46] He adds to the case another, very different instance of anonymity in Mark's passion narrative.[47] Although Mark refers by name to Pilate (15:1) and evidently expects his readers to know that Pilate was the Roman governor, in the case of the high priest Caiaphas he does not give his name but refers merely to "the high priest" (14:53).[48] The continued hostility of Caiaphas and other high priests from the family of Annas to the Christian community in Jerusalem, up to at least 62 CE, would have made it diplomatic for Christian traditions formed in Jerusalem in that period not to refer explicitly to the name of Caiaphas in an account of the death of Jesus.

Theissen himself does not take the notion of "protective anonymity" further, but there is at least one other anonymous person in Mark's passion narrative who could be regarded as complicit in the events that led to Jesus' arrest and could therefore have needed the protection of anonymity.[49] This is the woman who anointed Jesus (Mark 14:3–9). Like the two nameless men in Gethsemane, this woman is peculiarly unspecified. Not only is her name not given, but there is no indication at all of who she is. Her introduction in verse 3 is remarkably abrupt and unexplanatory: "a woman came." Whether she belongs to the household or is a guest or has simply come in from the town is unexplained, as is her connection with Jesus. But what makes her anonymity quite extraordinary and not at all

45. Theissen, *Gospels*, 186–87. With regard to the man with the sword, Theissen is far from the first to make this argument. For example, H. B. Swete, *The Gospel according to St Mark*, 3rd ed. (London: Macmillan, 1909), 352, wrote: "During the early days of the Church of Jerusalem when the evangelical tradition was being formed, prudential reasons (cf. Jo. xviii.26) may have suggested reticence as to the name of the offender and even the fact of his connexion with the Christian body."

46. Theissen, *Gospels*, 188–89.

47. Ibid., 171–74.

48. The other evangelists name him Caiaphas (Matt. 26:57; Luke 3:2; John 18:13–14, 24), although Luke does not name him in the passion narrative itself (22:54) and readers of Luke might have difficulty knowing whether Annas or Caiaphas were in charge of the proceedings that condemned Jesus.

49. The argument that follows is presented in a little more detail in Bauckham, *Jesus*, chap. 8.

comparable with the many unremarkable cases of anonymity in Mark's Gospel are the words of Jesus that conclude the pericope: "Truly I tell you, wherever the good news is proclaimed in the whole world, what she has done will be told in remembrance of her" (14:9). This statement that her story will be told not merely to make known what she did, but "in remembrance of *her*," seems in straight contradiction to her anonymity in the story, and commentators have often noted the problem without offering any convincing solution. It is true that in ancient narrative women are more often anonymous than men, but this type of prejudice is unlikely to be present in this particular narrative, which ends by commending the woman so highly and in terms unique within this Gospel.[50]

A solution can be found in Theissen's notion of protective anonymity. At the time when this tradition took shape in this form in the Jerusalem church, this woman would be in danger were she identified as having been complicit in Jesus' politically subversive claim to messianic kingship. Her act, in its context of the last days of Jesus in Jerusalem, would easily be seen as the anointing entailed by the term Messiah, comparable with the anointing of kings in the Hebrew Bible.[51] The woman was acknowledging or even designating Jesus as the Messiah ben David. She may have acted purely on her own initiative, or she may have planned it in association with others who wished to take Jesus by surprise and so encourage him to undertake the messianic role about which he seemed ambivalent. Admittedly, it would no doubt be very surprising for the Messiah to be anointed by a woman, but she could have been seen in the role of a prophet, like Samuel, inspired by God to recognize and designate his Anointed One (cf. 1 Sam. 16:1–13).[52]

Not all scholars who think the woman's act had messianic significance in its original historical context think that Mark's narrative preserves that significance,[53] while not all scholars who think Mark sees messianic significance in the anointing

50. It is tempting to compare "in remembrance (μνημόσυνον) of her" with "Do this in remembrance (ἀνάμνησιν) of me," spoken by Jesus at the Last Supper, but among the Gospels only Luke, who does not have these words about the woman, has Jesus say, "Do this in remembrance of me" in his Last Supper narrative (22:19: the words are in the longer text).

51. Most recently Craig A. Evans, *Mark 8:27–16:20*, WBC 34B (Nashville: Thomas Nelson, 2001), 359, with references to others who argue for this view; and see also Edwin K. Broadhead, *Prophet, Son, Messiah: Narrative Form and Function in Mark 14–16*, JSNTSup 97 (Sheffield: Sheffield Academic Press, 1994), 37 n. 2. For the anointing of kings in the Old Testament, see 1 Sam. 10:1; 16:1, 13; 1 Kings 1:39; 19:15–16; 2 Kings 9:3, 6; Ps. 89:20.

52. So Elisabeth Schüssler Fiorenza, *In Memory of Her: A Feminist Theological Reconstruction of Christian Origins* (New York: Crossroad, 1985), xiii–xiv; Richard A. Horsley, *Hearing the Whole Story: The Politics of Plot in Mark's Gospel* (Louisville: Westminster John Knox, 2001), 217–18. Schüssler Fiorenza's view is repeated, with updated references, in Elisabeth Schüssler Fiorenza, "Re-Visioning Christian Origins: In Memory of Her Revisited," in *Christian Origins: Worship, Belief and Society*, ed. K. J. O'Mahony, JSNTSup 241 (Sheffield: Sheffield Academic Press, 2003), 240–42.

53. E.g., J. Keith Elliott, "The Anointing of Jesus," *ExpTim* 85 (1973–1974), 105–7; Elisabeth Schüssler Fiorenza, *Jesus: Miriam's Child, Sophia's Prophet* (London: SCM, 1994), 95.

think this was originally intended or perceived.[54] Reasons for denying that the anointing, either historically or in Mark's story, carries messianic significance are: (1) Anointing the head in the context of a banquet was by no means confined to kings,[55] but was a common custom at feasts. (2) The messianic significance is not explicit in Mark's text.[56] (3) Mark's narrative "goes on to interpret the festal gesture in terms of death and burial rather than of messianic commissioning."[57] The first point is correct and therefore means that the messianic significance is not self-evident but dependent on the context, including the wider context in Mark's passion narrative outside this story itself. The second point can be answered by referring to Mark's narrative of Jesus' riding the colt into Jerusalem. The messianic significance is left implicit, but it can hardly be doubted that it is implicit. The story of the anointing is similar. The third point poses a false alternative. What happens in the story is that Jesus recognizes the messianic significance of the anointing but interprets it according to his own understanding of his messianic vocation as entailing suffering and death. Just as readers of Mark know that Jesus' riding into Jerusalem on a colt does not signify messianic triumph of the generally expected kind but constitutes a journey to his death, so the messianic anointing by the woman is redirected by Jesus toward his burial, coherently with the characteristically Markan connection between messiahship and the cross.

What has not been generally recognized is the significance of Mark's placing of this story between his account of the plot by the Jewish authorities to arrest and kill Jesus (14:1–2) and his account of Judas's visit to the chief priests in order to offer to hand Jesus over to them (14:10–11). I have already pointed out that this is a typical Markan "sandwich" composition, indicating a close connection of meaning between the story that forms the two outer parts and the story that is sandwiched between them. We should surely understand that Judas reports the incident of the anointing to the chief priests, for whom it must constitute significant evidence that Jesus and his disciples are planning an imminent messianic uprising. Perhaps we should also suspect that it was this incident—with its unavoidable confirmation by Jesus that he will undertake the messianic role only on his own terms as a vocation to die—that led Judas to defect. Thus the anointing provides both added cause for the chief priests to take swift action against Jesus and also the means to do so in the shape of Judas's offer.

54. E.g., Charles E. B. Cranfield, *The Gospel according to Saint Mark*, 2nd ed., CGTC (Cambridge: Cambridge University Press, 1963), 415.

55. Kathleen E. Corley, "The Anointing of Jesus in the Synoptic Tradition: An Argument for Authenticity," *JSHJ* 1 (2003): 66–67; Richard T. France, *The Gospel of Mark*, NIGTC (Grand Rapids, Eerdmans; Carlisle:Paternoster, 2002), 552.

56. Presumably this is why many commentators do not even mention the possibility; cf. also Esther Yue L. Ng, *Reconstructing Christian Origins? The Feminist Theology of Elisabeth Schlüssler Fiorenza: An Evaluation*, Paternoster Biblical and Theological Monographs (Carlisle: Paternoster, 2002), 146–47.

57. France, *Gospel*, 552.

That the anointing is related in this way to the actions of the chief priests and Judas is not, of course, explicit in the story, but this is not a valid objection to it. There is similarly no explicit connection between the story of the withered fig tree and the demonstration in the temple, but most commentators believe that, by means of the Markan "sandwich" construction, the former functions as a comment on Jesus' attitude to and action in the temple. But we should also notice the surely studied reserve in Mark's passion narrative as to what led the Jewish authorities to suppose both that Jesus was so dangerous that action must be taken swiftly and that a charge of claiming messiahship could be made to stick and represented to Pilate as a political challenge to Roman rule. There are three events in Mark's narrative that explain this: Jesus' entry into Jerusalem, his demonstration in the temple, and his anointing by a woman. But in all three cases the messianic significance is notably subdued in Mark's telling. The author seems wary of making explicit the aspects of these events that made them construable as evidence for the charge on which Jesus was put to death, that is, that he was claiming to be the messianic "king of the Jews" and planning an uprising.

The messianic significance of all three events would have been clear to Mark's first readers or hearers, but Mark's apparent strategy of leaving it for them to perceive, rather than himself highlighting it, coheres rather strikingly with the strategy of "protective anonymity" in relation to certain characters in this narrative. What put these persons in danger in Jerusalem in the period of the earliest Christian community would be their complicity in Jesus' allegedly seditious behavior in the days before his arrest. Furthermore, the whole community was potentially at risk for its allegiance to a man who had been executed for such seditious behavior. We can readily understand that, just as the pre-Markan passion narrative protected certain individuals by leaving them anonymous, so it protected the community by not making too obvious the messianic meaning of the events that had constituted the chief priests' evidence for treating Jesus as a dangerously seditious figure. Just as the members of the Jerusalem church who first heard the narrative would know who the anonymous persons were, so they would understand the messianic significance of these events without needing it spelled out for them.

We are now in a position to understand why several of the persons who are anonymous in Mark's passion narrative are named in John, thus:

Table 8.1. Anonymous in Mark, Named in John

Mark	John
woman who anoints (14:3)	Mary, sister of Martha (12:3)
man who wields sword (14:47)	Simon Peter (18:10)
servant of the high priest (14:47)	Malchus (18:10)

These should not be regarded as instances of some alleged tendency for names to get added in the tradition. There is little evidence of such a tendency before the fourth century.[58] Moreover, such an explanation neglects the specificities of these particular cases in the passion narrative. As we have seen there may be very good reasons for the anonymity of these characters in Mark, while conversely such reasons would no longer apply at the date and in the place at which John's Gospel was written. Given, as we have argued, that John has independent access to such traditions, there is no difficulty in supposing that the names in John are historically accurate.

In the light of the messianic character of the anointing, John's dating of this event before the triumphal entry makes good historical sense. Jesus is anointed as the Messiah in Bethany the evening before riding into Jerusalem as the Messiah. But in spite of this plausible sequence of events, John has actually obscured the messianic significance of the anointing more than Mark has. Mary of Bethany does not anoint Jesus' head, but his feet, wiping them with her hair. Whatever the explanation for the coincidence[59] with Luke's otherwise very different story of an anointing of Jesus by a woman (Luke 7:38),[60] the effect of this feature in John is to highlight Mary's extravagant devotion to Jesus rather than the messianic meaning of anointing.[61] She takes the role not of a prophet, but of a servant. She performs the role of a servant washing a guest's feet—a role distinctively that of a servant or slave[62]—but does so in an extraordinarily lavish way.[63] (But it is not clear that letting down her hair would be seen as scandalous, as most scholars suppose, if Mary was unmarried, as most likely she was.)[64] Various reasons why John's account focuses on the anointing of the feet are plausible. It is possible that Mary anointed more than Jesus' feet, but that John focuses on the feet because he wishes to stress her humble devotion to Jesus and has in mind the significance of footwashing in his Last Supper narrative.[65] The significance could be that she anointed *even* Jesus' feet. If, as we have suggested, the beloved disciple was close to the Bethany family, he may have wished to emphasize as much as possible Mary's

58. Bauckham, *Jesus*, 43–45.

59. But even so there is the contextually appropriate difference that Luke's woman sheds tears on Jesus' feet, whereas there is no suggestion that Mary in John weeps. Nor does Mary kiss Jesus' feet, as Luke's woman does (Luke 7:38).

60. There are a variety of views on the tradition history, depending on such judgments as whether there was only one anointing or two, and whether John knew Luke's Gospel. Many think of some kind of "cross-fertilization of the two anointing stories" (Witherington, *Women*, 113) in the tradition.

61. Scholars who find messianic significance in the anointing in John 12 include Barrett, *Gospel*, 409; Andreas J. Köstenberger, *John*, BECNT (Grand Rapids: Baker Academic, 2004), 361. Those who think that John 12 certainly cannot suggest royal anointing include Dodd, *Historical Tradition*, 173; Lincoln, *Gospel*, 337.

62. See John Christopher Thomas, *Footwashing in John 13 and the Johannine Community*, JSNTSup 61 (Sheffield: Sheffield Academic Press, 1991), chapter 3; and chap. 9 below.

63. For (rare) parallels to the anointing of the feet in antiquity, see J. F. Coakley, "The Anointing at Bethany and the Priority of John," *JBL* 107 (1988): 241–56, here 247–48.

64. Keener, *Gospel of John*, 863.

65. E.g., Colleen M. Conway, *Men and Women in the Fourth Gospel: Gender and Johannine Characterization*, SBLDS 167 (Atlanta: SBL, 1997), 152.

remarkable love for Jesus. It is also possible that referring to the feet rather than the head of Jesus is actually another protective strategy that originally served to veil the seditious nature of the act. Mark's version protects Mary by not naming her; John's narrative names her (and identifies her by reference to her brother and sister) but hides the messianic significance of her act. In that case John's version, like Mark's, was originally formulated in a context of danger to those who had aided and abetted Jesus.

Finally, there may be a more theological point. If the significance is not that Mary anointed only the feet, but even the feet, then her action is more appropriate for anointing for burial than anointing the head would be. This reading would be consistent with the way that John's account ends, not with commendation of the woman, as in Mark, but with, first, Jesus' words about his burial,[66] then the assertion that Jesus will be leaving them (12:7–8). The whole story in John functions as another of the many passion predictions in this Gospel and serves to interpret Jesus' riding into Jerusalem the next day as the arrival of a king already anointed for his burial. It is in this sense that John's Mary is a prophet: she performs a prophetic sign of Jesus' destiny.

If we accept that in Mark's passion narrative Mary's anonymity is protective and that John correctly identified her, there is a further consequence that will complete our argument for the historical value of John's account of the Bethany family. Lazarus would have needed "protective anonymity" in a passion narrative originating in Jerusalem in the 40s even more than his sister Mary would. John's Gospel explicitly reports, already before the death of Jesus, that "the chief priests planned to put Lazarus to death as well" (12:10). Lazarus could not have been protected in the early period of the Jerusalem church's life by telling his story but not naming him. His story was too well known locally not to be easily identifiable as his, however it was told. For Lazarus, "protective anonymity" had to take the form of his total absence from the story as it was publicly told.[67]

---

66. The seemingly intractable problem of the precise meaning of John 12:7 cannot be discussed here.

67. This has already been suggested by Murray J. Harris, "'The Dead Are Restored to Life': Miracles of Revivification in the Gospels," in *Gospel Perspectives*, vol. 6, *The Miracles of Jesus*, ed. David Wenham and Craig Blomberg (Sheffield: Sheffield Academic Press, 1986), 312; Keener, *Gospel of John*, 836.

9

DID JESUS WASH
HIS DISCIPLES' FEET?

Few narratives in the Fourth Gospel have made as strong an impression on its readers over the centuries as that of Jesus washing his disciples' feet (John 13:2–11). Does its symbolic power stem from Jesus' own prophetic daring, as most readers have assumed, or from the evangelist's creative imagination? The legacy of the nineteenth-century liberals' distinction between historically reliable, early sources (Mark and Q) and late, theological fiction (John) endures, even if only subliminally, in the minds of many New Testament scholars and students. Uniquely Johannine narratives are still often attributed to narrative creativity in the service of theology, at some stage in the Fourth Gospel's history of development. At least the burden of proof tends to be thrust onto any who would maintain otherwise in any specific instance. That John is indebted to Gospel traditions independent of the Synoptic Gospels (whether or not he is also dependent on one or more of these) is now very widely accepted, but still rarely ensures a level playing field between John and the Synoptics when it comes to evaluating the historical value of their narrative traditions.[1] The issue has to be tackled both in general and in

Originally published in a slightly different form in *Authenticating the Activities of Jesus*, ed. B. Chilton and C. A. Evans, New Testament Tools and Studies 28/2 (Leiden: Brill, 1999), 411–29.

1. Johannine creativity in attributing words to Jesus calls for quite distinct treatment from Johannine creation of narratives about Jesus.

particular. In the case of the footwashing, the historical question is rarely discussed in more than a few sentences.[2] For many Johannine scholars the question is, in any case, of little interest. Others perhaps assume that, in the nature of this case, there is little to be said on either side of the issue. Must it not hang largely on a judgment of the historical value of Johannine narratives in general? In fact, there is a good deal more to be said.

Footwashing in Antiquity

In the first place, it is important to be clear about the nature and social significance of footwashing.[3] For the ancients, footwashing was as necessary and regular a chore as brushing teeth is for most modern people. Feet were protected by no more than open sandals, and so, after walking in the heat and in the dust and dirt of country roads or town streets, washing feet was necessary both for comfort and for cleanliness, especially before sitting down to a meal. Footwashing appears in the literature most often as preparation for a meal, and also as a duty of hospitality, either to expected guests or to passing strangers, who needed both to be refreshed after their journey and to be properly prepared for sharing a meal with the host. But it was certainly not a host's duty to wash his guests' feet himself. Either a slave or servant would do it, or the host would provide a basin of water and a towel for the guests to wash their own feet. Washing someone else's feet was an unpleasant task, which no one except a servant or slave could be expected to do. So menial a task was it that in a household with a hierarchy of slaves and servants, it would be the duty of the slaves, not of the servants who performed less demeaning tasks such as waiting at table.[4] It was, in fact, the quintessentially servile task, the one thing that no one else would do. In a household without servants, everyone washed their own feet.

Exceptions in ancient literature are all recorded precisely as exceptional cases. In most, if not all, such cases it is clear that the person washing another's feet is deliberately playing the role of a servant or slave. This is explicitly the case with Abigail (1 Sam. 25:41), Aseneth (*Jos. Asen.* 13.15; 20.1–5), and Favonius (Plutarch, *Pomp.* 73.6–7). In some other exceptional cases, the footwashing is clearly an exceptional act of devotion or flattery (Aristophanes, *Vespae*, 605–11; Meleager

2. Substantial arguments for the historicity of the footwashing are C. H. Dodd, *Historical Tradition in the Fourth Gospel* (Cambridge: Cambridge University Press, 1963), 59–63; J. A. T. Robinson, *Twelve More New Testament Studies* (London: SCM, 1984), 77–80.

3. For the evidence on which this section is based, see especially J. C. Thomas, *Footwashing in John 13 and the Johannine Community*, JSNTSS 61 (Sheffield: JSOT Press, 1991), chapter 3. Thomas himself is much indebted to B. Kötting, "Fusswaschung," *RAC*, 8:743–59.

4. Cf. P. K. Nelson, *Leadership and Discipleship: A Study of Luke 22:24–30*, SBLDS 38 (Atlanta: Scholars Press, 1994), 164.

in *Anthol. Pal.* 12.68;[5] Plutarch, *Mor.* 12.249d).[6] Even when the person washing the feet is not actually a servant or slave, the social significance of the act remains the same. In a society highly conscious of relative status, it would be unthinkable for this uniquely servile act to be performed for an inferior by a superior in the social scale. Exceptionally an inferior who is not actually a servant or slave may perform the act as a kind of extravagant expression of their willingness to be subject to the superior, but for a superior to perform the act for an inferior would be an incomprehensible contradiction of their social relationship.

Abraham was famous for his hospitality to strangers, on the basis of Genesis 18:1–8. Even though he treats his visitors as his social superiors (18:3), he has water brought for them to wash their own feet (18:4), or, in the Septuagint, for his servants to do so. No doubt, the translators, knowing from the text itself that Abraham has servants, thought it, in those circumstances, more hospitable for the guests not to be left to wash their own feet (cf. the similar difference between Hebrew and LXX texts in Gen. 43:24). But according to the *Testament of Abraham*, it was Abraham himself who washed the three guests' feet (A6.6; cf. B3.9), and who performs the same act when one of the three, the archangel Michael, visits him again (A3.6–9). Of course, these angelic visitors really are Abraham's social superiors, and it is only the B recension (3.6–9) that implies it was Abraham's regular practice himself to wash the feet of visiting strangers. This might be a Christian touch (since, as we shall see in the section "History of a Practice" below, early Christian hosts did wash their guests' feet themselves),[7] though in general it is the A recension that shows most signs of the Christian transmission of the text.[8] But in any case, the social significance of footwashing is not lost. Abraham, exceptional in his hospitality to strangers (A1.5; 4.6; B2.10), is the exceptionally humble host who treats all his guests as his social superiors.

The Johannine Interpretation of the Footwashing

The meaning of the footwashing in John 13 has been much debated.[9] Lacking the space to rehearse the debate, I can here argue only briefly for my own view, as a

5. The point in this case, not brought out by Thomas, is that the poet renounces any claim on the boy he loves because he sees him as cupbearer to Zeus on Olympus, thus too superior for anything other than the poet's metaphorical washing of his feet to be appropriate. The image is the extravagant opposite of a homosexual act, whose social significance would be the inferiority of the boy.

6. All these texts are quoted and discussed in Thomas, *Footwashing*, 37–40, 52–55.

7. Note that Origen, *Hom. Gen.* 4.2, treats Abraham's example of washing his guests' feet as one which Christians should follow.

8. E. P. Sanders ("Testament of Abraham," in *The Old Testament Pseudepigrapha*, ed. J. H. Charlesworth, 2 vols., ABRL 13–14 [New York: Doubleday, 1983–1985], 1:879–80) does not include B3.6–9 among passages he suspects Christians may have reworked.

9. See the survey of interpretations in Thomas, *Footwashing*, chapter 1; and the assessment of the main types of interpretation in R. B. Edwards, "The Christological Basis of the Johannine Footwashing,"

preliminary to considering the issue of historicity. The passage (13:1–20) provides the initial statement of the theme of Jesus' lordship in self-humiliation and service, which is the major overarching theme of John's passion narrative. That narrative culminates with Jesus' dying the death of slaves and criminals, while designated king of the Jews for all the world to see (19:19–21) and subsequently buried with the honor due to a king (19:39–41). It begins with the stark paradox of 13:3–5: Jesus, knowing that the Father had given him the uniquely divine lordship over all creation, undertook the role of a slave, performing for his disciples the act most expressive of servile status. The one who can claim the highest status in all reality, sovereign over all creation, humbles himself to the lowest human status, expressing his lordship in self-humiliating service for his social inferiors. A radical overturning of common cultural values with respect to status is implied.

There can be no doubt that John understands the footwashing in relation to the cross, where the Jesus who in chapter 13 undertakes the role of a slave finally dies the death of a slave. The footwashing both provides an interpretation of the meaning of the cross, as Jesus' voluntary self-humiliation and service for others, and also gains its own fullest meaning when seen in the light of the cross it prefigures. In this respect, it parallels the Synoptic accounts of "the institution of the Lord's Supper," accounts whose function in these Gospels is not to record the institution as such (only the disputed verse Luke 22:19b indicates that the rite is to be repeated by the disciples), but rather to provide an interpretation of Jesus' coming death. John's omission of such an account must be due, not only to the fact that he has already spoken of Jesus' death in eucharistic language in chapter 6, but also to the fact that he gives Jesus' death a sacrificial interpretation in his narration of the death itself (19:34, 36). This leaves him free to narrate a different symbolic action at the Last Supper, supplying a different perspective on the meaning of Jesus' coming death.

As has frequently been argued, John 13 provides two interpretations of the act of footwashing, one in Jesus' dialogue with Peter (vv. 6–11), the other in Jesus' speech to the disciples after resuming his seat (vv. 12–20).[10] The two interpretations are related, but distinct. Both are christological, taking their meaning from the fact that it is Jesus the Lord who serves as a slave, but the first is christological and soteriological, the second christological and exemplary. The first is a meaning that the disciples will not be able to understand until after the resurrection (13:7; cf. 2:22; 12:16), a clear indication that it is a meaning connected with Jesus' death.

---

in *Jesus of Nazareth: Lord and Christ*, ed. J. B. Green and M. Turner, I. H. Marshall FS (Grand Rapids: Eerdmans; Carlisle: Paternoster, 1994), 367–83. See now also the cultural anthropological interpretation in J. H. Neyrey, "The Footwashing in John 13:6–11: Transformation Ritual or Ceremony?" in *The Social World of the First Christians*, ed. L. M. White and O. L. Yarbrough, W. A. Meeks FS (Minneapolis: Augsburg Fortress, 1995), 197–213.

10. D. A. Carson, *The Gospel according to John* (Leicester: InterVarsity; Grand Rapids: Eerdmans, 1991), 465, sees a distinct, third interpretation in vv. 10–11, but if his exegesis is correct, it would be more appropriate to see these verses as providing a second development of the first interpretation.

This meaning is conveyed by Jesus' words only in a way that hides it to the disciples within the narrative (vv. 8–10), including the characteristically Johannine double entendre of verse 8b: "Unless I wash you, you have no share in me (μέρος μετ' ἐμοῦ)." At the literal level, this can mean that unless Peter's feet are washed he cannot share the meal with Jesus. At the level of true significance, it means that without the cleansing to be effected by Jesus' death, Peter cannot participate in the eternal life to be had in union with Jesus' life. Whereas this first, soteriological interpretation of the meaning of the footwashing cannot be understood by the disciples within the narrative, as Peter demonstrates, there is nothing about the second interpretation that could not be clear to them. It portrays Jesus' act as an example the disciples are to follow. If he, their Lord and Master, serves them as a slave, so should they serve each other. What is not beneath his dignity can certainly no longer be considered beneath theirs. Here the socially revolutionary nature of Jesus' act is evident in the abolition of relationships based on status, which is its consequence among the disciples. If footwashing is not beneath anyone's dignity, then nothing is. A social group in which each washes the feet of the others can have no social hierarchy, at least of the type symbolized by the limitation of such menial tasks to those of lowest status.[11]

The question arises whether the command in verses 14–15 is meant to be followed literally or whether footwashing here functions as a symbol of humble service. In light of the practice and significance of footwashing in the ancient world, this is surely a false dilemma. There is no indication that the command is not meant literally, but literal footwashing is a concrete instance of the practice of humble service in ordinary life. The reference is to the regular washing of feet, which the disciples, like everyone else, must practice. This ordinary, daily chore is what they should do for each other. Since it is the most menial task, which no one but a servant or slave would ordinarily think of doing, it is the extreme case that carries with it every less humiliating kind of service for each other that might arise. If this is not beneath them, nothing is.

Those exegetes who see in verses 14–15 the institution of a special religious rite of footwashing[12] miss the ordinariness of footwashing as one of the most frequent of life's chores. To confine mutual footwashing to a ritual context while

11. J. Massyngbaerde Ford, *Redeemer—Friend and Mother: Salvation in Antiquity and in the Gospel of John* (Minneapolis: Augsburg Fortress, 1997), chapter 8, understands the footwashing as an act of ritualized friendship. Friendship is probably the best ancient model for the kind of radically nonhierarchical relationships that mutual footwashing would symbolize and enact. In 13:13 Jesus says that the disciples rightly call him Teacher and Lord, for so he is (cf. also 16), but in 15:15 he says that he no longer calls them servants but friends.

12. Thomas, *Footwashing*, offers the fullest recent argument for such a view. He lists earlier views of this kind on pp. 14–16; for more recent advocates, see Edwards, "Christological Basis," 378–79; M. F. Connell, "*Nisi Pedes*, Except for the Feet: Footwashing in the Community of John's Gospel," *Worship* 7 (1996): 517–31. Many of the arguments for a rite of footwashing depend rather heavily on the hypothesis that the Fourth Gospel reflects and addresses a "Johannine community" with distinctive practices not necessarily found in other churches. Against this general hypothesis, see R. Bauckham, ed.,

continuing to treat ordinary footwashing as the task only of slaves would create a scarcely tolerable contradiction in the social significance of the act. This ritual (or "sacramental") understanding of the footwashing—for example, as a rite of remission of postbaptismal sin—is often connected with a blurring of the distinction between the two interpretations of Jesus' act provided in John 13.[13] Something of the soteriological significance of Jesus' act of washing his disciples' feet is carried over into the practice of footwashing as the disciples are to continue it, as was the case in the repetition of the eucharistic acts in the Lord's Supper. But here the analogy of the Lord's Supper has proved misleading. The eucharistic acts would have no particular meaning without their close connection to the soteriological significance of Jesus' death, but mutual footwashing has a clear meaning as the key to a rejection of social hierarchy and a new form of social relationships based on Jesus' example. There is no need to carry over the soteriological focus of the first interpretation in order to make sense of verses 13–20, which themselves contain no soteriological allusion and are fully intelligible in their own terms.

The kind of exegesis that blurs or abolishes the distinction between the two interpretations, usually by thinking of footwashing in the church as a rite with salvific significance, is partly motivated by a dissatisfaction with the idea of two different interpretations merely placed side by side, especially as this idea has often been connected with theories of sources and redaction,[14] which see the evangelist or the final redactor as in less than full control of his material. However, rejecting the ritual meaning of mutual footwashing does not mean that the two interpretations are unconnected. Both are developed from the fundamental meaning of Jesus' act: his expression of his lordship in self-humiliating service. Moreover, both can be seen in relation to Jesus' death, which for the first interpretation is the act of salvific service for others to which the footwashing points, while for the second interpretation it would be the culminating act of Jesus' self-humiliating service as an example for the disciples to follow. Those who follow Jesus in acting like a slave for others may also, like Jesus, incur a slave's death for others. The difference between the two interpretations is that one is concerned with the unique soteriological significance of Jesus' self-humiliation and service, while the second presents these as an example his disciples should follow.

This juxtaposition of the uniqueness and the exemplariness of Jesus' self-giving service is not at all incongruous. It is found elsewhere in the New Testament, notably in Mark 10:43–45 (a passage thematically close to John 13: see the section "John and the Synoptics" below) and in 1 Peter 2:21–24.[15] The well-known christological

---

The Gospels for All Christians: Rethinking the Gospel Audiences (Grand Rapids: Eerdmans; Edinburgh: T. & T. Clark, 1997).

13. Thus Thomas, *Footwashing*, chapter 4, argues forcibly against the view that there are two different interpretations.

14. One of the most recent discussions of this type is M. C. de Boer, *Johannine Perspectives on the Death of Jesus*, Contributions to Biblical Exegesis and Theology 17 (Kampen: Pharos, 1996), 283–92.

15. See also 1 John 4:10–12 and 3:16, pointed out by de Boer, *Johannine Perspectives*, 291–92.

passage in Philippians 2:5–11, which strikingly resembles John 13 in its fundamental themes, also combines these two aspects. In the passage often identified as a hymn (vv. 6–11), Jesus' self-humiliation in service and servile death are envisioned as unique, at least insofar as they lead to his unique exaltation to the position of divine sovereignty over all things (cf. John 13:5), but the function of this passage in its wider context (vv. 3–5) is to exemplify the kind of self-denying humility toward each other that the Philippian Christians are encouraged to practice. That the fourth evangelist should highlight both aspects in relation to the footwashing is not at all surprising, and needs no theories of sources and redaction to explain it. This also means that no confidence can be placed in attempts to argue that one of the two interpretations is older and the other added. While this may be the case,[16] we have no way of knowing it. Our consideration of the historicity of the footwashing must manage without such speculations about Johannine tradition history.

Original Creation or Interpretation of Tradition?

In considering the historicity of the footwashing, we shall follow three lines of inquiry: the first considering evidence within the Fourth Gospel; the second the evidence of the relationship between John 13:1–20 and sayings of Jesus in the Synoptics; the third the evidence of the Christian practice of footwashing outside the Gospels.

As far as the internal evidence of the Fourth Gospel itself is concerned, much depends on our general views about the Johannine narratives of which this is one. A remarkable fact, though it is rarely remarked on, perhaps because it is considered too obvious to merit comment, is the relatively small number of events in Jesus' ministry that the Fourth Gospel recounts. Compared with the Synoptic Gospels, John's narratives are characteristically much longer, inviting the reader or hearer into a more reflective participation in a narrative whose form often provides significant indications of the meaning of the event recounted, while many narratives also incorporate or precede passages in which Jesus himself draws out the meaning of the events. In selecting rather few events to include in his Gospel, John has left himself the space to expound their significance at length. Whatever might be the relationships between John and the Synoptic Gospels, it is scarcely credible that John did not have far more stories about Jesus available to him than he includes in the Gospel (cf. 20:30). This being so, his selection is no doubt determined by the potential of the stories for the kind of interpretation they receive within the Gospel. But given the scope for selectivity that he must have had and given that some of the stories most important to him (such as the cleansing of the temple or the feeding of the five thousand) were, as we can tell from their parallels in

---

16. But the parallel with Mark 10:43–45 (see "John and the Synoptics" below) tends to suggest otherwise.

the Synoptics, certainly traditional, an easy resort to free creation of narratives, which has often been attributed to him, would seem unnecessary. John's genius as a narrator and interpreter of the story of Jesus seems to lie in telling the traditional stories in such a way as to indicate and incorporate profound and extensive reflection on their meaning. Since he undoubtedly does this in some cases, the onus of proof would seem to lie with those who attribute to him in other cases a kind of theological fiction, consciously inventing stories as carriers of the theological meaning he wishes to propound.

Of course, an argument that all John's narratives have a basis in tradition cannot show that all such traditions are historically reliable, but it can dispel the residue of suspicion about specifically Johannine narratives that the scholarly tradition of emphasizing John's theological creativity has left. That suspicion derives from the older view of the fourth evangelist as dependent on all three Synoptic Gospels and having no other Gospel traditions available to him. This view is held by few today. Without it there is no good reason to attribute to John's theological creativity the free creation of narratives ex nihilo, as distinct from and in addition to the interpretation of existing stories.

A further consideration is more specific to the footwashing. Jesus' statement that Peter cannot understand what he is doing but will do so "later" (μετὰ ταῦτα: 13:7; cf. 13:36), that is, after the resurrection, is paralleled earlier in the Gospel by two statements of the evangelist to the effect that the disciples did not understand at the time, but did so after Jesus' resurrection (2:22) or after his glorification (12:16). In one case the reference is to a saying of Jesus that was already known in the tradition (2:19; cf. Matt. 26:61; Mark 14:58), in the other case to an event, Jesus' entry into Jerusalem on a donkey, which was already known in the tradition (12:14–15). The probability is that in chapter 13, as in the other two cases, John sees, with postresurrection hindsight, a deeper significance in a feature of the traditions of Jesus' words and deeds, rather than creating an event to which he attributes such significance.

John and the Synoptics

There is a saying of Jesus well attested in the Synoptic traditions to the effect that the greatest among the disciples must be their servant. It is found in a variety of contexts, of which those closest to John 13 are Luke 22:24–27 and Mark 10:41–45 = Matthew 20:24–28. Whereas Matthew[17] has followed Mark's version of this pericope closely, Luke's version differs considerably and probably derives from another source.[18] The two versions of our saying (the greatest as servant:

17. The following discussion assumes Markan priority.
18. So, e.g., I. H. Marshall, *The Gospel of Luke*, NIGTC (Exeter: Paternoster, 1978), 811; J. Nolland, *Luke 18:35-24:53*, WBC 35C (Dallas: Word, 1993), 1062–63.

Luke 22:26–27a; Mark 10:43–44) show little verbal correspondence but close resemblance in sense. The same is true of the sayings of Jesus that are placed before and after it and to which in both cases it is very closely linked. The sequence must represent an early tradition, which we have in two pre-Lukan forms:

Table 9.1. Two Forms of a Servanthood Saying

Luke 22:24–27	*Mark 10:41–45 = Matthew 20:24–28*
The disciples dispute who is the greatest	The disciples indignant at the request of James and John to sit beside Jesus
(A) Kings of the Gentiles	(A) Rulers of the Gentiles
(B) Greatest as servant	(B) Greatest as servant and slave
(C) Jesus as servant	(C) Jesus as servant
	(D) Ransom

In both versions of this sequence, the fact that saying (B) is related to saying (C)—so that explicitly or implicitly it is because of Jesus' example of service that greatness among the disciples is defined in terms of service—brings this sequence much closer to John 13:12–20 than other occurrences of saying (B). Moreover, in both versions Jesus' service is probably to be understood as culminating in his death. This is explicit in the Markan version in the close link between (C) and the ransom saying (D). In Luke, the placing of the sequence at the Last Supper following the institution of the eucharist and the prediction of the betrayal suggests that saying (C) should be connected with Jesus' closely approaching death, just as John's placing of the footwashing at the Last Supper suggests the same connection. However, in neither the Markan nor the Lukan version is it clear in what Jesus' service prior to his death consists.[19] The general image of servant or slave in Mark's version becomes the more specific image of the servant who waits at table in the two questions that are unique to Luke's version of (B) (v. 27a). This coheres with a striking occurrence of the same image elsewhere in Luke (12:37) and with the Lukan setting at the Last Supper. But whether Luke's version is meant to imply that Jesus' serving is his actual waiting at table at the Last Supper is unclear, especially as in 22:14–21 Jesus is reclining at table, not waiting at table, and indeed presiding at the meal, not serving. In both versions, it is probably best to think of Jesus' whole ministry as one of self-giving service culminating in his death as the giving of his life for others.

It is Luke's version of this sequence that has usually been seen as especially close to John 13:1–20.[20] Luke's version is part of Jesus' "farewell discourse"[21] at the Last Supper, as John 13:12–20 is the beginning of the much longer "farewell discourse" in John (whereas Matthew and Mark have no such discourse). But it

19. For Luke, see the full discussion by Nelson, *Leadership*, 160–71.
20. For various views of the relationship, see ibid., 161–65.
21. Ibid., 97–119.

is doubtful how much significance can be attached to this. Luke or his tradition has highlighted the relationship of this material to Jesus' death by placing it on the last occasion on which Jesus teaches his disciples prior to his death, just as John has done with the footwashing and its interpretation. But Mark's placing is functionally similar, since he locates it after the third of the three passion predictions (Mark 10:32–34) and closely preceding Jesus' entry into Jerusalem. Moreover, whereas the table setting is explicit within Luke's version of saying (B) itself (22:27a), the correspondence with John is not as close as might at first appear. Luke refers to waiting at table as the servant's role. This is a different role from washing feet, and a less menial one, which, in a household with a number of slaves and servants, would be performed by the servants, whereas footwashing would be left to the slaves. The image of waiting at table, while it evokes a humble, serving role, is rather less shockingly demeaning than that of footwashing. While it is tempting to classify Luke 22:24–27 and John 13:1–20 among the rather numerous instances of shared tradition exclusive to Luke and John, it is doubtful whether the contact between John and Luke at this point is in fact significantly greater than that between John and Mark 10:41–45.

Saying (B), the "greatest as servant," also occurs in another context represented in all three Synoptics:

Table 9.2. The Greatest Servant

Matthew 18:1–5	*Mark 9:33–37*	*Luke 9:46–48*
Disciples dispute who is the greatest	Disciples dispute who is the greatest	Disciples dispute who is the greatest
	(B) First as servant	
Jesus takes a child	Jesus takes a child	Jesus takes a child
(E) Entering kingdom like a child		
(B) Greatest like a child		
(F) Receiving child is receiving me	(F) Receiving child is receiving me	(F) Receiving child is receiving me
		(B) Greatest as least

The core of this tradition consists of the narrative material and saying (F). It may well be Mark himself who has added saying (B), in a form that looks like an abbreviated form of the version in Mark 10:43–44 (which lacks πάντων ἔσχατος but has all the other vocabulary of the version in Mark 9:35). It is unlikely to be an independent version of the saying. Matthew's and Luke's changes stem from the recognition that, whereas the saying is appropriate to the context in that it speaks of the reversal (or abolition) of social status among the disciples, it is inappropriate to the extent that a child, though lacking social status, is not a servant. Both therefore transfer the saying into Jesus' words subsequent to his taking the child and adapt it to the example of the child by removing the "servant" terminology.

The Matthean and Lukan versions of saying (B) are not independent versions, but sufficiently explained as adaptations of Mark 9:35 to the context. Finally, Matthew has also transferred saying (E) to this context from its Markan context in the other Synoptic pericope featuring children, where Mark and Luke have it but Matthew omits it (Matt. 19:13–15; Mark 10:13–16; Luke 18:15–17). It forms an appropriate companion to Matthew's version of saying (B), which follows it in Matthew 18:3–4. The conclusion must be that it is unlikely that any of the three Synoptic versions of saying (B) in this tradition are independent versions, but all stem originally from the form in Mark 10:43–44.

Finally, one more Synoptic version of saying (B), the "greatest as servant," occurs in Matthew 23:11 in a quite different sequence of sayings. Whether this is Matthew's abbreviation of the version in Mark 10:43–44/Matthew 20:26–27 or an independent version from Matthew's special tradition, it is impossible to be sure. It is likely enough that such a saying should circulate widely and appear in more than one collected sequence of sayings, as is the case with the saying that follows it here (Matt. 23:12; cf. Luke 14:11; 18:14).

Thus we have two independent versions of sayings (B) and (C) connected within a sequence of sayings that contrasts kingship among the Gentiles with service among the disciples of Jesus and roots this contrast in Jesus' own example:

> The kings of the Gentiles lord it over them;
> and those in authority over them are called benefactors.
> But not so with you:
> rather the greatest among you must become like the youngest,
> and the leader like one who serves.
> For who is greater, the one who is at table or the one who serves?
> Is it not the one at table?
> But I am among you as one who serves.
>
> (Luke 22:25–27)

> You know that those who are considered rulers over the Gentiles lord it
>   over them,
> and their great ones tyrannize over them.
> But it is not so among you;
> but whoever wishes to become great among you must be your servant,
> and whoever wishes to be first among you must be slave of all.
> For the Son of Man came not to be served but to serve,
> and to give his life a ransom for many.
>
> (Mark 10:42–45)

There is also another plausibly independent version of saying (B):

> The greatest among you will be your servant.
>
> (Matt. 23:11)

It should be noted that in John 13:1–20 there are no verbal parallels at all with these Synoptic sayings, except that δοῦλος occurs both in John 13:16 and in Mark 10:44 (= Matt. 20:27). But John 13:16 is a saying paralleled in Matthew 10:24, where δοῦλος occurs.

Though verbally unrelated, John 13:1–20 has strong thematic similarities with Luke 22:25–27 and Mark 10:42–45. How are these to be understood? The question arises whether John is dependent on nothing more in the tradition than a version of these Synoptic sayings, and has created the narrative of the footwashing as a vivid illustration of the point made in these traditional sayings of Jesus. It has not seldom been suggested that the footwashing is an imaginative construction on the basis of Luke 22:27.[22] Such a process seems to lack parallels. While Gospel scholars sometimes suggest that the evangelists or their traditions have created narrative settings for traditional sayings, the creation of a narrative to *replace* a traditional saying has been suggested with any plausibility at all only in the case of parables,[23] where the traditional saying could not have been retained in the context of the narrative. There is no convincing example in John.[24] In the case of the footwashing, there is no reason why John should not have included a version of the sayings in Luke 22:25–27 and Mark 10:42–45 as Jesus' interpretation of his action, had these sayings been the source from which he created the narrative. That he has created not a setting for the sayings, but a narrative replacement of the sayings is implausible. Moreover, it should be observed that in Jesus' interpretation of the footwashing, John does cite two traditional sayings of Jesus, highlighted by the "Amen, amen, I say to you" formula, which John often uses to mark out traditional logia. These have parallels in the Synoptics (John 13:16; cf. Matt. 10:24–25; Luke 6:40; John 13:20; cf. Matt. 10:40; Luke 10:16),[25] but in different contexts, unrelated to the "greatest as servant" sayings.

22. E.g., C. K. Barrett, *The Gospel according to St. John*, 2nd ed. (London: SPCK, 1978), 436; for earlier supporters of this view, see J. A. Bailey, *The Traditions Common to the Gospels of Luke and John*, NovTSup 7 (Leiden: Brill, 1963), 36 n. 7.

23. Notably, the suggestion that the parable in Luke 13:6–9 is the origin of the story of the barren fig tree (Mark 11:12–14, 20–21): see W. R. Telford, *The Barren Temple and the Withered Tree*, JSNTSS 1 (Sheffield: JSOT Press, 1980), 13–14.

24. The suggestion (e.g., by M. Davies, *Rhetoric and Reference in the Fourth Gospel*, JSNTSS 69 [Sheffield: JSOT Press, 1992], 256) that John's narrative of the raising of Lazarus (11) is based on the parable of the rich man and Lazarus (Luke 16:10–31) is entirely unconvincing. Lazarus (Eleazar) was one of the most common Jewish names of the period, so that the coincidence of the name is of no significance. John's Lazarus is not raised so that he may warn unrepentant Jews of the punishment that awaits them in the next life, as it is suggested Luke's Lazarus should be (though the request is refused). It is impossible to see how Luke's parable could have generated John's narrative.

25. Cf. also Matt. 18:5 = Mark 9:37 = Luke 9:46, where a version of this saying makes reference to the child Jesus takes as an example of the lack of status required of disciples. In Luke 9:46 this brings it into combination with a version of the "greatest as servant" saying. But this is the version of the latter furthest from resembling John 13 (since it makes no reference to servant or serving), while John 13:20 is similarly closer to Matt. 10:40 than to Mark 9:37 or Luke 9:46.

If the Synoptic sayings are not a source of John's footwashing narrative, then they can be invoked in support of the historical value of John's narrative by the criterion of coherence. The two independent versions, Luke 22:25–27 and Mark 10:42–45, provide this series of sayings with good attestation in the tradition, indicating that Jesus both spoke of leadership among his disciples as the role of the slave or the servant of all,[26] and also spoke of his own example to them in the same terms. The embodiment of these ideas in a striking, even extreme instance of what he meant—washing the disciples' feet—is coherent with the Synoptic sayings, with Jesus' practice of enacting symbolic and demonstrative illustrations of his teaching, widely evidenced in the Gospel traditions, and with the hyperbolic style characteristic of Jesus' teaching.

History of a Practice

Outside John 13 there is only one New Testament reference to a Christian practice of washing the feet of fellow Christians. In 1 Timothy 5:10, the good works expected of a widow include that she has "shown hospitality, washed the saints' feet, helped the afflicted." The association with hospitality is not unexpected in the light of the general evidence about footwashing from the ancient world, and tends to preclude the possibility that the footwashing here is a religious rite. Rather, among the good works expected of widows is that they should perform for their houseguests the footwashing that, had they not been Christians, they would have expected a slave or the guests themselves to perform. Besides hospitality in their own homes, another possible context for the widows' footwashing, suggested by a passage of Tertullian I shall cite below, is the agape meal, at which the feet of all who arrived for the meal would have to be washed in some way. That footwashing is here mentioned among the good works of widows in no way implies that only widows practiced it in the context addressed by 1 Timothy.

This passage joins the scattered evidence from the following centuries for the Christian practice of footwashing. Except in connection with this other evidence, it might not be especially significant, while the later evidence alone could not be presumed to refer to a practice going back to the New Testament period were it not for 1 Timothy 5:10. Together the evidence is sufficient to indicate a widespread practice, highly distinctive to early Christianity, which originated at an early date. The fact that 1 Timothy 5:10 itself clearly presumes an established practice should be noted, and makes it very unlikely that it reflects the influence of the Fourth Gospel.

26. The subversion of social status in the community of the disciples is a theme also more widely attested in the tradition of the sayings of Jesus: e.g., Mark 10:31 and parallels; Matt. 23:12 and parallels.

J. C. Thomas has collected and discussed the relevant patristic evidence,[27] but his discussion is marred by his view that, like his interpretation of John 13, this material evidences a widespread religious rite of footwashing in early Christianity. On the contrary, most of the evidence is best understood as referring to the practice of washing the feet of fellow Christians (or others) on occasions when footwashing would take place in any case. There need be no special significance in the footwashing itself, only in the fact that Christians are performing the act.

Tertullian writes of the way a non-Christian husband might be expected to regard his Christian wife, especially the good works and religious meetings for which she would leave his home:

> For who would suffer his wife, for the sake of visiting the brethren, to go round from street to street to other men's, and indeed all the poorer, cottages? Who will willingly bear her being taken from his side by nocturnal convocations, if need so be? Who, finally, will without anxiety endure her absence all the night long at the paschal solemnities? Who will, without some suspicion of his own, dismiss her to attend the Lord's Supper which they defame? Who will suffer her to creep into prison to kiss a martyr's bonds? Nay, truly, to meet any one of the brethren to exchange the kiss? To offer water for the saints' feet? To snatch (somewhat for them) from her food, from her cup? To yearn (after them)? To have (them) in her mind? If a pilgrim brother arrive, what hospitality for him in an alien home? (*Ad Uxorem* 2.4)[28]

The husband's concern is probably envisaged as primarily for the dishonor such activities by his wife would bring on his own reputation. Some of the activities are of dubious propriety or worse, especially in view of the persistent pagan rumors about what happened in secret Christian meetings during the hours of darkness. But there is also evidently a concern about activities that demean the wife (and thereby her husband), such as entering the homes of the poor and honoring convicted criminals (the martyrs in prison). Washing the feet of the saints (perhaps a deliberate echo of 1 Tim. 5:10) would be seen as a socially degrading act. We cannot here think of hospitality in the woman's home as the context, since the last sentence of the quotation excludes what in any case would not be conceivable in the case of the wife of an unbeliever. Probably, therefore, the most plausible context is the agape meal, at which, Tertullian elsewhere notes, "a peculiar respect is shown to the lowly" (*Apol.* 39), though the later evidence associating footwashing with visiting the sick (*Apost. Con.* 3.19) suggests, alternatively, that this could be in view. Elsewhere Tertullian seems to imply that Christians were known for

27. Thomas, *Footwashing*, chapter 5. His treatment of the patristic evidence is also criticized by R. B. Edwards in a review in *EvQ* 66 (1994): 278–80.

28. Quoted by Thomas, *Footwashing*, 140, in the translation by Roberts and Donaldson (Ante-Nicene Fathers).

practicing footwashing in a religious context (*Cor.* 8); reference to footwashing preceding the agape meal would be very plausible here too.

From the late fourth century come two references to washing the feet of those unable to do this for themselves. The *Canons of Athanasius* instruct bishops to serve at meals with their priests, and to wash the feet of those too weak to do this for themselves. The *Apostolic Constitutions* instruct deacons, as part of their ministry of visiting the sick, to wash the feet of "such of the brethren as are weak and infirm" (3.19).[29] While these references may seem to minimize the practice in envisaging it only as a service to those unable to wash their own feet, they also make clear that it is no religious rite. It is the regular footwashing for comfort and hygiene, such as before a meal. Bishops and deacons are not to think it beneath their dignity to perform this ordinary but servile act for those who needed it done for them.

Other references to the practice, by Origen, Chrysostom, Pachomius, Caesarius of Arles, Sulpicius Severus, Sozomen, and Benedict of Nursia clearly envisage hospitality to strangers as the context, whether in private homes or in monastic communities,[30] while Caesarius also, like the *Apostolic Constitutions*, associates it with visiting the sick.[31]

Some of the evidence Thomas cites for footwashing as a rite signifying forgiveness of sins is not really such. Some passages mean that the meritorious act of washing the feet of others procures forgiveness of sins for the one who washes (Ambrose, *Spir.* 1.15) or procures prayers for his forgiveness by those whose feet he has washed (Cassian, *Inst.* 4.19; Caesarius, *Serm.* 202), while Augustine understands Christ to be daily cleansing our feet (metaphorically) from sin by interceding for us, with no apparent reference to an actual ritual practice (*In Joan. Ev.* 56.5; 58.5).[32] However, there is good evidence that, from at least ca. 300 onward, in certain parts of the Western church, there was a common practice of washing the feet of the newly baptized.[33] Ambrose, reflecting on the fact that this custom was observed in Milan but not in Rome, cites the view of some that footwashing was to be observed as a practice of hospitality only, not as a ritual element in the sacrament of baptism. His response is that the former "belongs to humility," the latter "to sanctification" (*Myst.* 3.5).[34] This makes a clear distinction between the special soteriological significance attached to the footwashing that in some churches accompanied baptism, and the significance of the common Christian

29. The two passages are quoted by Thomas, *Footwashing*, 130, 131–32.

30. The relevant passages are quoted by Thomas, *Footwashing*, 132–34, 141, 143–45.

31. *Serm.* 60.4, quoted by Thomas, *Footwashing*, 145.

32. All these passages are quoted by Thomas, *Footwashing*, 158–61.

33. The evidence, from the Synod of Elvira, Ambrose, Augustine, and Caesarius of Arles, is quoted by Thomas, *Footwashing*, 142–43, 145, 178.

34. Quoted by Thomas, *Footwashing*, 178. Caesarius (*Serm.* 104.3, quoted by Thomas, *Footwashing*, 145) says of the baptized: "Let them receive strangers and, in accord with what was done for themselves in baptism, wash the feet of their guests."

practice of footwashing as part of the hospitality offered to strangers and guests. The latter is not a religious rite, but a feature of everyday life, which Christians expressed their humility—their disregard of social status—in undertaking. As late as the sixth century it is clear that the practice was a stumbling-block for some high status Christians, who felt it to be degrading.[35] The socially radical significance of Christian footwashing persisted throughout the patristic period.

The practice of footwashing following baptism may well have been based on John 13:5–10, from which its soteriological significance and its connection with baptism could have been derived. The everyday practice of footwashing—in hospitality and visiting the sick—is also associated in the texts with John 13, as obedience to Jesus' command that his example be followed (vv. 14–15). These texts make it clear that the command was understood to apply to ordinary occasions when footwashing would be natural and necessary, requiring that Christians should not on these occasions hesitate to perform the act, which would otherwise be the duty of slaves. Though for the period from the first century to the third the only clear evidence is that provided by 1 Timothy, Tertullian, and Origen,[36] the incidental character of these references is indicative of a practice taken for granted and well known, despite its countercultural nature. The nature of our evidence for early Christianity in the first three centuries makes it unsurprising that references are not more plentiful. The evidence we have is sufficient to suggest a practice established already in the first century independently of the influence of the Fourth Gospel.

Footwashing was one of the most countercultural practices of early Christianity, symbolizing most radically the status-rejecting ideals of the early Christian communities. Its origin calls for explanation. It might be a practice initiated within earliest Christianity, under the inspiration of those sayings of Jesus that require his disciples to relate to each other by humble service rather than by self-aggrandizing lordship. John's story of the footwashing might then be an etiological myth, projecting the origin of this distinctive practice back into Jesus' ministry. But such a speculation is less plausible than the obvious alternative: that, just as Jesus dined with outcasts and blessed children, so also he washed his disciples' feet.

35. Caesarius, *Serm.* 202, quoted by Thomas, *Footwashing*, 133.
36. Cf. also, less clearly, Cyprian, quoted by Thomas, *Footwashing*, 141.

10

JEWISH MESSIANISM
ACCORDING TO THE
GOSPEL OF JOHN

1. Introduction

In 1872 William Sanday wrote:

There is no stronger proof of the genuineness and of the authenticity of the fourth Gospel than the way in which it reflects the current Messianic idea.[1]

Originally published in *Historical and Literary Studies in John: Challenging Current Paradigms*, ed. Peter M. Head and John Lierman, WUNT 2 (Tübingen: Mohr Siebeck, 2007), 34–68. Reprinted by permission of the publisher.

1. W. Sanday, *The Authorship and Historical Character of the Fourth Gospel* (London: Macmillan, 1872), 124. By "authenticity" Sanday means that the author was a participant in the events he recounts. The preceding sentence reads: "It is almost superfluous to point out how difficult, how impossible it would have been for a writer wholly *ab extra* to throw himself into the midst of these hopes and feelings [i.e., of those who during Jesus' ministry expected him to conform to popular messianic expectation], and to reproduce them, not as if they were something new that he had learned, but as part of an atmosphere that he had himself once breathed." This is a kind of psychological argument that seems to have carried much more conviction in the nineteenth century than it does in the twenty-first. It is hard now to know what weight to give it, but that what is suggested would have been "impossible" is surely too strong a judgment.

It is not my intention in this chapter to make so strong a claim. I think that the accuracy and detail with which the "messianic" ideas current in Palestinian Judaism in the period before 70 CE are reflected in the Gospel of John are one of several striking ways in which this Gospel reflects good knowledge of pre-70 Jewish Palestine. This does not necessarily guarantee the historical veracity of the Gospel's account of Jesus and his history, since a fictional story can be told with good historical verisimilitude.[2] But it is a feature of the Fourth Gospel all too neglected by those many scholars who read it as reflecting the situation of the "Johannine community" in relation to its local synagogue at the end of the first century rather than the situation in Jewish Palestine in the time of Jesus. The more the Gospel can be shown to correspond to the latter, the more we must take seriously that the evangelist's intention was to write a story set in the past—a past represented with historical realism rather than imagined with allegorical reference to the present.

Just as the Gospel of John is often more precise and detailed than the Synoptics in such factual matters as geography and chronology, so, as we shall see, its portrayal of Jewish "messianic" expectations in the time of Jesus is also, on the whole, more precise and detailed. I put "messianic" in quotes because in the title of this essay and up to this point I use it imprecisely to refer to expectations of eschatological figures of several kinds. If we follow the usage of our sources (including the Gospel of John), one of the two such figures that are of most importance in the Gospel—the prophet like Moses—should probably not be called a "Messiah." I shall drop the loose use of "messianism" after these introductory remarks.

Since Sanday wrote we have learned a lot more about Jewish eschatological expectations in the first century, both from closer study of the sources available in Sanday's time and from sources not then available (including some of the relevant Pseudepigrapha and especially the Dead Sea Scrolls).[3] This enables us to be more precise and detailed in our estimate of the accuracy of John's precision and details. Of course, more sources and closer study tend to generate more controversy. I cannot enter here into all the scholarly debates about Jewish "messianism" in the Second Temple period, but I shall attempt at least to argue briefly for my own position on debatable issues that are most pertinent to the material in the Fourth Gospel.

It is, of course, true that John's presentation and, especially, selection of Jewish "messianic" views in the Gospel serve his own literary and theological aims. But this does not invalidate the task we undertake in this essay, which is to examine these views on their own terms—apart from any further role they may play in

---

2. Cf. the more cautious remark of C. H. Dodd, *Historical Tradition in the Fourth Gospel* (Cambridge: Cambridge University Press, 1963), 120.

3. This is even true of the discussion in C. H. Dodd, *The Interpretation of the Fourth Gospel* (Cambridge: Cambridge University Press, 1953), 87–93, which shows its datedness in that it puts John's indebtedness to Jewish messianic ideas under the heading of his relationship to "Rabbinic Judaism." But it remains in some respects a useful discussion.

the Gospel—and to assess their plausibility as views held by Palestinian Jews in the time of Jesus. I therefore differ significantly from Marinus de Jonge's methodological principle that it is necessary *first* "to investigate how these references to Jewish . . . beliefs function in the setting in which they occur, and within the Gospel as a whole" *before* trying to assess the evangelist's reliability in reproducing such beliefs.[4] Indeed, I am inclined to think that this method of procedure prejudices de Jonge's investigation, inclining him to think that the views the Gospel attributes to Jewish contemporaries of Jesus have been formulated for the sake of their role in John's own christological purposes, including a critique of other Christian christological views, and relate only in a generally vague way to actual (non-Christian) Jewish views. The alternative approach adopted in this chapter may serve at least to redress the balance.

This chapter is confined to Jewish "messianism" and does not include consideration of similar aspects of Samaritan belief, even though these are certainly relevant to the Fourth Gospel (4:25–26, 29). Samaritan expectations of an eschatological figure require a separate discussion, which is beyond the scope of the present essay.

2. Three Eschatological Figures (1:19–21)

In the opening scene of the Gospel's narrative a delegation from the temple in Jerusalem inquires who John the Baptist is. Evidently John's behavior suggests that he must cast himself in one of the roles that were assigned to various eschatological figures in Jewish expectation. When John denies that he is the Messiah (ὁ χριστός), two other possible self-identifications are put to him and he denies that he is either of them. The three possibilities John denies are the Messiah, Elijah, and the prophet. The Messiah, as throughout the Gospel, is the Davidic royal Messiah. The Gospel, as we shall see, consistently distinguishes the Messiah from "the prophet," but nowhere else in the Gospel is there evidence of three different eschatological figures. If "the prophet" is to be understood as the eschatological prophet like Moses (Deut. 18:15–19), then it could be that those who question John are suggesting two different prophetic figures with whom he might identify himself: the returning Elijah and the Mosaic prophet. This is the view of most commentators.

There certainly was an expectation of the return of the prophet Elijah, based on Malachi 3:23–24 (LXX 3:22–23; English versions 4:5–6) and apparent in Sirach 48:10–11; *1 Enoch* 90:31; 4Q558 1.2.4; *LAB* 48.1; Mark 9:11–12; Matt. 17:10–11 (cf. Luke 1:16–17) as well as in rabbinic literature. From these texts it

---

4. M. de Jonge, "Jewish Expectations about the 'Messiah' according to the Fourth Gospel," *NTS* 19 (1973): 247.

is natural to see Elijah's eschatological ministry of restoration and reconciliation[5] as the role of a prophet, like that of the historical Elijah. But there is also evidence that the returning Elijah was understood as the eschatological high priest. The *Targum of Pseudo-Jonathan* to the Pentateuch identifies Elijah with Phinehas the grandson of Aaron[6] and sees Phinehas-Elijah as the one who will be sent as high priest at the end of days.[7] This tradition no doubt has an exegetical basis.[8] One factor must have been that Scripture does not record Phinehas's death (in its reliance on the silence of Scripture this is an interesting parallel to the case of Melchizedek in Heb. 7:3), along with the fact that Phinehas was given "a covenant of perpetual priesthood" (Num. 25:13; cf. *Num. R.* 21:3). Another factor is that both figures are noted in the biblical narratives for their "zeal" in slaughtering idolaters.[9] Finally, a decisive factor in the identification of Phinehas and Elijah must have been the parallel between the eternal "covenant of peace" made by God with Phinehas[10] and Malachi 2:4–7, which refers to God's covenant of peace with Levi and describes "the priest" as a "messenger of YHWH of hosts." This links Phinehas with "the messenger of the covenant" (Mal. 3:1), who is Elijah, and the covenant of peace with Elijah's eschatological ministry of reconciliation (Mal. 3:24[4:6]).

The evidence of the Targums and rabbinic literature does not enable us securely to date this tradition of Phinehas-Elijah as the eschatological high priest to the first century CE.[11] In Justin's *Dialogue*, the Jew Trypho maintains that it will be Elijah's role to anoint the Messiah.[12] This could presuppose that Elijah is the eschatological high priest but need not do so, since in the Hebrew Bible kings may be anointed by prophets[13] as well as by high priests,[14] and in the case of the Messiah the most relevant precedent might be David's anointing by the prophet

5. On this, see R. Bauckham, "The Restoration of Israel in Luke-Acts," in *Restoration: Old Testament, Jewish and Christian Perspectives*, ed. J. M. Scott, JSJSS 72 (Leiden: Brill, 2001), 439–48.

6. See M. Hengel, *The Zealots*, trans. D. Smith (Edinburgh: T. & T. Clark, 1989), chapter IV B, for a fuller study of the evidence; and R. Hayward, "Phinehas—the Same Is Elijah," *JJS* 29 (1978): 22–34, for a theory that links the origins of this identification with John Hyrcanus.

7. *Tg. Ps.-J.* Exod. 4:13; 6:18; 40:10; Deut. 30:4; cf. Num. 25:12.

8. Hayward, "Phinehas," denies this because the exegetical basis is not apparent in *LAB* 48.1, the oldest witness to the identification of Phinehas and Elijah, but it is characteristic of Pseudo-Philo's *LAB* to use traditions that have exegetical bases without making these bases explicit.

9. Phinehas: Num. 25:11–13; cf. Sir. 45:23; 1 Macc. 2:26, 54; 4 Macc. 18:12; *LAB* 47.1; Elijah: 1 Kings 19:10; cf. Sir. 48:2; Phinehas and Elijah identified: *Pirqe R. El.* 29.

10. Num. 25:12; Sir. 45:24.

11. The life of Elijah in *Liv. Proph.* 21, which says nothing of his eschatological role (unless 21:3 refers to the eschatological judgment), does say that Elijah was "of Aaron's tribe" (21:1), but it is by no means certain that this text should be dated as early as the first century CE.

12. *Dial.* 8.4; 49.1. Since this was not a Christian view, we may assume that Justin here accurately reflects a Jewish view.

13. 1 Sam. 10:1; 1 Kings 1:45; 19:16 [Elijah]; 2 Kings 9:1–7.

14. 1 Kings 1:39, 45; 2 Chron. 23:11; S. Talmon, "The Concept of Māšîaḥ and Messianism in Early Judaism," in *The Messiah*, ed. J. H. Charlesworth (Philadelphia: Fortress. 1992), 88–90.

Samuel (1 Sam. 16:1–13). But we have a first-century witness to the identification of Phinehas with Elijah in Pseudo-Philo's *Biblical Antiquities*. There God tells Phinehas that, instead of dying, he will be hidden away until he returns as Elijah in the days of the kings. Then

> you will be lifted up into the place where those who were before you were lifted up, and you will be there until I remember the world. Then I will make you [plural] come and you [plural] will taste what is death. (*LAB* 48.1)

This passage is clearly connected with the tradition found in *4 Ezra* 6:26; 7:28–29; 13:52; 14:9; *2 Baruch* 76:2, according to which, not only Elijah, but a whole group of people who never died will return at the end and only then die. It is not explicit in *LAB* 48.1 that Phinehas-Elijah will return as the eschatological high priest, but it must be implied in an expectation that Phinehas, recipient of a covenant of eternal priesthood and the greatest high priest after his grandfather Aaron, will return at the time of the end.

Therefore it is very possible that in John 1:19–21 the three eschatological figures represent the three roles of king, high priest, and prophet. These are the three human leaders that a properly restored Jewish theocracy would require, just as the historical David ruled with the aid of the high priest Zadok and the prophet Nathan (cf. 1 Kings 1:43–45). Such an eschatological trio appear together in only two extant Jewish texts, both from Qumran. The Community Rule refers to the regulations that must be obeyed "until the prophet comes, and the Messiahs of Aaron and Israel,"[15] while the collection of texts known as 4QTestimonia cites, in succession, three passages from the Torah: Deuteronomy 18:18–19 (the prophet like Moses); Numbers 24:15–17 (Balaam's prophecy of the star and the scepter, which was usually interpreted as referring to the Davidic Messiah); and Deuteronomy 33:8–11 (the blessing of Levi, probably taken here to refer to the eschatological high priest).[16] While the eschatological high priest and the Davidic Messiah appear elsewhere in literature produced by the Qumran community,[17] the eschatological prophet like Moses probably does not.[18] The fact that the community seems not to have been interested in the eschatological prophet makes it the more impressive that he is nevertheless included in the two passages just cited. These are evidence that it was assumed that all three offices would require to be filled in the messianic age.

15. 1QS 9.11. On whether this sentence is a later addition to the text of the Community Rule, see J. VanderKam, "Messianism in the Scrolls," in *The Community of the Renewed Covenant*, ed. E. Ulrich and J. VanderKam (Notre Dame, IN: University of Notre Dame Press, 1994), 212–13.

16. 4Q175.5–20.

17. See J. J. Collins, *The Sceptre and the Star: The Messiahs of the Dead Sea Scrolls and Other Ancient Literature* (New York: Doubleday, 1995), chapter 4.

18. It is questionable whether 4Q521 2 2 and 11QMelch 2 refer to this figure, as Collins, *Sceptre*, 117–22, argues.

A. S. van der Woude argued that the three figures in John 1:19–21—the Davidic Messiah, Elijah the high priest, and the prophet—actually represent the expectations of the Qumran community, and that the delegation of priests and Levites ask John the Baptist about all three because they associate him with the Qumran community.[19] Raymond Brown objected to this on the grounds that "the Qumran Essenes insisted on a priesthood of pure Zadokite lineage ... and there is no evidence that Elijah was a Zadokite priest."[20] This is not a cogent objection, since, if the Qumran community identified the eschatological high priest with Elijah, they would probably also have identified Elijah with Phinehas, who, as Aaron's grandson and the third Israelite high priest, had credentials superior to those of any descendant of Zadok. However, there is no evidence that the community did identify the eschatological high priest, the Messiah of Aaron, with Elijah, though this certainly cannot be ruled out. But there is no need to suppose that the expectation of three eschatological figures as such was unique to the Qumran community or the Essenes. The general consideration that the ideal constitution of Israel required all three offices,[21] which would easily be deduced from the Hebrew Bible, must have required that all three offices were to be filled by ideal occupants in the messianic age.

Our evidence seems to indicate that popular expectation (reflected in the Gospel of John itself in later chapters) focused on either the Davidic Messiah or on the eschatological prophet (or both). This was because both figures could and often were understood as savior figures who would deliver Israel from her pagan oppressors. From this perspective the rarity of reference to the eschatological high priest in our extant texts outside the writings of the Qumran community, which had especially priestly interests, is not surprising, but does not mean it would not have been taken for granted that there would be a high priest in the messianic kingdom. It is noteworthy that those who ask John the Baptist whether he is Elijah are priests and Levites (John 1:19), but perhaps it is even more important that the delegation from Jerusalem comprises religious experts who can be expected to know about all three eschatological figures and are not in this instance motivated by any particular interest in one or another of them. In the attempt to discover who John claims to be, they run through the whole gamut of possibilities. The only kind of eschatological figure they exclude is an angelic deliverer (Michael or Melchizedek), presumably taking it for granted that John is not an angel from heaven.

3. The Prophet

After 1:25 there is no further reference in the Gospel to Elijah or to the eschatological high priest. For those in the narrative who identify Jesus as one of the figures

---

19. A. S. van der Woude, *La secte de Qumran* (Louvain: Desclée de Brouwer, 1959), 121–34.

20. R. E. Brown, *The Gospel according to John (I–XII)*, AB 29 (New York: Doubleday, 1966), 50.

21. Cf. the claim of Josephus that John Hyrcanus "was accounted by God worthy of three of the greatest privileges, the rule of the nation, the office of high-priest, and the gift of prophecy" (*Ant.* 13.299).

of Jewish eschatological expectation, he is either "the prophet" or "the Messiah." These two categories are evidently alternatives, such that in 7:40–41 some people in the crowd claim that Jesus must be "the prophet," while others think he is "the Messiah." At this point it is essential to distinguish John's own Christology from the forms of Jewish expectation he attributes to his characters. It is probable that John intends to present Jesus as fulfilling the prophecy of a prophet like Moses as well as those of the royal Messiah. But he does not represent his characters as assimilating or confusing these two categories, though there are three passages (1:45; 6:14–15; 7:31) which have been thought to show such an assimilation. Some scholars have supposed that when Philip tells Nathanael, "We have found him about whom Moses in the law and also the prophets wrote" (1:45), Philip refers to the prophecy of a prophet like Moses in Deuteronomy 18:18–19[22] alongside prophecies of the royal Messiah in the prophets. But the Pentateuch contains two of the most popular prophecies of the royal Messiah: Genesis 49:9–10 and Numbers 24:17. There are more allusions to these two texts in the literature of early Judaism[23] than there are to Deuteronomy 18:15–19. They were popular because they were the most ancient messianic prophecies and because they were in the Torah, regarded as the most authoritative part of the Jewish Scriptures. In view of these messianic prophecies in the Torah, there is no reason to think that Philip's words identify Jesus as any figure other than the royal Messiah. Whether the people in 6:14–15 or 7:31 combine the categories of eschatological prophet like Moses and royal Messiah we shall discuss below.

3.1. The Prophet Like Moses in Jewish Literature

Outside the New Testament, we have two kinds of sources of information about expectation of the prophet like Moses in late Second Temple Judaism. One is direct literary references to this figure as part of the eschatological expectation. The other is the accounts by Josephus of popular leaders who, in first-century Jewish Palestine, appear to have adopted such a role for themselves. Evidence in

22. This is argued at some length by M.-É. Boismard, *Moses or Jesus: An Essay in Johannine Christology*, trans. B. T. Viviano (Minneapolis: Fortress; Leuven: Peeters, 1993), 25–30; see also B. F. Westcott, *The Gospel according to St. John* (London: John Murray, 1889), 26; J. H. Bernard, *A Critical and Exegetical Commentary on the Gospel according to St. John* (Edinburgh: T. & T. Clark, 1928), 1:62; M.-É. Boismard, *Du baptême à Cana (Jean, 1, 19–2, 11)*, LD 18 (Paris: Du Cerf, 1956), 92–93; R. E. Brown, *The Gospel according to John*, AB 29 (New York: Doubleday, 1966), 1:86; D. A. Carson, *The Gospel according to John* (Grand Rapids: Eerdmans, 1991), 159. But there is even less reason to think that the reference is to Gen. 28, as C. K. Barrett, *The Gospel according to St John*, 2nd ed. (London: SPCK, 1978), 183, does. How could Philip be expected to anticipate Jesus' allusion to Gen. 28 in 1:51?

23. Gen. 49:9–10: 1QSb 5.27–29; 4Q252 5.1–5; *4 Ezra* 12:31–32. Num. 24:17: Sir. 36:12; CD 7.18–21; 4QTest (4Q175) 9–13; *Sib. Or.* 5:155–61; Josephus, *BJ* 6.312–314; and the use of the nickname Bar Kokhba for the leader of the Second Revolt. From these last two instances it would seem that Num. 24:17 was the main scriptural inspiration of both the Jewish revolts against Rome.

the first of these categories is remarkably sparse.[24] Twice in 1 Maccabees there is reference to a prophet to come in the future: "until a prophet should come" (4:46), "until a trustworthy prophet should arise" (14:41). The expectation is of a prophet who would deliver oracles to make the divine will known with regard to specific issues. But it is not at all clear that a single, final prophet is envisaged. The promise of a prophet like Moses in Deuteronomy 18:15–19 may well lie behind the expectation, but the text need not be interpreted as referring to a single individual. A passage in which Philo clearly alludes to Deuteronomy 18:15–19 is similar in that it probably does not envisage a single eschatological prophet,[25] but rather expects that whenever Israel is obedient to God a prophet will arise. Philo also assumes that the role of such a prophet will be to give oracles from God disclosing the future or the divine will (*Spec.* 1.64–65).

If these references are not to the eschatological prophet, we are left with only the two Qumran references already mentioned in the last section (1QS 9.11; 4QTest 5–8).[26] We should probably assume that, whereas in the Qumran texts it will be the eschatological high priest who will teach and interpret the law in

24. C. L. Blomberg, *The Historical Reliability of John's Gospel* (Downers Grove, IL: InterVarsity, 2002), 120, following C. H. Talbert, *Reading John* (London: SPCK, 1992), 132–33, writes: "Expectation of a 'new Moses'-like Messiah . . . appears in *2 Baruch* 29.3 and 8 and in several later rabbinic sources." *2 Bar.* 29.3 refers to the Messiah, and there follows an extended description of the paradisal state of the world in the Messiah's time, one feature of which is the descent of manna from heaven. This does not seem to me sufficient to identify the Messiah here with the eschatological prophet like Moses. The accounts of the Messiah later in *2 Baruch* (39.7–40.3; 72.2–73.1) suggest the royal Messiah of David, and suggest also that the same Messiah is indicated in these passages as in 29.3. Later rabbinic tradition sometimes developed the idea of parallels between the activity of Moses and that of the Davidic Messiah, but there seems no reliable evidence that the two figures of the prophet like Moses and the Davidic Messiah were merged in the first century.

25. H. M. Teeple, *The Mosaic Eschatological Prophet*, JBLMS 10 (Philadelphia: SBL, 1957), 66–67, argues: "Philo's remark that the Prophet will appear 'suddenly' indicates that Philo's source is in Jewish eschatological thought, even though he himself does not develop it along that line." I do not see that this is a necessary deduction. Philo's phrase "appearing suddenly" (ἐπιφανεὶς ἐξαπιναίως) may be no more than an interpretation of the biblical statement that God will "raise up" a prophet (Deut. 18:15, 18).

26. I agree with Collins, *Sceptre*, 111–15; VanderKam, "Messianism," 227–30; and other scholars, that references in the Qumran texts to the future "Interpreter of the Law" (CD 7.18; 4QFlor 1.1.11) and the one "who shall teach righteousness at the end of days" (CD 6.11) are not to the eschatological prophet, but to the eschatological high priest, the Messiah of Aaron. Collins, *Sceptre*, 117–22, also argues that "his messiah" in 4Q521 2.2.1 is the eschatological prophet depicted in Isa. 61:1. (In this Collins is followed by C. A. Evans, "Jesus and the Dead Sea Scrolls from Qumran Cave 4," in *Eschatology, Messianism, and the Dead Sea Scrolls*, ed. C. A. Evans and P. W. Flint [Grand Rapids: Eerdmans, 1997], 96–97.) This depends on attributing to "his messiah" (line 1) what it is said that God will do in lines 11–12. But "his messiah" is parallel to "the holy ones" (line 2), and it may be that we should read the plural "messiahs" and understand the reference to be to angels. But even if Collins is correct in connecting "his messiah" with the actions of God later in the fragment, it need not follow that the reference is to the or an eschatological prophet. By means of a rather obvious exegetical link with Isa. 11:2, Isa. 61:1 could well have been understood to refer to the royal Messiah. É. Puech, "Une Apocalypse Messianique (4Q521)," *RevQ* 15 (1992): 475–519, takes the Messiah of this text to be the royal Messiah, while A. Laato, *A Star Is Rising*, University of South Florida International Studies in Formative Christianity and

the messianic age, the prophet's role will be to give oracles from God on specific issues, which we have seen to be the function 1 Maccabees and Philo attribute to such a prophet, even if they do not envisage a single eschatological prophet, as the Qumran texts appear to do. This limited role would explain why the prophet nowhere else appears in the Qumran texts. Unlike the Messiahs of Aaron and Israel, he appears to have no role in the eschatological events.

3.2. Moses-Like Prophets Who Led Popular Movements

A very different concept of the eschatological prophet like Moses seems to be evidenced by Josephus's accounts of a series of figures who have been variously called "sign prophets" (Barnett,[27] Gray[28] and others[29]), "prophets who led movements" (Horsley),[30] "action prophets" (Horsley and Hanson),[31] "leadership popular prophets" (Webb),[32] and "wilderness revolutionaries" (Longenecker).[33] Such terms are intended to distinguish these prophets from oracular prophets, who did not lead movements. The prophets we are now discussing were like Moses primarily in being charismatic leaders of the people who led their followers to expect to participate in salvific events like those of the exodus and conquest. The individuals and groups recorded by Josephus and plausibly belonging to this category are:

1. Theudas, 45/46 CE (*Ant.* 20.97–99; cf. Acts 5:36)
2. The Egyptian, in the time of Felix (52–60 CE) (*BJ* 2.261–63; *Ant.* 20.169–72; cf. Acts 21:38)
3. Several unnamed figures in the time of Felix (*BJ* 2.258–60; *Ant.* 20.167–68)
4. An unnamed prophet, ca. 60–62 CE (*Ant.* 20.188)
5. An unnamed prophet, 70 CE (*BJ* 6.283–87)[34]

Judaism 5 (Atlanta: Scholars Press, 1997), 309–10, suggests the reference is to a heavenly figure like the Son of Man in the Parables of Enoch.

27. P. W. Barnett, "The Jewish Sign Prophets—A.D. 40–70: Their Intentions and Origin," *NTS* 27 (1980–1981): 679–97.

28. R. Gray, *Prophetic Figures in Late Second Temple Jewish Palestine* (New York: Oxford University Press, 1993), chapter 4. On pp. 198–99 she defends the use of this term against Horsley's objection.

29. E.g., C. A. Evans, *Jesus and His Contemporaries* (Leiden: Brill, 1995), 73.

30. R. A. Horsley, "'Like One of the Prophets of Old': Two Types of Popular Prophets at the Time of Jesus," *CBQ* 47 (1985): 454.

31. R. A. Horsley and J. S. Hanson, *Bandits, Prophets, and Messiahs: Popular Movements at the Time of Jesus* (San Francisco: Harper & Row, 1988), 135.

32. R. L. Webb, *John the Baptizer and Prophet: A Socio-Historical Study*, JSNTSup 62 (Sheffield: Sheffield Academic Press, 1991), 333.

33. B. W. Longenecker, "The Wilderness and Revolutionary Ferment in First-Century Palestine: A Response to D. R. Schwartz and J. Marcus," *JSJ* 29 (1998): 335.

34. Gray, *Prophetic Figures*, 201–2 n. 24, rightly classifies this figure with the "sign prophets"—against Horsley. Webb, *John*, 340, thinks it "is not entirely clear whether this prophet should be classified as a leadership prophet or a solitary prophet." He does give a lead, even though he does not continue in a leadership role for long.

6. Jonathan the Sicarius in Cyrene, after 70 CE (*BJ* 7.437–50; *Vita* 424–25).[35]

Although the last of these was active in Cyrene rather than Palestine, he had come from Palestine and is therefore evidence of ideas current in Palestinian Judaism.[36]

The following recurrent characteristics of these figures are notable:

- They claimed to be prophets. In all cases except (6) Josephus either says this explicitly or implies it by his own judgment that the man was an "imposter" (γόης).

- They took their followers into the desert. This is said of all except (1) and (5), and may well be implied in (1).

- They promised their followers "signs." This is said explicitly of (3) and (6), in which cases the signs would take place in the desert, and of (5).

- There is reference to liberation or deliverance. In the case of (3) Josephus says that these prophets promised "signs of liberation" (σημεῖα ἐλευθερίας) (*BJ* 2.259), while in the case of (5) the prophet predicted "signs of deliverance" (τὰ σημεῖα τῆς σωτηρίας). In the case of (4), where Josephus does not mention signs, he does say the prophet promised "salvation and the cessation of evils" (σωτηρίαν ... καὶ παῦλαν κακῶν, *Ant.* 20.188). Liberation from Roman rule is certainly included in these expectations.

- In two cases—(1) and (2)—Josephus records very specific expectations. Theudas promised that at his command the Jordan would part and allow him and his followers to cross on dry land. The Egyptian led his followers from the desert to the Mount of Olives, promising that at his command the walls of Jerusalem would fall, allowing them to enter the city, where he would rule.

It seems clear that these prophets and their movements were working with a new exodus typology—or, better, a new wilderness-conquest typology, since they seem to have expected not to repeat the exodus from Egypt itself but to repeat the events that followed it. They went into the desert in order to reconstitute themselves the people of God, becoming like Israel in the ideal period in the wilderness under Moses' leadership. From there they would repossess the land of Israel, taking it from Roman rule just as the Israelites under Joshua took it from Canaanite rule.

35. The Samaritan (*Ant.* 18.85–87) is often classified with these "sign prophets" (e.g., Webb, *John*, 333–34), but in my view should not be.

36. There appears to be only one recorded example of a similar figure in later Jewish history. In the reign of Theodosius (412–454) a Jew on the island of Crete claimed to be Moses himself and promised that he would part the sea and lead the Cretan Jews through it on dry land to the land of Israel (Socrates, *Hist. eccl.* 7.38.63–64).

To what extent they expected to conquer by force of arms is uncertain,[37] but they certainly expected spectacular divine intervention. The miracle Theudas expected was a repetition of the crossing of the Jordan by Joshua and the Israelites at their first entrance into the land, while that expected by the Egyptian corresponds to the fall of Jericho, which inaugurated the Israelites' actual conquest of the land from the Canaanites. The prophets themselves seem to combine the roles of Moses, the leader in the wilderness, and Joshua, the leader in the conquest of the land. But, of course, the reason Moses did not himself lead the people into the land was the people's rebellion against God and Moses' response to that (Num. 20:12; Deut. 1:37; 32:51). In the expectation of these first-century leaders and their followers the disobedience of Israel in the wilderness was certainly not going to be repeated. This time there would be no reason why the prophet who led them in the wilderness should not himself lead them into their inheritance in the land.

In understanding the importance of the desert for these prophets and their movements we do not have to choose between typological reference to the wilderness wanderings of Israel after the exodus from Egypt, as most scholars have proposed, and reference to the prophecy of Isaiah 40:3 ("In the wilderness prepare the way of YHWH"), which a few have recently suggested as an alternative.[38] Both contributed to the significance of the desert as it was perceived by the Qumran community,[39] who also thought that from their temporary residence in the desert they would reconquer the land. The typology and the prophecy can very naturally be combined, because the significance of the desert in the biblical prophecies of the new exodus is itself typological, looking back to the wilderness experience in the time of Moses.[40]

The "signs" that were promised by several, at least, of these prophets are described by Josephus as "signs of liberation [σημεῖα ἐλευθερίας],"[41] "unmistakable marvels and signs [τέρατα καὶ σημεῖα] that would be wrought in accordance with God's providence [κατὰ τὴν τοῦ θεοῦ πρόνοιαν],"[42] "signs of deliverance [τὰ σημεῖα τῆς σωτηρίας],"[43] and "signs and apparitions [σημεῖα καὶ φάσματα]."[44] The one word that is common to all these descriptions—σημεῖα—would seem to be of

---

37. In the two cases where Josephus provides two parallel accounts—(2) and (3)—Gray, *Prophetic Figures*, 117, 119, 200–201 n. 18, thinks that Josephus has "militarized" the account in *War* to assimilate these movements to those of the armed rebels in the same period, whereas the account in *Antiquities* better reflects the nonmilitary nature of the movements. But even she admits that the account of the Egyptian in *Antiquities* probably implies that he and his followers were armed, whereas Horsley, "Like One of the Prophets," 459–60, thinks the Egyptian's movement and the others were all nonviolent.

38. Longenecker, "Wilderness," argues against the proposals of D. R. Schwartz and J. Marcus to this effect.

39. Longenecker, "Wilderness," 328–35.

40. Isa. 35:1–2; 40:3; Ezek. 20:35–36; Hos. 2:14–15.

41. *BJ* 2.259.

42. *Ant.* 20.168.

43. *BJ* 6.285.

44. *BJ* 7.438.

special importance for understanding what Josephus means by these phrases.[45] In the Pentateuch and later Jewish literature, "signs" (or "signs and wonders") often describes the great acts that God performed for Israel through the agency of Moses, especially the plagues and the crossing of the Red Sea, but also the miracles in the wilderness.[46] It has therefore been supposed that the signs promised by the first-century prophets were the actual acts of deliverance that God would perform.[47]

However, Rebecca Gray has argued that Josephus's own usage, in his narrative of the exodus, suggests otherwise. Josephus there uses σημεῖα exclusively with reference to the three "signs" God gave Moses at the time of his commissioning by God at Mount Sinai (Exod. 4:1–9, 17). The only possible exception is a reference to "all those signs wrought by God in token of their liberation (πρὸς τὴν ἐλευθερίαν αὐτοῖς σημείων),"[48] which might include the plagues of Egypt but most probably refers, like the preceding references to σημεῖα, to the miracles given to Moses at Mount Sinai. The phrase is strikingly like one of those Josephus uses of the first-century prophets, as is also Moses' claim to Pharaoh and his magicians that these miracles were done through "God's providence (κατὰ . . . θεοῦ πρόνοιαν)."[49] The function of these miracles was not to accomplish deliverance but to give assurance that God's promise of deliverance is reliable and therefore also to authenticate Moses as God's agent who conveys God's message of coming deliverance.[50] Gray perhaps stresses the function of authenticating Moses a little too much at the expense of the function of giving confidence that God will deliver his people. Josephus rather emphatically makes the point that the signs performed the latter function for Moses himself (*Ant.* 2.275–76) as well as for the people. But clearly the two functions are very closely related.

It could be questioned whether Josephus's usage elsewhere[51] should control the meaning of the signs he mentions in connection with the first-century prophets. These prophets and their followers must themselves have used this language. It would be difficult otherwise to explain the prominence of it in Josephus's accounts of them, and, moreover, Mark 13:22 provides good evidence of its use with reference to such prophets independently of Josephus. The prophets need not have meant this language in exactly the sense in which Josephus elsewhere uses it. His meaning could in these instances be controlled by theirs, or he could have misunderstood them by assimilating their talk of "signs" to his own habits of thought. But there is one feature of the signs in his accounts of these prophets

45. Gray, *Prophetic Figures*, 123.

46. E.g., Exod. 7:3; 10:2; Num. 14:11, 22; Deut. 4:34; 6:22; 7:19; 26:8; 29:3; 34:11–12; Neh. 9:10; Ps. 78:43; 105:27; 135:9; Jer. 32:20–21; Sir. 45:3; Wis. 10:16; Bar. 2:11; *LAB* 9.7, 10; 19.11; Ezekiel the Tragedian, 132–50, 220–52, ap. Eusebius, *Praep. Ev.* 9.29.

47. E.g., Horsley, "Like One of the Prophets," 456.

48. *Ant.* 2.327.

49. *Ant.* 2.286.

50. Gray, *Prophetic Figures*, 125–28.

51. Gray, *Prophetic Figures*, 128–30, finds supporting evidence for the same usage in *Ant.* 10.25–29; 8.230–45, 408.

that can give us some confidence that Josephus's understanding of Moses' signs is at least close to their understanding of the function of the signs they expected. In two of the three cases—(3) and (6)—the signs are to occur in the desert. But the desert is not likely to have been the location of the deliverance itself. Rather, as is clear in the case of the Egyptian, it is when the people come out of the desert that God is expected to give them victory over the Gentile occupiers of the land. The signs in the desert must be "signs of liberation" or "signs of deliverance" in that they will assure the prophet and his followers that God is going to liberate or deliver them. At the same time, of course, by authenticating the message of the prophets about God's coming deliverance, the signs would also function as authentication of the prophets themselves.

Gray's understanding of the function of the signs can therefore be plausibly attributed to the prophets and their followers. This probably means that the collapse of the walls of Jerusalem, expected by the Egyptian, would not count as a sign: it is the deliverance itself, not a sign of it. The parting of the Jordan expected by Theudas might count as a sign of the deliverance to come,[52] since the original event in the book of Joshua functioned in this way (Josh. 3:10). We cannot tell what kind of signs the other prophets promised their followers, but since the signs were to be performed in the desert, it is at least a reasonable guess that they might have been thinking of the miracles of provision Moses performed for the people in the wilderness: the water from the rock, the manna from heaven, and the quail from the sea.[53] The miracle of water in the wilderness is echoed in Isaiah's prophecy of the way through the wilderness in the future.[54] Such repetitions of the miracles given through Moses in the wilderness could function for the first-century prophets and their followers as signs that God would lead them, as he had the Israelites of old, from the wilderness to conquer the land, and would at the same time authenticate the prophets as the expected prophet like Moses.

It is striking that the kind of eschatological,[55] Moses-like role that these popular prophets adopted is not to be found in the surviving literature of Second Temple Judaism, except in Josephus's accounts of these prophets and their movements, where the ideology at work is far from fully explicit and has to be reconstructed. It is true that the Qumran community shared the same pattern of expectation in that they lived in the desert and expected to come from the desert to reconquer the land from its Gentile rulers. But they did not expect a prophetic figure who would play the roles of Moses and Joshua in these events. Of course, only some of the literature of Second Temple Judaism has survived and the lack of reference to such a figure in non-Qumran Jewish literature, which has been preserved almost entirely through Christian traditions, might reflect the selectivity of Christians

---

52. Gray, *Prophetic Figures*, 131–32, too confidently denies this.

53. Cf. Exod. 16:13–17:6; Num. 20:2–13; 21:16–20; Ps. 78:15–31; *LAB* 10.7.

54. Isa. 35:6–7; cf. 12:3.

55. I do not share the hesitations Gray, *Prophetic Figures*, 141–43, has about the appropriateness of this term for these figures.

who preserved texts about the Davidic Messiah but not texts about the prophet like Moses. But it remains remarkable that there is such a contrast between the considerable popularity of the Moses-like charismatic leader evidenced by these accounts in Josephus and the lack of reference to such a figure in the extant literature of the period. It may be that this figure was much more popular among the common people than in the circles that produced the literature. It was the ordinary people who followed these prophets and it is likely that the prophets themselves were of humble origin rather than from the social elite. One of them, Jonathan the Sicarius, we know from Josephus was a weaver. We hear of no support from established religious leaders for any of these movements (unlike, for example, the movement led by Judas the Galilean that Josephus calls "the fourth philosophy," and unlike the Zealots).[56]

It is also instructive to compare, according to Josephus's evidence, the relatively frequent occurrence of these movements led by Moses-like prophets and the relatively infrequent occurrence of movements led by claimants to the role and status of royal Messiah. Of the latter there were three who led revolts following the death of Herod (ca. 4 BCE) in various parts of Herod's kingdom,[57] but we hear of no others until after the outbreak of the revolt in 66 CE. By contrast, Josephus refers to prophets who led movements in 45/46 (Theudas), in the period 52–60 (the Egyptian and several others), and ca. 60–62 (an unnamed prophet). For several decades before the revolt, Davidic messianism, it seemed, produced no popular movements, but the hope of a Moses-like prophetic leader spawned several. There may be two factors that explain this contrast. First, the festivals in the temple in Jerusalem must have been for many Palestinian Jewish peasants the most important source and encouragement for eschatological hopes of liberation. At Passover they relived the events of the exodus from Egypt and at Tabernacles they relived the experience of Israel in the wilderness. Both historical remembrances also carried future expectations—of a new exodus and of divine blessing in the age of salvation to come. The ceremony of the water-drawing that was central to the ritual of Tabernacles recalled the miraculous provision of water in the wilderness and anticipated the blessings of the future, when Israel "will draw water from the wells of salvation" (Isa. 12:3).[58] Attending these festivals would have been highlights of the year for the average Palestinian Jew and must have been formative for the religio-political outlook of many ordinary people. Moses, of course, was central

56. R. A. Horsley, "Popular Prophetic Movements at the Time of Jesus: Their Principal Features and Social Origins," *JSNT* 26 (1986): 12–14; D. Goodblatt, "Priestly Ideologies of the Judean Resistance," *JSQ* 3 (1996): 225–49.

57. On such figures see Horsley and Hanson, *Bandits*, chapter 3. Josephus, motivated no doubt by a desire to avoid suggesting that militant messianism was a significant feature of Judaism, carefully avoids messianic language in his accounts of these figures, but we should probably suppose that they claimed to be the royal Messiah and may well have claimed Davidic descent.

58. On Tabernacles and its eschatological significance, see H. Ulfgard, *Feast and Future: Revelation 7:9–17 and the Feast of Tabernacles*, CB (NT) 22 (Lund: Almqvist & Wiksell, 1989), 108–47.

to the narratives that were relived annually at these festivals. This fact must be connected with the popularity of prophets claiming to be the Moses-like leader of the new exodus-conquest.

The figure of the Davidic Messiah may also have been popular (as the Gospels suggest), but there is a significant difference between the two forms of expectation, along with their embodiment in actual movements in this period. The royal messianic claimants led armed revolts. The biblical story of David cohered with the expectation of defeating Israel's enemies by armed force, not excluding divine assistance but not excluding human violence either. But the movements led by popular prophets, even if some of them gave some place to the use of human force in the liberative events to come, were not essentially militaristic, but set their hopes on dramatic divine interventions, like those of Israel's early history. After the failed and brutally suppressed revolts of 4 BCE, there may well have been a sense that in pragmatic terms armed revolt against the Romans was unlikely to succeed. While the Sicarii, heirs of the "fourth philosophy," adopted a new strategy of assassination, many ordinary people will have found very attractive the expectation that liberation would come from God in the miraculous ways it did in the time of Moses and Joshua.

Of course, Josephus does not refer to any Moses-like popular prophets before Theudas (45/46 CE), and this may seem to make any conclusions we could draw as to popular expectations at the time of Jesus problematic. However, we should certainly not conclude from Josephus's silence that there were no such figures before Theudas. For the period 10–44 CE Josephus's narratives of events in Jewish Palestine are very sparse. He could not, for this period, depend on his own memory (he was born in 37 CE), as he could for the period from the governorship of Felix onward. His sources of information were evidently not plentiful. Prophets whose followers were few and whose movements were quickly suppressed need not have been remembered prominently enough to feature in Josephus's narratives. By way of positive evidence that ideas related to those that inspired the Moses-like prophets were already current in the time of Jesus, we have the figure of John the Baptist, who resembled them at least to the extent that he called the people into the wilderness in order to renew their identity as God's people there. While there are significant differences between John and the Moses-like prophets, there are also striking similarities,[59] which show that something of the same context of ideas and expectations that makes the Moses-like prophets of Josephus's accounts intelligible was already available at the time of Jesus.

3.3. The Prophet in John 6 and 7

On two occasions in the Gospel people think that Jesus must be "the prophet" (6:14; 7:40). The two occasions are connected with the two festivals that we have suggested particularly inspired the popular hope of a Moses-like prophetic leader.

---

59. Webb, *John*, chap. 10, provides a balanced account of the resemblances and the differences.

The events of chapter 6 occur when Passover is near (6:4), while in 7:37–44 Jesus and the crowd are in the temple on the last, climactic day of the feast of Tabernacles.

On the first of the two occasions, the belief that Jesus must be "the prophet who is to come into the world" results from seeing "the sign" Jesus performed (6:14), that is, the feeding miracle. In the later discussion the people ask Jesus for an authenticating "sign" (6:30) and refer to the manna in the wilderness as the kind of sign they seek, citing Psalm 78:24 (John 6:31). On the second of the two occasions, the idea that Jesus is the prophet results from his public announcement: "Let anyone who is thirsty come to me, and let the one who believes in me drink" (John 7:37–38). The scriptural quotation that Jesus adds in support combines Ezekiel 47:1 and Zechariah 14:8, both referring to the water that will flow from the temple in the age of salvation, while probably also alluding to Psalm 78:16, which refers to the miracle of water in the wilderness in Moses' time. Thus the Tabernacles theme of water is evoked in both its dimensions of remembrance and anticipation. On both occasions the people's response, hailing Jesus as the prophet, could not be more appropriately placed. The allusions to Psalm 78 in both contexts help create the parallelism: in each case the people are reminded of one of Moses' "signs" in the wilderness, first bread from heaven, then water from the rock. These are the sort of signs the popular prophets sought in the wilderness to authenticate themselves as the prophet like Moses and to authenticate their message of God's liberative action to come. Jesus seems to fit into this pattern of popular expectation and so the people respond to him much as they did to Theudas, the Egyptian, and the others.

In chapter 7 there is a clear distinction between the prophet and the royal Messiah. When some of the crowd decide Jesus must be the prophet, others continue to maintain that he is the Messiah (7:41), as many had done before (7:31). But many scholars suppose that the two figures are assimilated in chapter 6 when Jesus, hearing the crowd's identification of him as the prophet, "realized that they were about to come and take him by force to make him king" (6:15). In view of the clear distinction between the prophet and the Messiah both in 7:40–41 and in 1:20–21, it would seem inappropriate to conclude too readily that 6:15 fudges this distinction.

The popular prophets in Josephus's accounts provide one interesting parallel to John 6:15. According to Josephus's account in the *War* (though the briefer account in the *Antiquities* omits this), the Egyptian expected, having captured Jerusalem, "to set himself up as tyrant of the people (τοῦ δήμου τυραννεῖν), employing those who poured in with him as his bodyguard" (*BJ* 2.262). Josephus's use of τυραννεῖν here is no doubt derogatory, suggesting despotism.[60] Elsewhere, for example, "tyranny" is how he describes the rule of Abimelech over Israel: he

---

60. Τύραννος, a neutral term in earlier usage, had become generally a pejorative term by this period.

"transformed the government into a tyranny (τυραννίδα), setting himself up to do whatsoever he pleased in defiance of the laws and showing bitter animosity against the champions of justice" (*Ant.* 5.234). It seems rather significant that Josephus, while avoiding calling Moses a king, since the polity for which Moses legislated was a theocracy,[61] nevertheless has those who rebel against Moses' leadership of the people accuse him of "tyranny" (τυραννεῖν, τυραννός, τυραννικῶς, τυραννίς: *Ant.* 4.16, 22, 146, 149). Thus we probably cannot tell whether the Egyptian would have called himself "king,"[62] but a position of sovereign leadership over the people is entirely consistent with the the role of a prophet like Moses. Apart from Philo,[63] most Jewish writers of the Second Temple period[64] seem, like Josephus and following scriptural practice, to have avoided calling Moses king, but use other terms to describe his leadership.[65]

All that might therefore be problematic for understanding John 6:15 entirely within the paradigm of the prophet like Moses is the use of the *word* "king" (βασιλεύς). That the people should wish to set over them as leader or governor someone they identified as the prophet like Moses is entirely to be expected, but it seems unlikely they would have called this position kingship. This makes it probable that John's use of βασιλεύς (which he does not directly attribute to the people) is his own choice of terminology, just as Josephus chose to refer to the Egyptian's leadership by the term τυραννεῖν. John has chosen the word βασιλεύς to link this passage with the theme of true and false understandings of Jesus' kingship, which is an important theme in his Gospel. But he need not be understood to mean that the people in chapter 6 confuse the figures of prophet and Messiah.

One more passage in the Gospel requires our attention in the section. At the end of chapter 7 the Pharisees tell Nicodemus, "Search and you will see that no prophet arises from Galilee (ἐκ τῆς Γαλιλαίας προφήτης οὐκ ἐγείρεται)" (7:52). There is a significant text-critical issue: P[66], the earliest witness to this part of John, has the article ὁ before προφήτης, and this is supported by the Sahidic version but has no other support.[66] This reading could easily be explained as a scribal assimilation to ὁ προφήτης in 7:40.[67] But several scholars have accepted this reading with

---

61. W. A. Meeks, *The Prophet-King: Moses Traditions and the Johannine Christology*, NovTSup 14 (Leiden: Brill, 1967), 135.

62. Horsley, "Popular Prophetic Movements," 7–8, is probably too confident in asserting that he did not. If "the Egyptian" was an Egyptian Jew, he might be more likely to think "king" an appropriate title for Moses—and hence for himself—than Palestinian Jews would.

63. For Philo, see Meeks, *Prophet-King*, 107–17; for Moses as "king," cf. also *Sib. Or.* 11.38.

64. For rabbinic material, see Meeks, *Prophet-King*, chap. 4.

65. Cf. *T. Mos.* 11:10; *LAB* 9.10; 20.5; Josephus, *Ant.* 2.268; 4.11.

66. According to Boismard, *Moses*, 7 n. 20, "Bodmer Papyrus XV (P[75]) has a lacuna of some letters at this place. The editors of the papyrus reconstructed the text by adding the article in front of προφήτης, given the width of the lacuna, but this reconstruction has been challenged, rightly it seems."

67. So Barrett, *Gospel*, 333.

the article as original.[68] It would create a chiastic pattern of parallel statements about "the prophet" and "the Messiah" in 7:40–52 thus:

A   "This is really the prophet" (7:40)
  B   "This is the Messiah" (7:41)
  B′ "Surely, the Messiah does not come from Galilee, does he?"
        + reference to Scripture (7:41–42)
A′ "the prophet does not arise from Galilee"
        + implied reference to Scripture (7:52).

It is also claimed that this reading avoids the problem that at least one prophet, Jonah, did come from Galilee (2 Kings 14:25).[69] In fact, however, the instruction to Nicodemus is considerably more difficult to understand if we read ὁ προφήτης: "Search and you will see that the prophet does not arise from Galilee." This would only make sense if Scripture indicated that the prophet will come from somewhere other than Galilee, but the Hebrew Bible contains no indication at all of the eschatological prophet's place of origin and no text that could plausibly be read as indicating this. So far as we know, Deuteronomy 18:15–18 is the only text that was understood to refer to the prophet like Moses. It is easier to think the Pharisees overlook the case of Jonah (whose origin from Gath-Hepher is not mentioned in the book of Jonah, but only in 2 Kings 14:25).[70] The Pharisees are not here appealing to extra-scriptural traditions about the prophets (though it is not clear that at this time there was any such tradition that ascribed Galilean origin to any prophet)[71] but only to Scripture. "Search" means "search the scriptures," as in 5:39.

So it makes best sense for the Pharisees to say: "Search and you will see that no prophet arises from Galilee." But this does not make their statement irrelevant to the case of *the* prophet. Their argument is that, since Scripture does not refer to

68. Boismard, *Moses*, 7–8; Brown, *Gospel*, 1:325; G. R. Beasley-Murray, *John*, WBC 36 (Waco: Word, 1987), 121.

69. The only other case of a prophet whom the Hebrew Bible might indicate came from Galilee is Nahum, who is called "the Elkoshite" (Nah. 1:1). If this refers to a place Elkosh, the location is not known. Jerome identified it with a village in Galilee, but other identifications are also to be found in the Fathers. The name Capernaum probably means "village of Nahum," but the Nahum who gave it its name need not have been the prophet Nahum.

70. The life of Jonah in *Liv. Pro.* 10 shows how easily the information in 2 Kings 14:25 could be ignored; it says that Jonah "was from the district of Kariathmos near the Greek city of Azotus by the sea" (10:1).

71. Most commentators cite: "Thou hast no single tribe in Israel from which a prophet has not come forth" (*b. Sukk.* 27b); "Thou hast no city in the land of Israel in which there has not been a prophet" (*Seder Olam R.* 21). But there is no reason at all to think such traditions go back to the first century. *Lives of the Prophets* assigns a place of origin to every one of the twenty-three prophets whose lives it contains. Only one of these is in Galilee: Hosea is said to have come from "Belemoth of the tribe of Issachar" (5:1), which should indicate Galilee, though Torrey's identification of Belemoth with Ibleam (see D. R. Hare, "The Lives of the Prophets," in *OTP* 2:391 n. 5a) would place it outside Galilee in northern Samaria.

any prophet from Galilee in the past, there is not going to be any prophet from Galilee in the present or future: prophets do not come from Galilee. This covers the case of the eschatological prophet as much as any other. The Pharisees are not committing themselves to the expectation that there is to be a prophet of the kind the people mean when they think Jesus is the prophet, but by denying that someone from Galilee can be a prophet at all they exclude Jesus from any prophetic role. On this interpretation the chiastic structure suggested above for 7:40–52 remains valid, with "no prophet arises from Galilee" (A′) relating well enough to "the prophet" (A) and corresponding well enough to "the Messiah does not come from Galilee" (B′).

Finally, it is worth noting that some scholars detect in Jesus' discussion with the Jewish authorities in 7:15–19 and 18:20–21 (cf. also 7:47) the issue of whether Jesus is the true, that is, Moses-like prophet of Deuteronomy 18:15–19 or the contrasted deceiving prophet of Deuteronomy 13 and 18:20–22.[72] Deuteronomy 18:15–19, which was evidently the source of the rather formal expectation of the prophet at Qumran, played little if any part in the popular expectation of a Moses-like prophet that the crowds manifest in John 6:14 and 7:40. For this expectation it was not Moses as a teacher but Moses as leader, liberator, and agent of miraculous signs that provided the model for the prophet to come. Neither Jesus nor the Jewish authorities endorse this popular expectation. Instead, they debate Jesus' authority as a prophet according to the criteria given in the Torah. This distinction between popular and learned views of the Moses-like prophet is an interesting additional way in which John's account corresponds to what we can gather of such expectations from our other sources.

4. The Messiah

4.1. Messianic Titles

4.1.1. *"Messiah" in John.* The word χριστός occurs nineteen times in John, always with the article, except in two special cases (1:41; 4:25) and in the two occurrences of the phrase Ἰησοῦς Χριστός (1:17; 17:3). As in the Synoptics, it hardly ever occurs on the lips of Jesus himself (only 17:3), but is used by those who recognize him as the Messiah or discuss whether he is the Messiah. As in the Synoptics, the impression given is that the absolute usage, "the Messiah" or "the Anointed One," is a current Jewish usage, referring to the Davidic Messiah (cf. 7:42). As we have noticed, John makes this clearer than the Synoptics do by having his characters use "the Messiah" and "the prophet" as mutually exclusive terms for two different eschatological figures. He also strengthens the impression of reporting the oral usage of the term in Jewish Palestine by giving the Aramaic term itself in 1:41 (cf.

---

72. Meeks, *Prophet-King*, 56–61; P. N. Anderson, *The Christology of the Fourth Gospel: Its Unity and Disunity in the Light of John 6*, 2nd ed. (Valley Forge, PA: Trinity, 1997), 174–79.

4:25): Μεσσίας, a transliteration of מְשִׁיאָה. He must be reflecting some Aramaic usage, though it could be that of Aramaic-speaking Christians rather than that of non-Christian Jews.

4.1.2. *"Messiah" in Other Jewish Literature.*

Maurice Casey claims that "the fourth Gospel's use of the term 'Christ' is altogether unhistorical,"[73] because the determined, absolute usage, "the Messiah," was not current in pre-70 Jewish Palestine:

> This term was not a title in Second Temple Judaism, and the term "messiah" or "anointed" on its own was not specific enough to refer to the messianic son of David, nor to any single individual at all. . . . In the Christian church, however, "Christ" became a title for Jesus, and one which was central to the church's identity. . . . It is this Christian usage of the term "Christ" in Greek which appears in the fourth Gospel, where it reflects real debates between Johannine Christians and "the Jews."[74]

Evidence for the use of "Anointed One" (in Hebrew, Aramaic, or translated into other languages) with reference to a specific eschatological figure in early Jewish literature can be classified in three categories as follows.

1. The term is qualified by "YHWH's" ("the Lord's Anointed One") or by "his," "my," or "your," where these pronouns refer to God. This usage is universal in the Hebrew Bible when the term refers to the king, including instances that influenced the later use of the term for the ideal Davidic king of the future.[75] It is relatively common in references to the royal Messiah in literature of our period.[76]

2. In the Qumran literature the term is used for both the eschatological high priest and the eschatological king, and is usually qualified in these ways: "the Anointed Ones of Aaron and Israel,"[77] "the Anointed One[s?] of Aaron and Israel,"[78] "the Anointed One of Israel,"[79] "the Anointed One of righteousness."[80]

73. M. Casey, *Is John's Gospel True?* (London: Routledge, 1996), 59.

74. Ibid., 58. The same argument, though without reference to the Fourth Gospel, appears in P. M. Casey, *From Jewish Prophet to Gentile God* (Cambridge: James Clarke; Louisville; Westminster John Knox, 1991), 42–43. Casey discusses the evidence in detail in an unpublished seminar paper, given at the 1996 meeting of the SNTS: "The Use of the Term (א)יחישמ/יח/מ(ה) in Late Second Temple Sources Other than the Dead Sea Scrolls." Similar conclusions were reached by M. de Jonge, "The Use of the Word 'Anointed' in the Time of Jesus," *NovT* 8 (1966): 132–48; idem, "The Earliest Christian Use of *Christos*: Some Suggestions," in idem, *Jewish Eschatology, Early Christian Christology and the Testaments of the Twelve Patriarchs*, NovTSup 63 (Leiden: Brill, 1991), 110–14.

75. 1 Sam. 2:10; Ps. 2:2; 132:10.

76. *Pss. Sol.* 18: title, 5, 7; *1 Enoch* 48:10; 52:4; *2 Bar.* 39:7; 40:1; 72:2; apparently 4Q521 2.2.1.

77. 1QS 9.11.

78. CD 12.23–13.1; 19.10; 4Q266 10.1.12.

79. 1QSa 2.14, 20; 4Q382 16.2.

80. 4Q252 5.3, where the text continues: "the Branch of David." 11QMelch 2.18 refers to "the Anointed One of the Spirit." This corresponds to the use of the plural form "the anointed ones of his holy Spirit" (CD 2.12) to refer to the prophets. In 11QMelch "the Anointed One of the Spirit" is the

3. In a few cases we find the determined, absolute use, referring to the royal Messiah: "the Anointed One."[81] Later the rabbinic literature and the Targums have this usage frequently.

Casey and de Jonge unjustifiably ignore the absolute use of "the Messiah" in 1QSa 2.11–12, where the verb is disputed but the reference to "the Messiah" is not: either God causes the Anointed One to be born or God leads forth the Anointed One. The text goes on to refer to the (eschatological) high priest (line 12) and to the Anointed One of Israel (line 14). If lines 11–12 are read as "God will beget the Anointed One" (which computer enhancement technology apparently has confirmed as the reading of the manuscript), then this rather startling terminology can be explained as an allusion to Psalm 2:7 ("this day I have begotten you") and the reference is certainly to the royal Messiah, called in the Qumran texts "the Anointed One of Israel." Uses of "the Anointed One" in the Qumran literature are not numerous enough for this single example of the absolute use to be negligible. It cannot be maintained that the absolute use is found in Jewish literature only after 70 CE (when it is found in *2 Baruch* and *4 Ezra*).

What the evidence shows quite clearly is that the absolute use of "the Messiah" developed as an abbreviation of the biblical term "YHWH's Messiah."[82] The abbreviation is really no more ambiguous than the full phrase: "the Messiah" would naturally have been understood to be the Lord's Messiah. It should be noted that the examples from postbiblical Jewish literature that follow the biblical usage—category (1) above—are probably deliberately alluding to or imitating the biblical usage, especially Psalm 2:2.[83] In that sense they are rather literary. It would be understandable if the abbreviation "the Messiah" became common in ordinary speech before it did so in literature. It is significant that the Gospels, including John's reproduction of the Aramaic word, purport to reflect colloquial, not literary usage.

Moreover, William Horbury correctly points out that the fuller designations found in the Qumran literature—category (2) above—actually "imply the currency

---

messenger of Isa. 52:7, and seems also to be identified with the "anointed one" of Dan. 9:25 (or perhaps Dan. 9:26) and with the anointed figure who speaks in Isa. 61:1. The functions of this figure seem to indicate a prophet (so, e.g., Collins, *Sceptre*, 118–19), but it is possible that he is the royal Messiah: cf. Laato, *A Star*, 311–12.

81. 1QSa 2.12; *2 Bar.* 29:3; 30:1; *4 Ezra* 12:32; cf. *2 Bar.* 70:9 ("my servant the Anointed One"); *4 Ezra* 7:29 (probably the original text was "my servant the Anointed One"). I omit *Pss. Sol.* 17:32, where the Greek and Syriac versions both speak of "the Lord Messiah" or "the Messiah the Lord" (Greek: χριστὸς κύριος), but many scholars suspect the original had "the Lord's Messiah."

82. Laato, *Star*, 3; W. Horbury, *Jewish Messianism and the Cult of Christ* (London: SCM, 1998), 9–11. G. Dalman, *Words of Jesus*, trans. D. M. Kay (Edinburgh: T. & T. Clark, 1902), 290, argues that "as the Tetragrammaton was not pronounced, and as there was a reluctance to name 'God,' so here, as in other commonly used titles, the name of God was omitted, and only . . . 'the Anointed,' was said." This is a possible factor.

83. To which *1 Enoch* 48:10 certainly alludes; cf. *Rev.* 11:15; 12:10, where "his Christ" alludes to Ps. 2:2.

of the abbreviated form."[84] A phrase such as "the Anointed One of Israel" presupposes that the phrase "the Anointed One" can be used as short for "the Lord's Anointed One." The fact that the fuller phrases at Qumran presuppose the abbreviated one makes it easier to understand the fact that the abbreviated form actually appears once in the Qumran texts (1QSa 2.12). At Qumran however, "the Anointed One" could designate both the eschatological high priest and the eschatological ruler. This ambiguity required the fuller phrases "the Anointed One of Aaron" and "the Anointed One of Israel" for clarity. But we should not suppose that the same potential for ambiguity would make popular use of "the Anointed One" problematic outside Qumran. The eschatological high priest, though doubtless taken for granted, was not a focus of popular expectation, and, although he could, on the basis of biblical usage, quite properly be called "the Anointed One," in fact he is not so called in any Jewish literature other than the Qumran group's own writings. We have no clear evidence that the eschatological prophet was ever called "the Anointed One."[85]

So we do not need to suppose that the absolute use of "the Messiah" would only have become unambiguous after 70 CE, when, as Casey argues, "Judaism no longer had any prophets nor any anointed high priests officiating in the temple."[86] (Why should this have prevented talk of an anointed high priest or prophet to come in the future? The fact that pre-70 Judaism no longer had a Davidic king did not prevent reference to an anointed king to come in the future.) Outside Qumran, "the Messiah" was already unambiguous before 70, and especially in colloquial usage we may reasonably suppose it was already current. It is also plausible to think that, whereas in literature a wide variety of different ways of referring to the royal Messiah persisted, the simple "the Messiah" would have become more standard in colloquial use.

There has been considerable scholarly disagreement as to whether or to what extent there was a continuous tradition of Davidic messianism from the postexilic to the Roman period. It is undisputed, however, that it was in the early Roman period that the hope for a new David who would liberate the people from Roman domination became especially popular. It is therefore precisely in this period that we should expect the short term "the Messiah" to have become current in popular usage with reference to the royal Messiah.

4.1.3. *Other Messianic Titles.* Besides "the Messiah" (1:41) the first disciples use two other titles to express their recognition of Jesus as Messiah: the Son of God (1:49; cf. also Martha's confession in 11:27) and the King of Israel (1:49; cf. also the acclamation of the crowds in 12:13).

84. Horbury, *Jewish Messianism*, 9–10.

85. In 11QMelch 2.18 it seems that a prophetic figure is called "the Anointed One of the Spirit." I am not convinced by Collins, *Sceptre*, 117–22, that "his Messiah" in 4Q521 2.2.1 is an eschatological prophet.

86. Casey, *From Jewish Prophet*, 43.

4.1.3.1. *Son of God.* Opinions differ as to whether "the Son of God" is likely to have been a messianic title in Judaism. It certainly has a sound basis in passages of the Hebrew Bible that were read as messianic in late Second Temple Judaism: 2 Samuel 7:14; Psalm 2:7; and Psalm 89:26–27. The first of these passages, including God's words, "I will be his father and he shall be my son," is actually quoted with reference to the royal Messiah in 4QFlor 1.6–7, but this may be the nearest the literature gets to the actual title "the Son of God." There may be an allusion to Psalm 2:7 ("You are my son; today I have begotten you") in 1QSa 2.11–12, if that text is correctly understood to say that God "will beget the Messiah." But Psalm 2 itself certainly underlies other accounts of the royal Messiah,[87] thus making the use of "the Son of God" as a messianic title readily available. References to the Messiah as "my [i.e., God's] son" in the versions of *4 Ezra* (7:28–29; 13:32, 37, 52; 14:9) are commonly and plausibly thought to reflect an original "my servant,"[88] but since Psalm 2 is one of the messianic scriptures underlying *4 Ezra* 13 (cf. 13:35 with Ps. 2:6) it is quite possible that "my Son" is original and derives from Psalm 2:7. In the Ethiopic version of *1 Enoch* 105:2 apparently God refers to "my son" (though M. Black thinks Enoch is the speaker and refers to his son Methuselah),[89] but unfortunately these words do not survive in the Qumran Aramaic fragment that attests other parts of 105:1–2 (4QEn[c] 5.1.23–24) and it is dubious whether they belong to the original text. Finally, it remains controversial whether "Son of God" and "Son of the Most High" in 4Q246 2.1 refer to the royal Messiah or to a Gentile king who arrogates these titles to himself.[90] Despite strong arguments to the contrary, the context seems to favor the latter.

The evidence suggests that "the Son of God" could have been used as a messianic title, but that if so, it was relatively rare. This is perhaps surprising in view of the solid basis for it in texts of the Hebrew Bible that were widely read as messianic in this period. It is possible that the title was avoided because of the danger of a pagan misunderstanding of it as a matter of physical procreation. In that light it is interesting to recall the suggestion that, in Nathanael's confession (John 1:49), "the King of Israel" is added to "the Son of God" as an explanation that would, from this Jewish perspective, counter such a misunderstanding.[91] In any case, it is noteworthy that in this confession "the Son of God" is not placed second, as it

87. *Pss. Sol.* 17:23–24; 4QFlor 18–19; *1 Enoch* 48:10; *4 Ezra* 13:35.

88. See the full discussion in M. Stone, *Fourth Ezra*, Hermeneia (Minneapolis: Fortress, 1990), 207–8.

89. M. Black, *The Book of Enoch or I Enoch*, SVTP 7 (Leiden: Brill, 1985), 318–19.

90. See the review of scholarship as well as his own discussion (arguing for a reference to the Messiah) in Collins, *Sceptre*, chap. 7. More recently, Laato, *Star*, 313–16, follows Collins, while J. D. G. Dunn, "'Son of God' as 'Son of Man' in the Dead Sea Scrolls? A Response to John Collins on 4Q246," in *The Scrolls and the Scriptures*, ed. S. E. Porter and C. A. Evans, JSPSup 26, Roehampton Institute London Papers 3 (Sheffield: Sheffield Academic Press, 1997), 198–210, still thinks reference to a Gentile king "the most plausible hypothesis" (208).

91. B. Lindars, *The Gospel of John*, NCB (London: Marshall, Morgan & Scott, 1972), 119.

should be if it were understood as a higher or more adequate ascription than "the King of Israel." On Nathanael's lips it is no more than another title for the royal Messiah of Jewish expectation. We should probably suppose that John attributes to Nathanael a title he thought Nathanael could have known already from this Jewish tradition of messianic hope, but the fuller significance that early Christianity and John himself found in the title "the Son of God" accounts for the selection of a title that was rare in non-Christian Jewish usage but more common in Christian usage.

4.1.3.2. *King of Israel.* The title "the king of Israel" is used of the Davidic Messiah in *Psalms of Solomon* 17.42, where it has a significant position at the climax of the long description of the Messiah and his reign that precedes.[92] Although the Qumran texts call the Davidic Messiah "prince" (נָשִׂיא), following Ezekiel, rather than "king," the latter is found sometimes elsewhere[93] and has ample precedent in biblical passages that were interpreted messianically.[94] In fact, the testimony of all the Gospels that Jesus was crucified for claiming to be "King of the Jews"—usually considered historically indubitable—presupposes that "King of Israel" was a messianic title. There is a simple point about the use of language that is consistently neglected by Johannine scholars in particular: "Jews" (or, as some prefer to render Ἰουδαῖοι, "Judeans") was a term used by Gentiles. Palestinian Jews speaking to or writing for each other called themselves "Israelites" or their nation "Israel," but speaking to or writing for Gentiles would use "Jews."[95] The Gospel of John conforms almost entirely consistently to these facts of usage.[96] In the case we are considering, Nathanael (1:51) and the Jewish crowds (12:13) speak of "the King of Israel," but Gentiles (19:3), including Pilate (18:33, 39; 19:19) speak of "the King of the Jews," as do the chief priests speaking to Pilate (19:21). It therefore makes no sense for Meeks to claim that the "title 'King of the Jews' cannot have been derived from the messianic ideology of Judaism. It never occurs in the Old Testament, and

---

92. This reference is overlooked by Meeks, *Prophet-King*, 79 n. 1, who says that "King of Israel" is not, "to my knowledge," attested as a title for an eschatological figure in Jewish literature.

93. *Pss. Sol.* 17.21, 32, 42; *Sib. Or.* 5.108.

94. E.g., Ps. 2:6; 72:1; Jer. 23:5; Ezek. 37:24; Zech. 9:9.

95. K. G. Kuhn, "Ἰσραήλ, Ἰουδαῖος, Ἑβραῖος in Jewish Literature after the OT," *TDNT* 3:359–369; P. J. Tomson, "The Names Israel and Jew in Ancient Judaism and in the New Testament," *Bijdr* 47 (1986): 12–40, 266–89. The point is argued most recently, with additional evidence from the Palestinian Talmud, by P. J. Tomson, "'Jews' in the Gospel of John as Compared with the Palestinian Talmud, the Synoptics, and Some New Testament Apocrypha," in *Anti-Judaism and the Fourth Gospel*, ed. R. Bieringer, D. Pollefeyt, and F. Vandecasteele-Vanneuville (Louisville: Westminster John Knox, 2001), 176–212.

96. The very frequent use of "the Jews" in John is largely due to the fact that the evangelist himself, writing for Gentiles (as well as Jews), follows Gentile usage, as does, for example, Josephus. The use of "Jew" and "Jews" by Jesus and the Samaritan woman in chapter 4 does not break the rules: it is required to distinguish Jewish (Judean) Israelites from Samaritan Israelites. The rules are broken only in three cases, at least two of which are instances of the special Johannine usage of "the Jews" to mean "the Jewish authorities": 11:8; 13:33; 18:20 (whereas in 18:36 Jesus is addressing a Gentile).

in the literature of inter-testamental Judaism it appears, so far as I can discover, only twice."[97] "King of the Jews" is not a title to be distinguished from "King of Israel"; it is merely the latter put into Gentile or Gentile-friendly terms. For the same reason, it is entirely misleading to find theological distinctions between John's use of the two titles, as though one relates to "the true Israel" and the other to "the Jews" in a negative sense.[98] Since John was *obliged* by the rules of usage he consistently follows throughout his Gospel to use "King of Israel" and "King of the Jews" in the passages where the two titles respectively occur, it is also implausible to suggest that a theological difference constitutes an additional overtone in his usage.

4.2. The Origins of the Messiah

In chapter 7, the people raise two objections to the possibility that Jesus could be the Messiah:

> We know where this man is from; but when the Messiah comes no one will know where he is from. (7:27)

> Surely the Messiah does not come from Galilee, does he? Has not the scripture said that the Messiah is descended from David and comes from Bethlehem, the village where David lived? (7:41–42)

Both these objections are based on the fact that Jesus is known to come from Nazareth, but they seem to be mutually exclusive objections: either it will not be known where the Messiah comes from, or this *is* known but the Messiah comes from Bethlehem, not Galilee. There is no reason why John should not have put two alternative Jewish views of the Messiah's origins on the lips of the crowd: those who make the first objection need not be the same people as those who make the second.

Most discussions of 7:27 correctly refer to the idea of a hidden or unknown Messiah. There are really two different such ideas, though both entail the belief that God will "reveal" the Messiah or (with the same meaning) that the Messiah will "appear." Such expressions recur in Jewish messianic texts,[99] while the corresponding notion that up to his revelation the Messiah will have been hidden

97. Meeks, *Prophet-King*, 79 n. 1. (He refers to Josephus, *Ant.* 14.34–36; 16.311.) In the same passage, Meeks refers to the Markan passion narrative, which usually has "king of the Jews," but has "the Messiah, the king of Israel" in 15:32, but misses the significance of the fact that in the latter case the words are spoken by the chief priests, whereas in the other cases they are spoken by Pilate and the Gentile soldiers.

98. Meeks, *Prophet-King*, 82–83; and frequent variations on this distinction in much Johannine scholarship.

99. *1 Enoch* 62:7; *2 Bar.* 29:3; 30:1; 39:7; *4 Ezra* 7:28; 13:32; *Tg.* Jer. 30:21; *Tg.* Zech. 3:8; 4:7; 6:12.

by God is also sometimes explicit.[100] The general idea probably had a scriptural origin, like most messianic notions. Amos 4:13 LXX refers to God "announcing to humans his Messiah" (ἀπαγγέλων εἰς ἀνθρώπους τὸν χριστὸν αὐτοῦ), which must translate a Hebrew text different from the MT (where the MT has the very obscure מַה־שֵּׂחוֹ, the LXX's Vorlage must have had מְשִׁיחוֹ): "making known to humanity his Messiah." In the case of Isaiah 32:1–2, the LXX has understood the text in the following manner:

> For behold a righteous king will rule, and rulers shall govern with judgment. And the man will be hiding his words, and will be hidden (κρυβήσεται), as from rushing water, and shall appear (φανήσεται) in Zion, like a rushing river, glorious (ἔνδοξος) in a thirsty land.

This is valuable at least in attesting the idea of a hidden Messiah at an early date.

One of the two ideas of a hidden or unknown Messiah is that the Messiah will be a man who will not be known to be the Messiah until God reveals him to be. In the version that Justin attributes to his Jewish conversation-partner Trypho, the Messiah will not be identifiable even to himself until Elijah comes and anoints him, making him manifest to all (φανερὸν πᾶσι ποιήσῃ).[101] When Justin repeats the substance of this later in his work, the correspondence with Isaiah 32:2 is notable, suggesting that Justin was aware of this textual basis for the belief: "It is not known who he is, but when he shall become manifest and glorious (φανὴς καὶ ἔνδοξος), then it shall be known who he is" (*Dial.* 110.1). But in neither case is Justin describing a plausibly Christian view, and so he should be taken to report a Jewish view accurately. John's familiarity with some such notion seems clear from 1:26, 31–34. The Messiah was incognito among the crowds, unidentifiable even to John, until God revealed the Messiah's identity to John and thereby, through John's witness to this revelation, to Israel. Here John is not the Elijah who anoints Jesus and thereby reveals him to all. Rather, God himself anoints Jesus with the Spirit and thereby reveals him to John.

However, despite frequent assertions that this is the idea of the hidden Messiah to which 7:27 alludes, it is hard to see how this can be the case. According to 7:27, what is not known is where the Messiah comes from. In the tradition we know from Justin, what is not known is that the man already designated by God as Messiah is the Messiah. Where this man comes from can presumably be known. To explain 7:27, we seem to require a different idea of the hidden Messiah, one that is clearest in *4 Ezra*. This apocalypse says that the Messiah "will be revealed" (7:28; 13:32), that is, by God, and also refers to him as "the Messiah whom the Most High has kept until the end of days, who will arise from the offspring of David" (12:32; cf. 13:26). It seems clear that this Messiah is revealed when he

---

100. *1 Enoch* 62:6–7; *4 Ezra* 12:32; 13:26; *Tg.* Mic. 4:8.
101. *Dial.* 8.4; cf. 49.1.

comes from heaven (cf. 13:3, 25–26), and that the idea is influenced by Daniel 7:13, understood to mean that the clouds of heaven bring the Messiah to earth (cf. *4 Ezra* 13:3). Presumably this Messiah simply appears on earth and so it is true of him that "no one will know where he is from" (John 7:27). Since *4 Ezra* and *2 Baruch* are generally very close in their eschatological ideas, we can safely assume that the same notion lies behind the less explicit references in *2 Baruch* to the appearance of the Messiah (29:3; cf. 39:7). This idea of a Messiah who comes from heaven, influenced by the figure of "one like a son of man" in Daniel 7, also appears in *Sibylline Oracles* 5:414–27, and in the Parables of Enoch.

It is important to realize that the Messiah in these passages is the Davidic Messiah, not an alternative messianic idea of a transcendent Son of Man. These writings have understood the figure in Daniel 7 as the royal Messiah son of David, which is the only Jewish interpretation of Daniel 7 of which we have evidence. Since most of what little Daniel 7 says about the figure "like a son of man" refers to his kingdom (7:14), it was entirely natural for Jewish exegetes to suppose that he was the royal Messiah described elsewhere in Scripture as descended from David. But in that case the Davidic Messiah must come from heaven. Especially in relation to *4 Ezra* 12:32, where it is clear both that the Messiah is in some sense preexistent in heaven before he appears on earth and also that he is descended from David, scholars have been puzzled as to how these statements are compatible. The answer is available in *4 Ezra* 7:28: "the Messiah will be revealed with those who are with him." In 14:9 Ezra learns that he himself is going to be one of these: "You shall be taken up from among humankind, and henceforth you shall live with my Son [or servant?] and with those who are like you, until the times are ended." Phinehas-Elijah is also one of these favored people (*LAB* 48.1). Those who will be revealed with the Messiah are those people who, though born on earth, have not died but have been "kept" by God in heaven until the last times. It follows that we should think of the Messiah in *4 Ezra* also in this way.[102] At some time in the past he was born a descendant of David—in Bethlehem?—but is now being kept hidden by God in heaven until the time for him to be revealed.[103]

John 7:41–42 requires much less comment. The reference to the Messiah's origin from Bethlehem must be to Micah 5:2 (Hebrew 5:1, in connection especially with the reference to Jesse in Isa. 11:1), since a descendant of David need not otherwise

---

102. Stone, *Fourth Ezra*, 210, compares the case of Melchizedek in *2 Enoch* 71–72, where Melchizedek is born before the flood, but removed by Michael to be preserved in the paradise of Eden for a future role.

The case of the Elect One in the Parables of Enoch is more difficult than the Messiah in *4 Ezra*, since it is clear that he is in some way identified with the Davidic Messiah (there is considerable allusion to the key Davidic messianic texts Isa. 11 and Ps. 2), but it is hard to see how he can actually be descended from David if his identification with Enoch in 71:14 is original.

103. According to some later Jewish traditions, the Messiah son of David was born (in Jerusalem or in Bethlehem) at the time of the destruction of the first temple, and is kept hidden by God until the end: see, e.g., G. W. Buchanan, *Revelation and Redemption* (Dillboro, NC: Western North Carolina Press, 1978), 452–58.

be thought to come from Bethlehem (none of David's royal descendants in the Old Testament period did). We do not have specific evidence of (non-Christian) Jewish messianic interpretation of Micah 5:2 from the Second Temple period, but its messianic reference must have been obvious, especially through its thematic and verbal connections with Isaiah 11:1 (Bethlehem was *Jesse's* village; אצי occurs in both texts, suggesting their close relationship according to the exegetical principle of *gezera shewa*). But Micah 5:2(1) cannot be a source of the preexistence of the Messiah in this period, if, as we have argued, this "preexistence" was after his birth,[104] rather than, as Micah 5:2(1) would imply, before his birth.

4.3. The Signs Done by the Messiah

If beliefs about the Messiah's origin seem to the crowd in John 7 to count against Jesus' identification as the Messiah, another consideration seems strongly favorable to this identification: "When the Messiah comes, will he do more signs than this man has done?" (7:31). This is the most problematic statement in the Gospel about any of the eschatological figures. While, as we have seen, the prophet was popularly expected to perform signs, there is no clear evidence in extant Jewish texts that the Messiah was expected to do so.[105] Some scholars therefore take 7:31 as evidence that John merges the two figures of the Messiah and the prophet,[106] despite the clear evidence of this chapter itself that he does not. In some cases this idea of the merging of the figures reflects a confusion between John's own Christology and the ideas he attributes to his characters. For others, 7:31 has to be taken either as a formulation of the *Christian* belief that the Messiah does signs, which John shares, or as representing "the views of Christians of Jewish descent which it [the Fourth Gospel] criticizes."[107] But John's accurate reflection of Jewish ideas about eschatological figures in other cases suggests that we should accept this explanation only as a last resort.

In the absence of clear evidence in the extant Jewish texts, an informed guess may be made. Jewish messianism was not so much a tradition of ideas as a tradition of exegesis, and in all Jewish exegesis much depended on recognizing links between one passage and another. A link could easily be made between Isaiah 11:2 ("the Spirit of YHWH shall rest upon him"), which is at the heart of one of the principal texts of Davidic messianism, and Isaiah 61:1 ("the Spirit of the Lord YHWH is upon me, because YHWH has anointed me"). No other figures in the Hebrew Bible are said to be anointed with the Spirit of YHWH. The more obvious (at least to modern exegetes) identification of the speaker in Isaiah 61:1 as a prophet could well be overridden by the link with Isaiah 11:2. It is easy to

---

104. Horbury, *Jewish Messianism*, 58, 89, 95.

105. The point is made emphatically, perhaps overstated, by J. L. Martyn, *History and Theology in the Fourth Gospel*, rev. ed. (Nashville: Abingdon, 1979), 94–99.

106. E.g., Martyn, *History and Theology in the Fourth Gospel*, 113; Carson, *Gospel*, 319.

107. De Jonge, "Jewish Expectations," 259.

make further exegetical links from Isaiah 61:1 to Isaiah 42:7 and Isaiah 35:5–6 and perhaps Psalm 146:7–8.[108] In this way, such miraculous acts as opening the eyes of the blind and healing the lame could be understood as signs the Davidic Messiah will perform. Some support for this suggestion might be found in the much debated Qumran text 4Q521 2.2.7–14, where releasing captives, giving sight to the blind, raising up the downtrodden, healing the wounded, raising the dead, preaching good news to the poor, and enriching the hungry (acts mostly drawn from Ps. 146:7–8 and Isa. 61:1) seem to be ascribed directly to God, not to the Messiah. But similar exegetical moves could easily ascribe these to the Messiah of Isaiah 61:1.

4.4. The Messiah's Eternal Reign (12:34)

In 12:32–34 Jesus announces that "I, when I am lifted up from the earth, will draw all people to myself," and the crowd objects, "We have heard from the law that the Messiah remains forever. How can you say that the Son of Man must be lifted up? Who is this Son of Man?" The dialogue is perhaps not entirely realistic. Jesus has not used the term "the Son of Man" since verse 23, which is spoken to Andrew and Philip, though probably the crowd is understood to overhear. It seems unlikely that they could connect that use of the term with Jesus' saying in verse 32. But Johannine dialogue is sometimes stylized. The people respond as though what they have heard is one of Jesus' sayings about the lifting up of *the Son of Man* earlier in the Gospel: "Just as Moses lifted up the serpent in the wilderness, so must the Son of Man be lifted up" (3:14); "When you have lifted up the Son of Man" (8:28). The people do not know what Jesus means by the expression "the Son of Man" (cf. 9:36) but sense that he must be referring to some important personage and wonder if he means the Messiah. It is not necessary to suppose that they understand that Jesus' talk of the lifting up of the Son of Man refers to his death (which John explains to his readers in verse 33). For their objection to hold, it would be sufficient for them to understand "lifted up from the earth" (12:32) as some kind of removal from the earth.

The crowd's objection is that they "have heard from the law that the Messiah remains forever." Commentators usually refer to God's promise of an eternal dynasty to David in scriptural passages that were interpreted messianically in this period: 2 Samuel 7:12–13 ("I will raise up your offspring after you. . . . I will establish the throne of his kingdom forever") and Psalm 89:28–29, 35–37.[109] These passages are echoed in *Psalms of Solomon* 17, which is one of our best sources for Davidic messianism in the early Roman period. Verse 4 reads:

---

108. Compare the way Isa. 61:1 and Ps. 146:7–8 are linked in 4Q521, and Isa. 61:1 and Isa. 35:5–6 are linked in Luke 7:22–23; Matt. 11:5–6.

109. W. C. van Unnik, "The Quotation from the Old Testament in John 12:34," *NovT* 3 (1959): 174–79.

> Lord, you chose David to be king over Israel,
> and swore to him about his descendants forever,
> that his kingdom should not fail before you.

(The reference here to YHWH's oath alludes to Ps. 89:35.) This divine promise is then the basis for the prayer to God to raise up "the son of David" (17:21), whose liberating action and reign are then described (17:22–43). It is not then explicitly said that this reign is to be eternal, but if the Messiah is understood to be the final Davidic king (rather than the ancestor of a continuing line of successors to the throne of David), then the promise to David requires that his reign be eternal.

We may ask whether Davidic messianism had any *exegetical* basis for expecting one final Davidic king who would rule forever, and interpreting 2 Samuel 7 and Psalm 89 in such a way. A possible basis is Isaiah 9:7, which speaks of a single Davidic ruler who will maintain the kingdom forever, while Ezekiel 37:25, which speaks of David himself as the future king, says that "my servant David shall be their prince forever." John 12:34 could be alluding to such passages in the prophets, although we have no direct evidence of their application to the Davidic Messiah in extant Jewish literature of this period. In John 12:34 the crowd says that they "have heard *from the law* that the Messiah remains forever." There is no difficulty in taking ὁ νόμος here in the wider sense of the whole of Scripture, rather than the Pentateuch alone: it has this sense in 10:34; 15:25.

But there is in fact a prophecy in the Torah itself that was interpreted to mean that the Messiah's own reign would last forever. As ostensibly the oldest prophecy of the Davidic Messiah, Genesis 49:9–12 was specially prestigious. Verse 10 reads:

> The scepter shall not depart from Judah,
> nor the ruler's staff from between his feet,
> until Shiloh comes [or: until he comes to whom it belongs]
> and the obedience of the peoples is his.

If the enigmatic figure in the third line is taken to be the Davidic Messiah, then the implication could be understood to be that this Messiah's own reign will be forever. Otherwise the meaning would be that the scepter will depart from Judah when the Messiah comes, which is inconceivable in view of God's promise to David in 2 Samuel 7:12–13. This is the interpretation found in the fragmentary Qumran pesher on Genesis, which interprets Genesis 49:10 by referring also to Jeremiah 33:15–17:

> A ruler (שליט)[110] *shall [no]t depart from* the tribe of (משבט)[111] *Judah* [Gen. 45:10a]. While Israel has the dominion, there [will not] be cut off someone

---

110. שליט is an interpretative alteration of the text of Gen. 49:10a, which has שבט ("sceptre"). It doubtless constitutes an interpretation of שילה in Gen. 49:10b.

111. This interpretative addition to the text plays on the double meaning of שבט, which is used in Gen. 49:10a to mean "scepter" but can also mean "tribe."

who sits on the throne of David [cf. Jer 33:17]. For *the staff* (הם חקקק) is the covenant of royalty, [and the thou]sands of Israel are the standards. [*vacat*] *Until* the messiah of righteousness *comes*, the branch of David [Gen. 45:10b; cf. Jer. 33:15]. For to him and to his descendants has been given the covenant of the kingship of his people for everlasting generations, which he observed. (4Q252 5.1–5)

In *4 Ezra* and *2 Baruch* we find the notion of a temporary messianic kingdom (lasting four hundred years, according to *4 Ezra* 7:28), which is followed by the new creation and the resurrection (*2 Bar.* 30:1; 40:3; *4 Ezra* 7:28–32). They differ in that, according to *4 Ezra*, the Messiah will die, along with all other people alive at the end (*4 Ezra* 7:29), while according to *2 Baruch* he "returns with glory," that is, to heaven (*2 Bar.* 30:1). Even *2 Baruch*, however, does not ignore the scriptural promise that the Messiah will rule forever, but interprets "forever" to mean "as long as this world endures" (cf. 40:3; 73:1). So even this form of the messianic hope might be thought compatible with the objection of the crowd in John 12:34, but it is more likely that the notion of the temporary messianic kingdom is one that developed only toward the end of the first century, when *2 Baruch* and *4 Ezra* are to be dated.

4.5. No "Son of Man"

Finally, it is worth mentioning that, like the Synoptics, John confines the use of the term "Son of Man" to Jesus himself, except in 12:34 where the crowd is echoing—with puzzlement—Jesus' own use of the phrase. He goes further than the Synoptics in representing Jesus' use of the term as unintelligible to others, in the sense that they do not know to whom it refers. When Jesus asks the formerly blind man whether he believes in the Son of Man, the man asks, "And who is he, sir? Tell me, so that I may believe in him" (9:36), and similarly the crowd asks, "Who is this Son of Man?" (12:34). This comports with the growing consensus[112] that "the Son of Man" was not a messianic title in Judaism but, in Jesus' usage, an enigmatic form of self-reference, which could only be heard as carrying an allusion to Daniel 7:13 in contexts that make other forms of allusion to Daniel 7:13–14. The figure in Daniel 7:13–14 was not, in the late Second Temple period, interpreted as a transcendent messianic figure distinct from the Davidic Messiah, but as the Davidic Messiah himself.[113] John's account of Jewish messianic expectation is fully consistent with this.

112. But, for exceptions, see, e.g., D. Burkett, *The Son of Man Debate*, SNTSMS 107 (Cambridge: Cambridge University Press, 1999); C. M. Tuckett, "The Son of Man and Daniel 7: Inclusive Aspects of Early Christologies," in *Christian Origins*, ed. K. J. O'Mahony, JSNTSup 241 (Sheffield: Sheffield Academic Press, 2003), 164–90.

113. So *2 Bar.* 39–40; *4 Ezra* 13; *Sib.Or.* 5:414–27.

5. Conclusion

John's account of Jewish expectations of eschatological figures is not systematic. He merely attributes to his characters aspects of those expectations that are relevant to his narrative or his purpose in specific contexts. Nevertheless he makes some careful distinctions among such expectations, distinctions that are hardly necessary for his own christological purposes. While some statements do raise problems, careful examination reveals that nothing John ascribes to his characters is implausible in pre-70 Jewish Palestine. In particular, the expectation of a wonder-working prophet like Moses really was, as John depicts it, popular among the common people specifically in the pre-70 period, and probably not popular among the religious experts and leaders, to whom John does not attribute it. So far as it goes, our evidence shows that John knew pre-70 Jewish Palestine accurately and intended to set his story of Jesus plausibly within that chronological and geographical context.

11

MONOTHEISM AND CHRISTOLOGY IN THE GOSPEL OF JOHN

For many scholars, the Christology of the Fourth Gospel is the "highest" in the New Testament. In my view, this is a mistake, not in the sense of exaggerating the extent to which true and full divinity is attributed to Jesus in the Fourth Gospel, but in failing to recognize the extent to which this is also the case in most other parts of the New Testament. In my view, a Christology of divine identity, in which Jesus is understood to be included in the unique divine identity of the one and only God, the God of Israel, is pervasive in the New Testament writings, clearly expressed in some ways that are common to all or most of these writings, though also developed in distinctive ways in the most theologically reflective and creative of them. All these writings make deliberate use of the ways in which Second Temple Judaism expressed and defined the unique and exclusive divinity of the one God YHWH. They use these well-understood categories of Jewish monotheism in order to apply them also to Jesus, thus including him in the unique divine identity (for this argument in detail, see my book *God Crucified*).[1] The Fourth Gospel, like Hebrews, Revelation, and some of the Pauline writings, does this in especially full and unambiguous ways.

Originally published in a slightly different form in *Contours of Christology in the New Testament*, ed. R. N. Longenecker (Grand Rapids: Eerdmans, 2005), 148–66. Reprinted by permission of the publisher.

1. Richard Bauckham, *God Crucified: Monotheism and Christology in the New Testament* (Grand Rapids: Eerdmans, 1999).

Many recent scholars have recognized that the relationship between so-called high Christology (what I would prefer to call Christology of divine identity) and Jewish monotheism is an important theme in the Gospel of John. They see this in the passages of debate between Jesus and the Jewish leaders, where the latter accuse Jesus of "making himself equal to God" (5:18) or making himself God (10:33) or understand certain of his claims as blasphemous claims to divine identity (8:58–59; 10:30–31, 38–39). These debates in the Gospel are often thought to reflect debates going on in the Gospel's context between Christians and non-Christian Jews who found the Christian claims for Jesus incompatible with Jewish monotheism. There may be something in this, but the passages in question are too integral to the Gospel's developing narrative and its sophisticated narrative revelation of Jesus' identity to be mere reflections of external debates. In any case, this angle on the material runs the risk of explaining Johannine Christology in purely apologetic or polemical terms (or even, as a result, in purely sociological terms) and failing to appreciate the deeply theological roots of this Gospel's concern to integrate "high" Christology into Jewish monotheism. This is not the product of some kind of theological drift toward ever higher Christology and the problems this caused for monotheism. Rather, Jewish monotheism and Christology had been necessarily related to each other in Christian understanding of Jesus' identity from the beginning. Without belief in the unique and exclusive divinity of the God of Israel, the inclusion of Jesus in that identity could not have meant what it did.

Although there is much else to Johannine Christology, its relationship to monotheism is central to the Gospel and it has not usually been adequately understood. For this reason, we shall focus in this chapter on this aspect of Johannine Christology.

Monotheism in the Beginning

In the prologue to his Gospel, especially the first few verses, this Evangelist already establishes that Jesus is fully and truly divine in a way that does not compromise Jewish monotheism because he is included within the unique divine identity as understood in Jewish monotheism. Any Jewish reader of the Gospel would at once recognize the opening verses as a retelling or interpretation of the beginning of the Genesis creation narrative (Gen. 1:1–4). The two opening words ("In the beginning") are identical with the opening word(s) of Genesis, and the impression of the retelling of Genesis would be furthered by the repetition of these words in verse 2, the reference to the creation of all things by the Word in verse 3, and the key words "light" and "darkness" in verses 4–5 (cf. Gen. 1:3–5). Retellings or interpretation of the Genesis creation narrative are common in Jewish literature of this period. Some of them were especially concerned with the monotheistic message that YHWH was the sole Creator of all things, who designed and accomplished his creation entirely by himself. In fact, it was a key element in the common Jewish understanding of God's unique identity that he alone was the Creator of all things. This was perhaps the simplest way of making, as Jewish monotheism required, an absolute distinction between God and all other reality. God alone is Creator of all else; all other things were created by God.

John 1:3 echoes very emphatically this monotheistic motif: "All things came into being through it [the Word], and without it not one thing came into being." I translate the pronoun as "it" rather than "him" because at this stage of the prologue there has been no clear indication that the Word is to be understood as a personal agent, though this emerges in the course of the prologue. That all things were created by God through the instrumentality of his Word is very commonly said in Jewish statements about the creation (beginning with Ps. 33:6). It is simply a concise expression of the fact that in the Genesis creation account each act of creation is effected by God speaking. Although Genesis 1 itself does not use the term "word," it is easily understood as saying that all things were created by God's Word. When John uses the term "Word" in the opening verses of his prologue, he means simply this: the divine Word that all Jews, on the basis of Genesis, understood to have been active in the creation of all things. Moreover, there was no question of this Word's being something or someone created. As God's own word, it was intrinsic to God's own unique identity. To say that all things were created by the Word did not compromise the belief that God alone was Creator of all things, since his Word belonged to his own identity. In fact, to say as John does that all things came into being through the Word is precisely to categorize the Word as belonging to the identity of God rather than to the creation.

But John has already taken care in verse 1 to make it clear that, while the Word can be distinguished from God and said to be with him, the Word is also intrinsic to God's own unique identity. This is the only possible meaning a Jewish reader could find in the claim that the Word was already with God in eternity before creation ("in the beginning"). We do not need to postulate any background to these verses other than Genesis 1 and the tradition of Jewish creation accounts dependent on it that speak of God's Word as his instrument or agent in creation. We should not, with many scholars writing on the Johannine Prologue, use the term Logos, as though John's Greek word means more than simply "word." It carries no particular metaphysical baggage. It refers simply to God's Word as portrayed in Jewish creation accounts, and this is why it does not appear in John's Gospel after the prologue. In the prologue he uses the term to identify the preexistent Christ *within the Genesis creation narrative*, and so within the unique identity of God *as already understood by Jewish monotheism*. He therefore confines his use of the term to his retelling of the Genesis creation account (John 1:1–5) and to the statement that this Word of the creation account entered human history as the man Jesus Christ (1:14). From the perspective of the rest of the Gospel, for which the Word has now been revealed as the Son of the Father, the terms in which the incarnate Christ spoke of himself (primarily as Son) naturally supersede the term used in Jewish creation accounts.

Thus the opening verses of the Prologue, read in the light of the later statement that the Word became flesh and lived among us as Jesus Christ (1:14), include Jesus in the unique divine identity by identifying him with the Word that was with God in the beginning and that as God's agent created all things. It places Jesus unequivocally on the divine side of the absolute distinction between the one Creator and all other things. By identifying Jesus with an entity intrinsic to the divine identity—God's Word—it includes Jesus in that identity without infringing monotheism. The Word "was with God" but was not another besides God: it "was God" (1:1). Thus the Gospel begins by engaging with one of the most important ways in which Jews defined the uniqueness of the one God—as sole Creator of all things—and uses this way of understanding the unique identity of God in order to include Jesus within it.

The Divine Prerogatives

In the Jewish definition of the one God's exclusive divinity, as well as being sole Creator of all things, God was also understood as the sole sovereign Ruler of all things. One key aspect of this was his sovereignty over life and death (Deut. 32:39). God is the only living one, that is, the only one to whom life belongs eternally and intrinsically. All other life derives from him, is given by him and taken back by him. Another key aspect of God's sole sovereignty over creation was his prerogative of judgment: his rule is just, implementing justice, and therefore judging nations and individuals. Such divine prerogatives have to be understood, not as mere functions that God may delegate to others, but as intrinsic to the divine identity. Ruling over all, giving life to all, exercising judgment on all—these belong integrally to the Jewish understanding of who God is.

These divine prerogatives, intrinsic to divinity as such, are the focus of the first major passage in the Gospel in which Jesus speaks about his own identity in discussion with the Jewish leaders: chapter 5. Jesus defends his act of healing on the Sabbath by claiming God's unique prerogative of working on the Sabbath: "My Father is still working [i.e., his work did not cease with his creation of all things but continues in his sovereign rule over all things], and I also am working" (5:17). (Since people are born and die on Sabbaths, it is clear that God exercises his sovereignty over life and death and his prerogative of judgment on the Sabbath as on other days. Jesus claims to do the same.) The Jewish leaders take this to mean that Jesus "was making himself equal to God" (5:18), and the lengthy discourse of Jesus that follows shows that in one sense they are right but in another wrong. Jesus stresses that in all he does he is wholly dependent on his Father, such that he in no way sets himself up as a rival to his Father. In his radical dependence on God, he is not equal to God in the sense the Jewish leaders intend, but he is equal to God in the sense that what the Father gives him to do are the uniquely divine prerogatives. He does not simply act as God's agent in implementing some aspects of God's sovereignty. He exercises the full divine sovereignty as given him by his Father but as also fully his own: "just as the Father raises the dead and gives them life, so also the Son gives life to *whomever he wishes*" (5:21); "the Father judges no one, but has given *all judgment* to the Son" (5:22); "just as the Father has life in himself, so he has granted the Son to have *life in himself*" (5:26). Jesus thus shares in the divine identity as the only living one, the only giver of life, the only judge of all. He does so as the Son who is wholly dependent on his Father, but nonetheless fully and truly exercises these divine prerogatives. This means that the unique divine identity *includes* the relationship Jesus here describes between himself as the Son and God his Father.

Finally on this passage, we should note that from this inclusion of Jesus in the unique divine identity follows the worship of Jesus: "The Father . . . has given all judgment to the Son, so that all may honor the Son just as they honor the Father" (5:23). In the Jewish tradition, worship is intimately connected with monotheism. The only true God must be worshipped and he is the only one who may be worshipped. This is because worship is precisely the recognition of the unique divine identity. In Jewish religious practice it is worship that distinguishes the one God from all other beings who, however exalted, are his creatures and subject to his sovereign rule. In early Christian practice, therefore, the worship of Jesus indicates his inclusion in the identity of this one God.

The "I Am" Sayings

The Gospel of John contains two series of sayings of Jesus including the words "I am" (Greek *egō eimi*, where the pronoun *egō*, which is not always necessary in Greek, is used for emphasis along with the verb). One of these series is easily recognized by readers of the Gospel in English translation. In this series, known as "I am" sayings with predicates, the "I am" is followed by a noun. They are metaphorical sayings in which Jesus describes himself in some way as the one who gives salvation. There are seven such sayings:

I am the bread of life. (6:35, 41, 48)
I am the light of the world. (8:12; cf. 9:5)
I am the gate for the sheep. (10:7, 9)
I am the good shepherd. (10:11, 14)
I am the resurrection and the life. (11:25)
I am the way and the truth and the life. (14:6)
I am the true vine. (15:1)

Of course, in ancient Jewish literature the number seven is never insignificant. It is the number of completeness, and so the existence of these seven sayings scattered through the Gospel indicates the completeness of the salvation Jesus brings and gives. As a series of complementary metaphors they illuminate it from various aspects. We could compare them with the seven "signs" (miracles) in the Gospel, which also have to be counted before we realize that there are, in fact, seven of them. While the "I am" sayings with predicates are verbal descriptions of Jesus as the Savior, the signs he does show him to be the Savior in concrete demonstrations of his power to give life. Like the sayings, the signs illustrate the nature of the salvation Jesus gives in a variety of ways. In some cases, "I am" sayings with predicates correlate with signs: Jesus supplies bread to the five thousand and declares himself "the bread of life"; Jesus opens the eyes of the blind man and declares himself "the light of the world"; Jesus raises Lazarus from death and declares himself "the resurrection and the life." In other cases, the signs and the sayings are independent of each other.

However, our main concern at present is not with this series of seven "I am" sayings with predicates, but with another series of "I am" sayings, known as absolute "I am" sayings. In these, the words "I am" (Greek *egō eimi*) stand by themselves without a predicate. These are less easy to identify in English translations, because the translators adopt a variety of translation strategies in order to make intelligible English of them. In one case at least, most translations render the two Greek words literally as just the two English words "I am." This is the best known of the absolute "I am" sayings and occurs in 8:58, where Jesus says: "Truly, truly, I tell you, before Abraham was, I am." On hearing this, the Jewish leaders take up stones to stone him for blasphemy (8:59). It is clear that here the phrase "I am" indicates not only Jesus' claim to have preexisted Abraham, but also some kind of claim to divine identity, taken by his hearers to be blasphemous. Precisely why it constitutes a claim to divine identity is less easy to determine, but before attempting to do so we must first identify this absolute "I am" saying as one of a series of seven scattered, like the seven "I am" sayings with predicates, through the Gospel.

The seven are these: 4:26; 6:20; 8:24; 8:28; 8:58; 13:19; 18:5, 6, 8 (treating these three occurrences in chapter 18 as a single saying repeated). In most of these cases except 8:58, the NRSV translates *egō eimi* as "I am he." In 6:20, the translation is "It is I," but in all cases the NRSV helps English readers to recognize the resemblance between all these sayings by giving the literal translation "I am" in a footnote. Not all scholars agree that all seven sayings belong together as a series of comparable statements. This is mainly because in some cases the Greek can be given an ordinary meaning. In the first of these sayings (4:26), Jesus is replying to the Samaritan woman, who has just spoken about the Messiah. Jesus' words (literally: "I, the one who is speaking to you, am") can easily be read as having an implied predicate in the antecedent reference to the Messiah. In other words, Jesus says: "I am he," meaning, "I am the Messiah." This is probably how the Evangelist expects us to suppose the Samaritan woman understands Jesus, since she goes on to ask her friends and neighbors whether it can be true that he is the Messiah (4:29).

In the second of the sayings (6:20), Jesus, walking on the water, is approaching the terrified disciples in the boat, and, to reassure them, says (literally): "I am; do not be afraid." Here "I am" can be understood, quite naturally in Greek, as "It is I": Jesus is simply identifying himself to the disciples. Matthew and Mark use the same phrase in their versions of this story.

A similar meaning can be understood in the last of the sayings, in chapter 18, where the soldiers come to arrest Jesus in Gethsemane. Jesus asks them, "For whom are you looking?" and when they reply, "Jesus of Nazareth," Jesus responds, "I am," meaning "I am he" or "It is I." However, in this case, we may be suspicious as to whether this ordinary meaning of the phrase is sufficient to explain the passage, since the reaction of the soldiers is to fall to the ground (18:6), and since Jesus' words "I am" actually occur three times (18:5, 6, 8), suggesting that this may be an emphatic climax of the series of such sayings.

While in these three cases out of the seven, an ordinary meaning is possible and may even be superficially obvious, in the other four cases no such ordinary meaning is available and the phrase "I am" is as strangely incomplete in the Greek as it is in a literal English translation. In these cases, there is no plausible antecedent in the context, as though Jesus could be saying "I am that one about whom we have just been speaking." In one case (8:24), the puzzlingly incomplete nature of the phrase is clear in the response of Jesus' interlocutors. Addressing the Jewish leaders, Jesus says: "you will die in your sins unless you believe that I am." They respond: "*Who* are you?" (8:25)—in other words, "What do you mean, 'I am'? 'I am' *who*?" Jesus is equally obscure when he uses the phrase again in 8:28: "When you have lifted up the Son of Man, then you will realize that I am." He can hardly mean, "I am the Son of Man," because "the Son of Man" is itself an enigmatic way of referring to himself that Jesus' hearers in the Gospel do not understand. In these two verses Jesus is clearly making some remarkable kind of claim, which is obscure to his hearers. Only when he uses the phrase a third time (8:58), saying, "Before Abraham was, I am," do they realize that he is claiming divine identity and react accordingly.

Since in these cases, as well as in 13:19, the phrase "I am" cannot be given an ordinary meaning, it is best to take all seven occurrences as a set, while understanding those where an ordinary meaning is possible as instances of double entendre. This evangelist is fond of double meanings. In many such cases, Jesus' hearers take his words in the superficially obvious sense and thereby miss his real meaning, which is a symbolic or otherwise more profound significance in the words. First-time readers or hearers of the Gospel will probably, like the Samaritan woman herself, take Jesus in 4:26 to mean, "I am the Messiah you just mentioned." While this is not wrong, readers who study the Gospel more carefully will find that, in the light of later occurrences of the phrase, there is a deeper meaning: Jesus is claiming not just messiahship, but divine identity. At this stage in the Gospel narrative, however, such a claim is not made explicit on the surface of his words. Similarly, in 6:20, first time readers will probably again give the phrase an ordinary meaning ("It is I"), though here the context, evocative of Old Testament theophanies, might already suggest to well-informed readers that more is implied. But in chapters 7–8 the issue of who Jesus really is becomes the central and explicit topic in discussion among Jesus' hearers and between Jesus and his hearers. Here the special significance of "I am" becomes unavoidable and finally, in 8:58, serves to cap the whole discussion as Jesus' climactic declaration of his identity, understood by the Jewish leaders as blasphemous. The fuller meaning implicit in the earlier occurrences can now be recognized by hindsight. And when, in chapter 18, this phrase on Jesus' lips provokes the soldiers to fall prostrate on the ground before him, attentive readers will not, with chapter 8 in the background, be surprised.

We may reasonably conclude that the Evangelist has distributed two series of seven "I am" sayings through his narrative: those with predicates describe who Jesus is for believers, as the giver of salvation, while the absolute "I am" sayings state more directly who he is in himself, his divine identity, which forms the basis for his salvific role. But exactly how does the phrase "I am" express divine identity? One suggestion, most often made specifically with reference to 8:58, where Jesus' hearers understand the phrase as blasphemous, is that "I am" is a form of the divine Name, the tetragrammaton (YHWH). In Exodus 3:14, when God reveals his Name to Moses, he interprets it as meaning "I am who I am" (this is one of several possible translations of the Hebrew), and then uses just the first of these three Hebrew words as a form of the Name: "Thus shall you say to the Israelites, 'I AM has sent me to you.'" A difficulty in regarding this as the background to the absolute "I am" sayings in John is that neither the Septuagint Greek version nor any known Greek translation of Exodus 3:14 uses the translation *egō eimi*, the Greek phrase in John. (LXX has *egō eimi ho ōn* ["I am the one who is"] and *ho ōn apestalke me* ["The one who is has sent me"].) This is not an insuperable difficulty. Like most of the New Testament writers, John not only uses the Septuagint as his regular form of the Old Testament text, but also knows the Hebrew text and, when the point he is making requires it, may allude directly to the latter. Perhaps he based the absolute "I am" sayings directly on the Hebrew of Exodus 3:14.

However, there is another explanation of them which is preferable, at least as their primary meaning, because it explains much more about this whole series of seven sayings. The Septuagint uses *egō eimi* in Deuteronomy 32:39 and on several occasions in Isaiah 40–55 (41:4; 43:10; 46:4 [here the phrase is repeated: *egō eimi egō eimi*]) to translate the Hebrew phrase, *'ănî hû'*, which is usually translated in English as "I am he." In the two cases (Isa. 43:25; 51:2) where the MT Hebrew has the more emphatic form of the same phrase, *'ānōkî 'ānōkî hû'*, the Septuagint has the double expression: *egō eimi egō eimi*. This phrase "I am he" is an extraordinarily significant one. It is a divine self-declaration, encapsulating YHWH's claim to unique and exclusive divinity. In the Hebrew Bible, it occurs first in what are almost the last words God himself speaks in the Torah, where it is an emphatically monotheistic assertion: "Behold, I, even I am he; there is no god besides me" (Deut. 32:39). In New Testament times, the passage was frequently read as an eschatological prophecy of the salvation God would achieve for his people in the end times. As such, it links closely with the prophecies of Deutero-Isaiah (Isa. 40–55), where this form of divine self-declaration recurs several times (in Hebrew: Isa. 41:4; 43:10, 13, 25; 46:4; 48:12; 51:12; 52:6). These chapters of Isaiah were for early Christians the most important biblical prophecies of the endtime salvation of Israel and the nations and the source of many quotations and allusions throughout the New Testament, including the Gospel of John. Their proclamation of eschatological salvation is intimately linked to their emphatic assertion of the absolute uniqueness of the God of Israel, who in these chapters constantly asserts his unique deity in contrast with the idols of the nations who are no gods, and defines his uniqueness as that of the eternal Creator of all things and the unique sovereign Ruler of all history. His great act of eschatological salvation will demonstrate him to be the one and only God in the sight of all the nations, revealing his glory so that all the ends of earth will acknowledge him as God and turn to him for salvation. All this is summed up in the divine self-declaration "I am he."

The occurrences of the phrase vary somewhat in the MT Hebrew and in the Septuagint Greek (which at one or two places may have translated a variant Hebrew original). But, whether we suppose John to have been working solely with the Septuagint or (as I think likely) to have known also the Hebrew, it is striking that his series of seven absolute "I am" sayings corresponds even numerically to its Old Testament source. The Septuagint has *egō eimi* in three instances (Deut. 32:39; Isa. 41:4; 43:10) and the double *egō eimi egō eimi* in four (Isa. 43:25; 45:18; 46:4; 51:12), making seven in all. The MT Hebrew has the simple *'ănî hû'* seven times (Deut 32:39; Isa 41:4; 43:10, 13; 46:4; 48:12; 52:6) and the emphatic form *'ānōkî 'ānōkî hû'* twice (Isa. 43:25; 51:12), making a total count of either seven or nine, just as John's series could be counted either as seven or (since the last saying is repeated twice: 18:5, 6, 8) nine. In the series of seven absolute "I am" sayings of Jesus the complete (sevenfold) assertion of YHWH's unique and exclusive divinity made in the Hebrew Bible is repeated by Jesus as the one who achieves the eschatological salvation and the universal recognition of YHWH's unique divinity that it entails.

The "I am he" declarations are among the most emphatically monotheistic assertions of the Hebrew Bible, and if Jesus in the Fourth Gospel repeats them he is unambiguously identifying himself with the one and only God, YHWH, the God of Israel. It does not do justice to these sayings to see them, as some scholars do, merely as an expression of an "agent" or "emissary" Christology in the Fourth Gospel. This is a label for the notion that Jesus comes into the world as the agent of God who sends him (Jesus in John very often refers to his Father as "the one who sent me"). As God's agent, he has full powers to act for God. In a sense, as God's agent he stands in for God. There is no doubt that it is an important aspect of the understanding of Jesus in John that he does in this sense act as God's emissary. But when these ideas are put in their wider context in the

Fourth Gospel, including the absolute "I am" sayings, it is clear that it is not sufficient to suppose that God sends *someone else* to act as his agent in salvation. What this agent does is not something God can delegate to someone other than God, since it belongs to the uniquely divine prerogatives of the one God. Only one who truly shares the unique divine identity can give eternal life and reveal God's glory in the world. Jesus' absolute "I am" sayings express his unique and exclusive participation in God's unique and exclusive deity. Just as "I am he" in the Hebrew Bible sums up what it is to be truly God, so in John it identifies Jesus as truly God in the fullest sense.

We can appreciate this better when we attend not only to the phrase "I am"/"I am he" itself, but also to its contexts both in the Old Testament and in John's Gospel. The first Old Testament occurrence of the formula stresses the uniqueness of YHWH as sovereign over life and death:

> Behold, I, even I am he;
> there is no god besides me.
> I kill and I make alive. (Deut. 32:39; cf. 1 Sam. 2:6)

Similarly, the Jesus who tells the Samaritan woman that "I am he" (John 4:26) has already implicitly claimed to be more than a human Messiah by offering the living water from which eternal life springs (4:14), while in chapter 8 Jesus' self-declarations as "I am" are closely connected with his power to deliver from death (8:24, 51–53).

In Deutero-Isaiah, the divine "I am he" is linked closely with the uniqueness of YHWH's eternal sovereignty as the One who precedes all things and whom none shall succeed (Isa. 41:4; 43:10; 48:12). It is this uniquely divine eternity Jesus claims in John 8:58: "Before Abraham was, I am." Also in the Deutero-Isaianic usage, YHWH's "I am he" includes his claim to be the only Savior (Isa. 43:11–13; 46:4). YHWH is the only Savior because he is the only true God, and Jesus' identification with YHWH in John is similarly connected with the exclusivity of his salvific role. Jesus' hearers "will die in your sins unless you believe that I am he" (John 8:24)—because it is in his unique and exclusive identity with the one God that eschatological salvation is achieved.

In Deutero-Isaiah, an important element in the claim to unique divinity by YHWH is that, unlike the purported gods of the nations, he announces beforehand the things that are to come. This is not merely his power of prediction but his sovereign power to accomplish what he plans. It is associated with the "I am he" self-declaration in Isaiah 43:9–10, and it is this aspect of the unique divine identity that comes to the fore in John 13:19, where, having predicted Judas's betrayal (13:18; cf. 6:70), Jesus tells the disciples, "I tell you this now, before it occurs, so that when it does occur, you may believe that I am he." As in Deutero-Isaiah, this is not a matter of mere prediction but of Jesus' sovereignty over the events that lead to his death. When Judas goes to do what he must, it is at Jesus' express command (13:27), and when Judas arrives in Gethsemane with the soldiers, Jesus gives himself up to them, identifying himself for them with the words "I am he," repeated for emphasis once by the Evangelist and once by Jesus also (18:5, 6, 8). The formula of divine identity reminds us that this is Jesus' own sovereign accomplishment of what he had purposed, such that the disciples, seeing what he had predicted occur, should now believe that "I am he." We should also notice that this climactic seventh absolute "I am" saying brings Jesus' identity with YHWH into direct connection with his death. It is as the uniquely divine Savior, fulfilling the sovereign divine purpose, that Jesus goes voluntarily to his death, in order to complete his salvific work.

Also notable is the contrast between this scene and that in 8:58–59. In the latter passage, the reaction of the Jewish authorities to Jesus' utterance of the divine self-identification is to take up stones to kill him for blasphemy. In Gethsemane, however, the soldiers "stepped back and fell to the ground" (18:6). At the literal level of the narrative as ordinary history, no doubt they hear Jesus' words as no more than an identification of himself as Jesus, the man they are seeking to arrest, and are taken aback by the open directness of his admission of who he is. But, as in some other passages of Johannine narrative, there is a further, ironic level at which the characters act much more significantly than they understand. At this level, on hearing the claim to unique divine identity, "I am he," they fall down in worship, which is the only appropriate response to recognition of the one true God ("to fall to the ground" is frequently used of obeisance and prostration in worship). At the seventh absolute "I am" saying, which as seventh symbolically completes the revelation of the unique divinity of the one God in Jesus, both Gentiles (Roman soldiers) and Jews (the temple police) bow in worship and submission.

Probably the scene reflects one of the most significant passages in Deutero-Isaiah's prophetic account of the revelation of YHWH to the world in his eschatological act of salvation for Israel and the nations: Isaiah 45:18–24. This begins with an "I am he" declaration (though only in the Septuagint Greek: the Hebrew has "I am YHWH"): "I am he, and there is no other" (45:18), a statement then repeated in other terms in verses 19, 21, and 22, as YHWH proclaims to the nations whose idols have failed them, that he alone is the only God and the only Savior:

> I am God and there is no other besides me,
> a righteous one and a Savior, there is none but me.
> Turn to me and be saved, people from the end of the earth.
> I am God and there is no other.
> By myself I swear . . .
> that to me every knee shall bow,
> and every tongue shall swear by God. (Isa. 45:21–24 LXX)

This is the passage to which Philippians 2:9–11 alludes, reading it as referring to the final acknowledgment by every creature in creation of the divinity of the one God revealed in Jesus. John's scene in Gethsemane is, of course, no more than a symbolic anticipation of that eschatological goal. But it is the evangelist's way of indicating that Jesus' passion, which in Gethsemane he undertakes irrevocably in its totality, is both the achievement of salvation for all and the revelation of God's glory to all, such that the unique identity of the one God is demonstrated and wins the recognition of all.

Finally, we may return to the connections between the seven signs, the seven "I am" sayings with predicates, and these seven absolute "I am" sayings that we have studied. In their different ways, all three series of sevens reveal who Jesus is and the salvation he gives. Salvation in the Fourth Gospel can be summarized as knowing the true God and receiving eternal life from him. The signs reveal God's glory in Jesus and the salvation Jesus brings. As acts of evident divine power, they demonstrate what the sayings can only say, but the two sets of "I am" sayings make fully explicit what the signs signify. One series, the "I am" sayings with predicates, focus on Jesus as the only Savior in a variety of images instancing the inexhaustible fullness of what salvation means. In these sayings, as in the signs, it is implicit that Jesus can be the only Savior only because he is identified with the only God. To reveal the glory of God's unique identity, to give the eternal life that God alone has in himself, Jesus must himself belong to God's own unique identity. This is what the absolute "I am" sayings make fully explicit, in a sevenfold series of progressive clarity, in which Jesus utters the most concise and comprehensive expression of all that it means for God to be uniquely and truly God. They identify Jesus with God, not just in an abstract way, but in a way that the Scriptures associate with the universal revelation of God's unique divinity in his eschatological act of salvation for Israel and the nations. Jesus' identity with God is thus essential and intrinsic to his work of revelation and salvation.

Jesus and the Father as the One God

The second occasion on which the Jewish leaders take up stones to kill Jesus for blasphemy is in response to his statement, "I and the Father are one" (10:30). Although, so far as I am aware, it has not been suggested by other scholars, it seems to me very probable that this saying of Jesus alludes to the Jewish confession of faith in the one God, the Shema: "YHWH our God, YHWH is one" (Deut. 6:4). This was the most familiar of all monotheistic formulas, since devout Jews recited it daily. It is frequently cited in Jewish literature in the abbreviated form: "God is one"—a form in which it also appears in the New Testament (Rom. 3:30; Gal. 3:20; James 2:19). It says nothing about the unitariness of God's nature, but simply indicates that YHWH is the one and only God. It is true that in all Greek echoes of the Shema the word for one is masculine (*heis*), as we should expect, whereas in

John 10:30 it is neuter (*hen*). But this is a necessary adaptation of language. Jesus is not saying that he and the Father are a single person, but that together they are one God. That the Fourth Evangelist should have in this way incorporated Jesus into the affirmation of one God in the Shema is not especially surprising, since Paul had already done the same thing in a different way in 1 Corinthians 8:6.

Jesus' assertion of his oneness with the Father occurs twice more in the Gospel, both in Jesus' prayer to the Father in chapter 17. In both cases Jesus prays that his disciples "may be one, as we are one" (17:11, 22). This analogy between the oneness of Jesus and his Father, on the one hand, and the oneness of the disciples, on the other, has been used to argue that the former indicates no more than closeness of association or concurrence of will. But again the background in Jewish monotheistic reflection will clarify the issue considerably. Jewish writers sometimes assert that to the one God there corresponds "one" of something else in what belongs especially to him in the world: one temple, one altar, one law, and especially one chosen people (*2 Bar.* 48:23–24; Josephus, *Ant.* 4.201; *C. Ap.* 2.193). Their service and worship of the one God unites the people of God into one (Josephus, *Ant.* 5.111; Philo, *Spec.* 1.52; 4.159; *Virt.* 35). This Jewish topos, of course, in no way implies that God is a unity in the same sense as his people are, only that the divine singularity draws the singular people of God together into a relational unity. Similarly Jesus prays that his disciples be a single community corresponding to the uniqueness of the one God in which he and his Father are united (see also 10:16).

Whereas the absolute "I am" sayings express Jesus' divine identity without explicit reference to the Father, Jesus' statements of his oneness with the Father indicate that it is as Father and Son that God and Jesus relate within the unique divine identity. When, in chapter 10, Jesus goes on to defend his claim that he and the Father are one in the face of Jewish leaders' accusation of blasphemy, he ends by making yet another statement that provokes them to try to take legal action against them. This time it is: "the Father is in me and I am in the Father" (10:38; for this claim, see also 14:10, 11, 20; 17:20, 21). Evidently, this reciprocal indwelling—the closest conceivable intimacy of relationship—is the inner reality of the oneness of Father and Son. Their unity does not erase their difference, but differentiates them in an inseparable relationship. We should also notice that the terms "Father" and "Son" entail each other. The Father is called Father only because Jesus is his Son, and Jesus is called Son only because he is the Son of his divine Father. Each is essential to the identity of the other. So to say that Jesus and the Father are one is to say that the unique divine identity comprises the relationship in which the Father is who he is only in relation to the Son, and vice versa. It is in the portrayal of this intradivine relationship that John's Christology steps outside the categories of Jewish monotheistic definition of the unique identity of the one God. It does not at all deny or contradict any of these, but from Jesus' relationship of sonship to God it redefines the divine identity as one in which Father and Son are inseparably united in differentiation from each other.

Conclusion

The monotheistic theme in John is far from merely apologetic or polemical, designed to show, against Jewish objections to Christology, that divine Christology is not incompatible with Jewish monotheism. Rather, that Jesus belongs to the unique identity of the one and only God has theological roots in the deepest theological concerns of this Gospel. Its theme is the eschatological revelation of God's glory to all and his achievement of definitive salvation for all, as foreseen especially in Isaiah 40–55. The one true God reveals himself savingly only in the Son who can reveal God and communicate eternal life only because he is one with the Father. The unique and exclusive divinity of the only God can be revealed savingly in Jesus only because Jesus participates uniquely and exclusively in that divinity. Thus, without contradicting or rejecting any of the existing features of Jewish monotheism, the Fourth Gospel redefines it as christological monotheism, a form of monotheism in which the relationship of Jesus the Son to his Father is integral to who the one God is.[2]

---

2. This chapter was written for a context in which footnotes were inappropriate. The works to which I am most indebted in developing the argument of this chapter are: Mark L. Appold, *The Oneness Motif in the Fourth Gospel*, WUNT 2/1 (Tübingen: Mohr Siebeck, 1976); David M. Ball, *"I Am" in John's Gospel: Literary Function, Background and Theological Implications*, JSNTSup 124 (Sheffield: Sheffield Academic Press, 1996); Masanobu Endo, *Creation and Christology: A Study of the Johannine Prologue in the Light of Early Jewish Creation Accounts*, WUNT 2/149 (Tübingen: Mohr Siebeck, 2002); Andrew T. Lincoln, *Truth on Trial: The Lawsuit Motif in the Fourth Gospel* (Peabody: Hendrickson, 2000); Jerome H. Neyrey, *An Ideology of Revolt: John's Christology in Social Science Perspective* (Philadelphia: Fortress, 1988); Catrin H. Williams, *I Am He: The Interpretation of 'Anî Hû' in Jewish and Early Christian Literature*, WUNT 2/113 (Tübingen: Mohr Siebeck, 2000).

12

The Holiness of Jesus and His Disciples in the Gospel of John

At first sight the Gospel of John may not seem to have much to say about the holiness of Jesus and even less about the holiness of his disciples. The word ἅγιος ("holy") occurs just four times, with reference to God (17:11: "Holy Father"), Jesus (6:69: "the Holy One of God"), and the Holy Spirit (14:26; 20:22[1]).[2] However, there are four occurrences of the verb ἁγιάζειν ("to make holy, to consecrate, to sanctify") (10:36; 17:17, 19 [*bis*]), two of which refer to the consecration of Jesus' disciples (17:17, 19). A close examination of these occurrences of ἁγιάζειν in their contexts will show that the Gospel treats the holiness of Jesus' disciples as a significant theme closely related to the holiness of Jesus, the Father, and the Spirit. The occurrences of ἅγιος ("holy") will fall into place as we consider the significance of the uses of ἁγιάζειν ("to make holy").

Originally published in a slightly different form in *Holiness and Ecclesiology in the New Testament* ed. Kent Brower and Andy Johnson, Alex Deasley FS (Grand Rapids: Eerdmans, 2007). Reprinted by permission of the publisher.

1. There is also a variant reading that adds ἅγιον to πνεῦμα at 7:39, but this is readily explicable from the tendency of scribes to add ἅγιον in references to the Holy Spirit.

2. In the Johannine letters, ἅγιος is used only at 1 John 2:20, where "the Holy One" is probably Jesus, as in John 6:69.

Purity and Holiness

Before proceeding to examine our theme in the Gospel of John, there is a preliminary point to be made about the biblical notion of holiness. New Testament scholars are not always careful about distinguishing between holiness and purity in Old Testament and Jewish thought. Both terms are closely connected with the sanctuary and the cultic practice of the temple, but in different ways. Holiness belongs properly to God, and all persons and things given to God become holy. It is a paradoxical concept, in that holiness expresses what God intrinsically is, distinct from all creation, and yet it is also shared—in varying degrees—by all that belongs to God. For the people of God, holiness is an obligation because God is holy: "You shall be holy, for I YHWH your God am holy" (Lev. 19:2; cf. 11:44–45; 20:26). The holiness of the people of God entails both cultic and moral obligations that set them apart from the world in dedication to the service of God. It can be said both that God makes people holy (consecrates or sanctifies them) and that people make themselves holy (consecrate or sanctify themselves) (e.g., Lev. 21:8).

Purity, however, is what creaturely persons and things have if they are not defiled by such things as death, sexual emissions, childbirth, scale disease, or animals forbidden as food. Impurity of this kind—ritual impurity—is more like dirt than sin. For most people most of the time, it is unavoidable and not blameworthy, but it must be removed by ritual washing and, in some cases, sacrifice. However, there is also a type of defilement—moral impurity—that results from immoral behavior.[3]

Each of these major terms—holy and pure—has its own opposite, making two distinct pairs of antonyms (cf. Lev. 10:10; 11:47; Ezek. 22:26; 42:20; 44:23): "holy" (קֹדֶשׁ, ἅγιος) and "profane" or "common" (חֹל, κοινός or βέβηλος); "pure" or "clean" (טָהוֹר, καθαρός) and "impure" or "unclean" (טָמֵא, ἀκάθαρτος). For the sake of clarity, I shall restrict my English usage in this essay to "holy" and "profane," "pure" and "impure." Corresponding to each of these pairs of antonyms are two verbs, describing the movement from one state to the other. To make the profane holy is to "consecrate" or to "sanctify" (קָדַשׁ, ἁγιάζειν or ἁγίζειν),[4] while to make the holy profane is to "desecrate" or to "profane" (חָלַל, βεβηλοῦν). To make the pure impure is to "defile" or to "pollute" (טָמֵא, μιαίνειν), while to make the impure pure is to "purify" (טָהַר, καθαρίζειν). We can represent these relationships by two diagrams:[5]

3. On this generally neglected category, see especially J. Klawans, *Impurity and Sin in Ancient Judaism* (Oxford: Oxford University Press, 2000).

4. Jewish and early Christian Greek generally use ἁγιάζειν, which is otherwise rare, in place of the otherwise more common ἁγίζειν.

5. The diagrams are adapted from G. J. Wenham, *Leviticus*, NICOT (Grand Rapids: Eerdmans, 1979), 19.

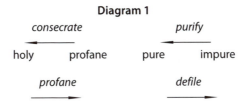

These show the way in which the two distinct systems of holiness/profanity and purity/impurity operate. But the systems are also related. All holy things are also pure, and all profane things are either pure or impure. The relationship can be expressed in a combination of the two diagrams,[6] thus:

Diagram 2

	consecrate		*purify*	
holy		profane &		impure
	profane	pure	*defile*	

From this diagram it appears that the state of being profane and pure is midway between holiness and impurity. It is the normal state of most persons and things. From this state it is possible to be elevated to holiness or degraded to impurity. The impure cannot become holy without first becoming pure, but the two processes involved—purification from impurity and consecration as holy—are distinct.[7] The impure should not come into contact with the holy and cannot do so without fearful results. If something holy is defiled, it is necessarily also profaned.

We are now in a position to distinguish John's use of these two sets of terms—those relating to holiness and those relating to purity. Three times he refers to Jewish practices of preserving purity (18:28)[8] and removing impurity (2:6; 3:25).[9]

6. This diagram is adapted from ibid., 19.

7. Some New Testament scholars speak of sanctification or consecration as including purification (e.g., H. Stettler, "Sanctification in the Jesus Tradition," *Bib* 85 [2004]: 159). But for the sake of clarity and conformity with Old Testament usage it is better to see purification as (in the case of impure persons or things) a necessary precondition or presupposition for consecration.

8. On the reasons why the chief priests may have feared defilement if they entered the praetorium, see R. Bauckham, "James, Peter, and the Gentiles," in *The Missions of James, Peter, and Paul*, ed. B. Chilton and C. Evans, NovTSup 115 (Leiden: Brill, 2005), 91–116. It is probably not the case that Gentiles or their houses were regarded as ipso facto ritually impure, but the chief priests may have feared contamination from the idolatry practiced in the praetorium or simply have been exercising extreme caution, as priests who must officiate at the sacrifices at the Passover, to avoid any possible source of impurity, such as human corpses or those of unclean animals.

9. In this case, it may be that the dispute is over whether John's baptism purifies from moral impurity (for this as John the Baptist's interpretation of his practice of baptizing, see Klawans, *Impurity*, 138–43), but the Gospel writer does not explain the point.

These references are simply matters of historical explanation.[10] But on two other occasions John refers to the purification of Jesus' disciples from the moral impurity caused by sin. Both are instances of John's frequent use of double meaning: using a term that has both an obvious, literal sense, but also an overtone of spiritual meaning. The first instance is when Jesus washes his disciples' feet. The word "clean" or "pure" (καθαρός) in 13:10–11 refers, on the literal level, to the cleanness of the body after it has been washed, but also, on a symbolic level, to the state of disciples who have been purified of sin by the forgiveness that Jesus' death is to procure for them.[11] Washing—especially the total immersion of which Jesus speaks in verse 10—is an appropriate symbol for this purification because washing was in many cases the form of ritual prescribed in the Torah for the removal of ritual impurity. But it was not a means of purification from moral impurity, and so it here functions symbolically.[12] The second instance is in 15:2–3, where the language of purification (καθαρίζειν and καθαρός) presumably refers, on a literal level, to pruning the vine,[13] but on a symbolic level it parallels 13:10. In 15:3 Jesus interprets the parabolic image to mean that the disciples have been purified (from sin) by his word.

These passages raise many questions we cannot answer here. What is important for our purpose is that, in line with biblical and Jewish ideas of purity and holiness, John understands the disciples to be purified from sin prior to their consecration to be holy (17:17–19). Purity is a presupposition for holiness but it is not the same thing. We might speak of a retrospective and a prospective aspect of salvation: purification deals with the entail of past sin, consecration with dedication to the service of God in the future.

The Festival of Hanukkah (John 10:22)

In John's Gospel, Jesus first uses the language of holiness in the context of the temple at the festival of Hanukkah, claiming that he is "the one the Father has consecrated (ἡγίασεν) and sent into the world" (10:36). Just as on other occasions in this Gospel Jesus' words relate to the themes associated with the festival he is attending in the temple,[14] so many scholars have postulated a connection

10. I disagree with the common view that the reference to purification in 2:6 has something to do with the meaning of the miracle at Cana.

11. For this understanding of the footwashing, see chap. 9 above.

12. This is also the case in Ezek. 36:25, which may be in the background to this passage.

13. The choice of the word καθαρίζειν (verse 2), not the most natural for viticulture, is probably determined by the symbolic meaning given to the image in verse 3. See C. S. Keener, *The Gospel of John* (Peabody, MA: Hendrickson, 2003), 2:996.

14. Besides the commentaries, see G. A. Yee, *Jewish Feasts and the Gospel of John* (Wilmington, DE: Michael Glazier, 1989); M. L. Coloe, *God Dwells with Us: Temple Symbolism in the Fourth Gospel* (Collegeville, MN: Liturgical Press, 2001), chapters 6–7.

between Jesus' reference to his consecration by the Father and the theme of the festival of Hanukkah.[15]

Hanukkah, the most recently established of the temple festivals and the only one not authorized in the Hebrew Bible, was also unique in being a festival that celebrated the temple itself. It commemorated the restoration of the temple to the worship of YHWH in 165 or 164 BCE,[16] following its profanation, two or three years earlier, by order of Antiochus IV Epiphanes. As part of his general proscription of specifically Jewish religious practices, Antiochus had made the Jerusalem temple a center of a pagan cult, for which an altar had been erected over the altar of burnt offering. This pagan altar was known as the "desolating sacrilege" (1 Macc. 1:54: βδέλυγμα ἐρημώσεως; cf. Dan. 11:31; 12:11). The restoration of the temple to the worship of YHWH was accomplished by Judas Maccabaeus, when he had defeated the Syrian army sufficiently for him to gain control over the temple. It included the purification of the temple from the defilements of pagan worship, the removal of the defiled and desecrated altar of burnt offering and the installation of a new altar, the reconsecration of the temple to YHWH's service, and the inauguration of sacrifices on the new altar of burnt offering. This recommencing of sacrifice to YHWH occurred on the same date (25 Chislev) as that on which pagan sacrifices had begun to be offered on the "desolating sacrilege" (1 Macc. 1:59; 4:52–54). The festival celebrating this restoration of sacrifice lasted eight days from 25 Chislev (1 Macc. 4:52–58). The Maccabees decreed that a festival on these dates should henceforth take place annually (1 Macc. 4:59).

From the point of view of the cultic acts involved, what Judas Maccabaeus had done to the temple entailed three processes: (1) the purification of the temple from defilement; (2) the (re-)consecration of the temple to YHWH, after its profanation; and (3) the restoration of sacrificial worship in the temple. The account in 1 Maccabees 4:36–59 (the fullest account we have) includes all three of these elements, and uses the standard vocabulary for each. In the case of (1) and

---

15. According to F. J. Moloney, *The Gospel of John*, Sacra Pagina (Collegeville, MN: Liturgical Press, 1998), 321, "Very few scholars make the link between the description of Jesus as 'consecrated' and the celebration of the Dedication." But at least since 1990 it has become common to recognize the link. Scholars who do so include E. C. Hoskyns, *The Fourth Gospel*, rev. ed. (London: Faber & Faber, 1947), 385; R. E. Brown, *The Gospel according to John (I–XII)*, AB 29 (New York: Doubleday, 1966), 400, 411; G. R. Beasley-Murray, *John*, WBC 36 (Waco: Word, 1987), 177; Yee, *Jewish Feasts*, 91; D. A. Carson, *The Gospel according to John* (Grand Rapids: Eerdmans, 1991), 399; C. H. Talbert, *Reading John* (London: SPCK, 1992), 165; M. W. G. Stibbe, *John*, Readings (Sheffield: Sheffield Academic Press, 1993), 118–19; B. Witherington, *John's Wisdom* (Louisville: Westminster John Knox, 1995), 191; F. J. Moloney, *Signs and Shadows: Reading John 5–12* (Minneapolis: Fortress, 1996), 149–50; Coloe, *God Dwells with Us*, chap. 7; Keener, *Gospel*, 1:822, 830; C. G. Kruse, *The Gospel according to John*, TNTC (Leicester: InterVarsity Press, 2003), 244; A. J. Köstenberger, *John*, BECNT (Grand Rapids: Baker, 2004), 316. It is remarkable that A. Guilding, *The Fourth Gospel and Jewish Worship* (Oxford: Clarendon, 1960), in chap. 9, a chapter devoted to the relationship between the "Feast of the Dedication" and the Gospel of John, made no reference to 10:36.

16. For discussion of the date and an argument for December 165, see J. VanderKam, "Hanukkah: Its Timing and Significance to 1 and 2 Maccabees," *JSP* 1 (1987): 23–40.

(2) our discussion of purity and holiness now enables us to distinguish the two and to recognize the characteristic vocabulary appropriate to each. The Gentiles had both profaned (βεβηλοῦν: 4:38, 44, 54) and defiled (μιαίνειν: 4:45) the altar. The Jews purified (καθαρίζειν: 4:36, 41, 43) the sanctuary and (re-)consecrated (ἁγιάζειν: 4:48) the courts of the temple. It is notable that the emphasis is on the profaned and defiled altar. This is not, however, specifically said to be purified, because the pagan altar was removed, the old altar of burnt offering was also removed and put into store, and a new altar was built (4:44–47). Apparently they did not know how to purify and to reconsecrate the old altar, but stored it with a view to a day when a prophet who could say what should be done with it would arise. As to the second of the necessary cultic acts, consecration, the account refers specifically only to the consecration of the temple courts. We should probably assume that the consecration of the new cultic objects, including the altar of burnt offering as well as the altar of incense, the lampstand, the table for the bread of the presence, and the holy vessels (4:49), is taken for granted as part of their installation. The sanctuary building was also reconstructed (4:48). The consecration of the courts is probably singled out for mention precisely because they were not, like most of the temple and its furniture, new.

Following purification and consecration, which included the installation of a new altar of burnt offering, the third stage was the inauguration of sacrificial worship at the new altar. For this, the account in 1 Maccabees uses the verb ἐγκαινίζειν (4:36, 54; 5:1) and the noun ἐγκαινισμός (4:56, 59), which in English versions of this passage are usually translated "to dedicate" and "dedication" (so, e.g., NRSV, JB; NEB has "to rededicate" and "rededication"),[17] but these translations are at best misleading, at worst incorrect. These English words suggest dedication to the service of God, which is the action we have called consecration. What is really meant by ἐγκαινίζειν and ἐγκαινισμός is "to inaugurate" and "inauguration." These are the plain meanings of the Greek words (from καινός, "new"), and they are also required by the context in 1 Maccabees: the new altar is "inaugurated" when sacrifices are offered on it (4:53, 56). The altar is not dedicated but inaugurated by means of its first use. This is what took place on 25 Chislev, the very day on which the old altar had been profaned through the offering of the first pagan sacrifices on the "desolating sacrilege" (1:59; 4:53–54). The parallel between the two is that in each case sacrifices were first offered on a new altar. Both the altar and the sanctuary could be said to be "inaugurated" (altar: 4:54, 56, 59; sanctuary: 4:36; 5:1) because worship in the sanctuary focused on the sacrifices on the altar of burnt offering. In both cases the reference is to the inauguration of sacrifices on the new altar. (Note also that the meaning "to inaugurate" suits

17. J. A. Goldstein, *I Maccabees*, AB 41 (New York: Doubleday, 1976), 272–73, 287, uses "restore" in 4:36 and 5:1, but "dedicate" in 4:54 and "dedication" in 4:56, 59. He supposes that ἐγκαινίζειν can have both meanings and that it is used here to translate more than one Hebrew root (284). This is mistaken both in thinking that the Hebrew חנך means "to dedicate" (see below) and in thinking that the Greek verb has both meanings.

very well the two New Testament occurrences of ἐγκαινίζειν: Heb. 9:19; 10:20, both with cultic reference.)

The reason that ἐγκαινίζειν has usually been translated "to dedicate" is not because of any evidence of Greek usage but because it has correctly been seen as a translation of the Hebrew root חנך.[18] This is the root from which the word Hanukkah (חנכה or חנוכה), the most common name for the festival, is derived. חנך has usually been understood to mean "to dedicate" and major reference works[19] still give this meaning, even though as long ago as 1972 S. C. Reif demonstrated it to be incorrect.[20] If "to dedicate" is understood in English to mean "to set apart for God, to consecrate to sacred use," then it is a misleading translation of חנך. This Hebrew verb means "to use for the first time, to initiate the use of." (As a compact translation I prefer "inaugurate" to Reif's "initiate," which has inappropriate connotations in English.) An instructive parallel to the events of the first Hanukkah is the use of חנך in 1 Kings 8:63, in the account of Solomon's inauguration of the temple. We are told that Solomon offered a vast number of sacrifices, and in this way he "and all the people of Israel inaugurated (ויחנכו) the house of YHWH." We then learn that, because the great bronze altar of burnt offering was not able to cope with all the sacrifices, Solomon "consecrated (קדש) the middle of the court that was in front of the house of YHWH" (8:64). Thus, as Jacob Milgrom explains,

> before Solomon could make the area around the altar an extension of the altar he had to consecrate it. By the same token one can assume that before Solomon could initiate the use (ḥnk) of the Temple, he first had to consecrate it (qdš).[21]

The parallel account in 2 Chronicles goes on to add that "they sacrificed the initiation offering (חנכת המזבח) for the altar seven days" (7:9). See also 2 Maccabees 2:9: Solomon "offered sacrifice for the inauguration [ἐγκαινισμοῦ] and completion [τελειώσεως] of the temple."

Milgrom finds the same sequence of consecration (קדש) followed by initiation of use or inauguration (חנך) in the case of the tabernacle in the wilderness. First Moses anointed (the usual means of consecration) and consecrated the tabernacle and the altar with all their accoutrements (Num. 7:1). Then the heads of the

---

18. Cf. Brown, *Gospel*, 1:402. In LXX (where there is an extant Hebrew *Vorlage*) ἐγκαινίζειν translates חנך four times, while four different nouns formed from ἐγκαινίζειν are used to translate חנכה fifteen times. On three occasions ἐγκαινίζειν is used to translate the Piel of חדש ("to renew, to restore").

19. E.g., D. J. A. Clines, ed., *The Dictionary of Classical Hebrew* (Sheffield: Sheffield Academic Press, 1996), 3:271. W. Dommershausen, writing on חנך in *TDOT* 5, correctly recognizes that the basic meaning is "to use for the first time," "to initiate" (19–20), but goes on to discuss it as though this were no different from "to dedicate" (20–21).

20. S. C. Reif, "Dedicated to חנך," *VT* 22 (1972): 495–501. Reif's case is strongly endorsed by J. Milgrom, *Leviticus 1–16*, AB 3 (New York: Doubleday, 1991), 592–95.

21. Milgrom, *Leviticus 1–16*, 593. For God's consecration (ἁγιάζειν) of Solomon's temple, see also 3 Macc. 2:9, 16.

tribes brought their offerings, which are called "initiation offerings for the altar" (חנכת המזבח: Num. 7:10, 11, 84, 88). These were gifts not for the consecration (dedication) of the altar but for the next ceremonial stage, the inauguration, when these offerings would be offered on the altar of burnt offering, thus initiating its use.[22] In the account of the consecration of the priests, the tabernacle, and the altar in Leviticus 8–9 the word חנך is not used, but there is the same sequence of consecration by anointing (8:1, 10–12, 30) and then inauguration by first use (9:1–24). The latter takes the form of Aaron offering one of each type of sacrifice on the consecrated altar.[23] Another instance where חנכה refers to the inauguration of the temple's sacrificial services is in the case of the second temple in Ezra 6:16–17.

It is likely that the precedents of the inauguration of the tabernacle and especially its altar as well as the inauguration of Solomon's temple lie behind the account of Judas Maccabaeus's restoration of the temple in 1 Maccabees 4:41–59. The fact that the latter speaks only once of consecration (ἡγίασαν) and with the temple courts (τὰς αὐλάς) as its object (4:48) may reflect 1 Kings 8:64, where Solomon consecrates (קדש, LXX ἡγίασαν) the middle of the temple court (LXX τῆς αὐλῆς) and this is the only act of consecration explicitly mentioned.

Our conclusions about the distinction between consecration and inauguration can be confirmed by study of Josephus's account of the restoration of the temple by Judas Maccabaeus (*Ant.* 12.316–26). This is based on the account in 1 Maccabees, but Josephus varies the key vocabulary. For the two stages on which 1 Maccabees focuses, purification and inauguration, Josephus uses the verb ἁγνίζειν (not to be confused with ἁγίζειν or ἁγιάζειν!)[24] as well as καθαρίζειν where 1 Maccabees has καθαρίζειν, and, where 1 Maccabees uses ἐγκαινίζειν (translating חנך), Josephus has the two verbs ἀνανεοῦν ("to renew") and ἀνακτίζειν ("to reestablish"). What Josephus says were renewed or reestablished are variously the temple itself, the sacrifices, the customs (τῶν ἐθῶν, evidently meaning the sacrificial practices) and the temple service (τῶν περὶ τὸν ναόν). Clearly, Josephus has understood ἐγκαινίζειν and ἐγκαινισμός in 1 Maccabees in the way we have argued it should be understood: as referring to the recommencement of sacrificial worship in the temple, centered on the sacrifices offered on the new altar of burnt offering. This, Josephus claims, is what happened on 25 Chislev, continued for eight days, and is commemorated annually in the temple on these dates thereafter. Why has he not used the terms ἐγκαινίζειν and ἐγκαινισμός, preferring the verbs ἀνανεοῦν ("to renew") and ἀνακτίζειν ("to reestablish")? The answer is probably that ἐγκαινίζειν and ἐγκαινισμός, strictly understood, suggest innovation rather than renovation or restoration. Since Josephus's whole

22. Milgrom, *Leviticus 1–16*, 593.
23. Cf. Ibid., 542–44, 571, 592–93.
24. LXX occasionally uses ἁγνίζειν to translate טהר, which is more commonly translated καθαρίζειν.

account stresses the restoration of the sacrificial worship as it had been before the desecration by Antiochus Epiphanes, he probably thought verbs with the prefix ἀνα ("re-") more appropriate.

Josephus does make one significant change to the account of events in this passage of 1 Maccabees. According to the latter, the priests offered incense on the new altar of incense, lit the lamps on the new lampstand, and set out the bread of the presence on the table before 25 Chislev (4:50–51), whereas the sacrifices on the altar of burnt offering commenced only on 25 Chislev. This makes the former actions not properly part of the inauguration, which is therefore restricted to the commencement of use of the altar of burnt offering and does not include the resumption of more minor aspects of the temple worship. Josephus, however, says that on the 25 Chislev all these activities recommenced: they lit the lights of the lampstand, burned incense, set out the bread on the table, and offered burnt offerings on the altar (*Ant.* 12.319).

Not only does Josephus redate the first three of these acts to 25 Chislev, but he also brings the kindling of lights on the lampstand forward into first place in the list. This must be connected with the fact that Josephus calls the annual commemorative festival not Hanukkah but "lights" (φῶτα). He explains this name "from the fact that the right to worship appeared (φανῆναι) to us at a time when we hardly dared hope for it" (*Ant.* 12.325). But his placement of the lighting of the lampstand as the first act on 25 Chislev shows that Josephus is certainly not ignorant of the more obvious connection of the name "lights" with the lights that were doubtless in his day lit on the first day of the festival in the temple. Whether the practice of lighting lamps in homes had already begun we cannot be so sure. This, the later usual way of observing Hanukkah (*b. Shabb.* 21b), may have begun only some time after the loss of the temple in 70 CE.[25] Not content with this obvious explanation, Josephus has added an explanation that relates to the historic significance of the original restoration of the temple worship. But "lights" was doubtless a popular name for the festival, alluding to a ceremony of lamplighting with which the festival began, whereas Hanukkah ("inauguration") was the more original and official name, describing the meaning of the festival.

Several names for the festival are attested in the literature. The Hebrew name (the days of) Hanukkah (חנכה) is first attested directly in the first century CE, in *Megillat Ta'anit*, which forbids fasting on the eight days of Hanukkah. But there can be no doubt that it is this Hebrew word that is translated into Greek as ἐγκαινισμός in 1 Maccabees (4:56, 59) and as ἐγκαινία in John 10:22 (the plural

---

25. The supposition of S. Zeitlin, "Hanukkah: Its Origin and Significance," *JQR* 29 (1938–1939): 8–9, that before 70 CE the people celebrated Hanukkah by marching through the streets with torches—a form of nationalistic celebration of the Maccabean liberation of Israel from the Syrians—and that later, for political reasons, this was transmuted into the custom of lighting lamps at home, seems to be pure speculation, while the distinction he makes between a religious festival and a political one is a misapprehension of the relationship between politics and religion in this period.

form is common for festivals in Greek). In 1 Maccabees the name of the festival is (the days of) the Inauguration of the Altar (ὁ ἐγκαινισμὸς τοῦ θυσιαστηρίου), for which the Inauguration (Hanukkah) was doubtless an abbreviation. But the second of the two letters prefixed to 2 Maccabees (1:10–2:18) calls the festival the Purification of the Temple (1:18: ὁ καθαρισμὸς τοῦ ἱεροῦ) or, more briefly, the Purification (2:16).[26] This concurs with the way the rather summarized account of the events in 2 Maccabees (10:1–8) calls what happened on 25 Chislev not the inauguration or restoration, but the purification (καθαρισμός: 10:5, cf. 7). This account seems to use "purification" as an overall description of all that was done to the temple (cf. also 14:36), and presumably means that the climax of the work was the completion of the purification on 25 Chislev. Perhaps the Purification was the name of the festival used in Egypt, where 2 Maccabees, an abridgement of the work of Jason of Cyrene, probably originated.[27] Since it was the sanctuary that was purified, while the altar was not purified but replaced, this name rather shifts the focus of the festival from the altar (as in 1 Maccabees) to the temple. We should note, however, that 2 Maccabees also preserves the name found in 1 Maccabees alongside its distinctive name when it announces the contents of the work: "the purification (καθαρισμόν) of the great temple and the inauguration of the altar (τὸν τοῦ βωμοῦ ἐγκαινισμόν) (2:19). The author probably knows that the Inauguration of the Altar was the original and standard name for the festival.

More remarkable is the way the first of the two letters prefixed to 2 Maccabees (1:1–9) apparently calls Hanukkah "the days of Tabernacles in the month of Chislev" (1:9; cf. 1:18). Evidently the eight days of Hanukkah could be thought to resemble the eight days of Tabernacles, with some of the ceremonies of the latter used for the former (2 Macc. 10:6–7), though the most characteristic feature of Tabernacles, the booths themselves, did not recur at Hanukkah.[28] It may be because of this association of the two festivals that the theme of light, with appropriate ceremonial in the temple, came to be part of the celebration of Tabernacles too (and is echoed in that context in John 8:12). In rabbinic times, at least the Hallel Psalms (Pss. 113–18) were part of the liturgy of both festivals.[29]

In conclusion to this section, we can be fairly confident that by the first century CE the official name of the festival was the Days of the Inauguration of the Altar, or Inauguration (Hanukkah) for short. The latter would be the most appropriate translation of ἐγκαινία in John 10:22.

26. J. A. Goldstein, *II Maccabees*, AB 41A (New York: Doubleday, 1984), 171, is probably right to claim that, following ἄγειν, these terms should be understood as the proper name of a festival.

27. T. Fischer, "First and Second Maccabees," *ABD* 4:443.

28. VanderKam, "Hanukkah," 32–34.

29. See J. VanderKam, "Dedication, Feast of," *ABD* 2:124.

Jesus the New Altar (John 10:36)

Scholars who have made a connection between Jesus' use of the word "consecrate" (ἁγιάζειν) in John 10:36 and the fact that he is speaking at the festival of Hanukkah (10:22: ἐγκαινία) have relied on the misleading translation of the latter as "Dedication" in all English versions, and taken the two Greek words to refer to the same action of consecration or dedication. Now that we have established that "Inauguration" (short for "Inauguration of the Altar") would be a better translation of the name of the festival, we must understand the connection differently. Jesus' consecration by the Father is to be seen as parallel not to the inauguration of the temple or altar but to the consecration of the temple or altar that would have preceded the inauguration. Of the three ritual stages of Judas Maccabeus's restoration of the temple—(1) purification, (2) consecration, and (3) inauguration by first use—the name of the festival refers to the third, but Jesus' consecration is equivalent to the second.

Scholars who have taken ἁγιάζειν as equivalent to the action indicated by the title of the festival have pointed out that John could not have used the verb ἐγκαινίζειν in 10:36 because it would be very unnatural to use this verb with a person as the object, whereas ἁγιάζειν can properly be used of the consecration of a person (for example, of Aaron: Lev. 8:12 LXX).[30] This is correct, but once we recognize the distinction between consecration and inauguration, there is a further reason why the former is applied to Jesus, not the latter. The inauguration to which the festival's title refers was accomplished by the offering of sacrifices for the first time on the new altar of burnt offering. We have seen that the title "Inauguration" properly referred to the inauguration of the new altar by its first use, but even if it were applied more loosely to the temple as a whole and the inauguration of worship in it, the focus of this worship would still be sacrifice on the altar of burnt offering. If Jesus is treated symbolically as the new temple or the new altar, sacrifice "in" or "on" him could not be a fact of the past, but an event still in the future at this point in John's narrative. God has already consecrated Jesus to be the place of sacrifice, but the sacrifice has not yet been offered.

The reference to Jesus' consecration in the context of the feast of Hanukkah must certainly be connected with the theme of Jesus as the new temple, fulfilling the meaning of the Jerusalem temple with eschatological newness, that runs prominently through the Gospel of John and has been highlighted in, among others, the passages that portray Jesus in the Jerusalem temple at other major festivals: Passover (2:13–22) and Tabernacles (7:37–39; 8:12).[31] For understanding this theme it is important to remember the two key and interrelated features of the meaning of the Jerusalem temple: it was the place in which God was graciously

30. E.g., Hoskyns, *Fourth Gospel*, 392.
31. See especially Coloe, *God Dwells with Us*, chap. 4 and 6; and the discussion of these passages in Keener, *Gospel of John*, ad loc.

present for his people in their midst, and it was the place of the sacrifices that, also in God's grace, provided God's people with access to his presence. Jesus is the eschatological fulfilment of these features in being both the new "place" of God's dwelling with his people and also the sacrifice, the final once-for-all sacrifice, that enables this presence of God among his people. While the two features are closely related, John's use of the symbolism of Hanukkah does not, as some scholars have argued, relate to Jesus as the new presence of God with his people but to the sacrifice he is going to offer when he is next in Jerusalem. In typically Johannine fashion, there are references forward to the death and resurrection of Jesus on the two previous occasions when the new temple theme is evoked in the context of temple festivals (2:19–22; 7:37–39) but in neither case is the imagery explicitly sacrificial. John reserves this for the last occasion when Jesus is in the temple prior to his death as the new Passover lamb on his last visit to Jerusalem. The occurrence of Hanukkah between Tabernacles and Passover makes it very appropriate for this purpose.

Hanukkah was unique as a temple festival whose theme was the temple itself. But the festival did not focus on God's presence as such but on the sacrificial worship. Whereas in the accounts of Solomon's inauguration of the first temple the visible presence of God's glory is the main focus (1 Kings 8:10–13; 2 Chron. 5:13–14; cf. 2 Macc. 2:8; 3 Macc. 2:9; and similarly for the tabernacle: Exod. 40:34–38), there is no reference to the presence of God in the temple in the accounts of Judas Maccabaeus's restoration of the second temple. There is no suggestion that the presence of God departed from the temple when it was desecrated and returned when sacrificial worship was resumed.[32] We must therefore reject the interpretation of John 10:36 offered by Mary Coloe, that, just as "in the Tabernacle and the Temple, God's glory dwells in [Jesus], consecrating him as a new House of God."[33] The thought here is not of Jesus as God's presence but of Jesus as the one God has consecrated for the offering of sacrifice. Probably we should think not of his consecration to be the temple as the place of sacrifice, but more specifically of his consecration as the new altar of burnt offering. Just as the altar installed by Judas Maccabaeus was a new one, so is Jesus the eschatologically new altar on which the final sacrifice is to be offered, not yet but soon, within the narrative time of the Gospel.[34]

32. For the (rather sparse) evidence that God was thought to inhabit the second temple as well as the first, see G. I. Davies, "The Presence of God in the Second Temple and Rabbinic Doctrine," in *Templum Amicitiae*, ed. W. Horbury, E. Bammel FS, JSNTSup 48 (Sheffield: Sheffield Academic Press, 1991), 32–36.

33. Coloe, *God Dwells with Us*, 153.

34. Various other suggestions of ways in which John 10:22–39 (and perhaps also chap. 11) echoes Hanukkah themes have been made: see Keener, *Gospel of John*, 1:821–23; E. Nodet, "La Dédicace, les Maccabées et le Messie," *RB* 93 (1986): 321–75; S. Motyer, *Your Father the Devil? A New Approach to John and the "Jews,"* Paternoster Biblical and Theological Studies (Carlisle: Paternoster, 1997), 124–25. These are less certain and not so directly related to our present theme of holiness, and so will not be discussed here.

Jesus' consecration to God's service is the reason for the title "the Holy One of God" that Peter ascribes to him in 6:69. The most characteristic way of making something or someone holy was anointing with oil (e.g., Exod. 29:36; 40:10; Num. 7:1 [these refer to the altar of burnt offering]; Exod. 30:23–30; Lev. 8:12; 16:32). Conversely, the significance of anointing is that it consecrates someone, sets them apart for God's service, makes them belong to the God whom the Hebrew Bible often calls "the Holy One." Aaron was called "the holy one of God" (Ps. 106:16) and Elisha "the holy man of God" (2 Kings 4:9) because they had been anointed with oil. The Messiah, that is, "the Anointed One" (and note that John makes sure his readers know what Messiah means: 1:41), or more properly "the Lord's Anointed One," is therefore by definition also "the Holy One of God." Though this is not attested as a messianic title in early Jewish literature, it is such a natural usage that we may probably assume it was used in that way. John 6:69 is the Johannine equivalent of the confession of Peter in the Synoptics, where Peter confesses Jesus to be the Messiah (Matt. 16:16; Mark 8:29; Luke 9:20). John's variation, "the Holy One of God," belongs to his tactic of running through a whole series of messianic titles at various points in his Gospel in order to apply all of them to Jesus (cf. 1:29, 34, 41, 45, 49; 4:42; 11:27; 20:28).[35] But it also creates a link with 10:36. It becomes clear that John places Jesus' anointing as Messiah prior to his coming into the world[36] and that he connects it especially with Jesus' mission to glorify God by sacrificial death.

From Christology to Ecclesiology

There are a series of close parallels between what Jesus says to "the Jews" at Hanukkah (10:23–38) and Jesus' prayer to the Father in chapter 17. The most important of these (listed in the table below) occur in the statements Jesus makes about himself and his relation to the Father in chapter 10 and in statements about the disciples and their relation to Jesus and the Father in chapter 17. The parallels are appropriate since 10:23–38 is the last of the occasions on which Jesus debates his own identity with the Jewish authorities in the temple, while chapter 17, following on chapters 14–16, concludes the part of the Gospel devoted to Jesus' teaching to and about his own disciples. The christological claims of chapters 2–10 come to a climax with those at Hanukkah: "I and the Father are one" (10:30) and "the Father is in me and I am in the Father" (10:38). Both become the basis for key requests that Jesus makes for his disciples in prayer to the Father, asking in each case that

35. In the Synoptics, Jesus is called "the Holy One of God" only by the unclean spirit (Mark 1:24; Luke 4:34). In context, the title is very appropriate, not because "holy" "is roughly synonymous with 'clean' . . . and the antonym of 'unclean'" (J. Marcus, *Mark 1-8*, AB 27 [New York: Doubleday, 2000], 188), but because the impure (unclean) should never come into contact with the holy or must suffer fearful consequences if it does. The demon fears Jesus most of all because he is "the Holy One of God."

36. For a limited parallel, see Jer. 1:5.

something true of Jesus and the Father should also be true for the disciples. It is characteristic of this Gospel that Jesus takes the relation he has to the Father as a model for the way the disciples relate to himself (and the Father).[37]

Table 12.1. The Hanukkah Speech and the Prayer to the Father

John 10	*John 17*
(30) the Father and I are one	(11) so that they may be one as we are one (21) that they may all be one (22) so that they may be one as we are one (23) so that they may be completely one
(36) the one whom the Father has consecrated	(17) consecrate them in truth (19) and for their sakes I consecrate myself, so that they also may be consecrated in truth
and sent into the world	(18) as you have sent me into the world, I have sent them into the world (21) so that the world may believe that you have sent me (cf. 3, 8) (23) so that the world may know that you have sent me and have loved them even as you have loved me
(38) the Father is in me and I am in the Father	(21) as you, Father, are in me and I am in you, may they also be in us (23) I in them and you in me (26) so that the love with which you have loved me may be in them, and I in them

The most significant christological statement in Jesus' words at Hanukkah, other than the two claims to unity with the Father, is the one we have been considering: Jesus as "the one whom the Father has consecrated and sent into the world" (10:36). That the Father has sent Jesus into the world is, of course, stated repeatedly throughout the Gospel, but here it is conjoined with the much more unusual claim that Jesus has been consecrated by the Father. It is very notable that the only other uses of the verb "to consecrate" (ἁγιάζειν) are the cluster of three occurrences in 17:17–19, and that here too there is a close connection between being consecrated and being sent.

Before turning to the consecration of the disciples, we must note that here it is not said that the Father has consecrated Jesus, but that Jesus consecrates himself (17:19).[38] These are complementary perspectives: in the Hebrew Bible it can be said

---

37. Cf. 13:20; 20:21. See also A. J. Köstenberger, *The Missions of Jesus and the Disciples according to the Fourth Gospel* (Grand Rapids: Eerdmans, 1998), 186–97; J. Ferreira, *Johannine Ecclesiology*, JSNTSup 160 (Sheffield: Sheffield Academic Press, 1998), chapter 6.

38. It is difficult to decide whether Jesus consecrates himself as the high priest who is to offer sacrifice or as the sacrifice itself. But the latter is more probable, since the theme of Jesus as high priest is not explicitly found elsewhere in the Gospel (but see J. P. Heil, "Jesus as the Unique High Priest in the Gospel of John," *CBQ* 57 [1995]: 729–45), whereas the theme of Jesus as the sacrifice is (1:29, 36). R. E. Brown,

both that God consecrates people (e.g., Exod. 31:12) and that people consecrate themselves (e.g., Lev. 11:44; Num. 11:18), and the two can be closely related (Lev. 20:7–8). In this case, there is the distinction between the Father's consecration of Jesus, setting him apart for the mission on which he sent him into the world (10:36), and Jesus' appropriation of that mission for himself at the crucial moment when he is going willingly to his death. It is because Jesus' self-consecration leads him to self-sacrifice on the cross that he does it "for the sake of" his disciples, "so that they also may be consecrated in truth" (17:19). By fulfilling the mission for which the Father consecrated him, Jesus makes it possible for his disciples also to be set apart for God's service. At the same time the holiness of the disciples derives from God (17:17), who has been addressed, uniquely, as "Holy Father" at the point where Jesus began to pray for his disciples (17:11).

As "Holy Father" occurs at the beginning of this part of the prayer (17:11b–19),[39] so the prayer for the disciples to be consecrated (17:17–19) forms the climax of the subsection, making an inclusio between "holy" (ἅγιε) in verse 11 and "consecrated" (ἡγιασμένοι) in verse 19b. Francis Moloney suggests that Jesus here takes up in turn the two words in his address to God as "Holy Father," asking God first, as Father, to exercise his fatherly care in protecting the disciples (17:11b–16) and then, second, as *Holy* Father, to make the disciples holy also (17–19).[40] But these two petitions are also closely connected by the theme of the disciples' relationship to "the world," a theme that runs through the whole section from verse 9 to verse 19. Jesus himself is leaving the world, but his disciples remain in it, and it is for his disciples in this situation that Jesus prays (17:11). Like Jesus, they are in the world but not of it, and therefore the world hates them, just as it hated Jesus (17:14). While Jesus was with them he protected them (17:12), but now that he is leaving the world, the Father must protect them (17:11b, 15). Furthermore, in order to fulfil the mission that is the purpose of their remaining in the world, they need not only protection, but also consecration. Consecration sets them apart from the world, as the holy distinguished from the profane. It puts them, as people devoted to the holy God, on God's side of the distinction between himself and the profane world that does not know him. But this does not take them out of the world (17:15). On the contrary, just as the Father has consecrated Jesus for his mission in the world, so the Father will consecrate the disciples for their mission in the world.

The Gospel according to John (XIII–XXI), AB 29A (New York: Doubleday, 1966), 766–67, attempts to combine the two possibilities.

39. For the tripartite structure of the prayer, see F. J. Moloney, *The Gospel of John*, Sacra Pagina 4 (Collegeville, MN: Liturgical Press, 1998), 458–59; Ferreira, *Johannine Ecclesiology*, chap. 3. Both scholars follow Jürgen Becker in dividing the prayer thus: (1) Jesus prays for himself (vv. 1–8); (2) Jesus prays for his disciples (vv. 9–19); (3) Jesus prays for future disciples (vv. 20–26). According to this analysis, "Holy Father" (v. 11b) does not open the second section of the prayer, but it does mark the beginning of the subsection that specifies what Jesus prays for the disciples.

40. Moloney, *Gospel of John*, 465–66.

In what does this consecration consist? We have already made clear that it does not include the disciples' purification from sin, which is only a precondition for consecration. The disciples have already been purified from sin (13:10; 15:3), though they continue to need ongoing forgiveness (13:10). Their consecration is still to come, from the point of view of Jesus when he prays 17:17–19. But even more decisively, their consecration parallels the consecration of Jesus himself, whereas Jesus needs no purification and so the disciples' purification cannot be modelled on his.

The common translation of ἁγιάζειν in this passage as "sanctify" has probably misled many English readers into supposing that the reference is to a process of being made ethically holy (since this is the meaning of "sanctification" in traditional Protestant theology). In fact, the reference is to an act of God that consecrates the disciples for his service, though it is an act that results in a state of holiness, that is, of having been set apart for God (hence the perfect passive participle ἡγιασμένοι in v. 19). But what is the act of consecration? Jesus' request to the Father, "Consecrate them by (or "in") the truth (ἐν τῇ ἀληθείᾳ) (your word is truth)" (17:17), is as difficult to interpret as many other uses of "truth" and "true" in John's Gospel, and there is also a question of whether the phrase "in truth" (ἐν ἀληθείᾳ) in verse 19 should be understood in the same way or simply as "truly" (equivalent to ἀληθῶς). The latter issue makes little difference to the overall sense. In the case of verse 17, an attractive option taken by some commentators[41] is that God consecrates the disciples by giving them his commandment(s) so that they may live lives obedient to him and so be holy. The thought that God has consecrated Israel by giving the commandments is common in rabbinic literature (e.g., *t. Ber.* 5.22; 6.9–14; *b. Shabb.* 137b), but it also makes good sense of the treatment of Israel's holiness in the Torah itself, where what sets Israel apart from the nations is the commandments. God consecrates Israel by giving the commandments, and Israel maintains holiness by keeping them (cf., e.g., Exod. 31:13; Lev. 11:44–45). Jesus, in his prayer, has already said that he has given his disciples God's word (17:14) and that they have kept it (17:6). Another interpretation of verse 17 is that God consecrates the disciples by means of the word of revelation of himself that Jesus has given them.[42] In this case, the reference backward would be especially to verse 8.

Yet Jesus *asks* God to consecrate them (17:17). The act is still future, as the fact that the consecration of the disciples follows from Jesus' self-consecration

41. E.g., Keener, *Gospel of John*, 2:1060.
42. E.g., C. K. Barrett, *The Gospel according to St. John*, 2nd ed. (London: SPCK, 1978), 510; B. Lindars, *The Gospel of John*, NCB (London: Oliphants, 1972), 528; Carson, *Gospel*, 566. A related view is that this revelation is the sphere in which the disciples are consecrated: H. N. Ridderbos, *The Gospel of John: A Theological Commentary*, trans. J. Vriend (Grand Rapids: Eerdmans, 1997), 555; Köstenberger, *John*, 495–96. Brown, *Gospel according to John (XIII–XXI)*, 761–62, implausibly takes the ἐν to mean both "in" and "by." He even allows the meaning "for," which would make excellent sense ("consecrate them for the truth") but is surely not possible.

to sacrificial death (17:19) also requires. So a better interpretation may be to understand God's word in verse 17 as simply a word of appointment and commissioning.[43] Then the way is open for us to think that the consecration of the disciples actually takes place in 20:21–23, when the risen Jesus turns his words in 17:18 into an address to the disciples: "As the Father has sent me, so I send you," and endows them with the Holy Spirit.[44] The Spirit is associated with sending here, as consecration is in 17:17–19. Perhaps we can conclude that, while the word of God sets the disciples apart for mission (17:17), the Holy Spirit enables the fulfilment of that holiness in the carrying out of the mission.[45] (Word and Spirit are closely connected in John, and both are connected with truth.) If so, all of this Gospel's holiness language coalesces around the consecration of Jesus and the disciples: The Holy Father consecrates Jesus the Holy One, who consecrates himself so that the disciples also may be consecrated, participating in the holiness of Jesus and the Father through the Holy Spirit.

Conclusion

Holiness is what distinguishes God as "other" than the world, and those who belong to God are thereby also distinguished from the world that does not know God. Yet God makes them holy, dedicated to him, not to remove them from the world, but to send them into the world to make God known. Jesus is the Holy One whom God has consecrated for his mission and, obedient to his Father, Jesus consecrates himself, especially with a view to his self-sacrifice on the cross. The holiness of the disciples relates to that of Jesus in two ways. First, it is because Jesus has accomplished his self-offering that the disciples can also be consecrated. Second, they are consecrated in order to continue Jesus' own mission in the world. There is a difference in that the disciples' mission is not to atone for the sin of the world, but it is similar in its demand for costly dedication to the service of God. As holy, the disciples are set apart from the world but, as in Jesus' case, this consecration is in the service of God's self-giving love for the world. They are distinguished from the world both for God's sake and for the world's sake.

43. Note that the idea of God's consecrating someone can come close to the idea of God's choosing them: 2 Macc. 1:25; Sir. 45:4.

44. It is very tempting to link consecration with the Holy Spirit with the image of anointing with the Spirit (cf. Acts 10:38), since anointing is a common means of consecrating, but the image in 20:22 is of the Spirit as breath in an act of new creation, not as oil.

45. Some such connection is made by J. H. Bernard, *A Critical and Exegetical Commentary on the Gospel according to St. John*, ICC (Edinburgh: T. & T. Clark, 1928), 2:574; Brown, *Gospel according to John (XIII–XXI)*, 766–67; G. M. Burge, *The Anointed Community: The Holy Spirit in the Johannine Tradition* (Grand Rapids: Eerdmans, 1987), 202.

13

THE 153 FISH
AND THE UNITY
OF THE FOURTH GOSPEL

Introduction

The final chapter of the Gospel of John has presented scholars with many problems, but probably those that have been most discussed are two: (1) the relationship of this chapter to the rest of the Gospel, and (2) the significance of the number 153 in 21:11.[1] In this chapter I shall argue for a solution to the second of these problems that also solves the first problem by demonstrating that chapter 21 is an integral part of the design of the whole Gospel.

J. H. Bernard's comment, "The Fourth Gospel was plainly intended to end with 20^{31},"[2] expresses what a very large majority of modern scholars have thought, though a few have dissented and considered chapter 21 an original part of the

This is a slightly different version of an article originally published in *Neotestamentica* 36 (2002); 77–88. Reprinted by permission of the publisher.

1. For a survey of attempted solutions to the riddle of the number 153, see George Beasley-Murray, *John*, WBC 36 (Waco: Word, 1987), 401–4.

2. J. H. Bernard, *A Critical and Exegetical Commentary on the Gospel according to St. John*, 2 vols., ICC (Edinburgh: T. & T. Clark, 1928), 687.

Gospel.[3] Some who regard chapter 21 as an "afterthought" or "appendix" added to an already complete Gospel hold it to come from the same author as the rest of the Gospel,[4] but Rudolf Bultmann, considering it "incontestable that chapter 21 is the work of a second hand, added later,"[5] made this, along with a few of the alleged aporias within chapters 1–20, the justification for extensive source and redaction criticism of the Gospel. In this, Bultmann has been followed by many others offering different accounts of the sources and processes of redaction that have produced the Gospel we have. Chapter 21 often functioned in twentieth-century Johannine scholarship as the "incontestable" evidence that the Gospel of John was not designed as a whole by a single author but had a history of composition by members of a Johannine school or leaders of a Johannine community. Thus the relationship of chapter 21 to the rest of the Gospel is an issue of considerable significance for our understanding of the composition of the whole Gospel.

W hether chapter 21 can be sufficiently distinguished from the rest of the Gospel on grounds of style to preclude its coming from the same author as the rest of the Gospel has been debated,[6] and many scholars have commented that the evidence is insufficient to prove or to disprove common authorship.[7] The latest work of Eugen Ruckstuhl (writing with Peter Dschulnigg),[8] a new and very much

3. E.g., Serge Besobrasoff (Bishop Cassian), "John xxi," *NTS* (1956) 3:132–36; Hartwig Thyen, "Entwicklungen innerhalb der johanneischen Theologie und Kirche im Spiegel von Joh 21 und der Lieblingsjüngertexte des Evangeliums," in *L'Évangile de Jean: Sources, rédaction, théologie*, ed. Marinus de Jonge, BETL 44 (Gembloux: Duculot/Leuven: Leuven University Press, 1977), 259–99; Paul S. Minear, "The Original Functions of John 21," *JBL* 102 (1983):85–98; Don A. Carson, *The Gospel according to John* (Leicester: InterVarsity; Grand Rapids: Eerdmans, 1991), 665–68; Thomas Brodie, *The Gospel according to John: A Literary and Theological Commentary* (New York/Oxford: Oxford University Press 1993), 572–82. Others are listed in Beverly Roberts Gaventa, "The Archive of Excess: John 21 and the Problem of Narrative Closure," in *Exploring the Gospel of John*, ed. R. Alan Culpepper and C. Clifton Black, D. Moody Smith FS (Louisville: Westminster John Knox, 1996), 249–50 n. 8.

4. E.g., Bernard, *John*, 687–88.

5. Quoted in John Ashton, *Understanding the Fourth Gospel* (Oxford: Clarendon 1991), 46.

6. Against common authorship, see especially M.-E. Boismard, "Le Chapitre XXI de Saint Jean: Essai Critique Littéraire," *RB* 54 (1947): 473–501; in favor of common authorship, B. de Solages and J. M. Vacherot, "Le Chapitre XXI de Jean est-il de la même plume que le reste de l'Évangile?" *Bulletin de Littérature Ecclésiastique* 80 (1979): 96–101; B. de Solages, *Jean et les Synoptistes* (Leiden: Brill, 1979), 191–235.

7. E.g., Barnabas Lindars, *The Gospel of John*, NCB (London: Oliphants, 1972), 622; Charles Kingsley Barrett, *The Gospel according to St. John*, 2nd ed. (London: SPCK, 1978), 577; John A. T. Robinson, *The Priority of John*, ed. J. F. Coakley (London: SCM, 1985), 111.

8. Eugen Ruckstuhl and Peter Dschulnigg, *Stilkritik und Verfasserfrage im Johannesevangelium*, NTOA 17 (Freiburg: Universitätsverlag; Göttingen: Vandenhoeck & Ruprecht, 1991); cf. Eugen Ruckstuhl, *Die literarische Einheit des Johannesevangelium: Der gegenwärtige Stand der einschlägigen Erforschung*, Studia Friburgensia 3 (Freiburg: Paulus-Verlag, 1951), new ed., NTOA 5 (Freiburg: Universitätsverlag; Göttingen: Vandenhoeck & Ruprecht, 1987); Eugen Ruckstuhl, "Johannine Language and Style," in *L'Évangile de Jean: Sources, rédaction, théologie*, ed. Marinus de Jonge, BETL 44 (Gembloux: Duculot; Leuven: Leuven University Press, 1977), 125–147. Martin Hengel (*Die johanneische Frage* [Tübingen: Mohr Siebeck, 1993], 239–42) attributes considerable importance to Ruckstuhl's work, and of the 1991 book says: "An dieser grundlegenden Monographie wird die künftige Johannesforschung, wenn sie den

strengthened version of his earlier argument, employs 153 (!) (cf. John 21:11) distinctive features of Johannine style and a careful methodology to demonstrate the stylistic homogeneity of the whole Gospel, including chapter 21. The fact that many of the stylistic features are inconspicuous and not imitable proves that this homogeneity reflects not the sociolect of a Johannine group, but the idiolect of a single author. This argument against sources (other than thoroughly assimilated ones) and multiple layers of redaction by a series of Johannine authors has yet to be properly addressed by proponents of source and redaction criticism. Very recently, Tom Felton and Tom Thatcher report stylometric work that they claim supports Robert Fortna's hypothesis of a signs source (including parts of chapter 21),[9] but the results seem too limited to establish the case. They are right to argue that statistical modeling and stylometry (not used by Ruckstuhl) should be applied to the Fourth Gospel, but they are surely not justified in simply dismissing the very thorough and methodologically quite sophisticated work of Ruckstuhl and Dschulnigg.[10]

However, the issue of stylistic homogeneity with the rest of the Gospel is not essential to the question with which we are presently concerned, that is, whether chapter 21 is a later addition to a Gospel that originally ended at 20:31, or an integral part of the design of the Gospel as a whole. It is possible to hold a single author responsible for all twenty-one chapters of the Gospel and at the same time to regard chapter 21 as an appendix, which that same author added subsequently to a Gospel originally designed to end at 20:31. It is also possible to consider that chapter 21 is dependent on a source that accounts for aspects of its style and vocabulary that distinguish it from the rest of the Gospel while also regarding it as composed in the form we have it by the author of the whole Gospel and designed by that author to be an integral part of the whole Gospel.

More decisive than the question of style in convincing most scholars that chapter 21 is an appendix added to a Gospel that was originally complete without it has been the impression that 20:30–31 reads so much like a conclusion that it must have been written to conclude the Gospel. Difficult as it is to dispel this impression, it is inaccurate. These verses claim to conclude the Gospel's account of the signs Jesus performed. They say that the signs that have been narrated (out of the many that could have been recorded) have been related in the Gospel so that hearers/readers may believe that Jesus is the Messiah and have life. These verses therefore conclude the Gospel's account of Jesus' signs and thereby complete the Gospel's main purpose, but there is no reason why they should be regarded as a conclusion to the Gospel itself.

Anspruch erhebt, wissenschaftlich ernstgenommen zu werden, nicht mehr vorbeigehen können" (241 n. 120).

9. Tom Felton and Tom Thatcher, "Stylometry and the Signs Gospel," in *Jesus in Johannine Tradition*, ed. Robert T. Fortna and Tom Thatcher (Louisville: Westminster John Knox, 2001), 209–18.

10. Ibid., 211.

It is important to realize that the miracle in chapter 21 is not another of the signs.[11] The Gospel up to chapter 20 narrates seven signs, which are identifiable as the seven events of which the Gospel itself actually uses the word σημεῖον (2:11; 4:54; 6:2; 6:14, 26; 9:16; 12:18; 2:18–19). These include the resurrection, which (contrary to a common assertion) the Gospel does call a sign (2:18–19). These seven signs manifest Jesus' glory so that people may believe in him. The great catch of fish in chapter 21 is not a sign in this Johannine sense, but a miracle with a quite different purpose. It symbolizes programmatically the mission in which the disciples are now to engage. After chapter 20, no more needs to be said about Jesus himself: the central, christological purpose of the Gospel has been fulfilled. But more does need to be said about the disciples, especially about the roles that the two disciples most prominent in this Gospel, Peter and the Beloved Disciple, are to play in the ongoing mission of the church. This different subject matter makes chapter 21 an epilogue, but an epilogue that there is no reason to doubt belongs to the original design and form of the Gospel. A comparison is often made between 20:30 and 21:25, as though the similarity is merely repetitive and demonstrates that 20:30 is part of the original conclusion while 21:25 is a part of a supplementary conclusion required by the addition of an appendix. But it seems to be overlooked that these two verses (20:30 and 21:25) differ in that the former speaks specifically of "many other signs" that "Jesus did" (πολλὰ . . . ἄλλα σημεῖα ἐποίησεν ὁ Ἰησοῦς), while the latter speaks generally of "many other things that Jesus did" (ἄλλα πολλὰ ἃ ἐποίησεν ὁ Ἰησοῦς). The variation surely deliberately distinguishes the conclusion to the Gospel's account of Jesus' signs from the conclusion to the Gospel as such.

The present study is not attempting a full argument for considering chapter 21 an integral part of the Gospel, and enough has been said to prepare the way for the contribution that can be made to such a case by an investigation of the number 153. This requires us to broach the subject of numerical composition in the Fourth Gospel.

Numerical Composition

New Testament scholars have rarely taken seriously the use of numerical techniques of literary composition by New Testament authors, but the evidence is mounting that such techniques were used in biblical and related literature.[12] Three

11. Here I differ strongly from Stephen S. Smalley ("The Sign in John xxi," *NTS* 20 [1964]: 275–88), who sees it as the seventh of the signs.

12. See the summaries of earlier studies of biblical texts in M. J. J. Menken, *Numerical Literary Techniques in John: The Fourth Evangelist's Use of Numbers of Words and Syllables*, NovTSup 55 (Leiden: Brill, 1985), 10–12, 16–23; also Charles Homer Giblin, "Structural Patterns in Jos 24,1–25," *CBQ* 26 (1964): 50–69; Gideon Bohak, "Greek-Hebrew Gematrias in *3 Baruch* and Revelation," *JSP* 7 (1990): 119–21; A. M. Cartun, "'Who Knows Ten?': The Structure and Symbolic Use of Numbers in the Ten Plagues:

such techniques have been identified: (1) The best known is gematria, involving the calculation of the numerical value of a word written in Hebrew or Greek letters. In Hebrew and Greek the letters of the alphabet also serve as numerals, and so every word has a numerical value, which is the sum of the numerical values of its letters. (2) Another technique is the measurement of sections of text by counting syllables or words.[13] (3) The number of occurrences of a particular word within a literary work (or a section of one) may be significant. Such techniques can also be combined.

M. J. J. Menken's dissertation, published in 1985, is a detailed study of the second of these techniques (with some reference also to the first) in selected sections of the Gospel of John.[14] Despite its publication in a well-known monograph series and despite its potentially considerable significance for the source and redaction criticism of the Gospel, this work has been more or less completely ignored.[15] Perhaps scholars who have consulted it have not found the case Menken makes for widespread numerical patterning in John compelling. Perhaps too many of the examples look as though they could be fortuitous. Perhaps the really convincing examples are buried in too great a mass of less compelling detail.

For our present purposes, it will be sufficient to extract from Menken's work three remarkable examples of numerical composition, which all involve both gematria and measurement by numbers of syllables or words. It seems unlikely that the phenomena in these cases are purely accidental, and they are sufficient to establish that this kind of technique occurs in the Gospel. (1) The prologue (1:1–18) consists of 496 syllables; 496 is a "triangular" number (it is the triangle of 31, i.e., it is the sum of the numbers from 1 to 31) and also a "perfect" number (i.e., it is equal to the sum of its divisors). This makes it a numerologically very significant number. Both types of number—triangular and perfect—are quite rare,[16] and they were of considerable interest for ancient mathematics and numerical speculation.[17] But the reason it seems virtually certain that this length of the prologue to John's Gospel is deliberately significant is that 496 is also the numerical

---

Exodus 7:14–13:16," *USQR* 45 (1991): 65–120; Jens Høyrup, "Mathematics, Algebra, and Geometry," *ABD* 4:611; Casper J. LaGuschagne, *Numerical Secrets of the Bible* (North Richland Hills, TX: Bibal, 2000); Richard Bauckham, *The Climax of Prophecy: Studies on the Book of Revelation* (Edinburgh: T. & T. Clark, 1993), 29–37, 384–407; D. S. Russell, "Countdown: Arithmetic and Anagram in Early Biblical Interpretation," *ExpTim* 104 (1993): 109–13; Richard Bauckham, "James and Jesus," in *The Brother of Jesus: James the Just and His Mission*, ed. Bruce Chilton and Jacob Neusner (Louisville: Westminster John Knox 2001), 134; Wilfried Warning, "Terminological Patterns and the First Word of the Bible: ראשית(ב)," *TynBul* 52 (2001): 267–74.

13. For this practice in ancient literature, see Menken, *Numerical Literary Techniques*, 3–10.

14. Ibid. Menken's work is confined to John 1:19–2:11; 5; 6; 9:1–10:21; 17.

15. I have seen no reference to it in any work of Johannine scholarship.

16. 496 is thirty-first in the series of triangular numbers, and third in the series of perfect numbers (after 6 and 28).

17. Menken, *Numerical Literary Techniques*, 27–29; Bauckham, *Climax of Prophecy*, 390–93.

value of the word μονογενής (John 1:14, 18).[18] The length of the prologue has clearly been designed to relate to its christological content and climax. (2) The section 1:19–2:11 consists of 1550 syllables, which number is the numerical value of the words ὁ χριστός (John 1:20, 25; cf. 1:41; 20:31).[19] (3) Jesus' prayer to the Father in 17:1b–26 consists of 486 words. This number is the numerical value of the word πάτερ, which both begins the prayer and is used five more times within it. To these three examples from Menken's work I can add a further example: (4) The name Jesus written in Hebrew as יהושע (the most common spelling of the name in the Hebrew Bible) and the words "the lamb of God" in Hebrew (שׂה אלהים) have the same numerical value: 391.[20] So when John the Baptist sees Jesus and says, "Behold the Lamb of God" (1:29, 35–36), he is interpreting the name Jesus by gematria. John's identification of Jesus as the Lamb of God is fulfilled when Jesus dies and the words of Exodus 12:46, referring to the Passover lamb, are quoted in 19:36.[21] The number of words that intervene between the first reference to Jesus in the narrative of the crucifixion (19:16) and the words quoted from Exodus (19:36), thus connecting the name Jesus with his identification as the Passover lamb, is 391.[22]

These four examples provide sufficient basis for considering whether the number 153 in 21:11 relates to similar elements of numerical composition in the Gospel.

The Numerical Shape of the Beginning and End of John

There is a rather obvious difficulty about measuring the length of sections of the text of the New Testament by counting syllables and words: the existence of textual variants makes such calculations uncertain to a small but significant extent. Clearly, choices of textual readings should not be made merely because they suit a particular theory of numerical patterning in the text. On the one hand, there must be good text-critical support for the readings selected, but, on the other hand, it is not improper, where the textual evidence is not decisively in favor of

18. Menken, *Numerical Literary Techniques*, 20–21.

19. Ibid., 83–84. It is relevant that the words, "And he said to him, 'We have found the Messiah'" (1:41) occur at the center of the passage 1:19–2:11.

20. I owe this observation to Asher Finkel.

21. Quotation from Exod. 12:46 (cf. 10 LXX) and quotation from Ps. 34(33):21 should not be regarded as exclusive alternatives. The author is most likely relating these two scriptural passages, using the Jewish exegetical technique of *gezera shava*. See the good discussion in Bruce G. Schuchard, *Scripture within Scripture: The Interrelationship of Form and Function in the Explicit Old Testament Citations in the Gospel of John*, SBLDS 133 (Atlanta: Scholars Press, 1992), 133–40.

22. This calculation depends on reckoning inclusively from καί (19:17) to πληρωθῇ (19:36) according to the text in NA[27]. A different choice among variant readings could include the whole of v. 36 in the figure of 391 words.

one reading, to allow considerations of numerical literary technique to play some part in tipping the balance.

The section of the Gospel with which we shall be concerned is 20:30–21:25. The text on which our discussion is based is that of the twenty-seventh edition of Nestle-Aland, but with the following words that appear in that text omitted: αὐτοῦ in 20:30; οὖν in 21:11; ὁ Ἰησοῦς in 21:17; οὖν in 21:21; and τί πρὸς σέ in 21:23. All these omissions have good manuscript support. The words omitted in 21:17 and 21:23 appear in square brackets in the text of NA[27], indicating considerable doubt as to their originality, while the words omitted in 20:30; 21:11; and 21:17 were omitted in previous editions of Nestle-Aland. There is reason to consider the omission of τί πρὸς σέ in 21:23 the harder reading, since it leaves an incomplete sentence that scribes will have completed in conformity with verse 22. The author surely left the sentence incomplete in order to make the words "until I come" appropriately the last words of Jesus in the Gospel.

John's Gospel does not have two endings,[23] but a two-stage ending,[24] the two parts of which (20:30–31 and 21:24–25) frame an epilogue (21:1–23). The numerical data help to make this clear. The sections 20:30–31 and 21:24–25 both consist of forty-three words.[25] We have already noticed that the prologue to the Gospel (1:1–18) consists of 496 syllables. The epilogue shows its correspondence to the prologue in that it consists of 496 *words*. This is confirmation from numerical data of the frequently made observation that chapter 21 is an epilogue that balances at the end of the Gospel the prologue at the beginning. We may also note that the epilogue itself falls into two sections (21:1–14, 15–23) and that the first has 276 words. Like 496, 276 is a triangular number (the triangle of 23). But whereas in the prologue the number 496 is the numerical value of a key word in the prologue (μονογενής), this is not the case in the epilogue. None of the significant words in the epilogue has the numerical value of 496. Nor do any of the significant words in the epilogue appear to have numerical values of any special significance.

However, this does not mean that gematria is absent from the Epilogue. The Epilogue contains a number, 153 (21:11), that contemporary readers familiar with gematria might well suspect of having such significance. One suggested explanation

---

23. I am not persuaded by the interesting proposal of Gaventa, "Archive of Excess," to the effect that chapters 20 and 21 constitute two different endings of the Gospel, each to be read as following directly chapter 19. She notes that "the third time" (21:14) presupposes chapter 20 (245), but fails to account for this feature that directly contradicts her proposal. It is also implausible that "again" in 21:1 refers to events prior to Jesus' death rather than to resurrection appearances.

24. Brodie, *Gospel*, 572–73, thinks there is a three-part conclusion, the first part being 19:35. It is true that there are significant links between 19:35 and (especially) 21:24–25, but I do not think that 19:35 can be considered the first part of the Gospel's conclusion. It refers only to one event in the Gospel's story. Moreover, its size (twenty words) sets it apart from 20:30–31 and 21:24–25 (forty-three words each).

25. This is pointed out by Carmelo Savasta, "Gv 20,30–32 e 21,24–25: Una Doppia Finale?" *BeO* 43 (2001): 130.

of the number is that it is the numerical value of the Hebrew בני האלהים.[26] This would be very appropriate as a kind of equivalent to μονογενής in the prologue. The theme of the prologue is christological, that of the epilogue ecclesiological. The prologue tells of the unique Son of God who comes into the world so that those who believe in him may become "children of God" (1:12: τέκνα θεοῦ). The miraculous catch of 153 fish in the epilogue is a symbol of the ingathering of these children of God through the church's mission, of which 11:52 (τὰ τέκνα τοῦ θεοῦ) also speaks. But there is a problem in this proposal. Given that the gematria in the prologue relates to the Greek word μονογενής, it is not clear why the gematria in the epilogue should relate to the Hebrew phrase בני האלהים. We should expect the number 860, which is the numerical value of the phrase τέκνα θεοῦ. The use of a Hebrew phrase would be explicable if the reference were to a passage in the Hebrew Bible, but the only occurrences of this phrase in the Hebrew Bible (Gen. 6:2, 4; Job 1:6; 2:1) are not even conceivably relevant. Perhaps the reason is that, whereas the number 153 makes an extraordinarily large catch in a single net, 860 would be completely inconceivable. Thus it is possible that 153 is intended to be the value by gematria of בני האלהים, but for the time being we should also remain open to other explanations—which need not be incompatible.

The 153 Fish and Ezekiel 47

Like 496 and 276, 153 is a triangular number, the triangle of 17. This is un-likely to be accidental. There are not very many triangular numbers (153 is the seventeenth of the series) and they were well known to ancient people interested in such things. One other triangular number appears explicitly in the New Testa-ment: the number of the beast, 666 (Rev. 13:18), has multiple significance both by gematria and by virtue of its "triangular" character.[27] An explanation of 153 that recognizes its character as the triangle of 17 would be the most satisfying. Such an explanation was offered by John Emerton,[28] who pointed out that the numerical value of the two Hebrew names גדי and עגלים in Ezekiel 47:10 is 17 and 153 respectively. The passage tells how the stream of water that will issue

26. H. Kruse, "'Magni pisces centum quinquaginta tres' (Jo 21,11)," *VD* 38 (1960): 129–48 (though he preferred to explain 153 as the numerical value of קהל האהבה, "the church of love"); J. A. Romeo, "Gematria and John 21:11—The Children of God," *JBL* 97 (1978): 263–64.

27. Bauckham, *Climax of Prophecy*, 384–407.

28. John A. Emerton, "Hundred and Fifty-Three Fishes in John xxi.11," *JTS* 9 (1958):86–89. Peter A. Ackroyd, "The 153 Fishes in John xxi.11—A Further Note," *JTS* 10 (1959): 10, responded by pointing out that among the many different Greek transliterations of En-gedi and En-eglaim in the manuscripts of Ezek. 47:10 LXX, two have numerical values that add up to 153 (ηγγαδι = 33 and = αγαλλειμ 120). In reply, John A. Emerton, "Some New Testament Notes," *JTS* 11 (1960): 335–36, pointed out that these two Greek forms of the names do not appear together in any one manuscript, while they could explain the figure 153 but not reflect its triangular character as the triangle of 17, to which the Hebrew text of Ezek. 47:10 does correspond.

from the new temple will flow down to the Dead Sea, turning it into a fresh water lake, where people will stand on the shore fishing all the way from the spring of Gedi (En-gedi) to the spring of Eglaim (En-eglaim): "It will be a place for the spreading of nets; its fish will be of a great many kinds" (Ezek. 47:10). In favor of seeing an allusion to this passage in the number 153 is a further remarkable fact about it that Emerton failed to notice: the word Gedi (גדי) in Ezekiel 47:10 is the 153rd word in this chapter of Ezekiel. Thus both the word Gedi itself and the combination of Gedi and Eglaim link the numbers 17 and 153. Noticing this fact it would have been easy for the writer of John 21 to relate it to the fact that 153 is the triangle of 17.

Gematria was often used to associate, as in some way equivalent, two different words that have the same numerical value.[29] In exegesis this technique could be used to substitute, in interpretation, a word with the same numerical value as a word in the text. In this way, the fact that the words בני האלהים have the numerical value of 153 becomes more relevant. Since Eglaim and "children of God" have the same numerical value, the author of John 21 could take Eglaim to signify "the children of God." The fact that he must be working with the Hebrew phrase בני האלהים, rather than a Greek one, is now entirely understandable, since he is engaged in exegesis of the Hebrew text of Ezekiel 47:10. Thus the 153 fish of John 21:11 constitute a reference to Eglaim in Ezekiel 47:10 and at the same time are to be understood as signifying "the children of God," since this phrase has the same numerical value (153) as the word Eglaim. If the author interpreted Eglaim by gematria, we should expect he would also have interpreted Gedi by means of another word with the same numerical value (17). Although we can only guess his interpretation, the most probable is that he associated Gedi with the word זבח ("sacrifice"), which has the value of 17. The new life symbolized by the river of Ezekiel 47, which makes people children of God, has its source in the temple, the place of sacrifice. As we shall see, according to this Gospel's interpretation of Ezekiel 47, it has its origin in the sacrificial death of Jesus, who is both the new Passover lamb and the new temple.

The plausibility and appropriateness of this explanation of the number 153 become more apparent when we consider two earlier allusions to Ezekiel 47 in the Gospel. The first is in 7:38: "as the Scripture says, 'From his breast shall flow rivers of living water' (ποταμοὶ ἐκ τῆς κοιλίας αὐτοῦ ῥεύσουσιν ὕδατος ζῶντος)."[30] As is well known there is no biblical text to which this scriptural citation conforms at all closely. It should probably be understood as a conflation of words from two or three texts, which have been connected by means of the exegetical technique of *gezera shava* (which links texts in which the same words occur). The primary reference is to Ezekiel 47:1, with a secondary reference to Zechariah

---

29. Examples in Bauckham, *Climax of Prophecy*, 386–87; Russell, "Countdown," 112.

30. I take the view that the words ὁ πιστεύων εἰς ἐμέ should be connected with verse 37, not with the scriptural quotation in verse 38.

14:8 and perhaps also a reference to Psalm 78:16. I give the NRSV's translation of the Hebrew because I think that the author is working with the Hebrew text of these passages:

> Then he brought me back to the entrance to the temple; there, water was flowing (מים יצאים) from below the threshold of the temple toward the east (for the temple faced east); and the water was flowing down from below the south end of the threshold of the temple (והמים ירדים מתחת מכתף הבית הימנית), south of the altar. (Ezek. 47:1)

> On that day living waters shall flow out (יצאו מים חיים) from Jerusalem. (Zech. 14:8)

> He made streams come out of the rock,
> and caused waters to flow down like rivers (ויורד כנהרות מים). (Ps. 78:16)

The phrase in Ezekiel 47:1 that the NRSV translates as "from below the south end of the threshold of the temple" could be more literally translated "from below the right-hand shoulder (כתף) of the temple." The word כתף usually means "shoulder" (of humans or animals), but can also mean the "side" of a mountain or building. John's use of this text has exploited the possible meaning "shoulder." Jesus is the new temple from which the living waters flow, and so Ezekiel's "from below the shoulder/side of the temple" can be translated as "from his breast" (ἐκ τῆς κοιλίας αὐτοῦ). In light of this interpretation of Ezekiel 47:1 in John 7:38, we can detect another allusion to the same text in 19:34: "one of the soldiers pierced his side (πλευράν) with a spear, and at once blood and water came out." This combines the image of Jesus as the new Passover lamb, from which blood flows, with that of Jesus as the new temple, from which water flows. The allusion to Ezekiel 47:1 seems to have been recognized by apocryphal literature[31] (whence also the Christian artistic tradition) and the Ethiopic version of John 19:34, in which the side is specified as the right side (not, as one might expect, the left side, nearer the heart). We can now see that John 21:1–14, with its allusion to Ezekiel 47:10 in 21:11, continues the same interpretation of Ezekiel 47.

The 153 Fish and John 20:30–31

We have still not exhausted the significance of the figure 153. It seems also to be linked to the first part of the Gospel's conclusion (20:30–31) in the following way. That passage states that the signs done by Jesus have been recorded in the Gospel so that readers may believe that he is the Messiah, the Son of God, and through believing have life. That, of course, also describes what the catch of

---

31. *Acts of Pilate* Greek B11.

153 fish in the narrative of chapter 21 parabolically illustrates: people coming to faith in Jesus and to new life as children of God. The keywords of 20:30–31 are: sign, believe, Christ, life. Each of these four words occurs for the last time in the Gospel in those verses. If we count the number of occurrences of these words in the whole Gospel up to and including this passage, the results are: σημεῖον 17, πιστεύειν 98, Χριστός 19, ζωή 36. The sum of the last three of these numbers is 153. So the number 17 and its "triangle" 153 are written into the whole Gospel in the form of these word statistics[32] and are implicit in 20:30–31.

As we have already noticed, the miraculous catch of fish is not, in the Johannine terminology, a sign. The signs are the miraculous events that are narrated in chapters 2–20 and whose purpose is to bring people to believe in Jesus as Messiah and to receive eternal life from him. The miraculous catch of fish does not have this purpose. Rather, its role in the Gospel is to depict symbolically the church's mission of bringing people to faith in Jesus and new life as children of God. It symbolizes what happens as a result of the signs. This relationship between the signs and the miraculous catch of fish corresponds perfectly to the way the numbers 17 and 153 are used in 20:30–31 and 21:11. According to 20:30–31 the signs (symbolic number 17), recorded up to that point in the Gospel, have been written so that people may believe in Christ and have life (symbolic number 153). The signs and the coming to faith are related, just as the number 17 and its "triangle" 153 are related. In 21:11 only the number 153 appears, for the 153 fish symbolize all the children of God, who become children of God, receiving eternal life, through believing in Jesus as the signs reveal him to them. This relationship between 20:30–31 and 21:10 also illustrates very clearly how the Gospel's epilogue (21:1–23) need not be read as an unexpected appendix added after what was originally the end of the book. John 20:30–31 concludes the narrative of the signs; the epilogue depicts their effect in the mission of the church up to the parousia (21:23).

If the Gospel had originally ended at 20:30, it would no doubt have been possible for a redactor to have added an appendix corresponding numerically to the Gospel's prologue (496 words and 496 syllables respectively) and also to have added a second conclusion of the same length as the first (43 words in each case). If he had been close to the author or circle from which the Gospel originated, he could have known the exegesis of Ezekiel 47 that lay behind 7:38 and 19:34 and have been able to incorporate a very appropriate development of this into his newly written appendix. He could have created all the other close links between chapter 21 and other parts of the Gospel. All these things are possible, though they do not seem to me probable. But such a redactor could not have designed the number of occurrences, throughout the Gospel, of the key words of 20:30–31, such that

---

32. With the possible exception of the word μαθητής, which occurs seventy-seven times, these are the only cases in which the number of occurrences of specific words in the Gospel of John seem to me to have significance.

they produce the numbers 17 and 153. This phenomenon is surely attributable only to an author who meticulously designed the whole Gospel, including chapter 21, and intended the explicit appearance of the number 153 in chapter 21 as an integral feature of his Gospel.

The Beloved Disciple's Numerical Signature

Now that we have observed the remarkable extent to which the concluding sections of the Gospel play with word-counting and gematria (the latter in Hebrew), we shall be prepared to credit another very striking instance of such numerical design in chapter 21. The name of the beloved disciple according to the earliest extant traditions was John,[33] and, despite many other modern proposals (Lazarus, Nathanael, Thomas, Judas, Philip, Apollos, Matthias, even Paul),[34] this name is likely to be correct, since the beloved disciple was a well-known figure in the context of the Gospel's origin (21:23) and the Gospel is unlikely ever to have circulated without a name attached to it.[35] In the first century the name John was often written in Hebrew as יהוחנן,[36] which has the numerical value 129. The 129th word from the beginning of the Gospel's epilogue is the first word (ὁ) of the phrase "that disciple whom Jesus loved" (ὁ μαθητὴς ἐκεῖνος ὃν ἠγάπα ὁ Ἰησοῦς), which is the first reference to the beloved disciple in the epilogue (21:7). By means of the techniques of word-counting and gematria the name of the beloved disciple has been cryptically encoded in the narrative that leads to the concluding attribution of the Gospel to his testimony (21:24).

In fact, if we continue to count sections 129 words in length, we find that the fourth such section in chapter 21 ends with the last word of verse 24, which concludes the Gospel's last statement about the beloved disciple.[37] That this is intentional may be supported by a similar phenomenon with reference to Simon Peter. His Hebrew name שמעון has the numerical value 466. The 466th word of

33. Richard Bauckham, "Papias and Polycrates on the Origin of the Fourth Gospel," *JTS* 44 (1993): 24–69 = chap. 2 above.

34. See the detailed survey of virtually all suggestions in James H. Charlesworth, *The Beloved Disciple* (Valley Forge, PA: Trinity Press International, 1995), chapter 3. The rest of the book argues for Charlesworth's own proposal: Thomas. To those who have proposed Nathaniel, there can now be added D. Catchpole, "The Beloved Disciple and Nathanael," in *Understanding, Studying, and Reading*, ed. C. Rowland and C. Fletcher-Louis, John Ashton FS, JSNTSup 153 (Sheffield: Sheffield Academic Press, 1998), 69–92.

35. Cf. Martin Hengel, *The Four Gospels and the One Gospel of Jesus Christ*, trans. John Bowden (London: SCM, 2000), 48–56.

36. E.g., Yehoḥanan, son of the high priest Theophilus, appearing in the inscription on the ossuary of his daughter Yehoḥanah: Dan Barag and David Flusser, "The Ossuary of Yehoḥanah Granddaughter of the High Priest Theophilus," *IEJ* 36 (1986): 39–44.

37. Is it also significant that 129 = 3 × 43, and that 43 is the number of words in each of the two parts of the conclusion (20:30–31 and 21:24–25)?

chapter 21 is the last word of verse 22, the conclusion of Jesus' words to Peter and the end of the Gospel's account of Peter.

The purpose of chapter 21, as we have noticed, is to preview the church's mission to the world, but also more specifically to indicate the respective roles, in that mission, of the two disciples most prominent in this Gospel: Peter and the beloved disciple. While the former's role is to be the chief under-shepherd of Jesus' flock, the latter's role is that of the perceptive witness to Jesus, who finally embodies his witness in the form of the written Gospel. (I have argued elsewhere that the Gospel as a whole portrays the beloved disciple as the "ideal witness" to Jesus, who is therefore qualified to be the "ideal author" of a Gospel.)[38] In 21:7 the beloved disciple for the first and only time in the Gospel performs his role of witness within the Gospel's own narrative. Elsewhere he is portrayed as the one who observed what happened in the Gospel's narrative so that he can later witness to hearers/readers of his Gospel, but he does not elsewhere communicate what he sees and perceives to people within the Gospel's story. In 21:7, he recognizes Jesus ("It is the Lord!") and communicates this insight to Peter, who acts on it. It is appropriate that, as we have seen, the beloved disciple's own name is encoded numerically in the narrative precisely at this point, but the fact that his witness is to *Jesus* is also represented in numerical composition. The section 21:1–14 consists, as we have noted, of 276 words. The two central words (the 138th and 139th) of this section are the beloved disciple's own words of witness to Jesus: ὁ κύριος (21:7). Moreover, 276 is the "triangle" of 23. If we multiply this "triangular root" (23) of the length of the section by the "triangular root" (17) of the triangular number that occurs within the section (153), the sum is 391. This is the numerical value of the name Jesus in Hebrew (יהושע), a significant instance of gematria that already, as we have observed, underlies the text of the Gospel in 1:29, 35–36; 19:15–36.

A common reaction to the kind of study we have pursued in this chapter is expressed in George Beasley-Murray's comment on one of the proposals for understanding the number 153 in terms of gematria: "It is altogether too complicated for the ordinary reader of the Gospel to perceive, and too much even for most modern scholars to guess without being initiated into this particular mystique."[39] In response to this, we should observe, in the first place, that the "ordinary reader" who perceives none of the instances of numerical composition that we have discerned will not find anything in the Gospel unintelligible. Even in the case of the number 153, if the "ordinary reader" takes it merely as a remarkably large number of fish in a single net, this understanding is sufficient to make adequate sense of the story. The numerical literary techniques add dimensions of meaning to the text for those who discern them, but they are not required for understanding the

38. See chapter 3 above.
39. Beasley-Murray, *John*, 403.

message of the Gospel and they do not impede "ordinary" readers who are not likely to discern them.

It may be that some aspects of numerical composition were not expected to be directly discerned by readers, but were thought to give appropriate form to the text, as ways of conforming the lengths and proportions of the text to its meanings. But we should remember that counting the number of syllables or words in a text was not as unfamiliar an activity then as it is now: it was regularly done to determine the price of manuscripts and for scribes to check the accuracy of their transcriptions.[40] Gematria was a well-known practice, which took such popular forms as the graffito found in Pompeii: "I love the girl whose number is 545."[41] Triangular and perfect numbers were known to everyone with a little education and were widely regarded as significant numbers. Furthermore, such New Testament writers as the authors of Revelation and the Fourth Gospel certainly considered their literary productions as something very like the Jewish Scriptures, and they were familiar with the learned exegetical techniques employed in the exegesis of those Scriptures, involving such numerical techniques as gematria and counting the words of sections of text. It is entirely plausible that they would have expected to have some learned readers who would study their work with the same kinds and degree of meticulous exegesis as the Hebrew Scriptures were studied by careful exegetes such as themselves. The analogy of the Hebrew Scriptures, as studied in first-century Judaism, would easily suggest that they should not confine their compositional work as authors to the obvious surface of the text, readily discernible by the "ordinary reader," but should also embody deeper and hidden meaning in, among other things, the numerical structures of their work.

Finally, it is essential to remember that few "ordinary readers" of an early Christian work such as the Fourth Gospel would read it alone, with only the resources of their own knowledge to assist their comprehension, as modern readers do. Reading (which for most "ordinary readers" was hearing) took place in community. Aspects of the text that were not obvious could be explained by teachers who had some training in scriptural exegesis and who may have given time and trouble to studying the text. In envisaging the original reception of a work such as the Fourth Gospel, we need not only to allow for the oral context, which meant that such a text should make some degree of immediate sense to most listeners, but also to recognize that such a text could also be intended to be studied by especially competent readers who could share their understanding with others.[42]

40. Menken, *Numerical Literary Techniques*, 12–13.

41. G. Adolf Deissmann, *Light from the Ancient East*, trans. L. R. M. Strachan (London: Hodder Deissmann, 1910), 276.

42. A relevant and fascinating study that came to my attention only after I had completed this essay is George J. Brooke, "4Q252 and the 153 Fish of John 21:11," in idem, *The Dead Sea Scrolls and the New Testament* (London: SPCK, 2005), 282–97.

Index of Modern Authors

INDEX OF ANCIENT PERSONS

Index of Place Names

Index of Scripture and Other Ancient Writings

Old Testament

298

Old Testament Apocrypha

New Testament

Old Testament Pseudepigrapha

Scrolls from the Judean Desert

Early Christian Literature (except New Testament)

Other Ancient Greek and Roman Literature

Rabbinic Literature

Babylonian Talmud

'Abodah Zarah
8b 169
25a 142

Baba Qamma
65b 153n70
94a 153n70

Berakot
34b 158n94

Besah
16a 159

'Erubin
63a 153n70

Gittin
56a 138, 140, 141, 143, 145, 161

Hagigah
13a 158

Ketubbot
66b–67a 148
66b 145, 146, 147
67a 146

Menahot
41b 158n93
45a 158

Nedarim
50a 139n12

Qiddushin
66a 44

Sanhedrin
11a 156
43a 168, 169
74a 158n93

Semahot
47a 166n124

Shabbat
13b 158
21b 261
137b 268

Sotah
48b 156

Sukkah
27b 224n71

Ta'anit
19b–20a 141
20a 169, 170

Temurah
30b 153n70

Yoma
31b–32a 43
35b 165n120
52b 153n70

Mishnah

'Abot
1:6–7 168n133, 169
2:8 169

Hagigah
2:2 168n133

Hallah
4.10 168n133

Pesahim
1–2 44

Qiddushin
4:14 153n70

Shabbat
1:4 157, 161

Sukkah
5:2–4 134

Ta'anit
4.5 144n35

Palestinian Talmud

'Abodah Zarah
3.1 156
43d 153n70, 156n88

'Erubin
22a 159n100

Horayot
3.5 156

Ketubbot
5.11 145, 146

Megillah
73b 153n70, 156n88

Mo'ed Qatan
82d 153n70
54 153n70

Pe'ah
17d 153n70
70 153n70

Pesahim
30b 158n93
41 158n93
113b 153n70

Sanhedrin
9 158n93
21b 158n93
23d 152n68
58 152n68

Shabbat
11d 153n70, 156n88

Sotah
9.13 156

Ta'anit
4.2 139n12

Yebamot
6c 153n70, 156n88

Tosephta

Berakot
5:22 268
6:9–14 268

'Erubin
3.17 159

Ketubbot
5.9 145, 146
5.10 146

Shabbat
1.17–19 157

Sotah
13.3 156

'Abot de Rabbi Nathan (ARN)

A6 141, 142, 143, 145, 148n52
A17 147
B13 141, 145, 148n52